Sovereignty without Power

What did independence mean during the age of empires? How did independent governments balance different interests when they made policies about trade, money, and access to foreign capital? *Sovereignty without Power* tells the story of Liberia, one of the few African countries to maintain independence through the colonial period. Established in 1822 as a colony for freed slaves from the United States, Liberia's history illustrates how the government's efforts to exercise its economic sovereignty and engage with the global economy shaped Liberia's economic and political development over the nineteenth and twentieth centuries. Drawing together a wide range of archival sources, Leigh A. Gardner presents the first annual estimates of Liberia's economic performance and uses these to compare it to its colonized neighbors and other independent countries. Liberia's history anticipated challenges still faced by developing countries today and offers a new perspective on the role of power and power relationships in shaping Africa's economic history.

Leigh Gardner is Professor of Economic History at the London School of Economics and Political Science and a Research Affiliate at Stellenbosch University. She is the author of *Taxing Colonial Africa: The Political Economy of British Imperialism* (2012) and co-author (with Tirthankar Roy) of *Economic History of Colonialism* (2020).

Cambridge Studies in Economic History

Editorial Board

Cambridge Studies in Economic History comprises stimulating and accessible economic history which actively builds bridges to other disciplines. Books in the series will illuminate why the issues they address are important and interesting, place their findings in a comparative context, and relate their research to wider debates and controversies. The series will combine innovative and exciting new research by younger researchers with new approaches to major issues by senior scholars. It will publish distinguished work regardless of chronological period or geographical location.

A complete list of titles in the series can be found at:
www.cambridge.org/economichistory

Sovereignty without Power

Liberia in the Age of Empires, 1822–1980

Leigh Gardner

London School of Economics and Political Science and Stellenbosch University

CAMBRIDGE
UNIVERSITY PRESS

CAMBRIDGE
UNIVERSITY PRESS

University Printing House, Cambridge CB2 8BS, United Kingdom

One Liberty Plaza, 20th Floor, New York, NY 10006, USA

477 Williamstown Road, Port Melbourne, VIC 3207, Australia

314–321, 3rd Floor, Plot 3, Splendor Forum, Jasola District Centre,
New Delhi – 110025, India

103 Penang Road, #05–06/07, Visioncrest Commercial, Singapore 238467

Cambridge University Press is part of the University of Cambridge.

It furthers the University's mission by disseminating knowledge in the pursuit of
education, learning, and research at the highest international levels of excellence.

www.cambridge.org
Information on this title: www.cambridge.org/9781009181105
DOI: 10.1017/9781009181082

First published 2023

A catalogue record for this publication is available from the British Library.

ISBN 978-1-009-18110-5 Hardback

Cambridge University Press has no responsibility for the persistence or accuracy of
URLs for external or third-party internet websites referred to in this publication
and does not guarantee that any content on such websites is, or will remain,
accurate or appropriate.

For Steve

.

Contents

Figures

Maps

Tables

Preface

"We've had independence since 1847. We should have something much better than this." Jimmy Korkollie said this as we walked along Broad Street in Monrovia on a Saturday in April 2017. The sidewalks on either side of the wide grassy median were busy, lined with small businesses selling clothes, airtime for mobile phones, or household goods. Interspersed between the shops were empty buildings, gutted shells left at the end of the civil wars that ravaged Liberia from 1989 until 2003.

Jimmy had worked as a tour guide for the past four years, part of a small group of Liberians attempting to revive a tourist industry which had been one of many economic casualties of the conflict. When he was growing up in Monrovia, his father had worked as a waiter in the Ducor Palace Hotel. In the 1970s, it was one of the only five-star hotels in sub-Saharan Africa. Postcards from the time show guests relaxing by the pool and enjoying the view from the top of Ducor Hill over the Atlantic Ocean. The views are still there, but the hotel became home to squatters displaced by the war and stands today as another shell, the building stripped down to concrete foundations which still frame the outlines of hotel rooms and elevator shafts.

I had arrived in Liberia for a research trip a few days before, in part to try to answer Jimmy's question about how political independence had shaped Liberia's economic development over the long run. My previous work had focused on the legacies of European colonial rule. In the twenty-first century "renaissance" of African economic history, this has been a key focus for historians and economists attempting to understand the historical roots of Africa's continued poverty.[1] My own research had

---

[1] Gareth Austin and Stephen Broadberry, "The Renaissance of African Economic History," *Economic History Review* 67, no. 4 (2014): 893–906; Johan Fourie, "The Data Revolution in African Economic History," *Journal of Interdisciplinary History* 47, no. 2 (2016): 193–212; A. G. Hopkins, "The New Economic History of Africa," *Journal of African History* 50, no. 2 (2009): 155–77; Stelios Michalopoulos and Elias Papaioannou, "Historical Legacies and African Development," *Journal of Economic Literature* 58, no. 1 (2020): 53–128. For a review of the literature on the economic history of colonialism, see

focused on the finances of colonial states and the ways in which European officials had built a tax base and then used the resources of the state to shape patterns of economic development.[2] A key part of this work was understanding how colonial governments mediated relationships between indigenous producers and the global economy through policies relating to trade and money. This research showed that colonial governments drew on the resources of metropolitan states to build infrastructure and promote economic growth in the short run but at the same time invested little in human capital or broad-based economic development.[3]

Like most economic historians of Africa, I had never really given Liberia much thought before. Liberia has a rich historiography of its own, including excellent economic histories, but it rarely, if ever, appears in comparative work on Africa's economic history.[4] It was an accidental discovery in the UK National Archives in 2011 which started me on the road that would lead me to walk down Broad Street with Jimmy six years later. I was reviewing the archival records of the West African Currency Board, the institution that issued the colonial currency of British West Africa. The West African shilling, as it was called, was tied to the British pound and most research on colonial currencies has argued that while this suited the needs of British officials and merchants transacting between Britain and its colonies, it was not particularly good for colonized countries. Within these records, I stumbled on a file of correspondence about the use of British colonial currency as the primary medium of exchange in Liberia.[5]

Reading this file raised many questions for me. The first and most obvious was why Liberia, an independent country, would choose to

Leigh Gardner and Tirthankar Roy, *Economic History of Colonialism* (Bristol: Bristol University Press, 2020).

[2] Leigh Gardner, *Taxing Colonial Africa: The Political Economy of British Imperialism* (Oxford: Oxford University Press, 2012).

[3] Alfonso Herranz-Loncan and Johan Fourie, "'For the Public Benefit'? Railways in the British Cape Colony," *European Review Economic History* 22, no. 1 (2018): 73–100; Elise Huillery, "History Matters: The Long-Term Impact of Colonial Public Investments in French West Africa," *American Economic Journal: Applied Economics* 1, no. 2 (2009): 176–215; Remi Jedwab and Alexander Moradi, "The Permanent Effects of Transportation Revolution in Poor Countries: Evidence from Africa," *Review of Economics and Statistics* 98, no. 2 (2016): 268–84; Remi Jedwab, Edward Kerby and Alexander Moradi, "History, Path Dependence and Development: Evidence from Colonial Railroads, Settlers and Cities in Kenya," *Economic Journal* 127 no. 603 (2017): 1467–94; Leonard Wantchekon, Marko Klasnja, and Natalija Novta, "Education and Human Capital Externalities: Evidence from Colonial Benin," *Quarterly Journal of Economics* 130, no. 2 (2015): 703–57.

[4] George Brown, *The Economic History of Liberia* (Washington, DC: The Associated Publishers, 1941); F. P. M. van der Kraaij, *The Open Door Policy of Liberia: An Economic History of Modern Liberia* (Bremen: Bremer Afrika Archiv, 1983).

[5] TNA CO 554/69/4.

adopt a colonial currency. Why didn't it have its own currency? By the 1920s, when the correspondence in this file was written, having a national currency had become a key signal of sovereignty in addition to an important tool of fiscal management. The answer, which appears in Chapter 5, was that Liberia had established its own currency – the Liberian dollar – after independence but that the limited resources of the Liberian government combined with the need to service foreign debt denominated in pounds made it expedient to adopt the West African shilling instead. The story of Liberia's monetary history led to a set of wider questions about how states not under formal colonial rule managed the same relationships with the global economy that I had already investigated for colonial states. How similar or different was the experience of independent states? Did interventions by more powerful states linked to money and debt simply replicate the conditions of formal colonial rule as theories of neocolonialism would suggest? Or did formal recognition of sovereignty – even in the context of relative poverty – change the story in some way that might help answer Jimmy's question? What did sovereignty mean in the age of empires?

Liberia has a complicated and unique history. Its origins as a political unit date to 1820, when a ship called the *Elizabeth* set sail from New York to West Africa carrying a group of eighty-six freeborn African Americans. The voyage was organized and sponsored by the Society for the Colonization of the Free People of the United States (more commonly known as the American Colonization Society or ACS). The ACS was a private organization led primarily by white slave owners who feared that the presence of freeborn African Americans would threaten the stability of the system of slavery in the United States, but it built on a diverse array of calls for emigration coming from both white and black voices during the eighteenth and nineteenth centuries.[6] The migrants on the *Elizabeth* and subsequent ships had a difficult start, as discussed in Chapter 3, and for the next two decades occupied a tenuous position in communities along what was historically known to Europeans as the Malagueta or Grain Coast, after a type of pepper prized by Portuguese traders. During the 1840s, disputes over the power of the ACS administration to impose tax on British merchants ultimately led a group of African-American migrants to declare Liberia an independent country in 1847. It has remained an independent state, recognized as such by other governments, ever since.

---

[6] Amos Sawyer, *The Emergence of Autocracy in Liberia: Tragedy and Challenge* (San Francisco: ICS Press, 1992): ch 2; Beverly C. Tomek and Matthew J. Hetrick (eds), "The Past, Present and Future of Colonization Studies," in *New Directions in the Study of African American Recolonization* (Gainesville: University Press of Florida, 2017), 1–32.

From 1847 until 1980, a government dominated by those same migrants and their descendants – known as Americo-Liberians – would expand its reach over the indigenous population of the interior but allowed that population little say in how it was governed.[7] They maintained a distinct and exclusive political culture which looked to the United States and Europe rather than West Africa for its inspiration. In 1980, a group of indigenous soldiers led by Samuel Doe overthrew and killed President William Tolbert. After a period of brutal repressive rule, Doe himself was killed in 1989, and battles between competing factions in the fourteen years that followed resulted in the death of around 10 percent of the population and the displacement of many more.[8]

This unusual history has made it difficult for historians to classify Liberia, which may be one of the reasons it does not appear often in comparative work. Some, like Nigerian historian Monday B. Akpan, describe it as essentially a settler colony; others as a de facto (if not formally recognized) colony of the United States.[9] However, this book argues that Liberia had more in common with other independent states than it did with countries under formal colonial rule. It was, for example, hardly alone in being ruled by a narrow elite, particularly during the nineteenth century when representative institutions were few and far between in all regions of the world. Historically, limited government has been the exception, not the rule, and in all periods of history, most of the world's population has been governed by what Douglass North, John Wallis, and Barry Weingast call "natural states," in which coalitions of elites cooperate in limiting violence in exchange for rents derived from exclusive control over trade or other resources.[10] Nor was it unusual for that elite being foreign in its outlook; the same could be said of much of Latin America, for example, or the United States. Even independent countries under indigenous leadership laid claim to territory not traditionally under their rule, often under pressure from colonial governments to justify their spheres of influence. Under Yohannes and Menelik, for

---

[7] This phrase is not universally accepted in histories of Liberia. See, for example, Robtel Pailey, *Development, (Dual) Citizenship and Its Discontents in Africa: The Political Economy of Belonging to Liberia* (Cambridge: Cambridge University Press, 2021). For consistency with earlier historiography, I have retained it here.

[8] Stephen Ellis, *The Mask of Anarchy: The Destruction of Liberia and the Religious Dimension of an African Civil War* (London: Hurst & Company, 2007), 312–16.

[9] Monday B. Akpan, "Black Imperialism: Americo-Liberian Rule over the African Peoples of Liberia, 1841–1964," *Canadian Journal of African Studies* 7, no. 2 (1973): 217–36; Bronwen Everill, *Abolition and Empire in Sierra Leone and Liberia* (Basingstoke: Palgrave Macmillan, 2013), 178.

[10] Douglass C. North, John Joseph Wallis, and Barry R. Weingast, *Violence and Social Orders: A Conceptual Framework for Interpreting Recorded Human History* (Cambridge: Cambridge University Press, 2009), ch 2.

example, what became Ethiopia expanded from its traditional highland center to incorporate the region of Tigray and other territories to the south and east.[11] The centralization and extension of the authority of Siam (Thailand) over previously autonomous provinces like Chiang Mai occurred in similar circumstances.[12]

These nuances make colonialism – and also sovereignty – difficult to define precisely. Given the different forms foreign intervention could take, does it make sense to talk about sovereignty in the cases of Liberia, Siam, or Ethiopia at all? Both terms are multidimensional, and any definition of either must leave room for numerous shades of gray. Standard approaches to the concept of sovereignty in political science divide it into several dimensions, reflecting its both internal and external features. Stephen Krasner, for example, provides four separate ways of using the term: international legal sovereignty; Westphalian sovereignty, or freedom from external intervention in internal systems of governance; domestic sovereignty, or internal control over those governed; and interdependence sovereignty, or the role of the state in regulating flows of information, goods, capital, and so on.[13] It is not necessary for all of these to be equally present; states in possession of international recognition may still endure foreign intervention in internal systems of governance and may not have full domestic legitimacy. Drawing on these dimensions of sovereignty, this book defines formal colonialism as (1) international recognition of foreign control and (2) foreign control over internal administration, which is sufficiently extensive to create what Mancur Olson calls an "encompassing interest."[14] As Chapters 6 and 7 show, the establishment of an encompassing interest had real material consequences for patterns of economic development when compared to more limited forms of foreign administrative control. This definition still leaves considerable room for variation and questions about how particular places should be defined. However, the history of Liberia and other countries explored in this book shows that even when constrained by limited

---

[11] Richard J. Reid, *Frontiers of Violence in North-East Africa: Genealogies of Conflict since c. 1800* (Oxford: Oxford University Press, 2011), ch 4.

[12] Christopher Paik and Jessica Vechbanyongratana, "Path to Centralization and Development: Evidence from Siam," *World Politics* 71, no. 2 (2019): 295; Thongchai Winichakul, *Siam Mapped: A History of the Geo-body of a Nation* (Honolulu: University of Hawaii Press, 1994).

[13] Stephen Krasner, *Sovereignty: Organized Hypocrisy* (Princeton: Princeton University Press, 1999): 11–12. See also Robert Jackson, *Sovereignty: The Evolution of an Idea* (London: Polity Press, 2007).

[14] Mancur Olson, The Rise and Decline of Nations: Economic Growth, Stagflation and Social Rigidities (New Haven and London: Yale University Press, 1982), 48.

resources and more powerful states, sovereignty did matter in shaping the long-run development of political and economic institutions.

African economic history's neglect of Liberia – and also Ethiopia, which remained independent apart from a brief period under Italian rule – means that it has little to offer in answer to the questions I began to ask after reading about Liberia's use of British colonial currency. Histories of other regions had more to say about the exercise of sovereignty by independent countries in what is now the developing world during the nineteenth and early twentieth centuries when much of that world was still under the control of European empires.[15] In Asia and Latin America, the economic development of independent countries was often stifled by a lack of resources. Borrowing abroad was more expensive for independent countries than for colonies, which made the construction of the infrastructure needed for economic expansion costly. They also faced external pressures from expanding empires, and the process of economic development and state-building in independent states was shaped by the interaction between these external pressures and the structure of internal politics. Internally, they had to manage debates about how they responded to changes in the world around them through policies on trade, currencies, debt, taxation, and investment, among other areas, and these policies helped determine how fast their economies grew and how the proceeds of that growth were distributed.

This book uses a case study of Liberia during the nineteenth and twentieth centuries to investigate these questions in an African context. While it is not the first book on the economic history of Liberia, it is the first to provide annual measures of Liberia's economic performance over this period, which can be compared with data from other countries. Taking an explicitly comparative perspective makes it possible to tell a new story of Liberia's economic history, which looks beyond local specificities to place Liberia in the wider context of independent states during the imperial age. While Liberia is just one small country, case studies like this one have several uses in evaluating causal explanations.[16] Mary Morgan proposes two ways in which case studies are used in social

---

[15] Anne Booth, "Night Watchman, Extractive, or Developmental States? Some Evidence from Late Colonial Southeast Asia," *Economic History Review* 60, no. 2 (2007): 241–66; Victor Bulmer-Thomas, *The Economic History of the Caribbean since the Napoleonic Wars* (Cambridge: Cambridge University Press, 2012), ch 7; Ewout Frankema and Aline Mase, "An Island Drifting Apart: Why Haiti is Mired in Poverty while the Dominican Republic Forges Ahead," *Journal of International Development* 26, no. 1. (2014): 128–48; Sevket Pamuk, *The Ottoman Empire and European Capitalism, 1820–1913: Trade, Investment and Production* (Cambridge: Cambridge University Press, 1987).

[16] Gary King, Robert O. Keohane and Sidney Verba, *Designing Social Inquiry: Scientific Inference in Qualitative Research* (Princeton: Princeton University Press, 1994), 211

science. Exemplary cases "are known, used and re-used because the case itself stands out as unique in some way." Other cases may be ordinary in and of themselves but may prompt new questions or new approaches to a question.[17] Perhaps greedily, this book hopes to be both, in both bringing a new perspective to Liberia's unique history and by using Liberia to prompt new questions about the link between sovereignty, power, and economic development in African (and global) economic history.

Chapter 1 presents new quantitative data and gives an overview of Liberia's economic history from 1847 to 1980. Part I examines the economic, political, and social foundations of what became Liberia. Chapter 2 assesses what we know about the indigenous economies of the region, drawing on anthropological records and historical accounts to examine the structure of markets and states before the arrival of the first African-American migrants. Chapter 3 focuses on the African-American migrants who would eventually become the Americo-Liberian elite, using new data on both the migrants and those who remained behind in the United States to examine the characteristics of that elite and the origins of cleavages that would later shape Liberia's economic policies.

The remainder of the book focuses on the Liberian government's exercise of economic sovereignty and the impact of its policies on different parts of the population. Part II begins with Liberia's declaration of independence in 1847 and examines the challenges the Liberian government faced in exercising its newly acquired sovereignty. Chapters 4–7 focus on areas in which tensions emerged between national sovereignty and elite prosperity: trade, money, sovereign debt, and foreign financial controls. Part III focuses on the ways in which Liberian elites used the external recognition of Liberia's sovereignty as a source of rent, beginning in the 1920s until the civil war in the 1990s. Chapters 8–10 examine foreign aid, concessions to foreign investors, and the creation of the Liberian "flag of convenience" in 1948. The book concludes by reflecting on lessons which might be drawn from the Liberian case for understanding the economic history of African countries after their own independence in c. 1960.

---

[17] Mary S. Morgan, "Exemplification and the Use-Values of Cases and Case Studies," *Studies in History and Philosophy of Science* 78 (2019): 6.

Acknowledgments

Like most book projects, this one has developed over a long time and would not have been possible without the support of numerous people and institutions. My trip to Monrovia in April 2017 was intended primarily to visit the Center for National Documents and Records Agency (CNDRA), where the then-Director General P. Bloh Sayeh provided both material support and enlightening conversation. I also visited the archives of the *Daily Observer*, where I received invaluable guidance from Bai Best and Satta Sonie. Outside the archive, I learned a great deal from conversations with Bill Allen, Nakomo Duche, Felix Gerdes, Nyda Mukhtar, Molley Shaffa, Lu Tolbert, and Moses Wreh.

Like much else in Monrovia, Liberia's national archives bear the scars of the civil war, and to write this book required the use of records in a number of other archives and libraries around the world. The Liberia collection at Indiana University was particularly valuable for material from the nineteenth century, and without the assistance of Verlon Stone, Megan Starr, and Mireille Djenno, this project would not have been possible. Archivists at the United Nations archives, particularly Colin Wells and Jacques Oberson, the UK National Archives (TNA), the US National Archives and Records Administration (NARA), the Library of Congress, the Herskovits Library at Northwestern University, and the Schomburg Center for Research in Black Culture at the New York Public Library also provided valuable assistance. Electronic resources were kindly provided by the Seeley G. Mudd Manuscript Library at Princeton University and the Pan-Am Historical Foundation. One archive that would be of great benefit to studies of Liberian economic history is the archive of the Firestone Rubber Company. Unfortunately, neither Firestone nor the Bridgestone Corporation, which acquired Firestone in 1990, has made this material available to researchers.

Travels to this diverse array of archives also required significant material support. The initial research into Liberia's monetary history was part of a Leverhulme-funded research project (Money in Africa, Grant #F/00

052/D). Subsequent travels were funded by the LSE's Research Infrastructure and Investment Funds (RIIF), and the Economic History Department. The digitization of Liberian currency objects held by the Smithsonian Institutions, depicted in Chapter 5, was supported by the LSE's Knowledge Exchange and Impact Fund. Permissions to use images for the cover were kindly granted by the Smithsonian National Museum of American History and the Smithsonian Museum of African Art.

Over the course of ten years, this project has benefited from conversations with too many people to list here. Michael Watson at Cambridge University Press was the first to encourage me to turn what I had imagined as a series of papers into a book. Numerous colleagues have read draft chapters or provided particular advice on their areas of specialty. These include Olivier Accominotti, Gareth Austin, Carolyn Biltoft, William Clarence-Smith, Bill Collins, Jari Eloranta, Bronwen Everill, Jennifer Foray, Johan Fourie, Tony Hopkins, Sara Horrell, Jane Humphries, Cassandra Mark-Thiesen, David Meredith, Chris Minns, Gregg Mitman, Deborah Oxley, Marlous van Waijenburg, and Marianne Wanamaker. Rebecca Simson not only commented on a draft chapter but also shared her previous experience working in Liberia and contacts from her time there. Jutta Bolt provided the map of West African soil quality in Chapter 2 and the accompanying statistics, in addition to being a supportive interlocutor over the years in which the ideas in this book took shape. Jennifer Köhler provided me with the data on anthropological measures of state centralization used in Chapter 2. Michael Clemens and Jeffrey Williamson kindly provided their data on average tariff rates for the comparative analysis in Chapter 4. Eric Schneider provided the data on child stunting presented in Chapter 9 and helped me to understand their interpretation. Ellen Feingold collaborated in the creation of a small display based on this research in the Value of Money exhibition at the Smithsonian National Museum of American History, along with accompanying digital resources (https://americanhistory.si.edu/blog/dollars-liberia), helped with research on the origins and design of the first Liberian dollar, and gave me valuable advice on how best to display coins on book covers. Daisy Chamberlain and Juliana Jaramillo provided essential research assistance at various stages of the project.

Support wasn't only from colleagues and institutions. My parents have always been supportive and encouraging, even of a project like this one that didn't always seem feasible. My father, Robert Gardner, lent the critical eye of a physicist to many of the arguments made here, while my mother, Linda Gardner, accompanied me on several archive trips and made them much more enjoyable. Jennifer Foray was a welcoming host during travel between Chicago and Bloomington, Indiana. Most of all I have to thank my husband, Steve Broadberry, for helping me build spreadsheets of fragmentary archival data into something systematic and for reading more draft chapters than either of us can remember. This book is dedicated to him.

1 Reconstructing the Fragments
Liberia's Economic History, 1847–1980

> The rate of expansion of the economy of Liberia during the decade preceding 1961 surpassed that of almost any other country in the world ... Japan is the only country whose growth rate exceeded that of Liberia.
>
> Robert Clower et al., *Growth without Development*

> The fragments of the Geryoneis itself read as if Stesichoros had composed a substantial narrative poem then ripped it to pieces and buried the pieces in a box with some song lyrics and lecture notes and scraps of meat. The fragment numbers tell you roughly how the pieces fell out of the box. You can of course keep shaking the box.
>
> Anne Carson, *The Autobiography of Red*

Comparisons between Liberia and Japan during the 1950s appear frequently in histories of Liberia. They first originated in the *Monthly Bulletin of Statistics* published by the United Nations in May 1962, which noted that Liberia's rate of economic growth during the previous decade was the second fastest in the world after that of Japan. The same fact was then repeated in a study of Liberia's economy published in 1966 by a team of Northwestern University economists led by Robert Clower, quoted here. Other histories have also taken it up. US diplomat Charles Morrow Wilson, who spent part of his career working in Liberia, observed that "by 1954 and continuing through 1960, Liberia, with the single exception of Japan, led the entire world in the growth rate of what census statisticians like to call the real gross national product."[1] Journalist James Ciment writes in his 2013 book, "Liberia in the 1950s and early 1960s boasted the second-highest economic growth rate of any nation in the world, behind only Japan."[2] Beyond history books, it has a popular resonance: I first heard it in a conversation with P. Bloh Sayeh, then director of the Liberian national archives, during my 2017 visit to Monrovia.

---

[1] Charles Morrow Wilson, *Liberia: Black Africa in Microcosm* (New York: Harper and Row, 1971), 196.

[2] James Ciment, *Another America: The Story of Liberia and the Former Slaves Who Ruled It* (New York: Hill and Wang, 2013), 202.

1

From the vantage point of the twenty-first century, this seems a strange juxtaposition. Japan is one of the wealthiest countries in the world, and Liberia one of the poorest. According to the World Bank's World Development Indicators for 2017, a child born in Japan can expect to live more than twenty years longer than a child born in Liberia, and while 100 percent of the Japanese population has access to electricity, less than a quarter of Liberians do. Similarly, almost every Japanese adult is literate, but fewer than half of Liberian adults are. Visitors to Tokyo arrive at one of the two major international airports, take a direct train that glides between skyscrapers into the city center before transferring onto the city's expansive and efficient metro system. In contrast, the limited number of flights landing at Roberts Field near Monrovia in that year had a bumpy taxi over a runway first constructed during World War II and frequently shut down due to maintenance problems.[3] The only transport into the city is by car, over largely dirt roads overlooked by buildings half-destroyed by war and never fully reconstructed.

Japan and Liberia did not start in the same place when they began their rapid postwar ascents. Before wartime destruction delivered a sharp shock to the Japanese economy, it had been the first country in Asia to achieve modern economic growth after the institutional reforms of the Meiji Restoration in 1868.[4] In 1850, Japan's GDP per capita was $901, while Liberia's was $441. The unit is 1990 international dollars, which is frequently used to make comparisons in historical national accounting. Subsistence income on this metric is defined as $400, or a dollar a day for most of the population plus a small elite. Both countries were independent nations increasingly isolated by the growing influence of European empires in the regions around them, and both struggled to define their position alongside the growing economic and military might of Europe and the United States. Over the decades that followed, however, Japan was able to carve a path for Asian industrialization, build its own empire, and marshal enough resources to engage in a global war. In contrast, Liberia's economy remained stagnant across much of the late nineteenth and early twentieth centuries. It was not until the 1930s that a rapid influx of foreign investment and growing demand for rubber and iron ore produced the growth that would prompt the comparisons between the two countries in the 1950s.

Recent quantitative research in African economic history has made it easier to compare African countries both to each other and to those in

---

[3] A new terminal opened in Monrovia in 2019.
[4] Jean-Pascal Bassino, Stephen Broadberry, Kyoji Fukau, Bishnupriya Gupta and Masanori Takashima, "Japan and the Great Divergence, 730–1874," *Explorations in Economic History* 72 (2019): 1–22.

other regions over time.[5] This work has challenged a number of standard narratives about Africa and its role in the global economy over the long run. By various metrics, African countries were not necessarily substantially poorer in the nineteenth century than those of Asia and elsewhere. They also experienced periods of rapid growth, contrary to common narratives about African economic stagnation.[6] Unfortunately, this work has not been distributed evenly across African countries. Differences in the availability of statistics on population, government finances, production, and trade have led to significant inequalities in the volume of research addressing the period before 1950. British colonies have received the most attention, in large part thanks to a standard set of statistical reports – known as the Blue Books – which all British colonial governments submitted to London each year. French colonies follow close behind, allowing for comparisons between British and French colonialism. Portuguese and Belgian colonies occasionally feature, though much less frequently. By contrast, Liberia and Ethiopia have been almost entirely absent, leaving a significant gap in our understanding of how their forms of governance and interactions with the world economy shaped their economic performance over the long run.

This chapter helps fill this gap by providing the first annual reconstruction of Liberian economic performance since the middle of the nineteenth century. Since there is no equivalent of the British Blue Books for Liberia, this involves the compilation of data from various, mainly qualitative, sources. Reconstructing the story of Liberia's economic history in this way is not unlike Anne Carson's reconstruction of the life of the monster Geryon in her *Autobiography of Red*; it requires piecing together a tale from the scraps of information that have survived over the centuries. With such a fragmentary record there will certainly be grounds to quibble over details and interpretation. The aim of the chapter is to document the broad trends of Liberian development over the nineteenth and twentieth centuries and provide a foundation for the more detailed thematic chapters to follow. It provides a transparent accounting of how these statistics

---

[5] For reviews, see Gareth Austin and Stephen Broadberry, "The Renaissance of African Economic History," *Economic History Review* 67 (2014): 893–906; Johan Fourie, "The Data Revolution in African Economic History," *Journal of Interdisciplinary History* 47, no. 2 (2016): 193–212.

[6] Stephen Broadberry and Leigh Gardner, "Economic Growth in Sub-Saharan Africa 1885–2008: Evidence from Eight Countries." *Explorations in Economic History* 83 (2022) p. 101424; Ewout Frankema and Marlous van Waijenburg, "Structural Impediments to African Growth? New Evidence from Real Wages in British Africa, 1880–1965," *Journal of Economic History* 72, no. 4 (2012): 895–26; Morten Jerven, "African Growth Recurring: An Economic History Perspective on African Growth Episodes, 1690–2010," *Economic History of Developing Regions* 25, no. 2 (2010): 127–54; Morten Jerven, The Wealth and Poverty of African States: Economic Growth, Living Standards and Taxation since the Late Nineteenth Century (Cambridge: Cambridge University Press, 2022).

have been assembled to provide a basis for future improvements and in order to counter broad claims about the particular unreliability of African statistics.[7] This will, I hope, offer a blueprint which people researching other neglected countries – notably Ethiopia – might follow in order to build a more rounded and inclusive picture of Africa's long-run economic development.

Reassembling the Fragments

Struggles to obtain data on Liberia are no new problem. In 1901, a report on Liberia's trade and commerce submitted by the British consul to the Foreign Office stated: "Authoritative statistics being unavailable, all others which are obtained from business houses and steamship agencies are apt to be biased by nationality or business relations, and are consequently more or less unreliable. I prefer, therefore, not to give any."[8] True to his word, the consul duly submitted a trade report that lacked any statistics on trade. The position improved in the reports that followed, but in 1910, the report noted that "financial considerations have necessitated the suspension of the work of the statistical department of the government, and practically no information in respect to the trade and commerce of the country has been procurable for the last two years."[9]

One of the first comprehensive economic histories of Liberia, initially written as a London School of Economics (LSE) PhD dissertation in 1936, had much the same complaint. The author was an African American named George Brown, who had grown up in Kentucky and previously studied at Howard University in Washington, DC. In 1934, Brown enrolled in a PhD program at the LSE, where he took courses in anthropology, economics, and history and was particularly influenced by economic anthropologist Bronislaw Malinowski.[10] In his dissertation, and in the published book based on it, Brown lamented that "as official sources and accredited public documents on Liberian history are far from numerous, the research problems of selectivity give way almost wholly to the more difficult task of critically assessing such documents as do exist." In particular, he observed that "the absence of accurate and creditable records of national wealth, business surveys, investment values and

---

[7] Morten Jerven, *Poor Numbers: How We Are Misled by African Development Statistics and What to Do about It* (Ithaca: Cornell University Press, 2013).

[8] UK Foreign Office, *Report on the Trade and Commerce of Liberia for the Year 1901* (London: HMSO, 1902), 7.

[9] UK Foreign Office, *Report on the Trade of Liberia for the Year 1910* (London: HMSO, 1911), 3.

[10] Gregg Mitman, *Empire of Rubber: Firestone's Scramble for Land and Power in Liberia* (New York: The New Press, 2021), 168–72.

production statistics, agricultural, industrial employment and population censuses is a serious handicap." Also missing was information on "wages earned by indigenous persons working abroad, and philanthropic contributions from abroad." Without official sources, these had to be calculated from the "private, scattered, fragmentary and, in some cases, simply estimated records."[11] The fact that Brown thanks the Liberian president for use of his yacht during the period of his PhD research suggests that these problems were not a matter of access to government resources but rather indicate that such records were never produced to begin with. Data remained scarce even in 1962 after Liberia had enjoyed the period of economic expansion discussed in the previous section and the government had grown significantly in size. Robert Clower, leading the Northwestern University project, noted during his time in Monrovia that "a major bottleneck to effective planning in Liberia is likely to be the absence of any systematic records of statistics collected by government departments and central compilation of governmental regulations and activities."[12]

The successive difficulties faced by Cromie, Brown, and the Northwestern team have been compounded in more recent decades. Both environmental conditions and looting during the civil wars have taken their toll, particularly on records from the nineteenth century.[13] A recent survey of surviving archival holdings yielded just two boxes of material from before 1900.[14] The vast bulk of what remains dates from the presidency of William Tubman (1944–71) and beyond. Additional materials from these early periods can be found in the Liberia collections at Indiana University Library, and earlier material about Liberia survives in the national archives of its major trading partners and international organizations such as the League of Nations. However, even with this archival triangulation, much of Liberia's early economic history is the subject of only limited surviving documentation.

This lack of easily accessible data has made it difficult to compare Liberia with other countries in terms of the patterns of its development, particularly for the period before World War II. However, it remains possible to construct data series, which can be used for comparative work, by harvesting quantitative information from largely qualitative

[11] George Brown, *The Economic History of Liberia* (Washington, DC: The Associated Publishers, 1941), 323–26.
[12] Clower to D. Nemetz, PAS, January 24, 1962, Herskovits Library, Economic Survey of Liberia papers, Box 1, Folder 9.
[13] David M. Foley, "Liberia's Archival Collection," *African Studies Bulletin* 11, no. 2 (1968): 217–20; Myles Osborne, "A Note on Liberian Archives," *History in Africa* 36 (2009): 461–63.
[14] Gregg Mitman, E-mail to author, March 3, 2018.

sources. For example, the annual statements of the president of Liberia to the legislature frequently contain data on government finances and, less frequently, trade, which can be compiled into a mostly continuous data set. These are supplemented or checked by figures given in diplomatic correspondence or the media. Sporadic trade reports provide additional data on exports. The rest of the chapter presents annual data on population, government finances, and trade. It concludes by using these data to construct measures of GDP per capita, which are compared with other countries in Africa and around the world.

Population

Population data are one of the most basic categories of data needed to track patterns of development over time. Unfortunately, there are few reliable direct measurements of the population of African countries before the second half of the twentieth century, and almost none at all before the nineteenth. Gareth Austin writes that "all aggregate figures for the population of pre-colonial sub-Saharan Africa, or its major sub-regions are 'guesstimates' based on backward projection from colonial census reports."[15] More recently, Sarah Walters has noted that "despite considerable research, especially on the demographic impact of slavery and colonialism, knowledge of Africa's past population trends remains sparse compared with other world regions."[16] There are some isolated exceptions, such as John Thornton's study of the Kingdom of the Kongo from the sixteenth to eighteenth centuries, which relies on baptismal registers kept by missionaries in the region.[17] Colonial governments made some effort to calculate the population of their territories. However, the limited capacity of colonial states meant colonial administrations had to make do with uncertain estimates by district officers for most regions. Resistance to colonial taxation and forced labor recruitment also made many Africans reluctant to be counted.[18] The first

---

[15] Gareth Austin, "Resources, Techniques and Strategies South of the Sahara: Revising the Factor Endowments Perspective on African Economic Development, 1500–2000," *Economic History Review* 61 (2008): 587–624.

[16] Sarah Walters. "African Population History: Contributions of Moral Demography," *Journal of African History* 62 (2021): 183–200.

[17] John Thornton, "Demography and History in the Kingdom of the Kongo, 1550–1750," *Journal of African History* 18, no. 4 (1977): 507–30. For an update to these calculations, see John K. Thornton. "Revising the Population History of the Kingdom of Kongo," *Journal of African History* 62 (2021): 201–12.

[18] Dennis D. Cordell, Karl Ittman and Gregory H. Maddox, "Counting Subjects: Demography and Empire," in *The Demography of Empire: The Colonial Order and the Creation of Knowledge* (Athens: Ohio University Press, 2010).

censuses judged to be reliable were not produced until after World War II, and, in many countries, not until after independence.

Even by this fairly dismal standard, however, data for Liberia are limited. Only the early population of migrants from abroad is relatively well documented. From the 1820s, censuses were taken of the migrant population, giving details of not only their numbers but also their ages and the number of deaths that year.[19] Unfortunately, these censuses did not continue after 1843, and there was no attempt to extend these counts to include the indigenous population. The next census was not for more than a century, in 1962. As a result, there was considerable uncertainty as to the population of Liberia for much of its history as a state. In 1912, the American consul wrote in response to a request for a Liberian census that "there has never been an official census taken of Liberia as a whole, neither has there ever been, so far as I am able to ascertain, any enumeration in the cities and towns of the country or in the political subdivisions which are counties. Statements with reference to the population of Liberia are merely estimates."[20] Writing in the 1930s, George Brown noted that "the total population of Liberia is unknown. Estimates vary widely and apparently in the interests of the occasion."[21] In 1956, Philip Porter gave the list of estimates over time, reproduced in Table 1.1.

The most systematic estimate of the population prior to the 1962 census was a PhD dissertation by Porter, a geographer, who used aerial photographs taken earlier in the 1950s to build a count of "huts" around Liberia and then field research to estimate the number of occupants per "hut." By this method, his estimate was 744,340, plus or minus 50,000. This was not far off some of the lower estimates of the 1940s but below the total given by the 1962 census of 1.02 million, which was in itself significantly lower than some earlier estimates. The lack of previous complete censuses made the calculation of population growth rates impossible. To remedy this, the Liberian government began a population growth survey of 70,000 people in 1969.[22]

Without reliable historical censuses, estimates of the population of Liberia and other African countries before the middle of the twentieth century are made primarily by assuming a reasonable growth rate and projecting backward from the first reliable count. Patrick Manning uses

---

[19] For an example, see Charles Henry Huberich (ed), *The Political and Legislative History of Liberia* (New York: Central Book, 1947), 289.

[20] W. D. Crum to C. S. Hammond and Co., September 11, 1912, in NARA RG 84 UD 584 volume 2.

[21] Brown, *The Economic History of Liberia*, 41–42.

[22] Republic of Liberia, *The Population of Liberia* (Monrovia: Ministry of Planning and Economic Affairs, 1974).

Table 1.1 *Population estimates for Liberia*

Year	Estimate	Source
1862	500,000	G. Ralston
1888	Nearly 2,000,000	E. B. Gudgeon
1906	Nearly 2,000,000	Sir H. H. Johnston
1912	600,000 to 700,000	L. Jore
1919	700,000	R. C. F. Maugham
1927	3,500,000	Capt. T. H. W. Beard
1948	1,322,066	US Economic Mission
1949	1,000,000 to 1,100,000	K. R. Mayer
1954	More than 2,500,000	Treasury Department, Liberian Government
1955	1,500,000	Wile, US Embassy, Monrovia
1956	700,000	J. Josephus, Firestone Plantations Company Recruiter

Source: Porter, "Population distribution," p. 47.

the growth rate of India to develop new estimates for African countries.[23] The use of the Indian growth rate has been critiqued by Frankema and Jerven, who argue that India was far more densely populated than much of sub-Saharan Africa.[24] They argue that the growth rates of land-abundant countries in Southeast Asia are more appropriate. Figure 1.1 shows estimates of the Liberian population using these two different growth rates. In the Manning estimates, the early population was higher but growth was less rapid. In contrast, the higher growth rate assumed by Frankema and Jerven results in a lower estimate for Liberia's population in 1850.

However, one problem for both these Liberia estimates is the starting point from which backward projections are made. They rely on population estimates by the UN for 1950 and 1960, which were made before Liberia's first census, and were actually higher than the census total. For example, the 1960 UN estimate was 1,052,000, as compared with a total population in 1962 based on the census of 1,016,443. While the gap between these is relatively small (around 3.5 percent), using the 1962 figure for calculating the population by the same method used in Frankema and Jerven reduces the overall population throughout the period. In 1850, for example, the revised estimate of the population within the modern boundaries of Liberia was 295,768 instead of

[23] Patrick Manning, "African Population: Projections, 1850–1960," in *The Demographics of Empire: The Colonial Order and the Creation of Knowledge,* edited by Karl Ittman, Dennis D. Cordell and Gregory H. Maddox (Athens: Ohio University Press, 2010), 245–75.
[24] Ewout Frankema and Morten Jerven, "Writing History Backwards or Sideways: Towards a Consensus on African Population, 1850–2010," *Economic History Review* 67, no. 4 (2014): 907–31.

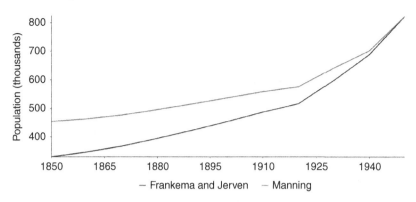

Figure 1.1 Alternative historical population estimates for Liberia
Source: Frankema and Jerven, "Writing history backwards and sideways," Manning, "African population."

330,073. This implies that using the Frankema and Jerven figures for Liberia would tend to bias per capita figures downward.

At the same time, it is also worth asking whether the growth rates assumed by Frankema and Jerven for the West African region as a whole are plausible for Liberia. Both Manning and Frankema and Jerven rely on what they refer to as "situational" revisions to growth rates, which attempt to take into account local events which may have affected fertility or mortality rates even if no direct evidence of the impact is available. Frankema and Jerven motivate their modification of Manning's situational adjustments largely with reference to the particular history of commercial expansion and colonial conquest in the region. For example, they argue that the West African growth rate likely differed from that of East Africa because the "integration of West Africa into the Atlantic economy through the so-called cash-crop revolution had been much further advanced in 1900 than the integration of other parts of tropical Africa in either the Atlantic or Indian Ocean trade networks."[25] Furthermore, they argue for adjustment in Manning's growth rates based on the fact that "colonial 'pacification' came earlier in West Africa," which "stabilized political relations and reduced investment risks." It was also "associated with growing domestic commercialization of rural and urban economies." These developments, along with colonial medical interventions such as smallpox inoculation, "created more favorable conditions for populations in West Africa to flourish."

[25] Frankema and Jerven, "Writing History Backwards or Sideways," 924–25.

Frankema and Jerven rely heavily on the experience of Ghana (colonial Gold Coast) in framing these estimates. However, there is considerable evidence to suggest that population growth rates in the Gold Coast may not fit the experience of Liberia well. As data presented later in this chapter show, the half-century from c. 1880 was, overall, a period of economic stagnation for Liberia, with frequent and often severe periods of shrinking. This had significant consequences for government finances, and government penury left little scope for the kinds of medical interventions which may have reduced mortality in Ghana. A report by the US Public Health Service, commissioned in response to an outbreak of yellow fever in Monrovia in 1929, noted, for example, that "Monrovia has no modern method of sewage disposal." Furthermore, it

has no municipal organization for the removal of garbahe [sic] and refuse . . . . The general method adopted is to dump all garbage and refuse in the back yard, in many instances it is the yard of the nearest neighbor who invariably returns a similar contribution. Once thrown out into the yard it is left to be disposed of by the numerous sheep, goats and other animal scavengers.[26]

Colonial governments could hardly be described as generous in terms of the provision of urban sanitation networks, but anecdotal evidence suggests that the position in Accra was better than in Monrovia. In response to an outbreak of plague, which killed 127 in 1908, construction began on the first pipe-borne water system – the Weija Water Works, which transported water to Accra from the Densu River – in 1914.[27] The availability of clean water led to declines in mortality from a variety of water-borne diseases, including dysentery, diarrhea, typhoid, and guinea worm. This is not to overstate the infrastructure of colonial Accra. There was, for example, no parallel provision of sewage disposal.[28] Still, studies of cities elsewhere in the world suggest that the provision of clean water had a dramatic impact on mortality rates, particularly through the decline in mortality not only from typhoid but also from the long-term health effects of surviving typhoid.[29]

[26] H. F. Smith, "A Report on Certain Phases of the Public Health Situation in Monrovia, Liberia, with Special Reference to Yellow Fever and Its Control," n.d., in Cambridge University Library RCMS 124/8, volume 1.
[27] Anna Bohman, "The Presence of the Past: A Retrospective View of the Politics of Urban Water Management in Accra, Ghana," *Water History* 4 (2012): 141–43.
[28] K. David Patterson, "Health in Urban Ghana: The Case of Accra 1900–1914," *Social Science Medicine* 13B (1979): 254.
[29] This is known as the Mills–Reincke effect. See Joseph P. Ferrie and Werner Troesken, "Water and Chicago's Mortality Transition, 1850–1925," *Explorations in Economic History* 45, no. 1 (2008): 1–16.

Without direct demographic data, it is difficult to know precisely how much these problems affected population growth, though there are suggestions from around 1960 that mortality remained high. In 1958, a report on public health by the United States Operations Mission in Liberia (USOM/L) stated that "the life expectancy and the infant mortality are not known in Liberia nor are there any other statistics that are worth talking about. It is, however, known that the infant death rate is quite high (estimated to be as high as 70%). It is also known that the maternal death rate is high, but nobody knows just how high." Disease burdens were also significant, according to the report.

The fact that we now have some fifty or more known cases of smallpox in one hospital and that we have had between 5–150 cases there since it was opened last February shows that, at least, one of the acute communicable diseases is prevelent [sic]. Our pre-spray malaria survey shows rates from 91–49% and even our post-spray surveys which are admittedly inadequate show a rate of between 62 to 19%, so we know that malaria is a big problem.[30]

A memorandum by a member of the Northwestern team noted that "although malaria is the largest single disease in Liberia, malnutrition and dysentery (in addition to malaria) are the causes of the absence of a 'population explosion' in Liberia. Another cause is the high infant mortality rate due to the ignorance of midwives."[31]

Some conclusions can be drawn from data collected from the 1960s onwards. In 1960, for example, life expectancy was higher in Ghana than in Liberia (forty-five as opposed to thirty-five), while mortality rates were higher in Liberia. Turning to fertility, Ghana's fertility rate (births per woman) was initially higher than Liberia's but declined faster. In studies of demography, trends over time are often more informative than comparisons of levels at a single moment.[32] The comparison of crude birth rates shown in Figure 1.2, for example, highlights the different trends between the two countries. In Ghana, fertility was higher initially but reached its peak around 1970. In Liberia, by contrast, fertility continued to increase until it peaked in 1981. An increase in fertility followed by an "irreversible" decline is one of the key stages in what demographers refer to as the demographic transition. In the first stage, high fertility rates and high mortality rates mean there is little or no population growth over the long run. When mortality rates fall, population expands rapidly as fertility rates

[30] "Public Health," USOM/L, Herskovits Library, Economic Survey of Liberia papers, Box 7, Folder 5.

[31] Memo to Survey Staff from Johnnetta Cole, April 24, 1961, Herskovits Library, Economic Survey of Liberia papers, Box 9.

[32] Tim Dyson and Mike Murphy, "The Onset of Fertility Transition," *Population and Development Review* 11, no. 3 (1985): 403.

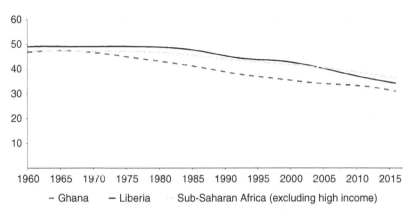

Figure 1.2 Crude birth rates per 1,000, 1960–2015
Source: World Development Indicators.

remain high and often increase. Owing to a variety of economic and social changes, fertility rates then begin to fall. In the final stage, low fertility rates and low mortality rates mean there is once again little or no population growth.[33] Research in historical demography has provided empirical evidence of this transition in a wide range of countries, from industrializing countries in eighteenth-century Europe to developing countries in the twentieth century. Placing Ghana and Liberia within this wider context suggests that Ghana began the demographic transition earlier than Liberia, making it difficult to believe that they would have shared the same growth rates across the twentieth century.

Figure 1.3 provides a reestimate of Liberia's population statistics, which reflect its later path in the fertility transition. The estimates are calculated by revising the starting point used in Frankema and Jerven's estimates, and by shifting the growth rate trend forward by ten years. This has the effect of dating the beginning of more rapid population growth during the twentieth century to the 1930s rather than earlier, which for Liberia reflects the beginnings of the period of economic growth discussed in the introduction to this chapter. This method produces figures for the nineteenth century which are somewhere between the two series in Figure 1.1: in 1850, 379,000 as compared to 330,000 (Frankema and Jerven) and 453,000 (Manning). To be sure, these estimates remain uncertain and there is much work to be done in the field of African

---

[33] Tim Dyson, *Population and Development: The Demographic Transition* (New York: Zed Books, 2010); Massimo Livi-Bacci, *A Concise History of World Population* (Chichester: John Wiley & Sons, 2017).

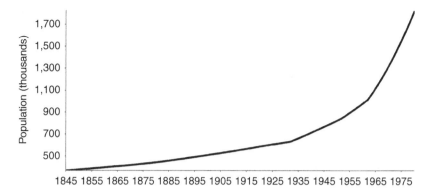

Figure 1.3 Recalculation of Liberia's population statistics
Sources: For figures up to 1962, see text. After 1962, see Liberia, *Statistical Handbook.*

historical demography to revise the "guesstimates" produced by backward projection under whatever assumptions. The role of internal migration, for one, remains imperfectly understood.[34] One aim of this book, however, is to broaden our understanding of long-run growth in Africa in order to sharpen the situational adjustments made for individual countries.

Public Revenue and Expenditure

Government finances are the next indicator considered in this chapter. Fiscal history has been an important strand in the quantitative economic history of Africa. What is taxed and how the proceeds are spent reflect wider political and economic characteristics of a country. Joseph Schumpeter argued that "the fiscal history of a people is above all an essential part of its general history. An enormous influence on the fate of nations emanates from the economic bleeding which the needs of the state necessitates, and from the use to which the results are put."[35] In global economic histories, the expansion of the public treasury is associated with the broader increase of government and legal capacity, itself related to economic development.[36]

---

[34] For a recent historical study of migration within Africa, see Michiel de Haas and Ewout Frankema, eds., *Migration in Africa: Shifting Patterns of Mobility from the 19th to the 21st Century* (London: Routledge, 2022).

[35] Joseph A. Schumpeter, "The Crisis of the Tax State," *International Economic Papers: Translations Prepared for the International Economic Association* 4 (1954): 6.

[36] K. Kivanc Karaman and Sevket Pamuk, "Different Paths to the Modern State in Europe: the Interaction between Warfare, Economic Structure and Political Regime," *American Political Science Review* 107, no. 3 (2013): 603–26; Noel Johnson and Mark Koyama,

In Africa, low population densities could make the collection of tax more difficult.[37] However, some African states did develop elaborate systems of taxation and tribute, often linked to the taxation of trade rather than land or income. More centralized states emerged particularly in areas where ecological diversity presented opportunities for specialization.[38] During the colonial period, the pressure to build local revenue sources came from the unwillingness of most metropolitan governments to sanction large financial transfers to their colonies.[39] How they did this depended on a combination of local political and environmental conditions.[40]

The Liberian government faced the same challenges as other states, colonized and independent. The prevailing theme in the historiography of the Liberian fiscal state is its almost constant insecurity, from the declaration of independence through the first half of the twentieth century. Monday Akpan, writing about the Liberian economy of the nineteenth century, noted that

> Of the many problems that beset the Liberian government of the nineteenth century, the most grave was perhaps the chronic penury of its treasury. This penury made it difficult to effect development in important areas like education, transport, communication and defense. It inhibited government efforts to occupy Liberia's territories effectively to prevent encroachment by European powers; and to implement a liberal or beneficent policy towards Liberia's indigenous African population.[41]

He supports this statement with fragmentary data on revenue and expenditures given in nominal terms for a series of benchmark years (see Table 1.2). This table hints at some of the main fiscal issues which dominate a fuller history. There is a steady but slow increase through

"States and Economic Growth: Capacity and Constraints," *Explorations in Economic History* 64 (2017): 1–20; Mark Dincecco, *Political Transformations and Public Finances in Europe, 1650–1913* (Cambridge: Cambridge University Press, 2011); Philip T. Hoffman, "What Do States Do? Politics and Economic History," *Journal of Economic History* 75 (2015): 303–32.

[37] Jeffrey Herbst, *States and Power in Africa: Comparative Lessons in Authority and Control* (Princeton: Princeton University Press, 2000).

[38] James Fenske, "Ecology, Trade and States in Pre-Colonial Africa," *Journal of the European Economic Association* 12, no. 3 (2014): 612–40; Leigh Gardner, "New Colonies, Old Tools: Building Fiscal Systems in East and Central Africa", in *Fiscal Capacity and the Colonial State in Asia and Africa, c. 1850–1960*, edited by Ewout Frankema and Anne Booth (Cambridge: Cambridge University Press, 2019), 193–29.

[39] Leigh Gardner, *Taxing Colonial Africa: The Political Economy of British Imperialism* (Oxford: Oxford University Press, 2012).

[40] See chapters in Ewout Frankema and Anne Booth, eds., *Fiscal Capacity and the Colonial State in Asia and Africa, c. 1850–1960* (Cambridge: Cambridge University Press, 2019).

[41] Monday Akpan. "The Liberian Economy in the Nineteenth Century: The State of Agriculture and Commerce," *Liberian Studies Journal* VI (1975): 1.

Table 1.2 *Estimates of revenue and expenditure*

Year	Gross revenue	Gross expenditure
1837	$3,500.00	Unknown
1847	$9,000.00	Unknown
1854	$48,046.98	$33,743.98
1878	$119,889.00	$124,166.63
1891	$151,940.90	$151,439.00
1892	$188,075.45	$165,943.60
1900	$255,000.00	$200,000.00
1905	$295,646.89	$286,427.73
1906	$357,433.39	$340,035.83
1907	$433,825.27	$426,436.16
1908	$382,356.00	$415,951.32

Source: Monday Akpan. "The Liberian Economy in the
Nineteenth Century: Government Finances," *Liberian
Studies Journal* VI (1975): Table 4.

the nineteenth century, but with setbacks in individual years, including deficits in 1878 and 1908. However, the table is fragmented, with large gaps between observations across crucial periods.

Figure 1.4 expands on this work by giving annual estimates of public revenue in constant prices from 1845 to 1980. For the nineteenth century, these estimates are based primarily on the annual statement of the Liberian president to the legislature.[42] Each year this statement would include reports on the statistics of Liberia's finances and trade for the year. Unfortunately, the original reports from this period have mostly not been preserved. However, the presidential statements themselves often give totals for revenue and expenditure, as well as sometimes more disaggregated figures. These data are supplemented by occasional figures from diplomatic correspondence or other archival sources. Where no direct observation has been found, linear interpolation is used to fill the gaps. Gray bars indicate observations from historical records. Figure 1.5 does the same for public spending.

The data are presented in constant US dollars. What currency to use for long-run figures in Liberia is not necessarily straightforward, as Chapter 5 documents in greater detail. After declaring independence, the Liberian government issued its own currency, the Liberian dollar, which was at least in theory issued at par with the US dollar. In practice,

---

[42] Accessed from IULC and CNDRA. Published in D. Elwood Dunn, ed., *The Annual Messages of the Presidents of Liberia 1848–2010* (Berlin: Walter de Gruyter, 2011).

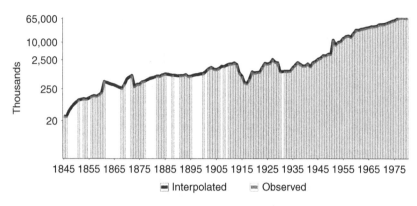

Figure 1.4 Real government revenue, 1845–1980
Constant 1950 US$

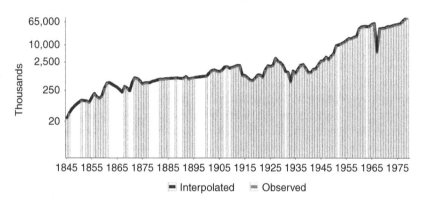

Figure 1.5 Real government spending, 1845–1980
Constant 1950 US$

however, the Liberian dollar was a paper currency issued without the backing of gold reserves or other assets. Through the nineteenth century, it was vulnerable to depreciation relative to gold-backed currencies. This led to the gradual substitution of British sterling, in an early example of "dollarization." In 1943, with assistance from the US military, Liberia changed from the British West African shilling to the US dollar. In the decades since, Liberia has continued to use the US dollar alongside the Liberian dollar. Presenting these figures in British sterling would be equally appropriate for some periods. The deflation of the series also presents difficulties. No systematic price data exist for Liberia across this period. Reflecting the change of currencies, price indices for British government spending are used up to 1943, after which US price series are spliced on. The two series are similar so in practice it makes little difference which is used.

The two figures show that the size of the government treasury expanded slowly in the first half-century following Liberia's declaration of independence, then more rapidly thereafter. However, it also shows the volatility of both revenue and spending. During the early period there were brief periods of rapid growth, in the 1860s and 1870s, but these were followed by sharp declines. A more substantial increase came around the turn of the century and lasted until the beginning of World War I. This was also followed by a sharp contraction, as was an increase of revenue in the 1920s. These fluctuations were small compared to the growth of government revenue during the postwar period. As the next section will show, this increase in revenue was linked to an expansion in foreign trade and investment.

Bringing the revenue and expenditure series together shows that more comprehensive data do not change the story of fiscal instability told by Akpan and others. Figure 1.6 shows the budget balance, measured as the surplus or deficit as a share of total revenue. The volatility of both revenue and expenditure resulted in frequent and substantial deficits. Even during phases when revenue was increasing rapidly, such as during the 1920s or the 1950s, spending kept pace with and often exceeded revenue. The Liberian government was thus frequently in financial trouble, even as it expanded in terms of both its share of the overall economy and its capacity.

Why were the public finances so volatile? In part, this is explained by the sources of revenue. Liberia, like other West African economies in the nineteenth century, relied heavily on the taxation of trade.[43] Tariffs charged on imported goods were the largest single source of revenue in Liberia until the introduction of an income tax in 1951, though efforts to diversify the sources of revenue – discussed in more detail in Chapter 7 – meant their significance declined over time. Still, since international trade was a key source of income with which Liberians paid direct taxes, these too tended to be more difficult to collect during periods of global economic crisis such as World War I or the Great Depression. The Liberian government had few means – peaceful or otherwise – by which to compel people to pay taxes, and its limited legitimacy with much of the population meant voluntary compliance was difficult to

---

[43] Gardner, *Taxing Colonial Africa*; Ewout Frankema, "Colonial Taxation and Government Spending in British Africa, 1880–1940: Maximizing Revenue or Minimizing Effort?," *Explorations in Economic History* 48 (2011): 136–49; Ewout Frankema and Marlous van Waijenburg, "Metropolitan Blueprints of Colonail Taxation? Lessons from Fiscal Capacity Building in British and French Africa, c. 1880–1940," *Journal of African History* 55 (2014): 371–400.

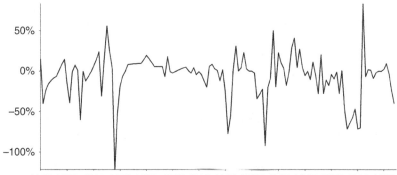

Figure 1.6 Liberia's budget balance, 1845–1980

build. Foreign companies operating in Liberia under concession agreements were offered generous tax exemptions as an enticement to investing in Liberia, so their contribution to the treasury was often less than it might have been.

Looking beyond the tax system, the Liberian government had few other means with which to mitigate sudden declines in revenue. It had no central bank until the 1970s. In its early decades, it would often turn to printing additional notes to satisfy short-run financial obligations, but this resulted in the depreciation of the Liberian dollar documented in Chapter 5. Once it began to use a foreign currency, this was no longer an option. It also accumulated substantial debts, as outlined in Chapter 6, but the introduction of foreign financial controls from 1906 also made this more difficult. In any case, neither of these mechanisms was sufficient to cope with the scale of the deficits accrued, and often the only real option was to cut spending, with difficult political consequences.

International Trade

Much attention is paid in African economic history to patterns of foreign trade, the third indicator reconstructed here. Trade links between Africa and the rest of the world have existed since antiquity. However, the volume of trade between Africa and Europe accelerated rapidly in the nineteenth century.[44] The abolition of the slave trade by most European

---

[44] Ewout Frankema, Jeffrey Williamson and Pieter Woltjer, "An Economic Rationale for the West African Scramble? The Commercial Transition and the Commodity Price Boom of 1835–1885," *Journal of Economic History* 78, no. 1 (2018): 231–367.

countries in the early nineteenth century did not immediately end the trade. However, exports of palm oil, groundnuts, and gum arabic gradually displaced the shipment of slaves across the Atlantic, as African merchants and elites responded to growing global demand.[45]

Since trade was a key source of both government revenue and commercialization in Africa, the level of exports has been interpreted by economic historians as a broad indicator of economic expansion.[46] While data on domestic agricultural production tend to be scarce, international trade is much better documented for most countries. For Liberia, however, no annual statistics of imports and exports survive before the early twentieth century. Instead, these need to be pieced together from sporadic reporting in qualitative sources, which for trade often leaves large gaps.

In the absence of regular annual statistics, exports can be estimated indirectly. The simplest method is through linear interpolation, as in the series used by Banks presented in Figure 1.7. Before 1908, the Banks' estimates show a steady increase in exports from 1850. This seems improbable given the turbulence of Liberia's economic history at the time. The period covered by the interpolation included a coup d'état in 1871, changing trade policies, and disputes with neighboring territories. It also included considerable volatility in the global economy, most notably the global depression of the 1870s and 1880s. Annual data reported for similar countries across the same period show significant annual variation rather than steady increases. Figure 1.8 gives nineteenth-century trade data for Liberia's neighbor, Sierra Leone, as an example. A more accurate way of filling in missing values builds on the close relationship between public revenue and the value of trade. As noted earlier, trade taxes were the most important source of revenue, and thus the two tended to move together. Where annual data are available, the correlation for the nineteenth century is very high: 0.93 for Sierra Leone for the period before World War I, for example.

Figure 1.9 gives estimates of the value of exports derived using this method. First, linear interpolation links the sporadic nineteenth-century estimates. Second, the ratio between exports and revenue is used to adjust

---

[45] Robin Law, ed., *From Slave Trade to "Legitimate" Commerce: The Commercial Transition in Nineteenth-Century West Africa* (Cambridge: Cambridge University Press); Paul Lovejoy, "Plantations in the Economy of the Sokoto Caliphate," *Journal of African History* 19, no. 3 (1978) 341–68; M. B. Salau, *Plantation Slavery in the Sokoto Caliphate: A Historical and Comparative Study* (Rochester: University of Rochester Press, 2017).

[46] Leandro Prados de la Escosura, "Output Per Head in Pre-Independence Africa: Quantitative Conjectures," *Economic History of Developing Regions* 27 (2012): 4.

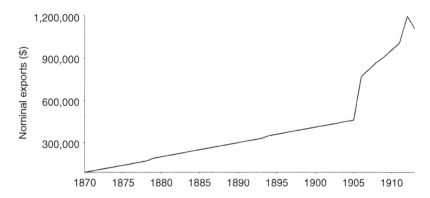

Figure 1.7 Interpolated estimates of Liberian trade, 1870–1914 (nominal values)
Source: A. S. Banks, "Cross-national time-series data archive," http://www.databanksinternational.com.

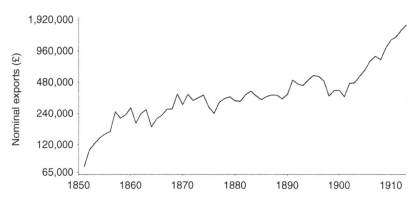

Figure 1.8 Sierra Leone exports, 1850–1913
Source: Sierra Leone, Blue Books.

the interpolation to take account of annual volatility in the data. These estimates provide the first overall picture of Liberian exports over this long period. There are two phases of rapid expansion: one in the middle of the nineteenth century and the second a century later.

During the first such boom, some Americo-Liberians built considerable fortunes as middlemen in the growing Atlantic trade. In between, there was a long period of stagnation punctuated by considerable volatility in the real value of exports. This period of stagnation began with the global depression of the 1870s, a period of economic retrenchment worldwide. The expansion of global trade resumed in the 1880s, and

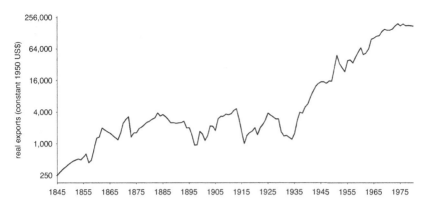

Figure 1.9 Real exports, 1845–1980 (in thousands of 1950 US$)
Source: See text.

Africa was among the fastest-growing regions in terms of export production. However, these data suggest that Liberia was seemingly unable to participate in this growth as it had in the middle decades of the century. As argued briefly in the next section and in more detail in Chapter 6, this was due primarily to the lack of investment in infrastructure comparable to other parts of West Africa. By contrast, the resumption of growth in the value of exports from the 1930s was linked to the rapid influx of foreign investment and production of exports by foreign concessionaires. During this period, as discussed in Chapter 9, the Liberian government aggressively courted foreign companies through the granting of large and generous concession agreements.

The primary exports in the early phase of growth were palm products and coffee. Figure 1.10 gives the value shares of specific exports by decade. While palm oil and palm kernels were exported across West Africa and thus do not generate much comment, there was great enthusiasm for Liberian coffee during this period: samples were even sent to the Great Exhibition of 1851. Data on coffee show a substantial increase through the nineteenth century. In the twentieth century, coffee exports were uneven, falling in the years leading up to World War I, then rising again during the interwar period, and falling to zero during World War II, before reviving during the second phase of growth after 1945. By the middle of the twentieth century, coffee was a minor contributor to Liberia's exports. During the 1930s, rubber became by far the most important export, comprising 82 percent of the total value of Liberia's exports on the eve of World War II. The export of rubber grew rapidly in

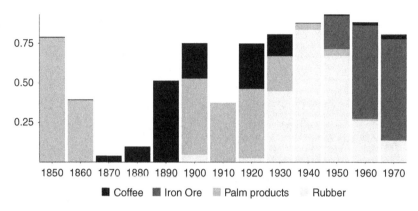

1850 1860 1870 1880 1890 1900 1910 1920 1930 1940 1950 1960 1970
■ Coffee ■ Iron Ore ▨ Palm products   Rubber

Figure 1.10 Export value shares by decade, 1850–1980
Note: Data are scarce for the 1870s and 1880s, but qualitative records suggest that it is likely that palm products and timber made up most of the remaining export value.

this period due to the establishment of the Firestone Rubber Plantation in 1927. Soon after World War II, however, rubber was overtaken by iron ore, which became the engine of the rapid growth that would prompt the comparisons between Liberia and Japan. Exports of iron ore grew from nothing in 1952 to 25 million tons twenty years later. Like coffee and rubber, however, the success of the Liberian iron ore industry was short-lived. By the early 1990s, the mines had ceased production entirely.

Real imports, shown in Figure 1.11, followed a similar pattern to exports. Data on the composition of imports is more fragmentary, but what data exists suggests that the nature of the goods imported shifted over time. During the nineteenth century, and particularly during the first decades after migrants arrived, imports were dominated by two classes of goods: those which could be traded with indigenous communities, particularly cotton textiles and tobacco, and goods largely consumed by the communities of migrants themselves. These included clothing, furniture and other household goods, and some foodstuffs including flour, salted fish, and meat.[47]

Some historians have interpreted the latter as an indication that emigrants scorned indigenous foods and subsisted on imports instead. William Allen, however, has shown that this was not the case, pointing to evidence from letters and other records suggesting widespread

---

[47] American Colonization Society, *Liberia Bulletin No. 20* (Washington, DC: American Colonization Society, 1902): 60.

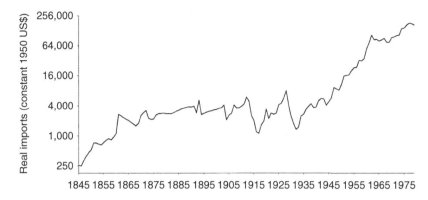

Figure 1.11 Real imports, 1845–1980 (in thousands of 1950 US$)

consumption of cassava and other African products.[48] Rather, food imports reflected what was to become a persistent problem in Liberia's economic history, namely the limited integration of local markets due to the high cost of transport from the interior to the coast. As a result, urban populations depended on imports of rice through most of the period, despite the fact that rice was widely produced locally. Rice imports increased rapidly with the expansion of rubber plantations and mining after World War II, as shown in Chapter 9.

Foreign trade was thus a key ingredient of Liberian economic development over the nineteenth and twentieth centuries. It was the main source of both economic growth and periods of shrinking, and on top of that underpinned government finances and the private incomes of the elite. The next section incorporates these figures with estimates of the shares of different sectors in the economy to build the first annual estimates of Liberian GDP per capita since 1847.

Liberian Historical National Accounts, 1845–2008

The three data series developed in this chapter can be used to construct the first estimates of Liberia's GDP per capita built from original archival data from 1845 to 1980. These estimates allow Liberia's economic performance since the middle of the nineteenth century to be compared to other countries, both in the region and farther afield. They show that

---

[48] William Allen, "Rethinking the history of settler agriculture in nineteenth-century Liberia," *International Journal of African Historical Studies* 37 (2004): 435–62.

Liberia's pattern of economic development over this period was characterized by considerable volatility, with the gains achieved during periods of rapid growth erased by economic shocks, both internal and external. While Liberia shared this characteristic with other West African countries, the pattern of growth in Liberia differed from that of the rest of the region.

Official GDP per capita data produced by the Liberian government begins only in 1964. Prior to that, there were two efforts to calculate Liberia's national income during the 1940s and 1950s. The first was an unpublished series compiled by a US government survey conducted in Liberia in 1959.[49] The second was by the Northwestern University team for the 1950s.[50] Subsequently, there has been only one attempt by an economic historian to estimate GDP per capita for Liberia before 1945. Leandro Prados de la Escosura's pioneering figures for a set of benchmark years from 1870 are based on extrapolating the relationship between terms of trade data and per capita income from the post-1945 period backward, using the largely interpolated trade data from Banks, replicated in Figure 1.7.[51] The estimates presented here use the archival data presented in previous sections of this chapter to calculate GDP per capita from the output side, dividing the economy into three sectors: the traditional sector (which includes agriculture and domestic industry and services), government, and the export sector. The method used is based on Broadberry and Gardner's estimates for eight other African countries, with some modifications due to data constraints.[52] These are outlined in more detail in Appendix 2.

In Liberia, as in other African economies, the domestic production of food and other goods for home consumption is the least well-documented of the three sectors discussed here, especially before the mid-twentieth century. In 1962, Northwestern economist Robert Clower described the agricultural sector as being divided among (1) foreign-owned plantations; (2) commercial farms; and (3) "tribal" farms producing for subsistence. Subsistence farmers made up the vast majority of those employed in agriculture, and of the labor force as a whole. He estimated, based on aerial surveys conducted during the 1950s, that there were some 150,000 "tribal farms" in production at that point. The plantation and commercial sectors had grown more recently and produced exports crops, primarily

---

[49] Report of the United States Internal Security Survey Team to Liberia November 16 to December 14, 1959, NARA RG 59, Entry A1 3107, Box 2.

[50] Robert W Clower, George Dalton, Mitchell Harwitz and A. A. Walters, *Growth Without Development: An Economic Survey of Liberia* (Evanston: Northwestern University Press, 1966).

[51] Prados de la Escosura, "Output Per Head in Pre-Independence Africa."

[52] Broadberry and Gardner, "Economic Growth in Sub-Saharan Africa, 1885–2008."

rubber.[53] The 1971 agricultural census painted a similar picture. It reported 128,076 agricultural holdings, with a total farm population of 681,702 (out of a total population of 1,362,000). Of these, 110,839 holdings produced rice, with an average size of 2.1 acres, and 73,103 produced cassava with an average size of 0.9 acres. These were the two main staple crops. There were 9,744 farms producing rubber, with an average size of 43.1 acres.[54]

The growth of plantation and commercial agriculture had prompted what Clower described as a slow process of commercialization in the subsistence sector, with the production of some traditional cash crops like cocoa, coffee, and piassava.[55] This had also been true in the first era of export expansion when indigenous farmers began to produce their own coffee and cocoa during the nineteenth century following the cultivation of both crops on settler farms near the coast.[56] However, this process was slowed by two factors: the high cost of transport from the interior, discussed in greater detail in Chapter 6, and in the twentieth century an institutional structure that gave the indigenous population little incentive to invest in agricultural productivity. This is discussed in Chapter 7.

Owing to the lack of systematic data on production in the subsistence sector, the estimates presented here follow the method used in early historical national accounts and assume that this sector grows in line with population.[57] In more recent work, the assumption that per capita consumption remains constant even as wider economies change has been challenged. To get a more accurate picture of how demand for food develops over time, newer estimates combine population data with estimates of income elasticity.[58] In estimates for other African countries, this

[53] Robert Clower, "Liberian Agriculture and Economic Development," Northwestern University Staff Paper, Liberian Economic Survey Papers uncatalogued.

[54] Republic of Liberia, 1971 Census of Agriculture: Final Report (Monrovia: Ministry of Planning and Economic Affairs, 1984).

[55] Robert Clower, "Liberian Agriculture and Economic Development," Northwestern University Staff Paper, Herskovits Library, Liberian Economic Survey Papers uncatalogued.

[56] Santosh C. Saha, "Agriculture in Liberia during the Nineteenth Century: Americo-Liberians' Contribution," Canadian Journal of African Studies 22 (1988): 234.

[57] P. Deane, Colonial Social Accounting (Cambridge: Cambridge University Press, 1953); R. Szereszewski, Structural Changes in the Economy of Ghana, 1891–1911 (London: Weidenfeld and Nicolson, 1965).

[58] N. F. R. Crafts, "English Economic Growth in the Eighteenth Century: A Re-Examination of Deane and Cole's Estimates," Economic History Review 29 (1976): 226–35; Paolo Malanima, "The Long Decline of a Leading Economy: GDP in Central and Northern Italy, 1300–1913," European Review of Economic History 15 (2011): 169–219; Carlos Alvarez-Nogal and Leandro Prados de la Escosura, "The Rise and Fall of Spain, 1270–1850," Economic History Review 66 (2013): 1–37; Stephen Broadberry, Johann Custodis and Bishnupriya Gupta, "India and the Great Divergence: an Anglo-Indian comparison of GDP per capita, 1600–1871," Explorations in Economic History 56 (2015): 58–75.

is done using real wages.[59] Unfortunately, very little price and wage data survive for Liberia before 1945, and thus it is not possible to apply the same approach here. Output for the government sector is measured by real government spending. As shown in the section on government finances, real government spending per capita grew rapidly in the first decades after Liberia's declaration of independence in 1847. Growth then slowed across the period from the middle of the 1870s until the early 1940s, when growth accelerated again. This follows broadly the pattern of real exports, used to measure output in the export sector. That these two should move in parallel is consistent with the importance of trade for government revenue.

To calculate GDP from these series requires applying the appropriate weights for the three sectors. Differences in definition mean the weights vary slightly between the US government, Northwestern University, and official Liberian government series, but all show a rapid growth of the export sector as a share of the overall economy. The time series of aggregate GDP is constructed from real output indices for the three main sectors, using the 1964 weights from Table 1.3.[60] This is then divided by population to produce estimates of GDP per capita.

Table 1.4 shows that in 1845, Liberian GDP per capita was $430, just above bare-bones subsistence, which is usually taken to be $400. This represents most people living at $1 a day, which was the World Bank's definition of poverty in 1990, plus an elite who were much richer, but were too few in number to have a significant impact on the average GDP per capita. It rose to around $500 in the two decades following the declaration of independence but then stagnated for a half-century before a period of rapid growth from the late 1930s. This growth was driven

Table 1.3 *Sectoral shares from Liberian national accounts, 1964*

	Traditional	Government	Export
1964	17%	7%	75%

Source: See text.

[59] Broadberry and Gardner, "Economic growth in Sub-Saharan Africa 1885–2008."
[60] See Appendix 2 for other estimates of sectoral weights.

Table 1.4 *GDP per capita in Liberia, Ghana, and Japan, 1850–1980*

	Liberia ($1990)	Ghana ($1990)	Japan ($1990)	Liberia/ Ghana (%)	Liberia/ Japan (%)
1850	441		901		48.9
1860	482				
1870	536		991		54.0
1880	540				
1885	574	654	1,085	87.8	53.0
1890	522	661	1,163	79.0	44.9
1901	469	696	1,356	68.1	34.6
1911	560	798	1,506	70.2	37.2
1920	490	815	1,866	60.1	26.2
1929	521	1,151	2,299	45.3	22.7
1938	533	1,142	2,671	46.7	20.0
1945	810	1,022	2,307	79.2	35.1
1950	1,084	1,122	1,921	96.6	56.4
1955	1,304	1,200	2,771	108.7	47.0
1960	1,885	1,378	3,986	136.8	47.3
1965	2,283	1,393	5,934	163.9	38.5
1970	2,796	1,424	9,714	196.4	28.8
1975	2,714	1,247	11,344	217.7	23.9
1980	2,596	1,157	13,428	224.4	19.3

Source: Broadberry and Gardner, "Economic growth in Sub-Saharan Africa"; Maddison, "Statistics on world population, GDP and per capita GDP."

largely by expansion in the export sector, though the government sector also grew during this period. It continued until the 1970s, after which it stagnated then declined by 1980.

For reference, Table 1.4 also gives GDP per capita in Ghana and Japan, the two comparator countries mentioned so far in this book. Appendix 2 expands the range of comparisons. It shows that Liberia and Ghana had similar levels of GDP per capita in 1884, but Liberia fell behind through the next few decades until the interwar period. At its lowest point in the early 1930s, Liberia's GDP per capita was less than 40 percent of Ghana's. In the 1940s, Liberia's rapid growth brought it back into parity with Ghana, and during the 1950s and 1960s, its GDP per capita was substantially higher than Ghana's.

This divergence is striking and signals a wider difference between Liberia and other West African countries. During the late nineteenth and early twentieth centuries, Liberia stagnated even as Ghana (then the Gold Coast) and most other West African countries enjoyed rapid growth based on the production of export commodities – in Ghana's case, cocoa. This growth was facilitated in no small part by the construction of railways. Construction of the Gold Coast railway began in 1898, and by the turn of the century it had reached the main cocoa-growing areas. For reasons discussed in Chapter 6, Liberia was unable to raise sufficient capital for railway construction and thus could not capitalize on export growth during the decades of globalization that preceded World War I.

Equally striking is Liberia's sudden growth from the 1930s, which allowed it to not only catch up with Ghana but actually exceed it by a substantial margin. This can be attributed to two factors investigated in greater detail later in the book. First was the establishment of the Firestone Rubber Plantation. While the plantation did not actually begin production until the 1930s, it also laid the groundwork for the rapid influx of foreign concession companies producing rubber, iron ore and timber during the two decades after 1945. It was these concession companies, and to a lesser extent the commercial farms related to them, which were largely responsible for the growth in exports, which in turn fueled the expansion of the government sector. This growth, and the uneven distribution of its proceeds, is the subject of Chapter 9. The second factor was foreign aid, examined in Chapter 8. Beginning during World War II, Liberia was a key recipient of foreign aid from the United States which contributed to improvements in road and port facilities.

Though Japan's per capita income was higher than that of the two African countries, comparison with Japan tells a similar story up to the 1930s, with Liberia falling steadily behind. The impact of the war on Japan's economy along with the acceleration of Liberian growth led to a short period of convergence in which Liberia regained its relative position of the late nineteenth century. The two grew at roughly the same pace during the 1950s before Liberia fell decisively behind from 1960. Its level of development was substantially lower and, as the rest of the book will explore, it did not have the same level of human capital and state capacity, leaving it vulnerable to periods of shrinking. During the civil war of the 1990s, Liberian GDP per capita dipped below the level of the nineteenth century, and subsequent growth has failed to regain the highs of the 1970s.

Conclusions

By bringing together the scraps of data on Liberia's economic history which have survived in a variety of qualitative sources, this chapter has provided a quantitative overview of Liberia's economic history since the middle of the nineteenth century. While the figures here can certainly be improved – and hopefully will be in future research – they tell a story of economic turbulence which is consistent with much of the existing historiography. However, they also allow Liberia's story to be compared with that of its neighbors in a systematic way for the first time.

From the data in Table 1.4 and the underlying series discussed earlier in the chapter, it is possible to separate Liberia's economic history into four periods. The first, dating from the 1820s until the 1870s, was a period of growth and expansion, as it was across much of the West African coast. Rising demand for African crops and forest products like palm oil paved the way for a rapid growth in the export of such goods. Americo-Liberian elites competed with indigenous merchants for a place in that growing trade, and some achieved considerable success in the coastal shipping of palm oil and subsequently coffee. Beginning with the global depression of the 1870s, Liberia's fortunes took a turn, both in absolute and relative terms. Like other such mercantile communities along the coast, Liberia's merchants began to lose their position of comparative advantage as steamships and larger European firms began to dominate. The construction of railways in neighboring countries saw more and more Liberian goods be exported out over land borders, with no benefit to the Liberian treasury. This downward trajectory was not reversed until the 1930s when the Firestone Rubber Plantation came into production. From then, exports of rubber and iron ore fueled rapid growth which saw Liberia catch up to Ghana and other African countries in terms of its per capita GDP.

The proceeds of this growth were unevenly distributed and accrued mostly to an urban elite in and around Monrovia. Inequality between regions and groups was not new to Liberia, as subsequent chapters will show, but it was certainly exacerbated by the specific pattern of growth during the middle of the twentieth century. The strains this placed on the political system began to emerge in the middle of the century, and in 1980 the unified rule of the True Whig Party finally fractured, ultimately leading to the civil wars which cost hundreds of thousands of lives and erased the economic gains of the period after World War II.

Liberia's story over the nineteenth and twentieth centuries is thus an extreme example of the pattern of growth observed in most countries before industrialization, characterized by phases of growth, which are then reversed by periods of shrinking.[61] The scale of the shrinking is due to a combination of limited economic diversification and institutional

---

[61] Stephen Broadberry and John Joseph Wallis, "Growing, Shrinking, and Long Run Economic Performance: Historical Perspectives on Economic Development," NBER Working Paper 23343 (2017).

weaknesses. Liberia's dependence on a small number of primary exports left it vulnerable to changing global demand for these products, and some of its biggest periods of shrinking came during global economic crises or the two World Wars. The most significant downturn, however, was during the civil wars of the 1990s, resulting from the failure of the Liberian political elite to redistribute economic gains more widely and allow a greater share of the population a voice in political decisions.

Subsequent chapters of the book explore how these two vulnerabilities emerged and developed over time. Part I of the book examines their foundations. Chapter 2 uses anthropological and archeological evidence to examine what we know about the economy of the "Grain Coast" before the arrival of migrants from the United States. Chapter 3 focuses on the migrants themselves, drawing together various collections of data to ask who came to Liberia and how the selection of migrants influenced its later history. Part II focuses on the Liberian government's struggles to exercise its new economic sovereignty in a region increasingly dominated by European influence. The dilemmas it faced and the solutions it found helped shape the impact of the long period of stagnation on the shape of Liberia's economy and society. In Part III, three chapters examine how the Liberian government under Americo-Liberian rule used strategic alienation of its sovereignty to help sustain the pace of economic growth and, in consequence, its own survival.

Part I

Foundations

2 Before the Dragons Came

> Before the dragon came ..., humans ruled the forest. Gola people and Kissi people and Loma people and Gio people. Vai people and Kpelle people and Kru people and Mano people. Bassa people and Krahn people and Grebo people and Gbani people. And these groups, they all ruled in their own way, prayed in their own way, told stories in their own way, loved in their own way. The people had many chiefs and each group had one prince to lead them. But the dragon said the forest was too small, and the ways of the people were not correct.
>
> Wayétu Moore, *The Dragons, the Giant, the Women: A Memoir*

In a memoir about her childhood during the Liberian Civil War, Wayétu Moore likens both the Americo-Liberian elite who governed the country up to 1980 and Samuel Doe, the man who overthrew them, to the mythical dragon Hawa Undu. When he came to power, Doe "promised that the forest would be for everyone again," but "those promises broke into tiny pieces."[1] In the eyes of five-year-old Wayétu, neither dragon had served the country well.

Many accounts of the Liberian Civil War blame long-standing inequalities and tensions between the Americo-Liberian elite and the indigenous majority for the eventual outbreak of violence. They point to Americo-Liberian policies of economic exploitation and political exclusion, along with assumptions of cultural superiority. At the same time, however, many histories of Liberia also pay little attention to the indigenous population other than as victims of elite predation. Stephen Ellis complains that much of Liberian historiography "is the history only of a few thousand settlers and their descendants in a country which, before the war of 1989, counted some 2,600,000 inhabitants."[2]

---

[1] Wayetu Moore, *The Dragons, the Giant, the Women: A Memoir* (Minneapolis: Greywolf Press, 2020), 31.
[2] Stephen Ellis, *The Mask of Anarchy: The Destruction of Liberia and the Religious Dimension of an African Civil War* (New York: New York University Press, 2007), 37.

And yet recent economic histories of Africa have shown that understanding the foundations of what became the Liberian economy before it was called Liberia is essential for understanding its later political and economic development.[3] If European colonizers could not treat their colonies as an institutional "blank slate" on which they could impose the institutions of their choice, Americo-Liberians were in even less of a position to do so given their lack of resources or access to external reinforcement.[4] Until the early twentieth century, the reach of the Liberian government into the interior was limited. Even after that, it relied heavily on indigenous institutions under policies of "indirect rule" which imitated those of colonized neighbors. Moreover, recent research into the relationship between the indigenous population and the Americo-Liberian elite suggests the divide between the two was not as wide as it once seemed.[5]

This chapter offers a sketch of the economic and political institutions of the region that became Liberia prior to the nineteenth century. It was then known to Europeans as the Grain Coast, depicted in the early eighteenth century by British cartographer Herman Moll in Map 2.1. The chapter then compares it to neighboring regions. Given the scarcity of data from the time, it relies on a variety of sources, including the accounts of early explorers, anthropological studies, and a range of biogeographic data. Its aim is to outline the economic and political foundations on which the Liberian state was built from the nineteenth century onward, which requires looking beyond the activities of the Americo-Liberians and understanding the role of indigenous economic agents.

Calculating the Unknowable

Neither a lack of evidence nor a failure to consult work already published has inhibited the expression of views about the economic backwardness of Africa in the period before European rule. On the contrary, opinions have been stated with a degree of conviction which sometimes appear to be inversely related to the amount of historical knowledge acquired.[6]

---

[3] Jutta Bolt and Leigh Gardner, "How Africans Shaped Colonial Institutions: Evidence from Local Taxation," *Journal of Economic History* 80, no. 4 (2020): 1189–223; Sanghamitra Bandyopadhyay and Elliott Green, "Pre-Colonial Political Centralization and Contemporary Development in Uganda," *Economic Development and Cultural Change* 64 (2016): 471–508.

[4] Leigh Gardner and Tirthankar Roy, *Economic History of Colonialism* (Bristol: Bristol University Press, 2020).

[5] William E. Allen, "Rethinking the History of Settler Agriculture in Nineteenth-Century Liberia," *International Journal of African Historical Studies* 37, no. 3 (2004): 435–62.

[6] A. G. Hopkins, *Economic History of West Africa* (London: Longman, 1973): 9.

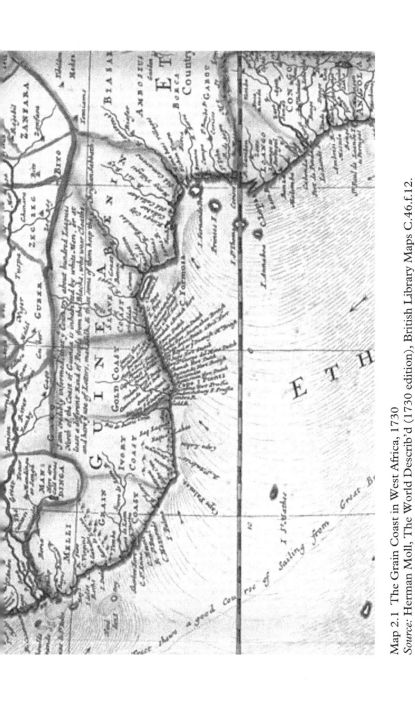

Map 2.1 The Grain Coast in West Africa, 1730

Source: Herman Moll, The World Describ'd (1730 edition), British Library Maps C.46.f.12.

Documenting the nature and workings of African economies before the beginning of European rule was one of the earliest tasks for scholars of the 1960s keen to stress that the colonial period was just a brief interlude in a longer economic history. In one of the landmark texts of the field, Hopkins argues that it is possible to reconstruct both an outline of indigenous economies as well as an approximate chronology and a framework for understanding regional variation. In 1982, Jan Vansina made a similar case, claiming that despite the scarcity of conventional sources, "knowledge about the past is often more substantial than is commonly realized."[7] Subsequent work has built on this foundation, not only using written records where they exist but also supplementing them with archaeological, linguistic, anthropological, and botanical evidence. Through these efforts, a rich historiography of indigenous societies and economies has emerged, building a picture of dynamic markets and producers engaged in extensive trade across long and short distances, undermining early claims about the "backwardness" of indigenous economies. Still, that evidence remains in many cases stubbornly indirect and relies heavily on proxy data from different periods for the comparison of different regions.

An early goal of research on Africa's pre-colonial economies was to challenge claims that African economies had operated under different, pre-capitalist rules. Such claims emerged from the "substantivist" school of economic anthropology based on Marxist notions of staged development. According to substantivists, trade and commerce in the pre-colonial period were not conducted for profit but rather for various social purposes. These arguments were connected to a wider view prevalent in the early twentieth century that "economic change in the sub-Saharan continent was largely absent or essentially exogenous."[8] Opponents of this view sought to show that economic incentives operated in Africa much like they did everywhere else. Robin Law, for example, uses data on prices in the Kingdom of Dahomey to counter the arguments of Karl Polanyi on the economic system of the kingdom. Polanyi had argued that economic activity of the highly commercialized kingdom was monopolized by the state, and prices were set according to social conventions. Using data on local prices, Law showed that despite administrative interventions in the price level, prices did fluctuate along with market conditions.[9]

[7] Jan Vansina, "Towards a History of Lost Corners of the World," *Economic History Review* 35, no. 2 (1982): 165.
[8] Gareth Austin, "Africa: Economic Change South of the Sahara," in *Global Economic History*, edited by Tirthankar Roy and Giorgio Riello, 251–70 (London: Bloomsbury Academic, 2019), 251.
[9] Robin Law, "Posthumous Questions for Karl Polanyi: Price Inflation in Pre-Colonial Dahomey," *Journal of African History* 33, no. 3 (1992): 387–420.

This does not mean that economic incentives were precisely the same in Africa and Europe. Environmental constraints and human geographies differed, and along with them people's choices about how and what to produce. Summarizing this early work, Gareth Austin notes that "while agricultural techniques varied across Africa, it is difficult not to see their prevailing features as specific responses to these physical conditions: a preference for land-extensive methods in the prevalence of itinerant pastoralism in herding areas, and various forms of hoe-based land rotation in arable ones."[10] These differences extended to the broader organization of society. While there remain debates about the origins of institutions and the reasons why they change, most theories accord at least some role to relative prices of factors of production in understanding the development of property rights. With low population densities, land was comparatively abundant in much of sub-Saharan Africa, and thus, the systems of individualized tenure that emerged in Europe and Asia were less common. Instead, African institutions were oriented less toward the control of territory and land and more toward the mobilization of labor by various means, including slavery.

This early work had the credibility of relying on direct evidence but, in consequence, was too patchy and anecdotal to be used in more quantitative analyses. To do more comparative quantitative work requires sacrificing the directness of evidence in exchange for comprehensive coverage of the continent and the ability to compare different regions to one another. Three primary measures are used: (1) population density and urbanization; (2) biogeographic data on soils or other features of the land; and (3) measures of institutional structure.

Population density and urbanization are often interpreted as proxies for levels of income in times and places when other data are not available, on the basis that "during preindustrial periods only relatively prosperous areas could support dense populations."[11] As discussed in the previous chapter, there is only limited direct evidence for the size of Africa's population (and therefore its density) before the twentieth century. As a whole, sub-Saharan Africa had lower population density than much of Europe or Asia, though higher than the Americas.[12] This is often believed

---

[10] Austin, "Africa: Economic Change," 254.
[11] Daron Acemoglu, Simon Johnson and James A. Robinson, "Reversal of Fortune: Geography and Institutions in the Making of the Modern World Income Distribution," *Quarterly Journal of Economics* 117, no. 4 (2002): 1232; Paul Bairoch, *Cities and Economic Development: From the Dawn of History to the Present* (Chicago: University of Chicago Press, 1988).
[12] Ewout Frankema, "The Biogeographic Roots of World Inequality: Animals, Disease, and Human Settlement Patterns in Africa and the Americas before 1492," *World Development* 70 (2015): 274–85.

to have had important implications for the structure of African societies and economies, limiting prospects for trade and specialization as well as the potential tax bases of African rulers.[13] As in all large regions, there was substantial variation within Africa in terms of the distribution of the population. Though data on population densities are fragmentary, it is clear that urban areas and "islands" of intensification in agriculture supported larger populations than more arid ones.[14]

For preindustrial societies, the link between population density, urbanization, and incomes is based on the ability of the land to produce sufficient food to support a larger population in which not everyone produces their own food. Another way to measure this is, therefore, to look at the quality of the land itself, an approach that has become increasingly common in quantitative economic history of Africa. Modern data are also used to estimate historical cropping patterns.[15] In this approach, modern data on soil quality are used as a proxy for pre-colonial incomes on the assumption that soil types are persistent over time and determine, at least in part, the ability of land in that region to support a surplus. From the perspective of econometric analysis, data on soil quality have several advantages: they are often easily accessible and already geocoded and can therefore be included in data sets that cover the whole of the continent. They are arguably more objective than the anecdotal accounts that inform historical studies of pre-colonial economic development. Finally, they allow for a more nuanced view of regional variation than broad estimates of total population.

However, they also have disadvantages. One is that soil mapping is an inexact science. The compilers of these maps face a constant struggle between, as one history of the field puts it, describing "the general kind of soil that tends to form in a particular climate" and preserving "a valid impression of the site-scale variability that occurs as a result of local geology, slope, internal drainage, vegetation cover and prior land use."[16] Human adaptations to particular local ecologies may mean that unpromising soils still have high yields. Specific soils may also be best for

[13] Gareth Austin, "Resources, Techniques and Strategies South of the Sahara: Revising the Factor Endowments Perspective on African Economic Development, 1500–2000," *Economic History Review* 61 (2008): 587–624; A. G. Hopkins, *An Economic History of West Africa* (London: Longman, 1973).
[14] Frankema, "Biogeographic Roots."
[15] Mats Widgren, "Mapping Global Agricultural History: A Map and Gazetteer for Sub-Saharan Africa, c. 1800 AD," in *Plants and People in the African Past: Progress in African Archaeobotany*, edited by Ana Maria Mercuri, A. Catherine d'Andrea, Rita Forniciari and Alexa Hohn (Cham: Springer Nature, 2018), 304.
[16] Nick Millea, "Soils Map," in *The History of Cartography, Volume 6: Cartography in the Twentieth Century*, edited by Mark Monmonier (Chicago: University of Chicago Press, 2015), 1448.

particular crops, and general maps may have difficulty accounting for gains from specialization. As one study of Liberia's geography put it,

There are many misconceptions about tropical soils. In general, they are neither so fertile as represented by the popular view, nor so infertile as is sometimes thought among scientific circles. The truth, which lies somewhere in between the two viewpoints, might be summarized as follows. Tropical soils vary greatly in capability; and for nearly every soil there is a proper use.[17]

Recent data also cannot account for change over time or for environmental shocks. Environmental histories of the African continent show significant variation across historical periods in broad climatic zones, the most dramatic example being perhaps the desiccation of the Sahara.[18] New innovations in environmental history have allowed for the reconstruction of droughts and other catastrophic events that may have had an impact on patterns of settlement and methods of production.[19] In response to this, Mats Widgren and co-authors have attempted to reconstruct from historical sources the agricultural systems of c. 1800 in Africa, rather than relying purely on twentieth-century data. They find that while climatic zones are important determinants of agricultural systems, there were many exceptions in which, for example, "areas of mixed farming or irrigation existed as islands of more intensive agriculture within the arid steppes."[20]

Soil quality serves as a proxy for the ability to support more complex, hierarchical societies. There are also more direct measures of the extent to which more centralized institutions of governance existed in Africa, although, as in the case of soil quality data, any systematic measures tend to be from a period long after the period of interest. Most commonly used for this purpose in quantitative economic histories of Africa is the *Ethnographic Atlas*, a database coded from secondary research in anthropology by George Murdock in the 1950s. The *Atlas* contains variables on a range of topics from political and family structures to methods of agricultural production and gender roles. Most often used in research in economics and economic history are measures of "jurisdictional hierarchy" which indicate the levels of authority above the village level, ranging

[17] Philip Wayland Porter, "Population distribution and land use in Liberia," London School of Economics PhD Dissertation (1956), 44.

[18] George Brooks, *Climate and Periodisation – Western Africa to c. 1860 AD: A Provisional Historical Schema Based on Climatic Periods* (Bloomington: Indiana University Press, 1985).

[19] David M. Anderson, "The Beginning of Time? Evidence for Catastrophic Drought in Baringo in the Early Nineteenth Century," *Journal of Eastern African Studies* 10, no. 10 (2016): 45–66.

[20] Widgren, "Mapping Global Agricultural History," 310.

from 0 to 4. Interpreting this measure as a proxy for levels of pre-colonial state centralization, econometric studies have linked it to current levels of economic development and political instability.[21] It has also been used in combination with soil quality data to test hypotheses about the relationship between environmental conditions and institutions.

Both the *Atlas* itself and its use by recent economics research have been the subject of critiques on a variety of grounds, from the accuracy of the data it contains to the ways in which recent work interprets it.[22] One issue is that the date of observation for many of the variables in Murdock's *Atlas* varies but is often much later than any period that can reasonably be classified as "pre-colonial" – the most common year is 1924.[23] Even for earlier observations, the interpretation is not clear. The nineteenth century was a period of considerable dynamism across much of sub-Saharan Africa, both politically and economically. Trade, migration, and political upheaval across the region make it difficult to distinguish between practices that had persisted from earlier and those that had emerged more recently.[24]

This brief review of efforts to document the development of pre-colonial economies in Africa points both to a growing consensus that such work is necessary for any comprehensive treatment of Africa's economic history and at the same time to the empirical challenges inherent in doing so. Direct data exist, but they are often patchy and anecdotal, making comparisons within Africa difficult. More comprehensive pictures require the use of proxy data that are subject to their own weaknesses of classification and interpretation. The rest of the chapter uses a combination of direct and indirect data to provide a sketch of the economy in the region of West Africa that became Liberia.

Population and Urbanization

The previous chapter documented the challenges of reconstructing Liberian population data going back in time. This section uses that data

---

[21] Stelios Michalopoulos and Alias Papaioannou, "Pre-Colonial Ethnic Institutions and Contemporary African Development," *Econometrica* 81 (2013): 113–52.

[22] For a review, see Denis Cogneau and Yannick Dupraz, "Institutions Historiques et Developpement Economique en Afrique: Une Revue Selective et Critique de Traveau Recents," *Histoire et Mesure* 30, no. 1 (2015): 103–34. There are ongoing efforts to update the *Atlas* to reflect more recent research. See Hans-Peter Muller, Claudia Kock Marti, Eva Seiler Schiedt and Brigitte Arpagaus, *Atlas Vorkolonialar Gesellschaften* (Berlin: Deitrich Reimer Verlag, 2010) and www.worlddevelopment.uzh.ch/en/atlas.html

[23] Morgan Henderson and Warren Whatley, "Pacification and Gender in Colonial Africa: Evidence from the Ethnographic Atlas," MPRA Working Paper 61203 (2014).

[24] Widgren, "Mapping Global Agricultural History," 309–10.

to compare Liberia's population density and urbanization levels with other parts of West Africa before the nineteenth century. As far as available evidence can show, the density of population in the area that became Liberia was low relative to neighboring regions. This was also reflected in the size of cities and towns. However, migration in the medieval and early modern periods had begun to change the human geography of the region prior to the beginning of the Atlantic trade.

Table 2.1 compares Liberia's population density with that of other West African states in c. 1850, using modern state boundaries and the population figures generated through backward projection in the previous chapter. It shows that Liberia's population density was lower than that of other parts of West Africa at that point. This is in accordance with qualitative historical evidence. Even in the late 1960s, there were extensive areas within Liberia with little habitation. In his 1969 report on the Kru, anthropologist Kjell Zetterstrom recounted that in Southeast Liberia,

vast areas are uninhabited. In Troh, we were told that it was more than a day's walk towards the north before on reached the first town. Troh chiefdom has three rather small towns. From Troh there is about 7 hours' walk to Duo which has three even smaller towns. From Duo there is another 3.5 hours walk before one reaches the first Toto-town. In eastern parts of Dino, the distances between towns are considerably less.[25]

Table 2.1 *Population densities, 1850*

	Population	Area	Population/km^2
Liberia	379,433	96,320	3.9
Sierra Leone	778,717	72,180	10.8
Cote d'Ivoire	1,033,828	318,000	3.3
Guinea	1,028,675	245,720	4.2
Ghana	1,981,047	227,540	8.7
Nigeria	13,539,371	910,770	14.9
Senegal	931,646	192,530	4.8

Source: For Liberian population estimates, see Chapter 1. Other population estimates are from Ewout Frankema and Morten Jerven, "Writing History Backwards or Sideways: Towards a Consensus on African Population, 1850–2010." *Economic History Review* 67, no. 4 (2014): 907–31. Area from World Bank, *World Development Indicators.*

[25] Kjell Zetterstrom, "Preliminary Report on the Kru," in IULC, Bai T. Moore papers.

However, such overall figures averaged across anachronistic boundaries can only tell us so much about the human geography of Africa. Despite having low average population densities, sub-Saharan Africa was home to numerous substantial cities and sites of more intensive cultivation. These then shaped local markets, trade routes, and often also the structure of states. Cities provided markets for their hinterlands and often acted as stops on longer trade routes. These, in turn, provided a source of revenue. In the absence of reliable quantitative data on the distribution of population, qualitative records can provide some insights into historical human geography. These include both early accounts from visitors to Liberia and later anthropological research. In general, these suggest that most Liberian communities were comparatively small, and that until the seventeenth century, this part of West Africa lacked the larger concentrations of population found in the Sudanic region.

In Liberia, settlement patterns reflected an economic system based on hunting, gathering, and shifting cultivation. For reference, Map 2.2 shows the distribution of ethnic and language groups in Liberia. In his work on the Dan (a Mande group), Martin Ford writes that "traditional Dan villages were impermanent, seldom remaining on the same site for more than a generation."[26] Among the Kpelle, Richard Fulton writes about new villages growing up around farms established by an individual and his wives. The initial founder would remain the head of the village, or Loi-Kalon, and controlled the distribution of usage rights for the surrounding land.[27] On the coast, among the Kru, people lived in villages called dako, comprising a small number of lineage groups (panton).[28]

The transitory nature of settlements makes it difficult to know exactly how large they were. A few larger commercial centers emerged at intersections between different types of land. For example, Handwerker writes that "Bopolu in western Liberia, has long been known as a major marketing town in an interlocking trade between coast and savannah."[29] Atherton's survey of archaeological research notes that the "remains of fortifications which used to surround many Liberian towns are also still found occasionally, especially when these were made of mud."[30]

---

[26] Martin Ford, "Kola Production and Settlement Mobility among the Dan of Nimba, Liberia," *African Economic History* 20 (1992): 56.

[27] Richard M. Fulton, "The Kpelle Traditional Political System," *Liberian Studies Journal* 1, no. 1 (1968): 2.

[28] Ronald W. Davis, *Ethnohistorical Studies on the Kru Coast* (Newark: Pencader, 1976), 23.

[29] W. Penn Handwerker, "Market Places, Travelling Traders, and Shops: Commercial Structural Variation in the Liberian Interior Prior to 1940," *African Economic History* 9 (1980): 3.

[30] John H. Atherton, "Liberian Pre-History," *Liberian Studies Journal* 3, no. 1 (1971): 109.

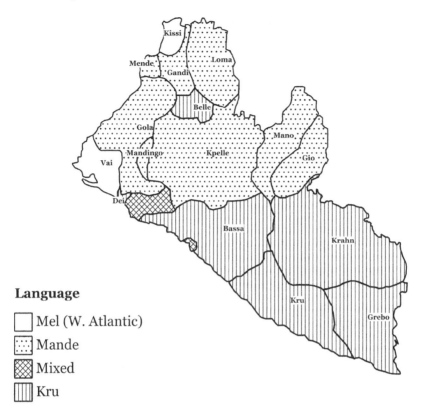

Language

☐ Mel (W. Atlantic)

▦ Mande

▩ Mixed

▥ Kru

Map 2.2 Ethnic groups in Liberia
Source: Duplicated from Stefan von Gnielinski, *Liberia in Maps: Graphic Perspectives of a Developing Country* (New York: Africana Publishing), p. 39.

During the early modern period, two factors began to change the distribution of the population in Liberia. The decline of the Malian empire followed by the arrival of Portuguese merchants began to draw new populations into the region. As a result of the political upheaval in the Sudan, several waves of Mande-speakers and others moved south into what is now the Liberian interior.[31] These groups retained links with the trans-Saharan trade and established a set of commercial centers. Handwerker describes the emergence of "double towns" of traders and

[31] Carl Patrick Burrowes, *Between the Kola Forest and the Salty Sea: A History of the Liberian People Before 1800* (Bomi County: Know Your Self Press, 2016), ch. 8; Augustine Konneh, *Religion, Commerce and the Integration of the Mandingo in Liberia* (New York: University Press of America, 1996), 9–11.

farmers which emerged in northern Liberia, including Borkeza, Zolowo, Zigita, and Zorzor.[32] At the same time, the expanding reach of the slave trade from the coast led to the development of what Hull describes as "a series of defensive settlements."[33] In the 1830s, an African-American missionary named George Brown – not, as far as this author knows, related to the author of the later *Economic History of Liberia* – went into the interior hoping to establish a mission station, and described one such settlement. King Brumney's Town, on the north bank of the St Paul's River had "a barricade around it, thickly set with plum trees, and about thirty booths within. And those people are of the Dey tribe. Their town covers about half an acre."[34]

Despite these changes, the distribution of the population remained closely linked to methods of agricultural production and their ability to support larger concentrations of population. Through much of what became Liberia, the ability to produce a surplus through cultivation was hindered by shortages of labor and the fragility of the soil. The next section considers the relative quality of Liberian soils and provides a brief outline of the methods of agricultural production.

Soil Quality and Agricultural Production

If they be farmers, point the to the soil, the fertility of which cannot be exaggerated, producing every thing a tropical clime can produce in ample abundance ... Labor and patience, two thirds of the labor, too, that it would take to support a man in the United States, will reward the workmen, thirty, sixty, a hundred fold – the profits will sweeten the toil. Reverend A. F. Russell, of Clay-Ashland, Liberia, quoted in the *African Repository* (1866)

It is amusing to one who knows, to read the windy letters from some of the Liberians, respecting the Agricultural resources and progress of that country. There positively is not, nor never has been a plow, a horse or a yoke of oxen, used in all the country. No man there has now or ever had, five acres of land cleared and in cultivation, and I am one of those who believe that it is impossible to clear the land, owing to the dense and rapid growth of the bush. William Nesbit, *Four Months in Liberia* (1855)

Migrants to Liberia in the nineteenth century gave widely divergent accounts of the economic potential of the country. While proponents of

---

[32] Handwerker, "Market Places," 11–12.

[33] Richard W. Hull, *African Cities and Towns Before the European Conquest* (New York: W. W. Norton, 1976), 19.

[34] George S Brown, *Brown's Abridged Journal Containing a Brief Account of the Life, Trials and Travels of Geo. S Brown, Six Years a Missionary in Liberia, West Africa* (Troy, NY: Prescott & Wilson, 1849), 69.

the colonization effort often extolled the fertility of the land, critics like William Nesbit accused them both of hyperbole and stressed the many challenges of agricultural production in Liberia. Based on soil quality measures, Nesbit and others like him were correct. However, anthropological and archaeological data suggests that indigenous people in the region adapted to the features of the soil by, as in other regions of Africa, adopting long fallow periods and practicing slash and burn techniques.

Map 2.3 compares Liberia to other parts of West Africa according to one measure of soil quality, the water-holding capacity of the soil. In systems of rainfed (rather than irrigated) crop production, the ability of the soil to retain water can be an important determinant of yields, acting as a failsafe in case of inadequate rainfall and determining the length of the growing season at the end of the rains. The map shows that Liberia is comparable to other countries in West Africa in having medium to low water-holding capacity, but with considerable regional variation. This is confirmed in Table 2.2, which gives descriptive statistics on the same measure.

In 1951, the US Department of Agriculture conducted a survey of the soils of Liberia based on a combination of fieldwork and aerial survey photographs.[35] Overall, it concluded that "the soils of Liberia are not rich, or fertile in the sense that a big crop with a high composition of plant nutrients can be harvested from year to year," contradicting some of the more optimistic assessments made on the basis of anecdotal data. "The soils of Liberia are not unlike those developed in other countries under forest and conditions of high rainfall and temperature. They have been extremely leached. They are low in total available bases and other nutrient elements." However, the report qualified this assessment by noting that "a very fertile soil is not necessary for the production of many crops. Although the soils of Liberia are not well-adapted to the production of certain crops, they are well adapted to others." According to the report, some 75 percent of Liberia's land area was comprised of land area particularly suited to the production of tree crops. This was reflected in the later success of coffee, cocoa, and rubber exports.

Hunting and gathering were prominent practices in many local economies. In his survey of the evidence for the coastal region, Amos Beyan writes that the Bandi, Mende, Loma, Kpelle, and Vai were all "gatherers and hunters before the fifteenth century."[36] Similarly, Holsoe argues that hunting and gathering was the dominant form of production across much

---

[35] US Department of Agriculture, *Reconnaissance Soil Survey of Liberia* (Washington, DC: US Government Printing Office, 1951).

[36] Amos Jones Beyan, "Transatlantic Trade and the Coastal Area of Pre-Liberia," *The Historian* 57, no. 4 (1995): 758.

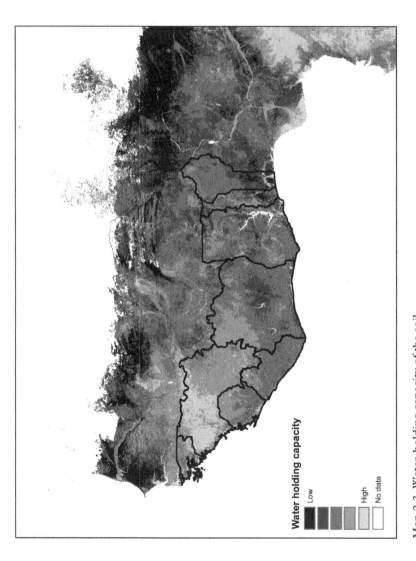

Map 2.3 Water-holding capacity of the soil

Source: Based on Johan G. B. Leenars et al. "Mapping Rootable Depth and Root Zone Plant-Available Water Holding Capacity of the Soil of Sub-Saharan Africa." *Geoderma* 324 (2018): 18–36.

Table 2.2 *Water-holding capacity of the soil in West Africa*

	Min	Max	Mean	Standard Deviation	Majority
Liberia	13	29	18	2	17
Benin	7	33	16.4	2.8	17
Cote d'Ivoire	10	29	17.8	2.4	18
Ghana	9	29	17.9	2.4	18
Guinea	13	33	22.6	2.8	22
Guinea-Bissau	13	29	20.7	2.6	20
Sierra Leone	14	29	19.9	2.7	22
Togo	8	29	16.9	3	16

Source: See Map 2.3.

of Liberia during what he calls the "pre-European" period.[37] In part, this reflected the difficulty of clearing Liberia's dense forest for cultivation.[38] However, the available evidence suggests hunting, gathering, and fishing were often complementary to cultivation, rather than substitutes.[39] For example, among the Kru, Zetterstrom writes, "many authors maintain that agriculture is a fairly recent introduction and that the Kru not very long ago were mainly hunters and gatherers. Their oral history to some extent supports this in that many of the most important characters in their tales and songs are hunters." However, he also observes that "their social organization is rather complex, a fact which hardly speaks for a recent shift from hunting and gathering to agriculture. The technique used is that of swidden cultivation and fallowing; the period of fallowing varying from 4–15 years." According to interviews conducted by Zetterstrom in the 1960s, the long fallow periods were both for biogeographical and historical reasons. "The reasons given for not staying in the same spot for any longer period of time were usually 'depletion of the soil and lack of moisture.' Another reason was that 'our forefathers did not practice it', i.e. staying in the same spot and using fertilizers."[40]

It is difficult to know the extent to which different groups relied on cultivation versus hunting and gathering. In 1958, Frank Livingston proposed that differences in the prevalence of the sickle-cell gene,

[37] Svend Holsoe, "Economic Activities in the Liberian Area: The Pre-European Period to 1900," in *Essays on the Economic Anthropology of Liberia and Sierra Leone*, edited by Vernon R. Dorjahn and Barry L. Isaac (Philadelphia: Institute for Liberian Studies, 1979), 63–65.

[38] Burrowes, *Between the Kola Forest and the Salty Sea*, 49.

[39] J. M. J. de Wet, "Domestication of African Cereals," *African Economic History* 3 (1977): 25.

[40] Zetterstrom, "Preliminary Report on the Kru," IULC, Bai T. Moore Papers.

a genetic adaptation to malaria exposure, could serve as an indicator of historical population densities and cultivation.[41] The agreement between his data and historical knowledge of farming practices varied. On the one hand, rice-growing groups like the Kissi, Kpelle, Loma, Vai, and Mende had comparatively high rates of sickle-cell prevalence, while the Ma and the Dan had lower rates. However, there were confounding examples. The Gola, who did not rely on rice cultivation, had rates of sickle-cell prevalence more comparable to those of the rice cultivators. Burrowes argues that some of these apparent contradictions can be explained by intermarriage, but that it may be more convincing to link sickle-cell prevalence to historically low population density than cultivation more particularly.[42] Archaeological evidence can also indicate the presence of rice cultivation. For Kpelle villages, Orr notes that finds of iron cutlasses, rawhide gloves, iron axes, hoes, rice-cutting knives, and mortars and pestles often coincide with areas of rice production.[43]

For both coastal and inland communities, rice was the primary staple crop, sometimes complemented by root crops, some of which were introduced through the Atlantic trade such as cassava.[44] In his study of the domestication of African cereals, de Wet notes that while the earliest record of rice cultivation in West Africa is from the twelfth century, it may have been cultivated much earlier. Originally a savannah plant, African rice was also cultivated in forest and upland areas. Asian rice was also introduced at some stage, but historical records do not often distinguish between the two.[45] For the Mano of northern Liberia, for example, upland rice was the primary crop with cassava second in importance.[46]

The methods of rice and cassava production in Liberia reflected adaptations to its relatively infertile soils.[47] The USDA report from 1951 noted that levels of nutrients in the soil were highest in land under virgin forest. Newly cleared land was thus more productive than land previously

---

[41] Frank B. Livingstone, "Anthropological Implications of Sickle Cell Gene Distribution in West Africa," *American Anthropologist* 60 (1958): 533–62.

[42] Burrowes, *Between the Kola Forest and the Salty Sea*, 210–11.

[43] Kenneth G. Orr, "An Introduction to the Archaeology of Liberia," *Liberian Studies Journal* 4, no. 1 (1972): 68.

[44] Burrowes, *Between the Kola Forest and the Salty Sea*, 225–26; George Schwab, *Tribes of the Liberian Hinterland* (Cambridge, MA: Peabody Museum of American Archaeology and Ethnology, 1947), 55.

[45] de Wet, "Domestication of African Cereals," 18.

[46] Zetterstrom, "Some Notes on Mano Beliefs," IULC, Bai T. Moore papers.

[47] This description is based on USDA, *Reconnaissance Soil Survey* and Johnetta Cole, "Notes on Traditional Occupations and Work Patterns of Tribal Liberians," Staff Paper No. 16, September 1962, in Herskovits Library, Northwestern Economic Survey papers, uncatalogued.

farmed – a difference described as the "forest rent" in other parts of West Africa.[48] Each year, small farms were made by clearing either virgin forest or the secondary bush which grew on land that had previously been planted. Clearing was done primarily by men between January and March, and the cleared foliage was left to dry and then burned in April. The 1951 survey showed that latosols after burning had more than double the amount of soluble phosphorous content of the topsoil, along with other nutrients, and therefore had a fertilizing effect. In May the rice was planted, primarily though not exclusively by women. Harvest season varied in different parts of the country but was usually between June and August. Once harvested, fields were left fallow to allow the regrowth of secondary bush, and a new piece of land was cleared the following year.

Even before the introduction of rubber, coffee, and cocoa exports, tree crops, particularly kola, were of early significance as trade goods in some parts of the region. The Dan of Nimba in northern Liberia began to grow kola nuts in order to exchange them for cloth, salt, tools, and sometimes rice and dried cassava during periods of seasonal food shortages in what was called the din lo, or "hunger exchange."[49] Palm oil was also produced locally and formed an important element of the diets of many people in the region. Palm kernels were less often cultivated than gathered from wild palm plants, as in this Kpelle oral history captured by Ruth Stone in 1970.

The story involves an orphan boy and a woman with no relatives who come together. After an introductory musical refrain, the story teller begins his narration. He describes the boy who, while walking along the path daydreaming, meets the woman. Hearing of his plight, she goes along with him and they gather palm kernels in the bush. The woman selects the finest kernels and admires one wistfully, wishing that it were a son. As she walks away, a child calls, "Mother wait for me."[50]

The iron ore that would later fuel such rapid growth in Liberia was known and exploited before the arrival of European merchants or African-American settlers, albeit at a smaller scale. Not all societies in the region practiced ironwork or metallurgy. Schwab noted that some Mano communities initially obtained iron from Kpelle smiths rather than producing their own. Later, the Mano replaced Kpelle iron with French trade iron supplied by Mandingo merchants.[51] Based on archaeological data, Will Schulze notes a particular concentration of ironworks in the

[48] Austin, "Resources, Techniques and Strategies," 599.
[49] Ford, "Kola Production," 52.
[50] Ruth Stone, "Meni-Pelee: A Musical-Dramatic Folktale of the Kpelle," *Liberian Studies Journal* 4, no. 1 (1972): 31–46.
[51] Schwab, *Tribes of the Liberian Hinterland*, 136.

southeast, particularly in northern Kpelle land at Fitua, Salayea, Palala, and other nearby places.[52] According to Ronald Davis, "Mt Gedeh has been known since the nineteenth century as a source of iron ore for local smelters. An iron smelting industry of unknown antiquity has been observed in the Putu mountains. This iron source may have been important in some way in the movement of peoples toward the coast."[53] Most iron production was done at relatively small scale, often for a single smith though some in large towns were built for two or three smiths.[54] Palala, in what is now northern Liberia, was an exception. Schulze describes the smelters there as being "of particular interest since they extend over a relatively large area and consist of a number of separate sites, some of which preserve a rather impressive witness of traditional iron smelting activities."[55]

The combination of soil quality data with evidence from historical accounts, archaeology, and anthropology illustrates that in terms of its biogeography, what became Liberia was similar to other parts of the wider West African region. Soils were often fragile, but people adapted to this by using long fallow periods. The comparatively low density of much of the Grain Coast region and its interior meant that hunting, gathering, and fishing were important components of food production for many people. However, this did not mean that there was no specialization or trade in this region despite limited domestic markets. Kola nuts, iron ore, and salt were produced for trade at both local levels and farther afield. The next section connects the institutions and social organization of indigenous Liberians to the resources and structure of economic production.

States and Societies

The structure of states reflected the population distribution and systems of agricultural production outlined earlier in the chapter. Most were decentralized, with hierarchies centered on villages or small groups of villages. There was no equivalent in Liberia to the highly stratified kingdoms to the north and east like Mali, Asante, or Benin. However, like other so-called stateless groups such as the Igbo of Nigeria, the indigenous people of Liberia did have effective institutions of governance, which could link more fragmented communities and help facilitate trade and coordination between them. There was also variation across

---

[52] Willi Schulze, "Early Iron Smelting Among the Northern Kpelle," *Liberian Studies Journal* 3, no. 1 (1971): 114.
[53] Ronald W Davis, "Two Historical Manuscripts from the Kru Coast," *Liberian Studies Journal* 1, no. 1 (1968): 45.
[54] Schwab, *Tribes of the Liberian Hinterland*, 136–37.
[55] Schulze, "Early Iron Smelting," 117.

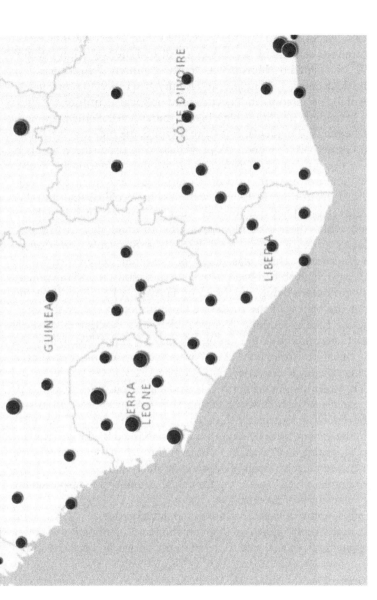

Map 2.4 Centralization of indigenous states in West Africa
Source: Constructed by the author from data coded by Jennifer Köhler. Larger dots indicate more centralized states.

space and time, and different degrees of centralization and stratification could occur within the same set of political traditions.

Map 2.4 shows societies in West Africa graded according to "jurisdictional hierarchy," a score of 1–4 indicating the number of layers above village level. According to this measure, the Grain Coast was one of the least centralized regions of West Africa. All of Liberia's ethnic groups score a "2," classified by Murdock as "petty chiefdoms." In their coding of the Murdock data set, Gennaioli and Rainer give Liberia a score of 0 for the share of the population under centralized political institutions.[56] Even Liberia's immediate neighbors have higher shares, even if only marginally in Sierra Leone (0.8 percent). For Cote d'Ivoire, the measure is 8.2 percent and Guinea 40.6 percent. As previously discussed, these numbers are subject to numerous criticisms and are no doubt spuriously precise. However, qualitative sources do not contradict the general conclusion that political institutions in Liberia were less hierarchical than in other parts of the region. They do, however, suggest a more dynamic political situation in which there were numerous substitutes for state institutions.

Murdock's primary source for Liberia was Schwab's *Tribes of the Liberian Hinterland*, which was based on research undertaken in the 1920s. George Schwab had been a Presbyterian minister and missionary in Cameroon before being appointed by Harvard's Peabody Museum, working at the behest of the Firestone Corporation, to study the characteristics of Liberia's ethnic groups.[57] Schwab's description of social organization suggested that the top of indigenous political hierarchies was the "clan chief" or "paramount chief," who had jurisdiction over a set of surrounding villages. These varied in size from just a few in Grebo areas in the southeast to larger units in the north.[58] It is not clear from Schwab's description the extent to which he was claiming that such structures had existed before the establishment of the Liberian government. Instead, he refers directly to the system of rural administration established by the government in Monrovia, writing that "when the tribes were brought under control by the Government, certain clan chiefs of outstanding ability and power were designated 'paramount chiefs' and given a nominal authority and responsibility over other clan chiefs of the area."

Subsequent anthropological research on political structures of the region suggests a more flexible system of fragmentation and coordination of power within a system of political rule centered in the village. In his study of the

---

[56] Nicola Gennaioli and Ilia Rainer, "The Modern Impact of Pre-Colonial Centralization," *Journal of Economic Growth* 12 (2007): 185–234.

[57] Gregg Mittman, *Empire of Rubber: Firestone's Scramble for Land and Power in Liberia* (New York: The New Press, 2021): 95–6.

[58] Schwab, *Tribes of the Liberian Hinterland*, 168.

Kpelle, for example, Richard Fulton writes that they were "organized around village groupings of various sizes," governed by the Loi-Kalon or "owner of the land." Village groupings originated when an individual and his wives, children, and other family set up autonomous households in a virgin part of the forest. Villages were "more or less autonomous," but would "attach their loyalties to the unit for protection and perhaps need for relationships higher than local structures could provide." However, the Loi-Kalon had limited authority over these villages, and Fulton noted that "there were even cases in which villages, feeling oppressed by their Loi-Kalon, would switch allegiances to a neighboring Kpelle king."[59]

Beyond the rise and fall of village alliances, there were several cross-cutting institutions in parts of Liberia which helped facilitate trade and diplomacy. Significant in the northern part of the country were the Poro and Sande secret societies. These had their own hierarchies, related to but not the same as village hierarchies. Richard Fulton finds that for the Kpelle, secret societies served a range of institutional purposes, from internal policing and certain judicial functions to diplomacy and communications between different groups and the legitimization of secular policies. This coordination occurred among the Kpelle without any pan-tribal Poro organization but instead relied on a set of shared norms and informal institutions.[60] For the Gola, too, authority centered in "the upper levels of secret society hierarchy and in the relationship between this hierarchy and the chiefs."[61]

Poro and Sande societies were largely restricted to the northern part of the country.[62] However, another set of coordinating institutions were craft guilds, in which smiths and other skilled craftsmen were connected across communities. Smiths in particular often held high positions in secret societies because their skills were needed for making ritual objects.[63] Schwab writes that

it was interesting to us to find guild fellowship everywhere in Liberia among those practicing the same handicrafts, regardless of clan or tribal affiliations. The weaver, the leather worker, or smith will always go to the home of a fellow craftsman, if there is one in the community, when visiting or passing through a place where he has neither friend nor relative.[64]

---

[59] Fulton, "The Kpelle Traditional Political System," 2.
[60] Richard M Fulton, "The Political Structures and Functions of Poro in Kpelle Society," *American Anthropologist* 74, no. 5 (1972): 1227.
[61] Warren L. D'Azevedo, "Common Principles of Variant Kinship Structures Among the Gola of Western Liberia," *American Anthropologist* 64, no. 3 (1962): 505.
[62] Warren L. D'Azevedo, "Tribe and Chiefdom on the Windward Coast," *Liberian Studies Journal* 14, no. 2 (1989): 94.
[63] Schwab, *Tribes of the Liberian Hinterland*, 145.
[64] Schwab, *Tribes of the Liberian Hinterland*, 121.

While anthropological data on Liberian state structures suggests limited levels of centralization, qualitative evidence offers a more dynamic picture of institutions in Liberia. They were likely less centralized than those of some states farther north, but the degree of centralization shifted over time as alliances between village groups rose and fell. The Poro and Sande societies, along with craft guilds, also provided links between village groups which helped overcome coordination problems.

Trade and Migration

As noted in the second section of the chapter, the interest of economic historians in the structure of institutions is partly driven by their historical role in facilitating trade and economic expansion. There is comparatively little data, even in proxy form, on the scope of trade within Africa during the medieval period. However, there is significant evidence – both anecdotal and archaeological – of extensive trade links within different regions of Africa prior to the beginning of the Atlantic trade. Salt, gold, kola, slaves, textiles, and other goods circulated along established trade routes and were often traded within cities and other market centers. Exchange often happened at a more local level between different types of agricultural producers, and in periods of localized harvest failure. The beginnings of the European trade along the Atlantic coast provide new sources of data, which show a rapid increase in the volume and variety of goods traded. The later prominence of the Atlantic slave trade often obscures the fact that European merchants originally came to the coast to trade in other goods, notably spices and gold. Slaves were initially traded between African ports, and then to sugar plantations on islands just off the coast, before the more famous triangular trade began.[65]

In writing about African trade, both before and after the arrival of European merchants, Liberia has tended to be neglected.[66] However, while there were few large population centers in Liberia prior to the seventeenth century, Liberia was linked to these wider trade networks. In his survey of Liberian marketplaces, Handwerker identifies "two largely distinct regional trading systems" on the coast and in the interior. Along the coast, increased trade did lead to the increased centralization of village groups, "in which chiefs controlled the limited supply of major trade goods

---

[65] Ralph A. Austen, *African Economic History: Internal Development and External Dependency* (London: James Currey, 1997); A. G. Hopkins, *An Economic History of West Africa* (London: Longman, 1973); John Thornton, *Africa and Africans in the Making of the Atlantic World, 1400–1800* (Cambridge: Cambridge University Press, 1998).

[66] Jelmer Vos, "The Slave Trade from the Windward Coast: The Case of the Dutch, 1740–1805," *African Economic History* 38 (2010): 29–51.

which were accumulated by isolated trading depots and/or periodically collected by merchant-men sailing the western coast of Africa." In the interior system, the arrival of the Mandingo led to the replacement of itinerant merchants with stationary trading centers where savannah and forest goods were exchanged. The primary goods traded over long distance were kola nuts, salt, and iron. These were exchanged by traveling merchants who would move between towns collecting trade goods.[67]

The location of what Europeans came to call the Grain Coast, after the malagueta pepper exported from the region, made it one of the earliest ports of call for Portuguese and other European merchants beginning in the fifteenth century. However, it was not a major center for the trade in slaves. Rather, it was one of the last regions of West Africa to begin the export of slaves and probably the smallest in terms of the number of slaves exported.[68] There are approximate data for the number of slaves exported from the region during this period, though these have been the subject of debate. Figure 2.1 compares the number of slaves who departed from the Windward Coast, a region that stretched from Cape Mount on the northern edge of what is today the Liberian coast to Assinie in modern Cote d'Ivoire. These data are from the Trans-Atlantic Slave Trade Database (TSTD) were established initially based on the work of Philip Curtin and extensively refined ever since.[69]

The TSTD has become an authoritative source of data on the scale and geographic distribution of the Atlantic slave trade. However, the limited body of research focused on the Windward Coast may make these numbers less certain than for other regions that have been studied more extensively. Jelmer Vos, for example, argues on the basis of the records of a Dutch company that traded in the area that the TSTD understates the number of slaves shipped from the Windward Coast because it does not account for the fact that ships on this route tended to stop at numerous places along the coast, picking up small numbers of slaves, then complete their cargoes in Elmina.[70] The TSTD, he argues, credits all of these slave exports to Elmina instead of to the Windward Coast. This fragmented structure of the trade contrasted with more centralized slave-trading farther east, where slave ships would often purchase all of their slaves from one of a few major centers like Bonny and Old Calabar. The Windward Coast few good natural harbors or navigable rivers, and has steep beaches and heavy surf restricted merchants to ship-based trade only.

---

[67] Handwerker, "Market Places," 4.
[68] Vos, "The Slave Trade from the Windward Coast."
[69] The Trans-Atlantic Slave Trade Database. 2019. SlaveVoyages. www.slavevoyages.org
[70] Vos, "The Slave Trade from the Windward Coast."

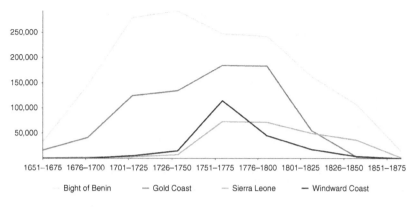

Figure 2.1 Numbers of enslaved people exported by region
Source: TSTD, data available from slavevoyages.org.

It is difficult to know what impact this trade had on the people and economies of what became Liberia. Considering the low density of the population, even this comparatively small export of slaves may have had an impact on agricultural production and family structures in the same way it did elsewhere. At the same time, however, some groups took advantage of the commercial opportunities offered by the trade without themselves being enslaved in great numbers. This, at least, has been the conventional wisdom about the Kru, many of whom "occupied intermediary positions as barracoon guards, lighter pilots, intelligence men, and even slave raiders. Kru traditions that they were never enslaved are doubtless oversimplifications, but it is probably true that slave traders more often than not appreciated Kru expertise and to some extent had to rely on it."[71] In return for their work, the Kru were able to buy cloth, guns, powder, metals, and other trade goods from European merchants, which they could trade themselves.[72]

Arrival of Hawa Undu

In April 1820, a new group of migrants arrived at Cape Mesurado. Among them were some of the eighty-six passengers on board the *Elizabeth*, the first ship sponsored by the American Colonization Society, which sailed from New York to Sierra Leone in January 1820. Many who were on that initial journey died of malaria and other tropical diseases after they arrived in West Africa, while others returned to the

---

[71] Ronald W. Davis, "The Liberian Struggle for Authority on the Kru Coast," *International Journal of African Historical Studies* 8, no. 2 (1975): 229.
[72] Zetterstrom, "Preliminary Report on the Kru," IULC, Bai T. Moore papers.

United States. Those that remained joined a group of thirty-four who arrived in Sierra Leone in 1821 on the *Nautilus* and thirty-seven who landed on the *Strong* in what was to become Liberia in 1822.

As this chapter has shown, these African-American migrants were not the first newcomers to settle along the Grain Coast, nor the first to try and integrate themselves into local trade networks. As Svend Holsoe writes, by the time they arrived "the indigenous Liberians who had more than three hundred years of contact with European traders and had made internal adjustments to new opportunities, were more or less prepared to meet the immigrants."[73] He points out that one difference between the African-American migrants and European merchants was their intention to settle permanently on the coast. However, this sort of permanent migration was already known in northern Liberia through the arrival of the Mandingo and other groups from the Sudan.

The aim of this chapter has been to provide a brief economic history of the region where these migrants landed. Often the story of Liberia is restricted to the history of the African-American settlements on the coast, with the indigenous population only depicted as victims of Americo-Liberian policy. But when the African-American settlers first arrived, they were a small group of migrants dependent for their living on some integration with local economic networks. They did this primarily by acting as middlemen in the existing trades between coastal producers and European merchants, much like the Mandingo had done in the north.

The region where those aboard the *Elizabeth*, the *Strong*, and the *Nautilus* landed was more decentralized than most parts of West Africa, though it had both coastal and internal trading economies which dated back centuries. According to most of the proxy measures currently used in African economic history, this suggests that this region was and would continue to be less developed than neighboring areas with higher population densities and more centralized institutions. But how predictive are such metrics of future economic performance? The previous chapter showed that Liberia's position of relative poverty in the region was not a constant and that in the middle of the twentieth century in particular it enjoyed levels of per capita income that outstripped most of the rest of West Africa. The nineteenth and twentieth centuries saw dramatic changes in African economies and their connections to an industrializing world. In Liberia, as elsewhere, growth and development were linked to the terms of the country's engagement with that global economy. The rest of the book explores how Liberia's sovereign status shaped that engagement.

---

[73] Holsoe, "Economic Activities," 74.

3   Black Americans in West Africa

We were black Americans in West Africa, where for the first time in our lives the color of our skin was accepted as correct and normal.

Maya Angelou, *All God's Children Need Travelling Shoes*

In a world dominated by white supremacy, a little bit of status goes a very long way. The Liberian ruling families were simultaneously members of a despised race and an internationally recognized polity. In a world that subjected the majority of black people to imperialism and/or racial segregation, the oligarchy was deeply conscious of its relatively privileged position within the world schema.

Ibrahim Sundiata, *Brothers and Strangers*

The previous chapter showed that trade and migration had helped shape the economy and political institutions of the region that became Liberia since the medieval period. During the nineteenth century, it was a new flow of migrants who would ultimately establish the Liberian state. These migrants are the subject of this chapter. Beginning in 1820 until the early twentieth century, some 16,000 African Americans traveled from the United States to West Africa under the auspices of an organization called the Society for the Colonization of the Free People of Color of the United States, more commonly known as the American Colonization Society (ACS). Their descendants became known as Americo-Liberians and dominated Liberia's political and economic institutions for the first century and a half of Liberia's existence as a nation. It was not until 1884 that Liberia elected a president, Hilary Johnson, who had been born in Africa and not the United States. It took nearly a century after that for a president of purely indigenous ancestry to come to power, when forces led by Samuel Doe overthrew the government of William Tolbert in 1980 and assassinated Tolbert. Like all previous Liberian presidents before him, Tolbert's ancestors had been born in the Americas. They left South Carolina in 1879, as part of a group inspired by what was known at the time as "Liberia Fever." The coup that overthrew him, which ultimately set the stage for the Liberian civil wars, followed decades of political exclusion and repression by the Americo-Liberians against the indigenous majority.

This violent end to the era Americo-Liberian dominance, and the hardships that era created for the majority of the population, has focused the attention of most histories of Liberia on cleavages between the indigenous and Americo-Liberian populations. However, this focus oversimplifies a more complex history. Neither the indigenous nor Americo-Liberian population were monolithic in their views or interests. For much of Liberia's history, divisions within the migrant community – economic, political, and social – were equally important in shaping Liberian government policy.

There is a substantial historical literature on the migrants and their fates. However, much of it considers only subsets of the migrants. The most widely cited is the study by Tom Shick which uses data on the first wave of migrants who departed from 1820 to 1843.[1] Other studies take a longer chronological view but focus on departures from particular US states or other subgroups, or sometimes even individual family stories.[2] There is also a substantial literature on the ACS and the politics of emigration.[3] This disparate historiography is rich in detail but makes it difficult to make more general statements about the community of migrants who ultimately became the Liberian elite.

This chapter uses a new, more comprehensive data set of the 16,000 migrants who left the United States for Liberia from 1820 to 1904 in order to understand the structure of the group of elites who would later make decisions of considerable consequence to Liberia's development,

---

[1] Tom Shick, *Behold the Promised Land: A History of Afro-American Settler Society in Nineteenth-Century Liberia* (Baltimore and London: Johns Hopkins University Press, 1980). His data are used in Antonio McDaniel, *Swing Low, Sweet Chariot: The Mortality Cost of Colonizing Liberia in the Nineteenth Century* (Chicago: University of Chicago Press, 1995), and Amos Sawyer, *The Emergence of Autocracy in Liberia: Tragedy and Challenge* (San Francisco: ICS Press, 1992).

[2] Caree Banton, *More Auspicious Shores: Barbadian Migration to Liberia, Blackness and the Making of an African Republic* (Cambridge: Cambridge University Press, 2019); Kenneth C. Barnes, *Journey of Hope: The Back-to-Africa Movement in Arkansas in the Late 1800s* (Chapel Hill and London: University of North Carolina Press, 2004); Claude Clegg, *The Price of Liberty: African Americans and the Making of Liberia* (Chapel Hill: University of North Carolina Press, 2004); Lisa Lindsay, *Atlantic Bonds: A Nineteenth-Century Odyssey from America to Africa* (Chapel Hill: University of North Carolina Press, 2017); Robert Murray, *Atlantic Passages: Race, Mobility and Liberian Colonization* (Gainesville, FL: University Press of Florida, 2021); Marie Tyler-McGraw, *An African Republic: Black and White Virginians in the Making of Liberia* (Chapel Hill: University of North Carolina Press, 2007).

[3] Recent contributions include Brandon Mills, *The World Colonization Made: The Racial Geography of Early American Empire* (Philadelphia: University of Pennsylvania Press, 2020); Beverly C. Tomek and Matthew J. Hetrick, eds., *New Directions in the Study of African American Recolonization* (Gainesville: University Press of Florida, 2017).

shaping its economy and the political institutions that governed it over the decades to follow.[4] It situates emigration to Liberia in the wider context of nineteenth-century migration in order to understand changing patterns of selection among those who went to Liberia, and how these contributed to the emergence of inequalities within the Americo-Liberian community. These inequalities in turn underpinned fierce political debates about trade policies, money, debt, and other aspects of Liberia's engagement with the global economy.

Voting with Their Feet: Migration in the Nineteenth Century

The people who went to Liberia joined a growing flood of migrants leaving their places of birth during the eighteenth and nineteenth centuries. The oft-cited 30 million European emigrants who moved to the United States during the age of mass migration were only part of the story. There were many others who moved shorter distances, from rural areas into cities or from densely populated regions to open frontiers. Some crossed different oceans, coming from Africa or Asia. Many went by choice, while others were coerced. Together, they reshaped both their destinations and their places of origin.[5]

People of African descent played an important role in these flows.[6] During the Atlantic slave trade, which peaked in the eighteenth century but continued until the middle of the nineteenth, some 12 million were forced to leave their homes to be enslaved in the Americas. Slave trading routes across the Sahara and along the Indian Ocean took still more. Debates continue on the complex ways that this massive coerced migration influenced the development of both African and American economies and societies.[7] The nineteenth century saw millions of enslaved

---

[4] Christopher Bayly argues that such capacities are one factor shaping divergences between countries. See Christopher A. Bayly, "Indigenous and Colonial Origins of Comparative Economic Development," World Bank Policy Working Paper 4474 (2008).

[5] David Eltis, "Free and Coerced Transatlantic Migrations: Some Comparisons," *American Historical Review* 88 (1983): 251–80; Sharla M. Fett, *Recaptured Africans: Surviving Slave Ships, Detention and Dislocation in the Final Years of the Slave Trade* (Chapel Hill: University of North Carolina Press, 2017); Kevin H. O'Rourke and Jeffrey G. Williamson, *Globalization and History: The Evolution of a Nineteenth-Century Atlantic Economy* (Cambridge, MA and London: The MIT Press, 2000), ch. 7.

[6] For a synthesis, see Ira Berlin, *The Making of African America: The Four Great Migrations* (New York: Penguin Books, 2010).

[7] This is now a large literature. For examples of different approaches to the question of how the slave trade impacted Africa, see Paul Lovejoy, *Transformations in Slavery: A History of Slavery in Africa* (Cambridge: Cambridge University Press, 2012); Nathan Nunn and Leonard Wantchekon, "The Slave Trade and the Origins of Mistrust in Africa," *American Economic Review* 101, no. 7 (2011): 3221–52; Klas Ronnback and Dimitrios Theodoris,

people sold or moved westwards from the Atlantic coast states of the Upper South to the new cotton plantations of the Lower South. The end of slavery opened up new possibilities for mobility by formerly enslaved people, not only in the United States but also in other parts of the Americas. Barbados, for example, saw more than 10 percent of its population emigrate after emancipation in 1833, mainly to other Caribbean islands in search of better wages or working conditions. Contemporaries described it as the "Ireland of the West Indies."[8] During the twentieth century, a substantial share of the African-American population chose to leave the South and migrated to northern cities, permanently reshaping the geographic distribution of the African-American population.[9]

Within these larger population shifts, smaller migrations like the movement to Liberia are often ignored. Kendra Field notes that voluntary movements of African Americans before the Great Migration "are frequently dismissed as demographically insignificant, regionally specific or otherwise exceptional."[10] During the antebellum period, the options available to African Americans wishing to migrate were extremely limited. Those who were enslaved could run away, and many did – most famously via Harriet Tubman's underground railroad. However, that choice came with the risk of violent punishment if caught. After the Civil War, legal constraints were eased but, thanks to vagrancy laws and other mechanisms intended to restrict the mobility of freedmen, not eliminated. Thus many looked for places outside the jurisdiction of the United States. Liberia was one such place, situated in the minds of migrants alongside Haiti, Mexico, and western states like Kansas and Oklahoma.[11] In her classic history of the Kansas "exodusters" in 1879, Nell Irvin Painter writes that "it is difficult to determine whether interest in Kansas migration grew out of the ground already prepared by Liberia Fever or it was the fruit of the same desire of Southern Blacks to escape oppression," noting

"African Agricultural Productivity and the Transatlantic Slave Trade: Evidence from Senegambia in the Nineteenth Century," *Economic History Review* 72, no. 1 (2019): 209–32; Warren Whatley, "How the International Slave Trades Underdeveloped Africa," *Journal of Economic History* 82, no. 2 (2022): 403–441. On the American side, claims about the ways in which slavery shaped the American economy remain fiercely contested. For examples of the two opposing views, see Edward E. Baptist, *The Half Has Never Been Told: Slavery and the Making of American Capitalism* (New York: Basic Books, 2014) and Alan L. Olmstead and Paul W. Rhode, "Cotton, Slavery and the New History of Capitalism," *Explorations in Economic History* 67 (2018): 1–17.
[8] Banton, *More Auspicious Shores*, 30–31.   [9] Berlin, *Making of African America*.
[10] Kendra T. Field, "'No Such Thing as Stand Still': Migration and Geopolitics in African American History," *Journal of American History* 102 (2015): 294.
[11] Field, "No Such Thing," 701–4; Berlin, *Making of African America*, 133–34. This tendency was not exclusive to the United States. The same was true of middle-class Barbadian migrants seeking to leave the jurisdiction of the British Empire. See Banton, *More Auspicious Shores*.

that "many of the organizational characteristics of planned migration to Kansas were common to the Liberia emigrationists."[12] Kenneth Barnes, writing about later emigrants to Liberia, describes this as a "paradox of American society": "while millions of Europeans were coming to the United States to follow their dream of political freedom and economic opportunity, thousands of black Americans ... were equally anxious to get *out* of this country."[13]

For its own part, emigration to Liberia has tended to be treated separately from other migrant flows because of the long and complicated evolution of ideas about African-American emigration to Africa. During the eighteenth century, several petitions were signed by African Americans from Massachusetts and Rhode Island in support of emigration to Africa.[14] The first of these movements to succeed in actually moving people to West Africa was initiated by Paul Cuffe, a Rhode Island merchant and abolitionist of mixed African and American Indian heritage. Using his own ships, he accompanied thirty-eight African Americans to Sierra Leone in 1815.[15] These early supporters of emigration schemes were, in the words of Steven Hahn, "educated, urban and entrepreneurial free men of color in the North." They imagined "what could be regarded as an early, civilizationist, variant of pan-Africanism: they searched for a site in Africa, Latin America, or the Caribbean where they might have the opportunity to enjoy freedom, to prosper, and to uplift the black masses by converting them to Christianity and petty bourgeois values."[16] The heavy costs of the venture, followed by Cuffe's death in 1817, meant that no subsequent group of migrants followed those initial thirty-eight.

While Cuffe's efforts enjoyed broad support among the African-American community, the same was not true of the ACS.[17] It took its inspiration not primarily from people like Cuffe but rather from white anxieties about the consequences of slavery for the new nation, for whom the emigration of those African Americans who were no longer enslaved

---

[12] Nell Irvin Painter, *Exodusters: Black Migration to Kansas after Reconstruction* (New York: Knopf, 1977), 145.

[13] Barnes, *Journey*, 1–2. Emphasis in original.

[14] Wilson Jeremiah Moses, "Introduction," in *Liberian Dreams: Back to Africa Narratives from the 1850s* (University Park, PA: Pennsylvania State University Press, 1998), xiii–xiv; James Campbell, *Middle Passages: African American Journeys to Africa, 1787–2005* (New York: Penguin Press, 2006), 15–16; Floyd J. Miller, *The Search for a Black Nationality: Black Emigration and Colonization 1787–1863* (Urbana: University of Illinois Press, 1975), ch. 1.

[15] Tyler-McGraw, *An African Republic*, 24.

[16] Steven Hahn, *A Nation Under Our Feet: Black Political Struggles in the Rural South from Slavery to the Great Migration* (Cambridge, MA, and London: Belknap Press, 2003), 320.

[17] Clegg, *The Price of Liberty*, 24–25.

provided one way out of the dilemma. Perhaps the best-known proponent of such a strategy was Thomas Jefferson, who argued that people who had been emancipated from slavery "should be colonized to such a place as the circumstances of the time should render most proper."[18] His reasons for advocating this separation were, first, that "deep-rooted prejudices held by whites" along with "ten thousand recollections, by the blacks, of the injuries they have sustained" would make it difficult for the two races to live together without conflict. In addition, he argued, there were numerous physical and intellectual differences which, according to Jefferson, meant it was advisable for enslaved African Americans to be located elsewhere after emancipation.

Though Jefferson himself was never a member or leader of the ACS, its early statements of purpose reflected very similar sentiments, and its leadership included a significant number of southern slaveholders. The first president was Bushrod Washington, who was there primarily because he was George Washington's nephew, rather than for any particular set of beliefs. Marie Tyler-McGraw argues that Washington "freed no slaves and made no personal sacrifice for colonization. Men like Bushrod Washington made it easier for skeptics to view colonization as a slaveholder's conspiracy or as a painless way to salve one's conscience over slavery while actually doing nothing."[19] In his opening address at the society's first annual meeting in 1818, Washington stated that colonization might lead "to the slow but gradual abolition of slavery" while at the same time noting that it provided a slave owner with a way to "emancipate his slaves without injury to his country."[20]

The ACS thus faced opposition from abolitionists and freeborn blacks in the north.[21] William Lloyd Garrison was an early supporter, but in the 1830s he changed his position, and, in the words of Bell Wiley, "charged that the society was seeking to strengthen slavery by providing token emancipation to salve guilty consciences and at the same time helping owners to get rid of useless bondsmen."[22] Many objected to the premise of emigration on the basis that, as Reconstruction-Era Senator Blanche Bruce argued, "the negro of America is not African, but American – in his

---

[18] Thomas Jefferson, *Notes on the State of Virginia* (Philadelphia: Prichard and Hall, 1788); electronic version accessed at https://docsouth.unc.edu/southlit/jefferson/jefferson.html.

[19] Tyler-McGraw, *An African Republic*, 28–30.

[20] "The First Annual Report of the Colonization Society," in *The Annual Reports of the American Society for Colonizing the Free People of Colour of the United States, Volumes 1–10, 1818–27* (New York: Negro Universities Press, 1969), 2.

[21] Tyler-McGraw, *An African Republic*, 26.

[22] Bell I. Wiley (ed.), "Introduction," in *Slaves No More: Letters from Liberia* (Lexington: University Press of Kentucky, 1980), 3. See also Barnes, *Journey*, 5.

physical qualities and aptitudes, in his mental developments and biases, in his religious beliefs and hopes, and in his political conception and conviction he is an American."[23]

Migrants to Liberia are thus portrayed less as active agents in their own destiny than as hapless pawns in a largely white effort to prevent emancipated African Americans from gaining any path to full citizenship in the United States. However, Everill writes that this approach "obscures the choices of those who did go, as well as the decision process of those who rejected extraterritorial emigration but chose to move within North America."[24] The agency of the migrants is key to understanding what became the Americo-Liberian community. Unfortunately, little direct evidence exists of the motivations of most migrants. While letters and other accounts do survive, they come from the relatively small number of literate migrants and are unlikely to be representative. There were no doubt active verbal discussions among both freed and enslaved people at religious gatherings and through communication networks between plantations, but these are not well documented.[25] This lack of evidence is not unusual. In his work on European migration to the United States, Dudley Baines notes that the majority of migrants leave no direct account of their motives for leaving their place of birth or choosing their destination. Instead, "historians have little choice but to infer motivation from indirect evidence, such as the ages, occupations, and marital status of the emigrants or the economic and social characteristics of the areas from which they came."[26]

Patterns of Migration to Liberia, 1820–1906

This chapter brings together for the first time data on the majority of migrants who went to Liberia during the nineteenth and early twentieth centuries. It builds on the work of previous historians of Liberia who took the first and most difficult step by compiling lists for specific periods from original primary sources. This includes lists of migrants compiled by Tom Shick (for migrants who went from 1820 to 1843), Robert Brown (1843–64), and Peter Murdza (1865–1904). As far as possible, these lists have been checked against original sources and in some cases additional

---

[23] Quoted in Painter, *Exodusters*, 143.
[24] Bronwen Everill, "'Destiny Seems to Point Me to that Country': Early Nineteenth-Century African American Migration, Emigration and Expansion," *Journal of Global History* 7, no. 1 (2012): 55.
[25] Hahn, *A Nation Under Our Feet*, 29–52.
[26] Dudley Baines, "European Emigration, 1815–1930: Looking at the Emigration Decision Again," *Economic History Review* XLVII (1994): 525.

data from these sources have been added and errors have been corrected. In addition, it includes a further 1,227 drawn from the archival records of the largest of the state societies, the Maryland Colonization Society.[27]

These lists are not always consistent in the data they record. All three lists kept by the ACS include name, age, status (freeborn or emancipated) until 1863, state of origin, literacy, occupation, and date of arrival in Liberia for each migrant. Brown notes that the lists may represent an upward bound on the number of possible migrants, writing that "many people simply did not appear at the dock when the ship sailed. Others changed their minds and, if the ship stopped at more than one American port, particularly if the second was in a northern state, they got off and vanished."[28] Other information appears in certain lists but not others. Mortality rates and return migration are only available for the 1820–43 sample, for example. The 1865–1904 list includes information on religion and more precise places of origin, while the lists kept by the Maryland Colonization Society record only names, ages, and places of origin. The quality of literacy and occupation data varies considerably within and between lists and is often somewhat patchy.

These data do not include everyone who went to Liberia. There were other state societies that sponsored smaller groups of migrants, about whom records are not as complete or accessible. It does not include the 346 migrants from Barbados who went to Liberia in 1865, owing to more limited data about the individual migrants and those who remained behind.[29] Similarly, the 4,675 recaptives brought to Liberia by the US naval vessels after they had intercepted slave ships are also not included, both because little is known about them as individuals and because the decisions which brought them to Liberia were largely made by others.[30] Both of these groups were, however, socially and politically significant in Liberia's history and will be discussed in more detail later in this chapter.

Figure 3.1 shows total migration in each year from 1820 to 1904. There were considerable fluctuations in annual number of migrants. The 1830s and 1850s alone account for just over half of all migrants that departed. A further 15 percent went during the 1860s, despite the disruption of the

---

[27] Tom W. Shick, *Emigrants to Liberia, 1820–1843* (Newark, DE: University of Delaware Press, 1971); Robert T Brown, "Immigrants to Liberia 1843 to 1865: An Alphabetical Listing," Liberian Studies Research Working Paper 7 (1980); Peter J. Murdza, Jr, "Immigrants to Liberia 1865 to 1904: An Alphabetical Listing," Liberian Studies Research Working Paper No. 4 (1975). For MCS migrants, see Maryland State Colonization Society Papers, Maryland Historical Society, MS 571, reels 25–27.

[28] Robert T. Brown, "Immigrants to Liberia 1843 to 1865," ii.

[29] Banton, *More Auspicious Shores*, provides a detailed accounting of the Barbadian migration.

[30] For more on recaptives, see Fett, *Recaptured Africans*.

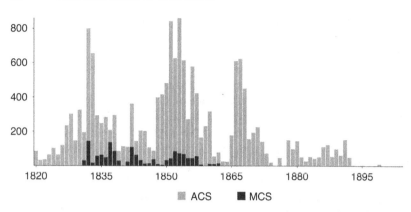

Figure 3.1 Annual migrants to Liberia, 1820–1904

Civil War causing a rapid fall in numbers during the first part of the decade. Adding the Barbadian migrants and recaptives to this period would increase the numbers still further. "Liberia fever" of the 1870s saw another surge, which comprised a further 6 percent of the total. After this the annual level of migration declined, though the society continued to send a steady, if small, number of migrants up to the early 1890s. Faith in the society was severely undermined by the "crisis" of 1892, when hundreds of migrants who came to New York to depart for Liberia were left stranded. The ACS, which had not anticipated their arrival, had no ships or resources with which to send them. After that there were only a few small groups of migrants, often selected specifically for the trip, the last in 1904.[31]

Previous histories of the ACS have suggested that this timing is particularly tied to events that heightened racial tensions, particularly the Nat Turner rebellion of 1831, the passage of the Fugitive Slave Act in 1850, and the end of the Reconstruction Era and consequent tightening of legal constraints on freedmen and women in the south in the 1870s.[32] For the 1830s and 1850s in particular, it is unclear whether the main channel by which these events influenced the number of migrants traveling to Liberia was through African-American demand or white anxiety about slave insurrections or instability. ACS revenues, which were primarily generated by auxiliary societies dominated by whites, also surged during these

[31] Barnes, *Journey of Hope*.
[32] Bronwen Everill, *Abolition and Empire in Sierra Leone and Liberia* (Basingstoke: Palgrave Macmillan, 2013), 57; Tyler-McGraw, *An African Republic*, 72, 79–80.

periods. In 1832, for example, the ACS's annual revenue increased to $42,065, up from $32,101 the previous year. Similarly, in the early 1850s, revenues increased from $64,973 in 1850 to $97,443 in 1851. The Society's biggest years for revenue collection were the years preceding the outbreak of the Civil War: $160,303 in 1859 and $104,546 in 1860.[33]

While the original intention of the ACS was to facilitate the emigration of freeborn African Americans, from the 1830s there was an increase in migrants who were manumitted from slavery on the condition that they migrate to Liberia. According to Eric Burin, manumitters hoped that the promise of emancipation would strengthen the reciprocal "bond" between enslaved people and their masters, which was otherwise fraying due to economic change. "The expectation of liberty, they declared, would arouse in slaves industry, dependability and loyalty; and the prospect of hard-working, reliable and filial bondpersons, they continued, would compel slaveholders to keep their promises of freedom."[34]

Numbers of manumissions from 1841 to 1860 were more than double those in the first twenty years of emigration to Liberia, which Burin puts down to changing emancipation laws, which made it more difficult for slave owners to emancipate their slaves, along with the deaths of many early colonizationists, who included manumissions in their wills.[35] Figure 3.2 shows the number of migrants by status from 1820 to 1863, when Abraham Lincoln's "Emancipation Proclamation" officially freed all those who remained in bondage. Migrant lists from shortly after that date pay homage to his executive order by describing emigrants as emancipated by "A.L. proclamation." It shows that during spikes in emigration in the 1830s and 1850s, numbers of both freeborn and manumitted migrants increased, though manumitted migrants became an increasingly important share of the total by the end of the period.

This shift is also reflected in the geographic origins of the migrants, shown by region in Figure 3.3. Given the opposition to the ACS among northern free black communities, it is perhaps not surprising that the majority of migrants, freeborn or otherwise, came from slave states in the south, broken down here into Upper South and Lower South. There are some exceptions to this. In particular, the spike in northern emigrants during the 1850s and 1860s may be particularly linked to the Fugitive Slave Act, which meant that even freeborn blacks in the north could be more easily stripped of their freedom.

[33] American Colonization Society, *The African Repository Vol XLV* (Washington, DC: American Colonization Society, 1869), 208.
[34] Eric Burin, *Slavery and the Peculiar Solution: A History of the American Colonization Society* (Gainesville: University Press of Florida, 2005), 35.
[35] Burin, *Slavery*, 45.

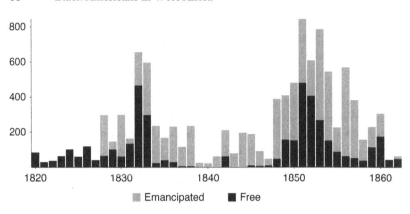

Figure 3.2 Migrants by status, 1820–1862

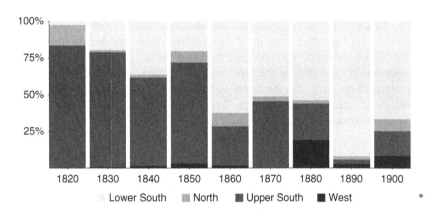

Figure 3.3 Regional origins of migrants by decade, 1820–1900

There was also a shift in sending regions from the Upper South to the Lower South. This reflected, in part, the distribution of the African-American population as a whole, which was overwhelmingly southern but shifted over time within the south. From 1790 to 1860, close to a million enslaved people were moved from coastal southern states to new plantations in places like Mississippi, Louisiana, and Alabama, so that by the later nineteenth century states in the "new

Table 3.1 *Gender balance of migrants by decade, 1820–1900 (%)*

	Female	Male
1820	43.8	51.6
1830	44.4	53.5
1840	45.8	51.8
1850	46.3	52.5
1860	46	53.2
1870	47.5	52.1
1880	46.2	52.8
1890	46.4	51.2
1900	58.3	41.7

Note: Gender has been assigned where possible based on first names of migrants. For some gender could not be assigned because the name was ambiguous or only initials were given. Percentages may not sum to 100.

south" were home to the majority of the black population.[36] The early dominance of the Upper South was also linked to the origins of manumitters, who were predominantly from the old south states of Virginia and Maryland. Even those who manumitted slaves from the "new south" were often born in those two states.[37]

The demographics of the migrants also provide suggestions as to their motivation. Gender and age data suggest that migrants traveled mainly in family groups. Table 3.1 shows that the gender balance was relatively equal throughout the period. There was also a comparatively high share of children among migrants to Liberia, as shown in Figure 3.4. This was different than some other African-American migrations. In his work on early migration to Pittsburgh, Peter Gottlieb noted a 1917 survey found that 76 percent were men between eighteen and forty.[38] This was, in part, due to the fact that movements to the north were often temporary, at least to start, linked to seasonal employment patterns.

Anecdotal evidence suggests that extended family connections between groups of migrants were often important in shaping patterns of migration. In her history of Virginia migrants, Tyler-McGraw writes of several family

[36] Richard H. Steckel, "The African American Population of the United States 1790–1920," in *A Population History of North America*, edited by Michael R Haines and Richard H Steckel (Cambridge: Cambridge University Press, 2000), 440–41.
[37] Burin, *Slavery*, 35.
[38] Peter Gottlieb, *Making Their Own Way: Southern Blacks' Migration to Pittsburgh, 1916–30* (Urbana and Chicago: University of Illinois Press, 1987), 29.

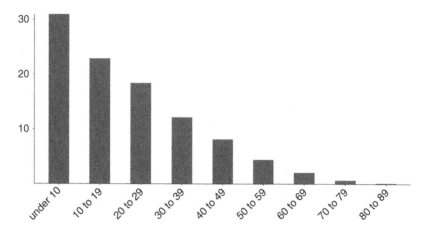

Figure 3.4 Age distribution of migrants
Source: See text.

groups, including cousins and also families like the Henry and Harris families from the Shenandoah Valley, or three sets of cousins from Southampton County. Members of these families were often encouraged to migrate by relatives who had gone previously and prospered, and family links provided networks of support for those who arrived in Liberia.[39] Lisa Lindsay tells a similar story of migrants from South Carolina who traveled on the *Joseph Maxwell* in 1852. Single men of working age like Church Vaughan, the subject of her biography, were joined by large extended families who were recruited in part by returning relatives.[40] A survey of potential migrants in 1826 conducted by Quakers central to the emigration campaign in North Carolina also illustrated the importance to many of migrating as a family group.[41] The vast majority of the Barbadian migrants, too, were couples with large families.[42]

Who Went to Liberia: Selection and Human Capital

A central question in research on migration is who chooses to migrate. Are the poorest or least educated more likely to migrate because of limited opportunities at home? Or are those who are wealthier or better educated more likely to be able to pay the costs of migration? The nature of the

[39] Tyler-McGraw, *African Republic*, 145–47.   [40] Lindsay, *Atlantic Bonds*, ch. 2.
[41] Clegg, *The Price of Liberty*, 59.   [42] Banton, *More Auspicious Shores*, 6.

surviving evidence often makes this a difficult question to answer, and conclusions vary, also because different types of migrants chose different destinations.[43] Many studies of migrants – as, for example, in the case of pre-famine Irish migration to the United States or Spanish emigration to the Americas – have found evidence of positive selection, implying that those who were wealthier or more skilled were more likely to migrate, due to the cost of migration as well as the difficulties of obtaining information about distant destinations.[44] However, there are contrary examples like Irish emigration during the famine, in which migrants came from poorer households and regions, and had lower human capital than those who did not migrate.[45]

There remains no consensus on the selection of African-American migrants out of the south; while earlier studies of the Great Migration to the north claimed that those who left the south were more literate and skilled than those who remained, more recent work has suggested otherwise. Within smaller flows of migrants to places like Liberia and Kansas, the issue of selection has not yet been addressed in a systematic way. Because previous studies of migrants to Liberia have focused only on certain groups of migrants, conclusions about the level of education attained by the cohort of migrants as a whole vary. Tom Shick, in 1971, argued based on the sample of migrants who went from 1820 to 1843 that "one fact about the emigrants, indicating their ability to understand the affairs around them, was the very large proportion of literacy, which was

---

[43] Ran Abramitzky and Fabio Braggion, "Migration and Human Capital: Self-Selection of Indentured Servants to the Americas," *Journal of Economic History* 66, (2006) 82–905; Yvonne Stolz and Joerg Baten, "Brain drain in the age of mass migration: does relative inequality explain migrant selectivity?," *Explorations in Economic History* 49 (2012): 205–20. Research on internal migration also reports varied results. Census data on migrants from the Dust Bowl in the 1930s, for example, shows little evidence of selection. See Jason Long and Henry Siu, "Refugees from Dust and Shrinking Land: Tracking the Dust Bowl Migrants," *Journal of Economic History* 78 (2018): 1018–24.

[44] Stephen Nicholas and Peter R. Shergold, "Human Capital and Pre-Famine Irish Emigration to England," *Explorations in Economic History* 24 (1987): 158–77; Blanca Sanchez Alonso, "Those Who Left and Those who Stayed Behind: Explaining Emigration from the Regions of Spain, 1880–1914," *Journal of Economic History* 60 (2000): 730–55.

[45] Ran Abramitzky, Leah Boustan and Katherine Eriksson, "Europe's Tired, Poor, Huddled Masses: Self-Selection and Economic Outcomes in the Age of Mass Migration," *American Economic Review* 102 (2012): 1832–1856; Dacil Juif, "Skill Selectivity in Transatlantic Migration: The Case of Canary Islanders in Cuba," *Revista de Historia Economica* 33, no. S2 (2015): 189–222. Debates about selection remain lively in the literature on Irish migration. See Joel Mokyr, *Why Ireland Starved: A Quantitative and Analytical History of the Irish Economy 1800–1850* (London and Boston: Allen and Unwin, 1983); Cormac O'Grada and Kevin H. O'Rourke, "Migration as Disaster Relief: Lessons from the Great Irish Famine," *European Review of Economic History* 1 (1997): 3–25.

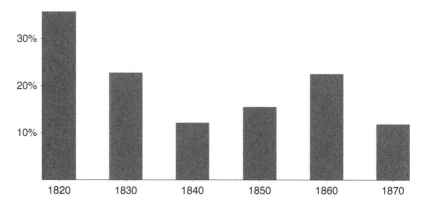

Figure 3.5 Literacy rates of migrants by decade of departure
Source: See text.

far greater than one might have suspected to be the case among either freed blacks or slaves in that period."[46] Claude Clegg, by contrast, remarks on the apparently low rates of literacy of particular groups of migrants from North Carolina.[47]

Using the combined database, Figure 3.5 gives literacy by decade of departure for migrants over the age of 13. Literacy rates were highest among those migrating in the 1820s, before falling sharply during the 1830s and 1840s then recovering slightly in the 1850s and 1860s. It is not clear from these data whether shifting literacy numbers came from changing demand from migrants or shifts in their regional origins due to ACS fundraising, emancipations, or other reasons.

Some baseline information about African-American literacy in the nineteenth century can help contextualize these numbers. The earliest US census to give data on individual African Americans was in 1850. However, censuses before the Civil War only enumerated freeborn African Americans, not those who were enslaved. It remains difficult to measure the literacy rates of enslaved people with any certainty, as literacy was, in the words of Heather Williams, "one of the terrains on which slaves and slave owners waged a perpetual struggle for control. Cognizant of the revolutionary potential of black literacy, white elites enacted laws in slave states to proscribe teaching enslaved and sometimes free blacks to

---

[46] Tom W. Shick, "A Quantitative Analysis of Liberian Colonization from 1820 to 1843 with Special Reference to Mortality," *Journal of African History* 12, no. 1 (1971): 47–48.
[47] Clegg, *Price of Liberty*, 205.

read or write."[48] John Malvin, born free in Virginia before migrating to Ohio, wrote in his autobiography of learning to read the Bible: "We obtained light to read by means of pine knots, which I would go out and find in the dark by feeling with my feet. I would carry them to the old man's cabin and put them in the fire-place. We did not dare to talk loud, lest we should be overheard, and had to confine ourselves to whispers."[49] Others recalled having been punished for trying to learn. Williams cites the case of Gordon Buford who "remembered that he and fellow slaves never learned to read and write because their master threatened to 'skin them alive' if they tried."[50] Efforts to measure the literacy of slaves during the antebellum period have used a variety of sources, including later testimonies collected by the Federal Writers Project in the 1930s, in which approximately 5 percent of respondents described learning to read and/or write while enslaved. Advertisements for runaways are another source, as they often indicated whether the runaway was literate. Studies of reconstruction also document numbers of literate slaves. Overall, a rough estimate of slave literacy in the antebellum South is around 10 percent.[51]

Dividing the sample of migrants by status makes it possible to compare their literacy against these benchmark rates. Figure 3.6a shows migrants who departed before 1863 by birth decade and compares them with the data from the 1850 census. Migrants who had been born enslaved were approximately as literate as their cohort, with literacy rates ranging from around 7 percent to around 15 percent. Among freeborn migrants, average levels of literacy were lower than the figures from the 1850 census. If these data are disaggregated by decade of arrival, as in Figure 3.6b, there are clear differences between the freeborn migrants of the 1820s, whose level of literacy was similar to the overall level for free-born African Americans, and the free-born migrants of the 1830s.

It may be that this is an unfair comparison, in that one set of people – the Liberian migrants – are being observed at the point of migration while the others were enumerated sometimes decades later. It is possible that the latter group learned to read later on. John Malvin recalls seeking donations and volunteers to set up schools for "several of the adult colored people of Cleveland, not having had the benefits of education

---

[48] Heather Williams, *Self-Taught: African American Education in Slavery and Freedom* (Chapel Hill: University of North Carolina Press, 2005), 13.

[49] John Malvin, *North into Freedom: The Autobiography of Johan Malvin, Free Negro, 1795–1880* (Cleveland, OH: Western Reserve Historical Society, originally published 1879; this edition 1996), 34.

[50] Williams, *Self-Taught*, 18.

[51] Janet Duitsman Cornelius, *"When I Can Read My Title Clear": Literacy, Slavery and Religion in the Antebellum South* (Columbia: University of South Carolina Press, 1991), 6–10.

(a)

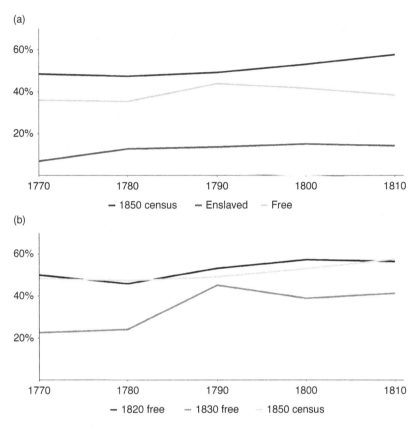

(b)

Figure 3.6 Migrant literacy by birth decade compared with the 1850 census
A. All migrants
B. Comparison of the 1820s and 1830s cohorts

before extended to them," who as a result "learned to read and write pretty well."[52] How widespread such opportunities were is unknown, but they may have impacted the literacy rates of people assessed later in their lives.

For early cohorts of migrants to Liberia, more comparable data are available from the 1843 census in Liberia. Just like in the United States, there were documented efforts to provide adult education to former slaves in Liberia. Figure 3.7 gives the share of literate migrants by birth decade, splitting the sample into those who arrived in the 1820s and 1830s. Note

[52] Malvin, *North into Freedom*, 63–7.

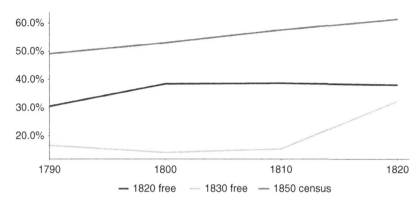

Figure 3.7 Migrant literacy from the 1843 Liberia census

that the Liberian census no longer distinguished people by status at birth so these figures include both those born free and enslaved. Literacy rates among the 1820s group remain below the literacy rates provided in the 1850 census, but they are significantly higher than those who arrived in the 1830s who were apparently unable to catch up despite efforts to offer adult education through the several adult literacy associations established in Liberia, such as the Ladies Liberia Literary Institute, founded in 1848.[53] These measures are perhaps closer to the 20 percent literacy which Bruce Sacerdote finds using the 1880 US census for African Americans born in slave states before 1865.[54]

Given the small scale of the migration to Liberia relative to the whole of the African-American population, it is perhaps more interesting to compare migrants to Liberia with those who migrated within the United States. The 1880 and 1900 US censuses allow for such comparisons. Research on the Great Migration of the interwar period has used census data to argue that migrants out of the south, and in particular migrants to the north, were more educated than those who remained in the rural south.[55] Some caution is needed in using this method. It offers no way to

[53] Shick, *Behold the Promised Land*, 55–6.
[54] Bruce Sacerdote, "Slavery and the Intergenerational Transmission of Human Capital," *Review of Economics and Statistics* 87, no. 2 (2005): 217–34.
[55] Stewart E. Tolnay, "Educational Selection in the Migration of Southern Blacks, 1880–1990," *Social Forces* 77 (1998): 499; Robert A Margo, *Race and Schooling in the South, 1880–1950: An Economic History* (Chicago: University of Chicago Press, 1990), 9; Thomas N. Maloney, "African American Migration to the North: New Evidence for the 1910s," *Economic Inquiry*

know for certain whether observed levels of literacy are the result of more literate people choosing to migrate, or migrants gaining better access to schooling after they have already migrated. In addition, these data are based on self-declarations to census takers, and there is considerable evidence to suggest people will declare higher levels of education in a more educated environment, as Claudia Goldin finds in her study of secondary education in the United States.[56] Literacy was a source of considerable social status in largely illiterate slave communities, and thus there may have been incentives to overreport.[57] In a paper using linked samples from the 1910 and 1930 censuses, which allowed the same individuals to be observed before and after migration, William Collins and Marianne Wanamaker found limited evidence for the positive selection of migrants, suggesting that the literacy skills of migrants to the north were most likely acquired after migration. They write that "this raises concern regarding the practice of using ex post migrant characteristics from cross-sections to make inferences about selection into migration."[58]

In the absence of a similar linked data set, however, we will have to assume for current purposes that the 1880 and 1900 censuses may overstate the literacy rates of other migrants, and interpret the figures accordingly. Figure 3.8 gives literacy by birth cohort from the 1880 and 1900 censuses for southern-born African Americans. It distinguishes between those who remained in the south, those who migrated to northern states, and those who went to the main destinations of what Steven Hahn calls "grassroots emigrationism," including Kansas and Oklahoma. In order to mitigate the effects of increasing literacy over generations, the data are based on the 1810–1850s birth cohorts only. These make up the bulk of the Liberian migrant sample.

The data show, as previous studies have noted, that African Americans born in slave states who migrated north were considerably more literate by 1880 than those who remained in the south. Whether this is because of selection or greater opportunities for post-migration education is not clear. Those who migrated to Kansas and Oklahoma were also more literate than those who remained in the south, but the gap is smaller

40 (2002): 1; Trevon Logan, "Health, Human Capital and African-American Migration before 1910," *Explorations in Economic History* 46 (2009): 188.

[56] Claudia Goldin, "America's Graduation from High School: The Evolution and Spread of Secondary School in the Twentieth Century," *Journal of Economic History* 58 (1998): 365.

[57] Hahn, *A Nation Under Our Feet*, 42.

[58] William J. Collins and Marianne Wanamaker, "The Great Migration in Black and White: New Evidence on the Selection and Sorting of Southern Migrants," *Journal of Economic History* 75 (2014): 959.

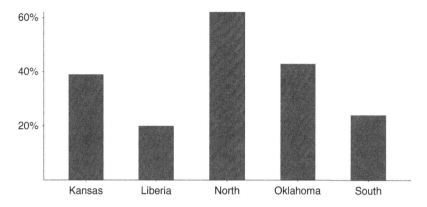

Figure 3.8 African-American literacy rates by destination

than for those who migrated north. "Exoduster" communities often struggled with limited economic opportunities in their destinations, along with the hostility of white residents, which may have affected both selection and opportunities for further education. Ira Berlin writes that "the settlements in Kansas, Oklahoma, Liberia and dozens of other migratory schemes spoke to the desperation of black Southerners."[59] Among these groups, however, migrants to Liberia are the least literate, with a rate closest to those who remained in the south.

Given the history of anti-literacy laws, occupation data may offer a better measure of human capital. In their study of linked samples, Collins and Wanamaker do find some evidence of positive selection in terms of skilled occupations for migrants to the north. Gottlieb does not investigate the question of selection directly, but in his study of migrants to Pittsburgh, he shows that for many migrants initial employment in some industrial enterprise provided a route to migration. For its part, the ACS was keen to encourage skilled migrants as the best route to the economic development of Liberia. Letters from migrants often stress that, even without capital, those who could perform some skilled trade often had an easier time making a living in West Africa. Peyton Skipwith, a mason, wrote to his former master of another freedman: "I am sorry to say that Erasmus is displeased with the Country because he is of no trade & therefore he sees no way to make a living."[60]

---

[59] Berlin, *The Making of African America*, 134.
[60] Peyton Skipwith to John H. Cocke, September 29, 1844, in Wiley, *Slaves No More*, 60.

Figure 3.9 Skilled and semiskilled adult male migrants

In the migrant list, occupation data are less comprehensive than literacy data. Most migrants have no occupation listed, which it is assumed here implies that they are unskilled, though as with literacy there are questions about the quality of ACS record-keeping in later decades. Still, there is enough information to provide some insights into the composition of migrants in terms of whether they had a skilled occupation or not. Figure 3.9 gives the share of adult male migrants – occupations are only infrequently listed for women – in skilled or semiskilled professions by decade of arrival. Skilled occupations included white-collar occupations like minister or doctor, of which there was a comparatively small number, particularly before the last couple of decades of Liberian migration. A much larger group was the semiskilled, which included carpenters, black-smiths, and other similar positions.[61]

The overall trend is similar to that of the literacy data, showing a more skilled group of migrants followed by declining shares of skilled and semiskilled migrants from the 1830s to the 1850s. The share then increased in the 1860s before declining again. At its highest, the share of skilled and semi-skilled men among the migrants was 28 percent. When compared to other migrant flows, this is a comparatively low share of men in skilled or semi-skilled occupations. Logan's analysis of African-American migrants to northern states gave the skilled share of African American as 38.9 percent in 1870. In their linked sample, Collins

---

[61] Occupational classifications follow Joe Ferrie and Jason Long, "Intergenerational Occupational Mobility in Britain and the United States Since 1850," *American Economic Review* 104 (2013): 1109–37.

and Wanamaker find a smaller share of skilled and semiskilled migrants, closer to the highest percentage in the migrant data.

Taken together, the comparisons offered in this section suggest that there was little if any positive selection of migrants to Liberia. If anything, following the first cohorts of migrants in the 1820s, migrants appear to have been negatively selected, with migrants to Liberia being less likely to be literate or in skilled occupations than those who went to other destinations in the United States. Contemporary observations by more affluent migrants attributed this to the migrants who had been emancipated only on the condition that they went to Liberia. Edward Wilmot Blyden, a clergyman who had emigrated to Liberia and became one of its fiercest advocates (and later critics) lamented in 1856 that emancipations had sent to Liberia "a set of worn-out, miserable wrecks of humanity who immediately upon their arrival are thrown upon the charity of the community."[62] It may also be that the combination of emancipated migrants and the institutional organization of the ACS made migration more feasible for lower-skilled migrants than was true for other destinations. Still, the data presented here are tentative and subject to uncertainties related to the quality of ACS records. With the increasing availability of digitized resources and the ability to process them it may be possible in the future to offer a more systematic analysis of who went to Liberia and who chose to stay in the United States. The next section will illustrate how inequalities between cohorts of migrants influenced the construction of Liberia's institutions.

Americans in West Africa

The communities of migrants established over the course of the nineteenth century were shaped not only by who chose to board a ship bound for West Africa but also by the difficult process of arriving and getting settled in the country. Mortality rates were high, and promises of land and support from the ACS frequently went unfulfilled, prompting many to try to return to the United States or go elsewhere. Accounts of these hardships may have dissuaded some potential migrants from traveling, and played a role in the declining share of literate and skilled migrants over time. The arrivals process also threw into sharp relief inequalities between skilled migrants with some capital, and those who arrived without either, which would continue to shape Liberia's politics in the decades to follow.

---

[62] Quoted in Hollis R. Lynch, *Edward Wilmot Blyden: Pan-Negro Patriot 1823–1912* (Oxford: Oxford University Press, 1967), 10.

For many families who migrated, the decision came at a heavy cost not only in terms of separation from home and kin but also in terms of lives. By the 1820s, West Africa was already legendary for its unhealthy climate. The British and French governments had begun collecting statistics on the mortality rates of soldiers posted overseas, and in Philip Curtin's synthesis of these data the "relocation cost" in mortality terms of Sierra Leone was some three times higher than the next highest, the Dutch East Indies. French soldiers in Senegal suffered lower mortality rates, but they were still higher than those of much of the West and East Indies.[63] However, it was also as a result of these deaths that advances were made in methods of prevention. The use of quinine, which until recently was the main method of malaria prophylaxis, was discovered the same year that the first group of ACS migrants went to West Africa.[64]

According to Tom Shick, "no problem was more devastating for the early settlers in Liberia than the disease environment."[65] Of the first eighty-six who arrived in March 1820, fourteen were dead by the end of the year. This included the entire Augustine family of Philadelphia, comprising thirty-year-old John, his twenty-five-year-old wife Nancy, and their three children, all of whom died of "fever" – probably malaria – on arrival. While few families were as unfortunate as the Augustines, many lost at least one member. Isaac Alexander, age twenty-nine when he arrived with his wife, Minty (twenty-five), and their two children, died by drowning in 1822. Their older son, James, had by that point already died of fever in 1820; the younger child would follow in 1830. In 1839, Minty succumbed to what contemporaries referred to as "diseased brain," which may itself have been a side effect of malaria. In response to these tragedies, many left or tried to do so. Some, like Thomas Camaran of New York, returned to the United States with his three children after the death of his wife, Ann, from fever. The Carey family of Philadelphia left for Sierra Leone under similar circumstances. Table 3.2 gives the causes of death of migrants up to 1843, the last year in which such data were compiled. By far the most important was malaria. Fever and infectious disease accounted for 40 percent of all deaths. Based on his analysis of mortality rates, McDaniel notes that "the calendar year of arrival was the most devastating time for the new arrivals in Liberia: approximately 43% of all deaths in the immigrant community occurred during that year."[66]

---

[63] Philip D. Curtin, *Death by Migration: Europe's Encounter with the Tropical World in the Nineteenth Century* (Cambridge: Cambridge University Press, 1989), Table 1.1.
[64] McDaniel, *Swing Low*, 87.   [65] Shick, *Behold the Promised Land*, 27.
[66] McDaniel, *Swing Low*, 77.

Table 3.2 *Causes of death for migrants to Liberia, 1820–1843*

	Male	Female	All
Fever and infection diseases	456 (40.2%)	420 (43.4%)	921 (42.0%)
Diseased brain	60 (5.3%)	34 (3.5%)	96 (4.4%)
Diseases of the lungs	97 (8.5%)	81 (8.4%)	188 (8.6%)
Consumption (tuberculosis)	99 (8.7%)	91 (9.4%)	193 (8.8%)
Childbirth and other gynecological	0 (0.0%)	56 (5.8%)	57 (2.6%)
Accidents and violence	119 (10.5%)	34 (3.5%)	156 (7.1%)
Circulatory and degenerative diseases	170 (15.0%)	138 (14.3%)	317 (14.4%)
Others and unknown	133 (11.7%)	113 (11.7%)	267 (12.2%)

Source: McDaniel, *Swing Low*, Table 4.5.

It did not take long after the first ship departed in 1820 before accounts of these and other hardships reached the United States. Tyler-McGraw writes, for example, of the family of James B. Barbour from Petersburg, Virginia, whose "family's fate in Liberia sobered his Virginia friends" and made it difficult for him to promote emigration without having to "acknowledge many deaths, including that of his well-known midwife mother."[67] Claude Clegg also argues that the sad fate of the *Nautilus*, a quarter of whose passengers died on arrival in 1828, stemmed interest in emigration. "For North Carolinians, the *Nautilus* was their death ship … Once information about the *Nautilus* company and the perils of colonial life in general, began trickling into North Carolina, the tide turned decisively against the colonization movement in the state."[68] Church Vaughan was initially supposed to travel in July 1852 with his brother, mother, and sister, but they changed their minds after hearing reports of conditions on the ground, and particular of attacks on Americo-Liberian settlements by the indigenous population. Vaughan went to Liberia alone in 1852 but left again several years later for Yorubaland, where he married and established what became a prominent Nigerian family.[69]

Accounts of those who survived often placed the blame for these deaths not only on the climate but also on the poor management of the ACS. William Nesbit wrote that new arrivals were housed for the first six months in "a long low brick building, divided off into little stalls or rooms, just large enough to admit a bed, table and a few chairs." The

---

[67] Tyler-McGraw, *African Republic*, 145.   [68] Clegg, *Price of Liberty*, 69.
[69] Lindsay, *Atlantic Bonds*.

stalls were "badly ventilated" and the "emigrants uncared for," so "of course a very large number of these deluded victims of the cupidity of Colonization agents, after a brief incarceration in that miserable place, breathing that stifled air, fall unwept, unhonored, and unsung, ... their corpses hurried out of sight only to give place to others following in their wake."[70] Nesbit was a known foe of the Society, which certainly shaped his account. However, even more neutral parties were critical of the conditions many migrants faced when they first came to Liberia. Augustus Washington's description of the "Receptacle," as the arrival building was known, was similar to Nesbit's – "an old, shabby, rickety building" in which "rooms (if they deserve such a name) are about six feet by nine, having one small window without glass, which must be closed during the rains and at night, thus making a suitable dungeon for a murderer."[71] Washington complained in particular about the lack of access to medical attention among those poorer migrants who were dependent on the Society for their provisions.

Migrants with either financial means or skills were often better equipped to survive the first year and establish themselves thereafter. "We northern emigrants by the *Isla de Cuba* have fared well enough and thus for ourselves have no very special public complaint ... Having some means of our own, we have all resided at the Cape in Monrovia, where we could more easily obtain medical attendance, comfortable houses, and tolerably good food," wrote Augustus Washington. He added that "I cannot encourage any body to come here who has not something of his own to depend on, aside from the aid he gets from the Society. Because every thing here is very dear for poor people."[72] These high prices offered opportunities for men with "only a little capital, and that in goods," but "if he does not have something to do with of his own it will go hard with him." Just a few years before, in 1846, Peyton Skipwith wrote to his mother that "all persons having any expectations to go to Monrovia should endeavor to accumulate some money if they possibly can and that is no hard matter to accumulate in the States."[73]

As early as 1828, sharp divides could be observed within the Americo-Liberian community. In that year, a report published in the *African Repository* distinguished between "the older class of settlers, fixed in comfortable dwellings ... successfully and actively employed in the coasting commerce, and the country trade" and a second class who were "slenderly fed, slenderly clad" and struggled to get by working for their

---

[70] Quoted in Moses, *Liberian Dreams*, 91.   [71] Quoted in Moses, *Liberian Dreams*, 206
[72] Quoted in Moses, *Liberian Dreams*, 205.
[73] Peyton Skipwith to Lucy Nicholas Skipwith, June 27, 1846, in Wiley, *Slaves No More*, 65.

better-off neighbors while attempting to get established.[74] Tyler-McGraw notes this diversity of experience in her account of migrants from Virginia: "urban free blacks with skills and literacy did relatively well in Liberia, while emancipated slaves and rural free blacks lacking those advantages tended to do less well."[75]

Fewer migrants went to Monrovia later in the century as new settlements were encouraged and there were reports that other destinations were healthier for new arrivals. Map 3.1 shows the distribution of Americo-Liberian settlements along the coast in 1900, and Figure 3.10 gives the share of migrants going to Monrovia over the decades. As early as 1825, ACS agent Jehudi Ashmun began establishing inland settlements along the St Paul River. These were intended to increase agricultural production, taking advantage of the fertility of the alluvial flood plains on the banks of the river as well as river transport to the coast.[76] New settlements were established through the nineteenth century, following the river and its branches, on land acquired through purchase and various other means (sometimes coercive) from indigenous leaders. Often these were established for particular large groups of migrants from the same origin, giving each its own unique character and culture. Sometimes these were reflected in the names of the new towns, as in the case of Virginia (established 1846), Louisiana (1843), or Kentucky (1847).[77] Some were named after ACS officials. Crozierville (1865), which became home to the Barbadian migrants, was named after Samuel and John Crozer, two Philadelphia colonizationists who had been aboard the *Elizabeth* in 1820 and had encouraged the Barbados migrants. Crozierville retained a distinct political culture, and in later decades would become a focal point of opposition to the Liberian government.

In addition to opening up new possibilities for agricultural production, these inland settlements also connected migrant communities to indigenous trade networks. By 1830, there was a road from Millsburg to Bopolu, a major commercial center mentioned in the previous chapter. Acting as intermediaries between the coast and the interior, migrants exchanged tobacco, gunpowder, salt, cotton cloth, beads, and a variety of other goods for agricultural and forest products, including palm oil, rice, camwood, and ivory. Some of these goods – particularly palm oil and camwood – were important Liberian exports before the development of sugar and coffee plantations.

---

[74] "Latest from Liberia," *African Repository* IV, no. 1 (March 1828), 14–25.
[75] Tyler-McGraw, *An African Republic*, 127–28.
[76] Gurley, *Life of Jehudi Ashmun*, 236.   [77] Shick, *Behold the Promised Land*, 75.

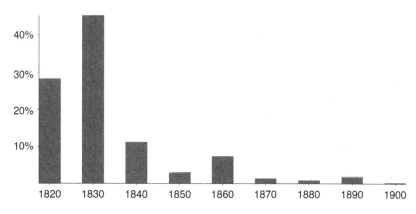

Figure 3.10 Share of migrants going to Monrovia

Trade provided an important lifeline to migrants in the interior. Though land on the river was more fertile than that on the coast, it still required more labor to clear and cultivate than most migrants could mobilize.[78] In addition, migrants had to adjust to a year sectioned by rainy and dry seasons, which Clegg describes as "probably one of the more discomforting adjustments that life in Africa required."[79] This change of seasons made agricultural production a process of trial and error even for those who had been farmers in the United States. As a result, life in Caldwell, Millsburg, and other new towns was a struggle for many of the migrants during early decades. Eventually, some succeeded in building prosperous plantations, growing the coffee and sugar which would fuel Liberia's first export boom in the mid-nineteenth century. They relied on labor from the recaptive population as well as poorer migrants.[80]

Contemporary evidence suggests that there was a process of spatial sorting in which better-off migrants remained in or went to Monrovia or other coastal settlements, while those with less capital were settled elsewhere. One result of this dispersion is that as early as 1843 there were considerable gaps in human capital within Liberia. Figure 3.11 gives literacy rates for other locations relative to that of Monrovia (which was 36 percent on average) from the 1843 census. It shows that higher literacy rates were found in coastal settlements like Edina, Bassa Cove, and Sinoe and lower rates in interior settlements like Caldwell, Millsburg, and New Georgia. This division was also reflected in occupation data from the

[78] Gurley, *Life of Jehudi Ashmun*, 230.   [79] Clegg, *Price of Liberty*, 80.
[80] Shick, *Behold the Promised Land*, ch. 5.

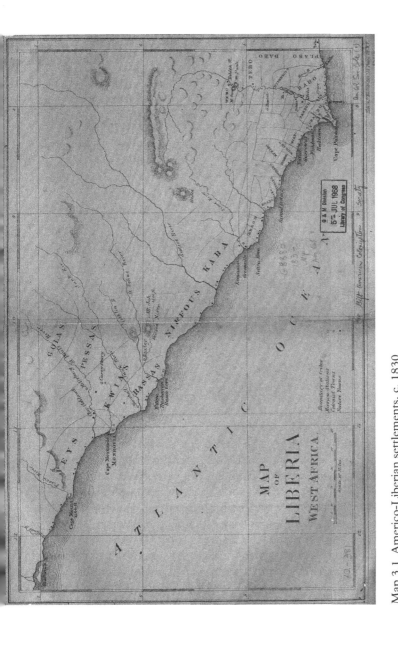

Map 3.1 Americo-Liberian settlements, c. 1830

Source: Based on Library of Congress, G8880 183-.N4 Am Col 1.

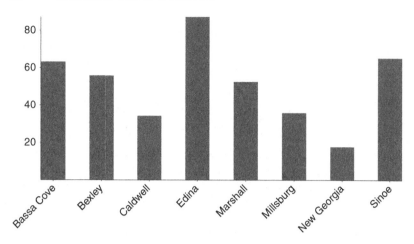

Figure 3.11 Literacy rates of adults in 1843 (Monrovia = 100)

1843 census, reproduced by Tom Shick. The interior settlements had a larger share of agricultural and unskilled workers, in contrast to Monrovia or other coastal settlements. In New Georgia, for example, 96 out of 120 inhabitants (or 80 percent) were either employed in agriculture or unskilled. In Monrovia, this total was 103 out of 463 (or 22 percent). To some degree these differences in occupational structure were by design; Ashmun, for example, had deliberately established Caldwell as a home for migrants aboard the *Hunter*, which arrived in 1825, the majority of whom were farmers.[81] New Georgia became home to a large number of the recaptives, and by the 1830s had become a "breadbasket" for the growing population of Monrovia.[82]

Unfortunately, the next Liberian census was not until 1962, so it is difficult to know whether there was any convergence in these rates over time through the provision of schooling. However, the migrant data going up to 1904 show similar gaps, with a literacy rate of 45 percent among adult males who gave their destination as Monrovia, as compared with an overall average of 25 percent for males. Other data are similarly suggestive. Data on trade presented in Chapter 4 show Monrovia's prominence as the main commercial center through the nineteenth and twentieth centuries. Through the twentieth century, Monrovia continued to attract African-American elites from W. E. B. Du Bois to Nina Simone, as well as migrants from other parts of Liberia. Amos Sawyer notes that during the

---

[81] Gurley, *Life of Jehudi Ashmun*, 232.   [82] Shick, *Beyond the Promised Land*, 66.

1960s, "Monrovia was at the terminus of the process of stepwise migration" from rural areas to the concession areas and finally to the capital.[83] Chapter 9 uses data from the 1962 census to show that at that point, people in Monrovia were better educated than in other parts of the country.

Making Liberia

In this consolidation of inequalities, the Americo-Liberian community bore some resemblance to other African-American communities in which new waves of migrants began to arrive. In Pittsburgh, for example, Gottlieb argues that "the reciprocal influences of the southern migrants and the establish black community strengthened the emerging class divisions."[84] Peyton Skipwith wrote in 1834 that "their is Some that hav come to this place that have got rich and a number that are Sufering. Those that are well off do hav the nativs as Slavs and poor people that come from America hav no chance to make a living for the nativs do all the work [sic]."[85]

These divisions – geographical, economic, and social – made their mark on Liberia's institutions and politics over the course of the nineteenth and early twentieth centuries. In its first decades as an independent country, Liberia was governed by the Republican Party which was dominated primarily by those few migrants who had arrived with the skills and capital to establish themselves as middlemen in the growing Atlantic trade in agricultural and forest products. This group was often referred to as the "merchant princes" owing to their dominance in both government and trade.[86] Many identified as mulattos, adding a racial dimension to economic and social divisions.

Poorer migrants often accused more established ones of profiting at their expense. Thomas Fuller, appointed by the ACS to travel to Liberia in 1851, reported meeting "a lady from Savannah, in Georgia, by the name of Mrs. Jackson" who was intending to go to Sierra Leone because Monrovia merchants "charged her twenty-five cents per quart for milk, twenty-five cents a-piece for fowls, and thirty-seven and a half cents per dozen for eggs."[87] Similarly, Delany's critical account noted that "some

---

[83] Sawyer, *The Emergence of Autocracy in Liberia*, 259.
[84] Gottlieb, *Making Their Own Way*, 7.
[85] Peyton Skipwith to John H. Cocke, February 10, 1934, quoted in Wiley, *Slaves No More*, 36.
[86] Dwight Syfert, "The Origins of Privilege: Liberian Merchants, 1822–1847," *Liberian Studies Journal* VI, no. 2 (1975): 109–28.
[87] Thomas Fuller, *Journal of a Voyage to Liberia* (Baltimore: John D Toy, 1851), 14.

few are wealthy and keep tolerable establishments; mostly, however, they are small affairs, low doggeries that deal out to the poor ignorant natives, rum, tobacco, cotton cloth, trinkets &c &c – in exchange for which they get Palm Oil, Camwood, &c, trading off these articles again to merchant vessels that frequently visit the coast." Augustus Washington wrote that "in nearly every town and county, there is a one-man power, for that county; a man may hold all the offices of government and besides be lawyer, merchant, judge, and agent for the Society, and, if he chooses, it is not difficult to turn the money and offices of these people into his own coffers."[88]

Resentments generated by what were seen as the abuses of the merchant princes, combined with the fading of the mid-century period of growth, helped consolidate opposition to the Republican Party. The interior communities along the St Paul River, including Crozierville, became what Amos Sawyer would later describe as "a hotbed of political agitation." In 1869, the True Whig Party was established in Clay-Ashland (formerly Kentucky) and defeated the Republican Party to elect Edward J. Roye as president.[89] As discussed in Chapter 6, Roye's efforts to raise capital abroad and reorient Liberia's commercial policies contributed to his overthrow in Liberia's first coup d'état in 1871.

Despite these divisions, the Americo-Liberian government managed to retain its position of dominance until 1980. In his history of Liberia, Gus Liebenow writes that

since 1822 the Americo-Liberian settlers and their descendants have become masters of the art of survival in a potentially hostile world. On many occasions in the past the very existence of the Republic was threatened either by an armed uprising on the part of the conquered tribal people or by the diplomatic and other victories of their colonial neighbors, the British and the French.[90]

This "art of survival" is the subject of Part II of this book. How did a government which had neither internal legitimacy nor much external support manage to stay in power over a period which saw the rise and fall of great empires? This is not a new question in Liberian history, but what this book shows is that, despite the singular character of Liberia's origins, the methods of survival adopted by Americo-Liberian elites were not necessarily unique. Liberia's declaration of independence in 1847 occurred just as other states, both old and new, were attempting to redefine their roles in a changing global economy. Only a tiny fraction

---

[88] Quoted in Moses, *Liberian Dreams*, 203.
[89] Sawyer, *The Emergence of Autocracy*, 160;
[90] J. Gus Liebenow, *Liberia: the Evolution of Privilege* (Ithaca: Cornell University Press, 1969), xviii.

of these enjoyed a position of dominance, political or economic, either within or outside their boundaries. The others faced many of the same dilemmas about how to define and exercise their sovereignty in a context of rapidly growing trade and increasing technological and financial inequalities between states.

Part II

The Art of Survival

4   Trade, Globalization, and Sovereignty

It is to be regretted that some foreign traders to this coast are disposed to attribute the enactment of this law to a feeling on our part hostile to their interests and to the interests of the aborigines, and to a desire entertained by us to enrich ourselves by monopolizing the native trade. With respect to their own interests, it is but just that foreigners should both feel and manifest some concern, and that they should endeavor, as much as possible, to guard them from detriment, so with regard to our own interests, we should be allowed to look after them in the best manner we can.

President Daniel Warner, annual message from March 1865,
after the passage of the 1864 Ports of Entry Law

On November 27, 1846, voters in the Commonwealth of Liberia decided by a slim majority to adopt a new constitution as an independent nation.[1] A Constitutional Convention was convened in Monrovia the following year and adopted the Declaration of Independence on July 26, 1847. It declared the Commonwealth of Liberia "a free, sovereign, and independent state, by the name and title of the Republic of Liberia."[2] While the Declaration listed numerous reasons for Liberia to become independent, its immediate origins were linked to trade.[3] "As our territory has extended, and our population increased, our commerce has also increased ... Questions have arisen, which it is supposed can be adjusted only by agreement between sovereign powers." These referred specifically to disputes between the Liberian administration and British traders from Sierra Leone. When faced with tariffs and restrictions on where they

---

[1] Joseph Jenkins Roberts, "Statement to the Council, January 1847," in *The Political and Legislative History of Liberia*, edited by Charles Henry Huberich (New York: Central Book, 1947), 808–9.

[2] Declaration of Independence, in Huberich, *Political and Legislative History*, 828.

[3] Tom W. Shick, *Behold the Promised Land: A History of Afro-American Settler Society in Nineteenth Century Liberia* (Baltimore: Johns Hopkins University Press, 1980), 103; Dwight Syfert, "The Liberian Coasting Trade, 1822–1900," *Journal of African History* 18, no. 2 (1977): 227–28.

93

could trade, British merchants challenged both the territorial jurisdiction of the Liberian government and its right to levy tariffs at ports it claimed. One such dispute at Bassa Cove prompted the British government to demand from the American government clarification on its position in West Africa. The American government denied all responsibility for Liberia, prompting the declaration of independence by a thin majority of Americo-Liberian settlers.

This chapter focuses on trade as one of three areas in which the newly established Liberian government sought to exert its control over the local economy. Subsequent chapters examine other avenues for the exercise of economic sovereignty, namely currency and public debt. Of the three, trade has received the most attention from historians of Liberia. Existing histories have focused particularly on the "ports of entry" laws that restricted the locations where foreign traders could operate. The enforcement of these laws, and their eventual abandonment in 1930, are thought to have played an important role in shaping the development of the Liberian economy. According to this story, the lack of access to foreign trade during the "closed door" era of the nineteenth century hindered Liberia's economic development compared to its neighbors. In contrast, under the "open door" policy adopted during the interwar period but championed most forcefully by President William V. S. Tubman (1944–71), foreign investment facilitated the exploitation of Liberia's natural resources and led to rapid economic growth which benefited foreign concessionaires and the Liberian elite, though not necessarily the majority of the population.[4]

This chapter compares Liberia's trade policy with that of other independent states for the century after the declaration of independence. Using new data on Liberian tariffs, it tells a different story than the standard narrative just outlined. Instead, the chapter shows that Liberia was not particularly "closed" to foreign influences during the first part of its history and that the ports of entry laws were less important in determining Liberia's relative position in West African trade than previous work has suggested. During the "open door" period, tariffs rose and invitations to foreign investors were selective rather than general. Overall, the chapter argues that, in Liberia as in other countries, the period was one of extensive experimentation in commercial policies in which debates about engagement with the global economy formed a foundational cleavage between Liberian elites.

---

[4] F. P. M. Van der Kraaij, *The Open Door Policy of Liberia: An Economic History of Modern Liberia* (Bremen: Bremer Afrika Archiv, 1983).

Responses to Globalization in the Nineteenth Century

Liberia's declaration of independence in 1847 came at a time of rapid expansions in global trade, migration, and capital flows.[5] The advent of rail and steam along with ever-growing demand for raw materials from the industrializing economies of Europe and North America changed the face of global commerce. Such was the impact of these changes that one textbook on modern economic history begins by observing that the "history of international relations since 1850 is largely an account of the problems, the solutions, the benefits and costs created by this upsurge of economic activity."[6]

Economic historians argue about whether this was the period when "globalization" first began.[7] Global trade links incorporating all regions of the world had already existed for centuries, ever since the first voyages from Europe to the Americas in the fifteenth century, a period which itself built on the commercial revolution of the medieval period. Early modern trade networks, including the Atlantic slave trade, had expanded rapidly alongside economic growth and improvements in shipping and navigation during the eighteenth century. To a certain extent, the nineteenth century built on this growth, although the scale of global trade expansion was unprecedented. The major shift of the nineteenth century was not only in the volume of trade but also in its character. In the past, the costs and risks of transport had restricted long-distance trade to elite goods for which elasticities of demand were sufficient to bear the cost. The trade expansions of the medieval and early modern periods were based on rare spices, precious metals, tea, sugar, and slaves, rather than bulkier agricultural produce more likely to be traded locally. This afforded local producers of less valuable goods, from food to manufactures, a certain degree of protection from foreign competition. The transport revolution of the nineteenth century changed this, and the period saw the emergence of regional specializations in the production of manufactured goods or raw materials.[8]

---

[5] Kevin O'Rourke and Jeffrey G. Williamson, *Globalization and History: The Evolution of a Nineteenth-Century Atlantic Economy* (Cambridge, MA: MIT Press, 1999); Ronald Findlay and Kevin O'Rourke, *Power and Plenty: Trade, War and the World Economy in the Second Millennium* (Princeton: Princeton University Press, 2009), ch. 7.

[6] James Foreman-Peck, *A History of the World Economy: International Economic Relations since 1850* (Brighton: Wheatsheaf Books, 1986), 1.

[7] Kevin O'Rourke and Jeffrey Williamson, "When Did Globalization Begin?" *European Review of Economic History* 6 (2002): 23–50; Dennis O. Flynn and Arturo Giraldez, "Cycles of Silver: Global Economic Unity through the Mid-Eighteenth Century," *Journal of World History* 13 (2002): 391–427.

[8] Giovanni Federico and Antonio Tena-Junguito. "World Trade, 1800–1930: A New Synthesis," *Revista Historia Economica* 37: 9–41; Findlay and O'Rourke, *Power and Plenty*.

Identifying winners and losers from this shift remains both complex and controversial. Dependency theorists in the 1970s tended to tell this story as one of winners in the "core" and losers in the "periphery," with foreign competition leading to deindustrialization in places like India and West Africa, which undermined their later development prospects.[9] More recent histories are more nuanced. Merchants and producers in the so-called periphery were as alive to the opportunities offered by global economic expansion as their Western counterparts, and the scale and scope of changes to the economies of regions outside Western Europe remain the subject of debate.[10] However, in many countries there were also groups of elites who pushed back against expanding foreign interests. Mexico, Argentina, and Peru were just a few of the many countries that saw "a wave of 'conservative nationalisms'" in the middle of the nineteenth century, before some, like Peru, shifted to more liberal trade policies later.[11]

For West Africa, discussion of this period centers on the end of the Atlantic slave trade and the subsequent rise of "legitimate commerce," or the export of agricultural and forest products. In 1973, A. G. Hopkins argued that this transition marked a period of "crisis" for West African states which had based systems of revenue generation on the trade in slaves.[12] New markets for palm oil, groundnuts, and other products offered Africans outside the warrior elite of the slave trade opportunities to increase their incomes and challenge existing hierarchies. Others have disputed this interpretation, arguing that in many parts of the region, elites were both able and willing to shift their resources – including enslaved people – to serve new markets. Plantations for production of raw materials emerged, manned by enslaved people who might in an earlier period have been exported.[13]

While the link to the Atlantic slave trade means that the terms of this debate are specific to West Africa, it can also be seen as part of a global history of political crisis and experimentation in the nineteenth century.

---

[9] See, for example, Fernando Henrique Cardoso and Enzo Faletto, *Dependency and Development in Latin America* (Berkeley: University of California Press, 1979); Walter Rodney, *How Europe Underdeveloped Africa* (Washington, DC: Howard University Press, 1981). For a more recent take, see Peter Evans, *Embedded Autonomy: States and Industrial Transformation* (Princeton: Princeton University Press, 1995).

[10] Christopher A. Bayly, *The Birth of the Modern World 1780–1914: Global Connections and Comparisons* (Malden, MA: Blackwell, 2004).

[11] Paul Gootenberg, *Between Silver and Guano: Commercial Policy and the State in Postindependence Peru* (Princeton: Princeton University Press, 1989), 9.

[12] A. G. Hopkins, *An Economic History of West Africa* (London: Longman, 1973).

[13] Robin Law (ed.), "Introduction," in *From Slave Trade to "Legitimate" Commerce: The Commercial Transition to Nineteenth-Century West Africa* (Cambridge: Cambridge University Press, 2009), 1–31.

It was not only in West Africa that governments and elites struggled to find the right response to the economic and technological changes of the period, and from the Americas to Asia to Africa they experimented with a variety of policy responses that tried to balance various imperatives and interests. The taxation of trade was the most important source of government revenue for virtually all states during this period. It was particularly important for new states with both low levels of capacity and tenuous authority over the people they governed.[14] Increasing trade volumes offered at least the opportunity to collect more revenue at a time when states were becoming increasingly bureaucratized. However, the desire to maximize revenue from the taxation of trade had to be balanced against the conflicting interests of those who either gained from the expanding trade or saw their livelihoods threatened by the erosion of the natural protection that distance and high transport costs had previously afforded. In his account of Peru's shift from protectionism to liberal trade policies, Paul Gootenberg writes that debates about trade were "primordial to Peru's difficulties in forming a cohesive state" after independence.[15]

Attempts to grapple with these dilemmas saw what Irwin describes as a "tremendous outpouring" of writing by classical economists.[16] Trade was a key topic for many, building on the work of Adam Smith in arguing for free trade on the basis of comparative advantage. Smith's ideas were not instantly adopted as orthodoxy, and the upheavals in global trade created by the Napoleonic wars provided plenty of material for debate. In 1807, William Spence argued that the cutting off of trade in wartime would not diminish Britain's national wealth because this lay in domestic production and internal trade. Countering this, Mill and Torrens pointed out the efficiency and productivity gains that trade could produce. By exploiting differences between countries in the costs of production, it might be that more of a particular good (like, for example, grain) could be produced indirectly through trade than directly by each individual country. This theory, known as the theory of comparative costs, was extended by David Ricardo in 1817. It was through the work of these and other classical economists that free trade became the orthodoxy of British economics during this period. However, as Irwin puts it, "despite their unanimity in extolling the virtues of free trade, the classical economists were acutely aware that certain groups were harmed by the policy and they did not

---

[14] J. H. Coatsworth and J. G. Williamson, "Always Protectionist? Latin American Tariffs from Independence to the Great Depression," *Journal of Latin American Studies* 36, no. 2 (2004): 205–32.

[15] Gootenberg, *Between Silver and Guano*, 11.

[16] Douglas A. Irwin, *Against the Tide: An Intellectual History of Free Trade* (Princeton: Princeton University Press, 1996).

entirely overlook those interests."[17] To compensate losers from globalization, they argued for either the gradual reduction of protective tariffs, which would allow for the reallocation of resources, or for direct compensation.

There were exceptions to this commitment to free trade. While most classical economists were particularly hostile to the Corn Laws, which restricted the import of grain into Britain to protect the interests of landlords and agricultural producers, Thomas Malthus took a different view. In a controversial 1815 pamphlet, he argued in favor of import restrictions on grain in order to maintain an independent supply. He argued that if grain exporters should for some reason refuse to trade, it would leave grain importers vulnerable to disruptions in their food supply. Further, he argued that it would have detrimental effects on the interests of landlords and prompt disruptions in the rural economy. In making this argument, Malthus joined people like Friedrich List in Germany, Augustine Cournot in France, and Henry Carey in the United States who were trying to develop a "new, positive case for protection" to counter the arguments of classical economists.

These same ideas informed debates among Americo-Liberian elites, who found it difficult to come to a consensus on the extent to which their new government should intervene in the market on their behalf. Some argued that protection was warranted based on Liberia's comparatively weak position in the world. One such case was put in 1858 by James Spriggs Payne, a minister who would later be president of Liberia, who submitted an essay titled *A Prize Essay on Political Economy: As Adapted to the Republic of Liberia* to the first National Fair intended to incentivize innovation in production.[18] In the essay, which won first prize, Payne argued for both greater reliance on domestic production and for at least some degree of protection. "Can we not dispose with a portion of the foreign food so abundantly imported into the country," he pleaded, "and substitue [sic] home products"? Further, he argued that

if "free trade" is becoming the general policy, it is between equals. It is folly to ignore our inequality in favor of a policy that must be injurious to us ... Liberia should not suppose that, if other governments embrace the doctrine of "free

---

[17] Irwin, *Against the Tide*, 92.
[18] J. S. Payne, *A Prize Essay on Political Economy: As Adapted to the Republic of Liberia* (Monrovia: G. Killian, 1860).

trade" and reduce its principles to reciprocal action, she can do the same; we are too young and too feeble, too unequl [sic] to the great nations of the earth, to attempt to operate with them on the great principles of strict reciprocity. However, he recognized that protectionist policies could do harm as well as good. To exclude foreign products, he wrote, "would subject the citizens to an imposition from home producers, by the prices and quality of the products they would then have in their power to put in the market."

Not all Liberians agreed with Payne, and how to engage with foreign trade and foreign interests became (and remains) one of the fundamental fault lines of Liberian politics. The two main political parties of the nineteenth century, the old Republican Party of Joseph Jenkins Roberts and the other "merchant princes," and the True Whig Party established by agricultural producers from the interior settlements, divided partly along these lines, with the Republican Party of Payne and other members of the merchant elite in favor of restricting the role of foreigners in the Liberian economy.[19] As the next section shows, however, these policy differences were often mitigated by the practical necessity of attracting foreign trade to ensure the financial survival of the new government. Even as Payne wrote his essay, both the Liberian government and members of the Americo-Liberian elite were acutely aware of their dependence on trade for both government revenue and private incomes. Payne's own family was among the more successful of the "merchant princes"; in the 1843 census, the firm of Payne and Yates was reported to have holdings worth some $34,000, and Payne himself would become president just a few years after winning his prize.[20]

Competing for Trade and Sovereignty

As Chapter 2 shows, there was already a lively trade on the coast of what became Liberia before the arrival of migrants from the United States. Trade in spices, slaves, and other commodities with European merchants from the fifteenth century drew indigenous communities toward the coast, establishing towns and factories.[21] In this it followed a pattern similar to other regions of West Africa, where the Atlantic trade prompted a reorientation of economic networks away from the interior and toward what Inikori refers to as the "Atlantic Basin" economies of western

---

[19] Van der Kraaij, *Open Door*, 23–4.
[20] Syfert, "The Liberian Coasting Trade," 226–27.
[21] Carl Patrick Burrowes, *Between the Kola Forest and the Salty Sea: A History of the Liberian People before 1800* (Bomi County: Know Your Self Press, 2016), 201; Syfert, "The Liberian Coasting Trade," 217–18.

Europe, western Africa, and the Americas.[22] Expanding commercial networks along the coast also provided opportunities for the newly arrived migrants. In that year, ACS administrator Jehudi Ashmun began using the society's ships to provision the new migrants, noting that it would be cheaper and more sustainable to engage in local markets than to rely on government funds and donations to provision them from the United States.[23]

Over the next several decades, Americo-Liberians became particularly involved in the "coasting trade," in which smaller ships moved African produce and foreign imports from main trading centers to the rest of the coast. Their role was similar to that of a number of other African and Eurafrican groups along the coast, from the settlers of Sierra Leone to the *habitants* of Senegal, who carved out a lucrative position as middlemen between European merchant ships and indigenous producers.[24] Over this period, a small shipbuilding industry emerged in Monrovia and the size of the Liberian shipping fleet increased steadily in the years leading up to the

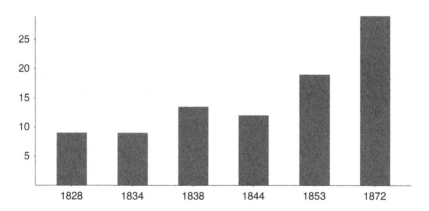

Figure 4.1 Estimated number of ships in Liberian fleet, 1828–1872
Source: Dwight N. Syfert, "The Liberian Coasting Trade, 1822–1900." *Journal of African History* 18, no. 2 (1977): 217–35

---

[22] Joseph Inikori, "Africa and the globalization process: western Africa, 1450–1850," *Journal of Global History* 2, no. 1 (2007): 70.

[23] Jehudi Ashmun, "Notes on trade," in *Life of Jehudi Ashmun, Late Colonial Agent in Liberia*, edited by Ralph Randolph Gurley (Freeport, NY: Books for Libraries Press, 1971), A42.

[24] See, for example, Raymond E. Dumett, "John Sarbah, the Elder, and African Mercantile Entrepreneurship in the Gold Coast in the Late Nineteenth Century," *Journal of African History* 14, no. 4 (1973): 653–79; Gabriele Cappelli and Joerg Baten, "European Trade, Colonialism, and Human Capital Accumulation in Senegal, Gambia and Western Mali, 1770–1900," *Journal of Economic History* 77, no. 3 (2017): 920–51.

declaration of independence. While most Liberian ships concentrated on the coasting trade along the coast, others went as far as Liverpool and New York.[25]

The success of the migrants in this trade depended in part on their ability to restrict foreign competition to specific locations along the coast, which then opened up opportunities for Liberian traders to distribute the goods they traded in other locations, linking to large indigenous markets in Bopolu and elsewhere. Thus the later Ports of Entry laws had early precedents in regulations promulgated by the ACS administration.[26] In 1822, Ashmun had recommended "prohibiting all foreign ships from trading to the settlement" of Monrovia. Four years later, the annual report of the administration referred to "regulations of the colony," which required "the barter to be carried on through factories established for the purpose."[27] An 1827 ordinance provided that

it shall not be lawful for any person or persons arriving on the African coast from abroad, except members of this Colony, to carry on trade, or communicate for the said purposes of trade, with the native inhabitants of any port or place situated on the said coast, between the mouth of the Grand Cape Mount River, towards the North-West, and the Colony factory near Poor, or Young Sesters River, towards the South Coast, both places included.[28] In 1836 an Act prohibiting smuggling reiterated the restriction of foreign trade to particular locations, and in 1837 a further law decreed that "no foreigner shall have the privilege of trading with another foreigner, nor with the natives within the limits of the Colony, without the intervention of a commission merchant of the Colony".[29]

These regulations followed the expansion of territory claimed by the ACS and were frequently challenged by both indigenous and foreign groups. There were frequent conflicts with indigenous communities when the Liberian migrants sought to intervene in their existing trading relationships with British merchants.[30] Foreign missionaries were accused of using their ability to import goods duty-free to undercut the profits of Liberian merchants and firms. In 1840, W. N. Lewis, the collector of customs for the Port of Monrovia filed a suit against the Reverend John Seys, superintendent of the Methodist mission, alleging that the mission had refused to pay customs duty on goods imported for

---

[25] Syfert, "The Liberian Coasting Trade," 229.
[26] This discussion is based on Nakomo Duche's notes on the Ports of Entry laws, which he kindly provided me in 2017.
[27] Huberich, *Political and Legislative History*, 345.
[28] Nakomo Duche, "Ports of Entry," quoting Huberich.
[29] Huberich, *Political and Legislative History*, 520–21.
[30] Syfert, "The Liberian Coasting Trade," 222.

the purposes of trade.[31] The defendant claimed that the merchandise had been used for "good works" of the mission. In part the case hinged on who had the final authority in determining Liberia's trade policy: the legislature in Monrovia or the Board of Managers of the ACS in Washington.

A similar question was raised in a suit brought against a British trader named John J. Jackson in 1841, alleging that Jackson had traded with "the natives, or fishmen, at Bassa Cove," in violation of the law.[32] In his instructions to the jury, Roberts addressed the question of whether what was then called the Commonwealth of Liberia had the power to regulate trade. It was "not a state," he acknowledged, "but it was a government," and as such "we may, and we do make laws for the regulation of our internal as well as our foreign commerce." This opinion was countered in 1844 in a letter from the commander of a British squadron, Captain Jones, who wrote to Roberts that the rights of "imposing custom duties, and limiting the trade of foreigners by restrictions, are sovereign rights."[33]

Liberia's declaration of independence was, in the end, the answer to these challenges. In 1847, Commander Murray wrote to the Commodore Sir Charles Hotham that "should the Liberians succeed in purchasing the whole coast line, and in having their sovereign rights acknowledged, they will of course endeavour to impose duties to enable them to raise revenue, and it is evident that British trade as it now exists will be interfered with."[34] Its formal right to regulate trade was soon acknowledged by the signing of treaties of commerce and friendship with Britain in 1848 and a number of other European powers, and the trade policies of the new Republic were merely a continuation of the policies it had adopted before. The next section considers the post-independence adoption of the ports of entry laws and their depiction by both contemporaries and historians.

Closing the Door: Ports of Entry Laws

The Ports of Entry laws thus served two purposes for the Liberian government and the merchant elite. First, the restrictions facilitated the collection of taxes on foreign trade by limiting the number of places where customs agents needed to be stationed.[35] In one of his first annual messages as the president of independent Liberia in 1849, Joseph

---

[31] Africa's Luminary, *Trial of the Suit Instituted by the Collector of Customs for the Port of Monrovia against the Superintendent of the Liberia Mission of the Missionary Society of the Methodist Episcopal Church before the Supreme Court of Liberia* (Monrovia: M.P.M Press, 1840).

[32] Account of the trial comes from Huberich, *Political and Legislative History*, 691–99.

[33] Quoted in Bronwen Everill, *Abolition and Empire in Sierra Leone and Liberia* (Basingstoke: Palgrave, 2013), 145.

[34] July 18, 1847, in FO 47/1.   [35] Syfert, "The Liberian Coasting Trade," 223.

Jenkins Roberts – himself a member of the "merchant princes" – proclaimed that the Liberian government could "only be sustained by a revenue derived from imposts". As a result, "it should watch cautiously over every occurrence that can possibly tend to obstruct the channel of its commercial enterprise." At the same time, the restriction of foreign trade to a few selected ports of entry also protected the coasting trade for Americo-Liberian merchants. In the assessment of both contemporaries and historians, these were contradictory aims.

As shown in the previous section, restrictions on the location of foreign trade already existed in Liberia at independence. However, the new Republic was quick to bring similar legislation into its own laws. An act passed in 1848 dictated that "no foreign transient trading vessel shall be allowed to trade within the limits of this Republic except at the regular ports of entry, nor shall any trade be made in the harbors of the Republic between foreigners and foreigners, nor foreigners and citizens, if said goods are to be landed in this Republic."[36] These were extended by the 1864 Ports of Entry Act, often referred to as the founding act of the "closed door" period but in actual fact simply a continuation of older sets of restrictions. It mandated that from January 1, 1865, "no foreign vessels, or vessels, arriving on the Coast of Liberia, from any port or place, or Liberian vessels engaged in the foreign trade shall be allowed to trade at any point or ports, but at Ports of Entry that are now or may hereafter be created by the Legislature of this Republic." Violators would be subject to a $5,000 fine.

The law remained in place, with some minor modifications, until the early twentieth century. Over that period, certain ports of entry were closed or opened, usually for financial reasons. River Cess, for example, was closed in January 1892 because it was a "needless expense to continue a Custom Office at that Port, there being no imports or exports by foreign vessels." However, by December 1892 it had been opened again by a Joint Resolution of the legislature. No reason was given. In 1900 it was closed again, the law making reference to "outrages" committed against Liberian merchants doing business there, and to a "great falling off of revenue at said port." The same Act mandated the Attorney General to investigate whether, as the abovementioned merchants claimed, the "outrages" could be "traceable to chiefs" in the area. New ports of entry were opened at the mouth of the Mannah River in 1886 and at Fishtown in Maryland County in 1906.

---

[36] An Act Regulating Commerce and Revenue, 1848, from IULC. Further legislation quoted later in this chapter from the same source.

There were also laws passed to strengthen the enforcement of the restrictions. In 1897, the legislature passed a law to limit the extent of the Ports of Entry to two miles inland from the coast, noting that the existing laws did not define such an extent and that foreign traders were taking advantage. In 1898, a Joint Resolution of the legislature restricted foreigners who were involved in agricultural production in Liberia from engaging in trade in the farming districts. It also fixed a punishment for any Liberians who were fronting for foreigners in the opening of any retail premises.

By the first decade of the twentieth century, however, there were moves to loosen the restrictions. In 1902, a Joint Resolution Respecting Trade noted that "numerous complaints have been made to the Government of Liberia that the trade policy of the Republic is restricted," and that a government commission on the condition of trade had come to the same conclusion. The resolution allowed foreign traders to expand to a variety of other locations, including Half Cavalla, Webo, and the town of Jenny. In 1909, this was expanded further by a law that allowed any foreigners established in the existing ports of entry to trade in the interior. The preamble stated that "the laws restricting foreign trade to Ports of Entry is [sic] obstructive to the development and expansion of our trade." A further loosening of restrictions came in 1923, and in 1930 the Ports of Entry laws were effectively abolished in the "Act Permitting unrestricted. trade in the Hinterland of Liberia, both to Citizens and Aliens." The preamble to the 1930 Act noted that "it is the desire of the Government to open the entire interior to trade and commerce."

The laws loosening or abandoning the trade restrictions referenced long-standing critiques of the policy by foreign merchants and other observers. A 1901 British trade report stated that "the present law forbidding any but Liberian citizens to establish business houses in the interior is a great hindrance to trade, as the natives, having as yet few requirements, will not take the trouble to bring their produce to the coast, not to mention that the roads are anything but safe owing to tribal wars."[37] A 1907 report drew much the same conclusion: "the present laws of the country are most detrimental to its development."[38] Even those sympathetic to Liberia doubted the wisdom of the law. Commenting on the Jackson case, the editor of *Africa's Luminary* wrote,

it cannot however be doubted, but that the visits of British vessels and other foreigners will not be as frequent to the settlements in Liberia, as perhaps they

---

[37] Foreign Office, *Report on the Trade and Commerce of Liberia for the Year 1901* (London: HMSO, 1902), 3.

[38] Foreign Office, *Report for the Year 1906 on the Trade of Liberia* (London: HMSO, 1907), 5.

might be, if they were allowed to trade with the natives, as well as the colonists. But whether the loss of their trade is more than made up to the colonies by the monopoly of the traffic with the natives, is, for wiser political heads than ours to determine.[39]

Historians have accorded the Ports of Entry law an important role in shaping Liberia's economic development over the course of the "closed door" period. Van der Kraaij attributes to the passage of the Ports of Entry laws the beginning of a "vicious circle" which explains "Liberia's failure to start even a beginning of economic growth prior to 1947." In this argument, the law "deprived the tribal people along the coast from a considerable portion of their (traditional) trade with European traders – and dissatisfaction with this law contributed to an increased armed resistance against the government."[40] Expenditures incurred fighting this resistance kept the government in a constant state of financial crisis. This account echoes later discussions of the "economic dysfunction" of postindependence African states in the late twentieth century, which argued that efforts by governments to remain in power undermined the economies of the countries they governed.[41]

Liberian trade did decline during the period from approximately 1870. Not much data are available on the size or profits of the coasting trade, but the data that do exist suggest that the size of the Liberian fleet declined dramatically (see Figure 4.2). At the same time, Liberia entered a long period of economic stagnation, which historians have attributed variously to growing competition from steamships to the effects of the ports of entry law. Van der Kraaij writes that after 1870, "trading activities had declined as a result of the Ports of Entry law."[42] The Liberian government itself blamed the ports of entry laws for deteriorating economic conditions. In the Act Permitting Unrestricted Trade of 1930, which finally abolished all regulations on the location of trade, the preamble noted that "the present slump in the trade of the Republic is partly attributed to restrictions" on the location of trade. However, neither British nor Liberian observers offered much in the way of empirical evidence on the extent of trade loss or how merchants selected the locations where they would trade.

Figure 4.3 gives data for a selection of years on the value of imports into the main ports of entry across both the closed door and open door periods. Map 4.1 shows the location of these ports along the Liberian

[39] Huberich, *Political and Legislative History*, 699.
[40] Van der Kraaij, *Open Door*, 12–13.
[41] See review in Catherine Boone, *Merchant Capital and the Roots of State Power in Senegal, 1930–1985* (Cambridge: Cambridge University Press, 1992), 2–3.
[42] Van der Kraaij, *Open Door*, 25.

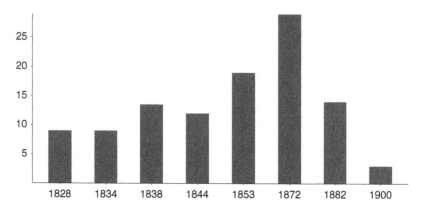

Figure 4.2 Decline of the Liberian fleet, 1828–1900
Source: Syfert, "Coasting trade".

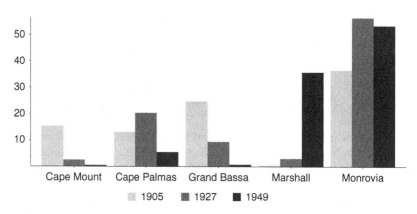

Figure 4.3 Value of imports by Ports (%)
Source: Report on the commercial and industrial activities of the
Republic of Liberia for the calendar year ending December 31, 1905,
in US Consulate Despatch Book, NARA RG 84, Entry UD 584, Vol 7;
Republic of Liberia Customs Service, Import, Exports and Shipping
Statistics for the Calendar Year 1927 (Monrovia, 1928), in IULC.

coast. If the ports of entry laws had artificially restricted the volume of
trade, it would be reasonable to expect that trade would expand to a wider
and more diverse range of ports after the laws were abandoned. However,
the data in the figure do not show this. Trade became more, rather than
less, concentrated in a few ports after the abolition of the law. Monrovia,

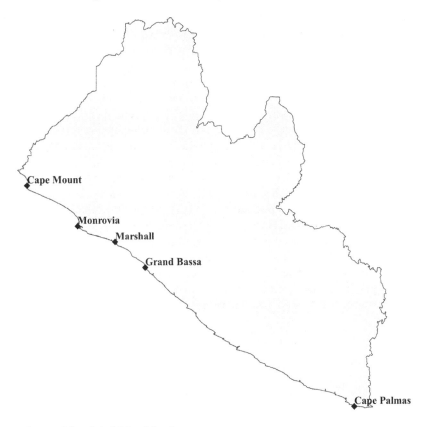

Map 4.1 Major Liberian ports

perhaps not surprisingly, features prominently in the value of imports in both periods. In 1905, when the ports of entry restrictions were still in place, it absorbed nearly 40 percent of the total value of imports. Following closely behind was Grand Bassa, which received about 25 percent of imports. Cape Mount and Cape Palmas, farther south, were also substantial ports. The trade of the other statutory Ports of Entry was negligible in value. However, by 1927, when the ports of entry laws still existed but after they had been liberalized, Grand Bassa and Cape Mount had faded in significance and Monrovia received more than 50 percent of total import value.

Monrovia maintained this level of significance in 1949, while the others – Grand Bassa, Cape Mount and Cape Palmas – all diminished. Marshall, which had not been a significant port in the first two years for which data are available, had grown dramatically and absorbed 35 percent of the total value of imports. The reason for its growth was its proximity to the Firestone Rubber Plantation, and the construction by Firestone of roads and port facilities.

It is worth noting here that Liberia was not the only country in West Africa to close or open ports as financial necessity dictated. In African colonies, too, colonial administrations made frequent judgments about whether a particular port or customs station would repay the staff needed to keep it running. In 1928, the British administration on the Gold Coast closed its port at Sekondi and opened another at Takoradi. A number of smaller ports like Dixcove, Elmina, Pram Pram, and Chama were closed from 1919 to 1921.[43] In his history of customs tariffs in the Congo Free State, Bas de Roo argues that studies of customs tariffs underemphasize the extent to which they also require state capacity to collect.[44] Given the Liberian government's constant financial difficulties, it was perhaps this aspect of the Ports of Entry laws that was more important than their protective function. The next section uses data on tariffs to question the extent to which Liberian trade policy can really be classified as protectionist during the "closed door" period.

Was the Door Really Closed? Liberia in Comparative Perspective

The largely qualitative histories of Liberian ports of entry laws make it difficult to assess how "closed" Liberia was compared to other independent countries. However, other trade policies provide more measurable indicators of openness. Tariffs, in particular, have been used by economic historians of trade and globalization to illustrate the different responses of countries around the world to the rapid expansion of trade in the nineteenth and twentieth centuries. When compared to other countries, Liberian tariff policies tell a different story than the one suggested by the history of the ports of entry laws alone. Liberian tariffs were considerably lower than those of Latin America, the most protectionist region of the world during the period before World War I, and not far from those of Asia, which was the least. They also did not vary much from those of British West Africa, which were similarly low.

Early histories of tariffs across the nineteenth and early twentieth centuries tended to focus on the experience of a set of "core" economies

---

[43] Gold Coast, *Blue Books* (Accra: Government Printer, various).

[44] Bas de Roo. "The Trouble with Tariffs: Customs Policies and the Shaky Balance between Colonial and Private Interests in the Congo," *Low Countries Journal of Social and Economic History* 12, no. 3 (2015): 1–21.

in Europe and the United States.[45] These histories told a broad narrative of a period of "openness" in the middle decades of the nineteenth century, followed by a "globalization backlash" which prompted a steady rise in tariff rates up to World War I, then an even sharper drift toward protectionism in the interwar period. Looking at a wider range of countries tells a different, and more complex, story. First, tariff policies varied enormously both between and within different regions of the world. In Latin America, for example, high tariffs were not a product of the interwar period but rather had been in place in many countries since shortly after independence. There were exceptions. Peru adopted more liberal policies during the years of the "guano boom" from 1850 to 1870. The United States also maintained very high tariffs, which were initially imposed during the Civil War to raise money for the federal war effort. In contrast, Asian countries had much lower tariffs during the period before World War I, though these ultimately caught up with those of Latin America during the interwar period.

The variation between countries and regions reflects the wide range of priorities and interests which could shape tariff policies. The need for revenue was one, but setting tariffs to maximize revenue was not necessarily straightforward. According to Douglas Irwin's study of the 1888 "tariff debate" in the United States, the extent to which higher tariff rates will generate more or less revenue depends on the elasticity of demand for imported goods.[46] If demand for goods is less elastic, higher rates will generate more revenue. If, however, consumers are sensitive to price increases for imported goods and can easily substitute domestically produced goods, higher tariffs will lead to a decline in the value of imports and therefore lower revenue. The tariff debate of 1888 split Democrats and Republicans on precisely this discussion. Protection for domestic industries and strategic coordination with major trading partners also played a role. Further, not all countries had full autonomy in setting their tariff rates; colonies or independent countries subject to unequal treaties often faced limits on the tariff rates they could set.

The setting of tariff rates was a frequent subject of deliberation for the Liberian legislature. Figure 4.4 shows Liberia's ad valorem rate over the course of the nineteenth and twentieth centuries. It started at around 6 percent, then rose progressively through the middle of the twentieth century to 15 percent, still low by global standards. This timeline seems

---

[45] Chistopher Blattman, Michael A. Clemens, and Jeffrey G. Williamson, "Who protected and why? Tariffs Around the World 1870–1938," paper presented to the Conference on the Political Economy of Globalization, Dublin August 29–31, 2002.

[46] Douglas A Irwin, "Higher Tariffs, Lower Revenues? Analyzing the Fiscal Aspects of 'the Great Tariff Debate of 1888'," *Journal of Economic History* 58, no. 1 (1998): 59–72.

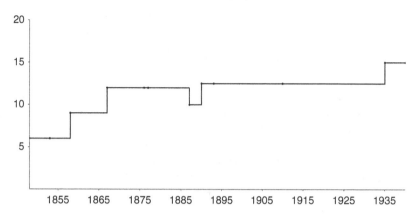

Figure 4.4 Ad valorem tariff rates in Liberia, 1848–1940
Source: Acts, IULC.

to contradict the timeline proposed by the history of the ports of entry law; as this was being eased through the 1920s, then finally abolished in 1930, tariffs were actually going up. Like many other governments of the period, Liberia did attempt to introduce some special rates. In the first tariff legislation introduced after independence, alcoholic beverages were taxed at twenty-five cents per gallon and soap at one cent per pound. Certain textiles, particularly more costly ones, were taxed at rates of 10 and 12 percent. Though records of the discussions about setting these rates have not survived, the targeting of more expensive consumer goods suggests that the Liberian government was using these special rates to target in particular the better-off class of Americo-Liberians as a source of revenue.

This may explain why they also seem to have had difficulty enforcing these rates. This particular set was repealed in December 1853, and the ad valorem rate remained at 6 percent. In 1855, a further duty of one dollar per gallon was levied on "all ardent spirits, wines, claret, cordials and malt liquors." In 1858, the ad valorem rate was raised to 9 percent. In 1860, an additional duty of 10 percent was levied on brown sugar, syrup, and molasses. These additional duties were suspended in 1861. In January 1870 the Legislature passed an act imposing a long list of higher special duties in particular categories of goods. This included a duty of five cents per pound on leaf and chewing tobacco, and fifty cents per gun on all rifles, pistols, and double-barreled guns. Brass kettles and pans were subject to a duty of five cents on each pound, and "all fine broad-cloths and cashmeres" had a duty of forty cents per yard. Each barrel of

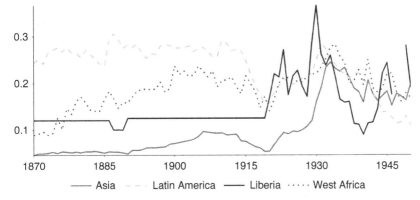

Figure 4.5 Average tariff rates, 1870–1948
Source: Data on Latin America and Asia from Michael A. Clemens and Jeffrey G. Williamson, "Why Did the Tariff-Growth Correlation Change after 1950?" *Journal of Economic Growth* 9, no. 1 (2004): 5–46. West Africa data from trade reports of the Gold Coast, Nigeria, and Sierra Leone. For Liberia see Ch. 1.

flour attracted a duty of one dollar and fifty cents, and each barrel of pork three dollars per barrel. Iron bars and hollow-ware were also subject to a variety of goods, as were kerosene and petroleum. However, this array of duties had little time to come into force before the Act was repealed a month later. The preamble to the repeal noted that the Act imposing the special duties "has not met the wants of the Government, and has greatly disappointed the people of this Republic, and has seriously deranged the payment of duties on imports and exports." In 1876, a simpler list of special duties on tobacco, guns, and alcohol was passed, but these were further revised in 1878.

How did Liberian tariffs compare with other countries over the same period? Figure 4.5 compares Liberia's average tariff rates with those of Latin America, Asia, and British West Africa. Average tariff rates, or the ratio of customs revenue to import values, are a standard measure of tariff protection which have the advantage of also accounting for special rates. In the absence of disaggregated revenue data for Liberia distinguishing customs revenue from other sources before 1920, ad valorem rates are used for the comparison. The Liberian government's difficulties in imposing special rates suggest this is a reasonable proxy. For the scattered years for which data are available, Liberia's average tariff rates are often below the ad valorem rate.

In this figure Liberia hardly stands out as a "closed" economy, with tariff rates below even those of colonized West Africa in the first decades of the period. During this period Latin American countries had some of the highest tariff rates in the world, ranging from 20 to 40 percent. In contrast, Asian countries had some of the lowest. This was in part linked to the greater degree of autonomy that most Latin American countries had in setting their tariff rates. The unequal treaties that forced open markets in countries like Japan and China often set low maximum tariff rates.

However, this was only part of the story. Michael Clemens and Jeffrey Williamson argue that both the tariff levels of trading partners and features of their internal markets explain the difference between the two regions.[47] Latin American countries traded mainly with the United States, which maintained high tariffs of its own. Their populations were also, on average, wealthier and better educated than those of Asian countries, and internal markets were better connected by railways. In contrast, Asian trade was more heavily intra-regional, or with European countries with lower tariffs, particularly Britain. Limited transport infrastructure provided domestic producers with a certain degree of natural protection. At the same time, frequent political instability increased the need of most Latin American countries for revenue and made it difficult for them to raise revenue through other types of taxes.

Applying this same logic to Liberia, its low tariff rates even during the era of the "closed door" are not surprising. During this period, Liberia's trade with the United States was limited, and Britain was its dominant trading partner. By the end of the nineteenth century, it was also surrounded by, and competed with, colonized territories where tariff rates were also low. Thus, while it had technical autonomy over its tariff rate – neither the treaties it signed with foreign powers after independence nor any of its loan agreements mandated a limit on tariff rates the way treaties in Asia had done – its trading partners and the rates of other countries in the region suggested lower tariffs as the most logical strategy.

The Liberian government did share with its Latin American counterparts both a desperate need for revenue as well as frequent internal revolts, which may explain why its tariff rates rose over time. However, balanced against this was its inability to police its boundaries. In much of West Africa, porous borders meant that high tariff rates could have a negative impact on tariff revenue, both because of the elasticity effects explored by Irwin in the case of the United States and because it was

[47] Michael A. Clemens and Jeffery G. Williamson, "Why Did the Tariff-Growth Correlation Change After 1950?" *Journal of Economic Growth* 9, no. 1 (2004): 5–46.

frequently possible to move goods between countries. An extreme case was British Gambia, which deliberately set lower tariffs than French Senegal and as a result raised substantial revenues through people smuggling goods across the long land border.[48] Equally, if Liberia were to have imposed high tariff rates, it would have been easy for many producers to simply cross the border to trade. Later chapters will show that differences in infrastructure development meant that there was a tendency for such cross-border trading to occur anyway.

What is known in histories of Liberia as the "era of the closed door" was hardly a period of autarky. The Liberian government, and many Liberian elites, depended on trade and its trade policies reflected efforts to increase revenue and trade volumes in a context of limited state capacity, porous land borders, and low tariffs among neighboring countries and trading partners. Tariffs were comparatively low and intended to raise revenue rather than to hinder international competition.

Reassessing Liberia's Trade Policy

Globalization during the nineteenth and twentieth centuries offered both challenges and opportunities for governments of the period, which in many cases were only just beginning to adopt the territorialized, bureaucratized forms that became standard by the end of this period. On the one hand, governments in all regions of the world had long turned to trade as a source of revenue to be tapped, and growing trade increased the amount of revenue that could be raised in this way. This was no less true for the Liberian government than it was for governments in Latin America, Asia, or even Europe. The taxation of trade, primarily through customs tariffs imposed on imports, provided the lion's share of the Liberian government's resources during this period. Trade was also an important source of income for the Americo-Liberian elites who dominated policy-making.

This dependence on trade revenue meant that the Liberian government was, from its very inception, outward looking in its orientation. Added to this was the limited domestic market which did not allow it any other real source of revenue. The risk of expanding trade and growing regional specialization was that industries which had enjoyed some degree of natural protection provided by transport costs were exposed to competition from other regions. From textile producers in India to grain farmers in Britain, globalization in the nineteenth century had its share of losers as

---

[48] Leigh Gardner, "The Curious Incident of the Franc in the Gambia: Exchange Rate Instability and Imperial Monetary Systems in the 1920s," *Financial History Review* 22, no. 3 (2015): 301.

well as winners, and it was often the lobbying of these interests that prompted some governments to adopt more protectionist policies. In Liberia, by contrast, there were few domestic industries that the Americo-Liberian elite had an interest in protecting, beyond access to trade. Rather, the industries the government most encouraged were precisely those crops that might be exported rather than those for which there was an extensive domestic market. The domestic market for Liberian producers was limited by the comparative poverty of much of the indigenous population, their fractious relationship with that population, and the lack of transport networks into the interior.

Global studies of trade policies suggest they could be motivated by a number of factors. High tariffs in Latin America, for example, were driven at least at first by the need for revenue, then later by the political influence of domestic industrialists. Liberia's ports of entry laws could be characterized in a similar way. Older studies have tended to treat them as a method of government protection for the enterprises of the merchant princes. This might have been part of their motivation. In his study of Peru, Gootenberg notes that "economic nationalism usually coalesces as a defensive reaction to new competitors, on the part of previously organized and advantaged groups and those closest to the existing state."[49] However, this chapter has shown that protectionism was not a consistent policy. Liberia's tariff rates through this period were comparatively low, closer to those of Asian governments whose trade policies were influenced by foreign interests than to those of Latin America. By this metric, Liberia did not appear to be especially protectionist even during the era of the "closed door."

This could suggest some inconsistency in policy, or, as this chapter argues, an alternative interpretation of the ports of entry laws. Anecdotal evidence surrounding the adoption and eventual repeal of these laws suggests they were driven as much by the limited administrative capacity of the Liberian state and its inability to establish customs houses at more than a few sites along the coast, as they were by the desire to keep trade out of the hands of indigenous merchants, who in any case were quite adept at evading feeble Liberian efforts at enforcement. Further, evidence on the distribution of trade from after the shift to the "open door" suggests they did not have the kind of impact that critics of the ports of entry laws, and later historians, have claimed. Instead of becoming more widely distributed along the coast after the repeal of the ports of entry law, foreign trade became even more concentrated at a few locations driven most likely by

---

[49] Gootenberg, *Between Silver and Guano*, 148.

the availability of infrastructure and the proximity to particular resources like rubber.

Even if the ports of entry laws were intended to be protectionist, inconsistencies in policy-making are perhaps not surprising for a new government within which opinions varied on the costs and benefits of engaging with foreign markets. The next three chapters will focus on money and foreign debt, two other areas in the exercise of economic sovereignty in which the Liberian government struggled to define the right level and manner of interaction with the global economy. They also show that, as in the area of trade policy, it was not alone in this struggle.

5   From Paper to Gold

Trade and protectionism were not the only subjects related to Liberia's economic sovereignty addressed in James Spriggs Payne's *Prize Essay on Political Economy: As Adapted to the Republic of Liberia*. He also had words of caution with regard to the issue of currency. "If the government puts into circulation a paper medium – negotiable only in the country – and promises to redeem it with specie at its treasury department, it certainly should know, at any moment, how much of this currency is in circulation, and should keep itself prepared to redeem it." If government failed to do this, he noted "some citizen, presuming on the faith of the government, may suffer embarrassment. His faith in monetary matters of the government wanes at this moment."[1]

Payne's warning would prove to be prescient. Shortly after the declaration of independence in 1847, the Liberian government issued its first national currency, the Liberian dollar. President Roberts saw the issue of a currency as part of the broader project of nation-building. On returning from a trip to London in 1854, Roberts recounted to the legislature that he had had "frequent conversations with S. Gurney, Esq., on the subject of a metallic currency which he thought we ought to have – as well for the conveniences of trade, as to mark the existence and the nationality of the Republic." In this conversation, Roberts noted that "in consequence of its limited pecuniary resources," it was unable to provide a metallic currency for itself.[2]

The man in question, Samuel Gurney, was the proprietor of Overend Gurney bank and a prominent abolitionist. During that trip, he volunteered to finance the coining of two hundred pounds worth of the new currency, along with the cutting of dies and the

---

[1] James Spriggs Payne, *Prize Essay on Political Economy: As Adapted to the Republic of Liberia* (Monrovia: G. Killian, 1860), 80.

[2] Joseph Jenkins Roberts, "Seventh Annual Message December 20, 1854," in *The Annual Messages of the Presidents of Liberia 1848–2010: State of the Nation Addresses to the National Legislature from Joseph Jenkins Roberts to Ellen Johns Sirleaf*, edited by D. Elwood Dunn (Berlin: de Gruyter, 2011), 83.

minting of one- and two-cent coins, on the condition that the Liberian government paid one hundred pounds on receipt of the coins. "I scarcely need say," reported Roberts, "that I accepted his proposition and that the work was put immediately in the hands of the coiner." He stressed both the economic and political advantages of this step, noting "the great facilities such a means of exchange will afford to the commercial transactions of the country, and the stamp of nationality a coinage always impresses upon the public mind, whether at home or abroad."

The same limits in pecuniary resources which forced Liberia to rely on British charity in minting its first coins also forced it to supplement its coinage with issues of paper money but not, as Payne had recommended, backed by any reserve of specie. The Liberian dollar was initially issued at par with the US dollar but like many inconvertible and unbacked paper currencies during this period, the Liberian dollar quickly depreciated in value relative to other currencies circulating in the region. By the end of the nineteenth century, it had been displaced as the primary medium of exchange in Liberia by foreign currencies – first British sterling and its colonial offshoots, then the US dollar from 1943. Despite various attempts to reverse this process of "dollarization" and return to a single currency, a dual currency system remained in operation into the twenty-first century.

During the decolonization era, monetary sovereignty was considered a potentially powerful tool for promoting post-independence development.[3] However, research on contemporary developing countries often stresses their limited range of options in exercising that sovereignty. Weak fiscal institutions leave their currencies prone to high inflation and currency crises.[4] Underdeveloped domestic financial markets force governments to borrow abroad. If local currencies depreciate relative to the currencies in which they have borrowed, they are vulnerable to debt crises and default. One potential solution is to peg to anchor currencies, but such pegs can lack credibility, leaving the remaining option the adoption of a "super hard peg" such as a currency board or full dollarization.[5] However, this requires

---

[3] A. Hazelwood, "The Economics of Colonial Monetary Arrangements," *Social and Economic Studies*, 3 (1945): 291–315; A. J. Schwartz, "Currency Boards: Their Past, Present and Possibly Future Role," *Carnegie-Rochester Conference Series on Public Policy* 39 (1993): 147–87.

[4] G. A. Calvo and F. S. Mishkin, "The Mirage of Exchange Rate Regimes for Emerging Market Countries," *Journal of Economic Perspectives* 17 (2003): 104.

[5] G. Selgin and L. H. White, "Credible Currency: A Constitutional Perspective," *Constitutional Political Economy* 16 (2005): 72–73. The example of Argentina illustrates the impact of limited credibility. See G. A. Calvo, *Money, Exchange Rates and Output* (Cambridge, MA: MIT Press, 1996), 127–48.

some loss of monetary independence. The adoption of a foreign currency, in particular, also has political costs. Currencies provide a symbol of national sovereignty, and losing this symbol can be politically damaging even if it provides economic benefits.

This chapter examines Liberia's monetary policy from 1847, focusing particularly on the circumstances which led it to abandon its monetary sovereignty from the late nineteenth century onwards.[6] Debates about the fate of the Liberian dollar reflected some of the wider divisions discussed in the previous chapter about the structure of Liberia's interactions with the global economy, and the tension between political imperatives and the limited capacity of the Liberian state.

Creating the Liberian Dollar

Joseph Jenkins Roberts' trip to London in 1854 came in the middle of a formative period in global monetary history. It was over the course of the nineteenth century that the system of national currencies taken for granted in the twenty-first century first came into being. Before that, currencies often circulated across a number of political units, competing with one another based on perceptions of stability and security. However, as state capacity increased and boundaries hardened, governments began to promote the use of their own currencies while restricting the circulation of others.[7] From then on, national currencies began to acquire political as well as economic meaning, a "stamp of nationality" as Roberts had put it.

This transition was gradual, and through most if not all of the nineteenth-century West Africa retained a currency system dominated by the overlapping circulation of multiple currencies. Some of these were indigenous and had circulated long before the arrival of the Portuguese on the West African coast in the fifteenth century. These included cowrie shells, gold dust, beads, and, particularly in the region that became Liberia, iron bars known as kissi pennies (see Figure 5.1). Textiles, livestock, and other crops also served as media of exchange.

European trade introduced new types of currency, including Indian textiles and crescent-shaped objects of copper, brass, or iron known as manillas, key currencies of the Atlantic slave trade.[8] During the nineteenth century,

---

[6] Parts of this chapter are reproduced from Leigh Gardner, "The Rise and Fall of Sterling in Liberia, 1847–1943," *Economic History Review* 67, no. 4 (2014): 1089–112.

[7] Benjamin Cohen, *The Geography of Money* (Ithaca: Cornell University Press, 1998), 32–34; Eric Helleiner, *The Making of National Money: Territorial Currencies in Historical Perspective* (Ithaca: Cornell University Press, 2003), 19–41.

[8] Eugenia W. Herbert, *Red Gold of Africa: Copper in Precolonial History and Culture* (Madison: University of Wisconsin Press, 1984); J. S. Hogendorn and H. A Gemery, "Continuity in West African Monetary History? An Outline of Monetary Development,"

Figure 5.1 Kissi penny
Source: Smithsonian National Numismatic Collection.

European coins were imported in growing quantities through the expanding export of cash crops. These were not initially tied to political spheres of influence but were rather associated with particular trades. The French five-franc coin, for example, was the primary medium of the groundnut trade in what would later become both British and French colonies.[9] Early histories of African monetary systems written in the middle of the twentieth century often claimed that the introduction of European currencies constituted a "revolution" in the monetary systems of the region, displacing the use of cowries, manillas, and other currency objects.[10] However, subsequent work has challenged this interpretation, showing that people continued to use alternative currencies like cowries and manillas until well into the twentieth century, even after the introduction of colonial coins and notes.[11]

African Economic History 17 (1988): 127–46; Jan S. Hogendorn and Marion Johnson, *The Shell Money of the Slave Trade* (Cambridge: Cambridge University Press, 2003); Marion Johnson, "Cloth as Money: The Cloth Strip Currencies of Africa," *Textile History* 11, no. 1 (1980): 193–202; James Webb, "Toward the Comparative Study of Money: A Reconsideration of West African Currencies and Neoclassical Monetary Concepts," *International Journal of African Historical Studies* 15, no. 3 (1982): 455–66.

[9] Leigh Gardner, "The Curious Incident of the Franc in the Gambia: Exchange Rate Instability and Imperial Monetary Systems in the 1920s," *Financial History Review* 22, no. 3 (2014): 295.

[10] Paul Bohannon, "The Impact of Money on an African Subsistence Economy," *Journal of Economic History* 19 (1959): 491–503; A. G. Hopkins, "The Currency Revolution in South-West Nigeria in the Late Nineteenth Century," *Journal of the Historical Society of Nigeria* 3, no. 3 (1966): 471–83.

[11] Jane Guyer, "Introduction: The Currency Interface and its Dynamics," in *Money Matters: Instability, Values and Social Payments in the Modern History of West African Communities* (London: James Currey, 1995), 1–34; Walter Ofonagoro, "From Traditional to British Currency in Southern Nigeria: Analysis of a Currency Revolution, 1880–1946," *Journal of Economic History* 39, no. 3 (1979): 623–54; Mahir Saul, "Money in Colonial Transition: Cowries and Francs in West Africa," *American Anthropologist* 106, no. 1 (2004): 71–84.

From the first establishment of migrant settlements on the coast, the ACS and other colonization societies issued their own token coins and notes. Figure 5.2 shows examples of some of these, issued by the ACS and Maryland Colonization Society, respectively. Little documentation about these currencies has survived, but it is unlikely that they circulated far outside the coastal settlements and were certainly not intended to be anything like a national currency. The text on the Maryland Colonization Society note, for example, suggests that the notes were intended to be used only at the Society store. Still, the design of these ACS tokens may have influenced the design of the first Liberian dollar coins, shown in Figure 5.3. Both feature a palm tree, reflecting Liberia's early dependence on palm oil

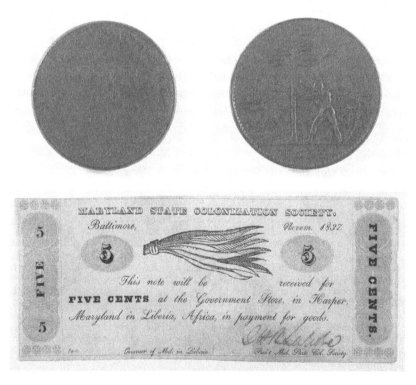

Figure 5.2 Colonization society tokens and notes
Source: Smithsonian National Numismatic Collection.

Figure 5.3 First Liberian dollar coin
Source: Smithsonian National Numismatic Collection.

exports, and a ship in the distance signifying the arrival of the migrants. Unlike the ACS token, however, the coiner of the first dollar coin replaced the ACS name with the image of an allegorical woman, wearing what is known as a Phrygian cap, or freedom cap, associated in classical imagery with freed slaves.[12]

The coiner in question was William Joseph Taylor, whose initials appear on the base of the neck of the female figure. Taylor was a London medalist and entrepreneur, one of a group in London during the nineteenth century who took advantage of the opportunities created for their profession by a world in which many new states wanted to establish their own currencies but did not have the industrial capacity to produce them. He is perhaps best known for what is referred to as the Kangaroo Office scheme, in which he attempted to establish a mint in Australia to convert gold nuggets produced by newly established mines – which were initially sold at a substantial discount – into stamped coins or ingots. The scheme took its name from a kangaroo that appeared on the coin designs. After shipping equipment to Australia at a substantial cost, the scheme folded when banks began purchasing gold at full value.[13] Taylor joined what would be a noteworthy club of somewhat shadowy foreign intermediaries who influenced Liberia's financial development in

---

[12] Yvonne Korshak, "The Liberty Cap as a Revolutionary Symbol in America and France," *Smithsonian Studies in American Art* 1, no. 2 (1987): 52–68; Eric Foner, *The Story of American Freedom* (New York: W. W. Norton, 1998), 14.

[13] John P. Sharples, "The Australian Tradesmen's Tokens Project, the James Nokes Proof Halfpenny and Problems of the Kangaroo office," *Journal of the Numismatic Association of Australia* 17 (2006): 42–52.

various ways. The next chapter, on public debt, will provide further examples.

There were several benefits to governments of adopting a national currency. One was the symbolic demonstration of sovereignty. A second, perhaps of more immediate practical use, was the fact that national money could contribute to the public finances through seigniorage revenue, or the difference between the nominal value of the money and the cost of producing it. For governments with weak fiscal systems, seigniorage could be an important "revenue of last resort," as Charles Goodhart described it.[14] In periods of fiscal crisis, more money could be produced to pay soldiers or civil servants or to honor contracts. In the years after Taylor minted the first Liberian dollar coins, this was a source of revenue to which the Liberian government resorted with some frequency, ultimately undermining the credibility of the currency. The establishment of the Liberian dollar was thus part of a wider set of efforts to create, as Benjamin Cohen writes, "tangible proof of one's rightful place in the family of nations."[15] However, as in the case of trade policy, the government was constrained in a variety of ways from exercising its monetary sovereignty. Subsequent sections examine the struggle to maintain the value of the Liberian dollar and its eventual displacement by foreign currencies.

Maintaining the Value of the Liberian Dollar

The Liberian government had few means with which to cope with the fiscal crises which afflicted it with some regularity over the course of the nineteenth century, as shown in Chapter 1. By the early 1860s, the Liberian Treasury – no central bank had yet been established – began to issue unbacked paper to pay military wages along with other government expenses. President Warner's second inaugural address in 1866 referred to "an immoderate expansion of paper currency notes, which had resulted in severe monetary distress upon the whole country" prior to 1864.[16]

---

[14] Charles A. E. Goodhart, "The Political Economy of Monetary Union," in *Understanding Interdependence: The Macroeconomics of the Open Economy*, edited by P. B. Kenen (Princeton: Princeton University Press, 1995), 452.

[15] Cohen, *Geography of Money*, p. 36

[16] Joseph Saye Guannu, ed., *The Inaugural Addresses of the Presidents of Liberia: From Joseph Jenkins Roberts to William Richard Tolbert Jr., 1848–1976* (Hicksville, NY: Exposition Press, 1980), 56.

Ironically, a similar issue also occurred subsequently during Joseph Payne's presidency, just ten years after he wrote his essay.[17] Payne's change of heart about the risks of paper money issues suggests that the weakness of Liberia's fiscal institutions left the government with limited options.

Paper money was issued in a variety of forms which were, according to a British trade report, "discounted by the mercantile houses at ruinous rates." It included what were referred to as "general government papers," or bills issued directly by the Secretary of the Treasury. These were used in payment to European merchants, who accepted them in exchange for goods at below par value but returned them to the government in payment of customs duties at par. They also included currency bills, which the same report described as "lithographed papers, issued in the form of banknotes and drawn upon the treasury," which only realized around a third of their face value. Municipal governments and county superintendents also issued their own bills, which could be used to pay customs duties.[18] The fact that such bills were widely used to pay taxes and as instruments of public spending (often at different rates) helps explain the difficulty in finding consistent totals for revenue and expenditure, discussed in Chapter 1. Payne, in his inaugural address in 1868, confessed that his government could not come to an accurate figure of the amount of Liberian currency and other forms of government paper in the hands of the public.[19]

In 1871, the state of the currency remained a source of concern to the Liberian government. At his inauguration, Payne's successor, Edward Roye, proclaimed that "we must have a sound par value currency," and proposed one of a series of measures to "relieve the depressed position of our currency," along with a growing domestic debt burden. One such measure was a turn to the international capital market. In that year the Liberian government raised its first loan in London, which is examined in greater detail in Chapter 6. Of the £100,000 that the loan ordinance authorized the government to raise, £25,000 was to be deposited in the Treasury as a basis for the issue of paper currency, thus curbing the

---

[17] US legation, Monrovia, to Department of State, May 30, 1875, in *US Department of State, Papers Relating to the Foreign Relations of the United States*, vol 2 (Washington, DC: Government Printing Office, 1875), 831.

[18] UK Foreign Office, *Report for the Year 1906 on the Trade &c. of Liberia* (London: HMSO, 1907), 15; Corporation of Foreign Bondholders, *Annual General Report of the Council of the Corporation of Foreign Bondholders* (London: CFB, 1903–4), 253.

[19] Guannu, *Inaugural Addresses*, 65–75.

depreciation of the Liberian dollar. A further £25,000 was to be used to pay off the floating internal debt.[20] In the end, only a small share of the loan proceeds actually reached the Treasury, and the effort to shore up the value of the currency failed.

The Liberian government was not the only new government in Africa to use paper money in this way or to suffer the consequences to its credibility. In southern Africa, the Orange Free State and the South African Republic, Afrikaner states which had achieved formal recognition not long after Liberia, were also struggling with what to do about their currency. In their early decades, with a limited tax base, both issued paper money of various kinds which quickly depreciated when more notes were issued, generally in response to fiscal crises. In the Orange Free State, the so-called blue backs were first issued in 1865. Despite various attempts to sustain their value, they depreciated to such an extent that they were no longer accepted in trade with coastal merchants, who would accept only wool or hides in payment. Prior to the discovery of gold in the South African Republic, paper money took the form of "mandaten" or a kind of government IOU used to pay government employees and buy ammunition. As with the blue backs, it quickly became impossible to say how many mandaten were issued. The Volksraad debated raising a foreign loan to redeem the notes but found it would not be able to do so except on punitive terms.[21]

Bordo and Flandreau argue that peripheral nations in the gold standard era had to choose between restricting foreign borrowing or sacrificing some control over their currency because the devaluation of local currencies could lead to debt crises.[22] In Liberia, servicing the loan as well as other sterling-denominated obligations became increasingly difficult as the Liberian dollar continued to decline in value. Actual data on exchange rates during this period are much rarer than anecdotal comments, but they do reveal something of the Liberian government's struggle to sustain the value of the dollar. In 1876, the *Statesman's Yearbook* – an annual reference of economic and financial data widely used by investors in London – reported revenue and expenditure in "paper currency" at an

---

[20] Guannu, *Inaugural Addresses*, 71.

[21] E. H. D. Arndt, *Banking and Currency Development in South Africa 1652–1927* (Cape Town: Juta, 1928), 73–104; Ellen Feingold, Johan Fourie and Leigh Gardner, "A Tale of Gold and Paper: A New Material History of Money in South Africa," *Economic History of Developing Regions* (2021), 36(2): 264–81.

[22] Michael D. Bordo and Marc Flandreau, "Core, Periphery, Exchange Rate Regimes and Globalization," *NBER Working Paper* 8584 (2001): 6

exchange rate of $7 to the pound (while the US dollar was worth just over $5 to the pound). In 1880, the government issued a new instrument – ten-year domestic bonds at 6 percent – in exchange for the paper currency still in circulation. Three years later, a law was passed providing for the removal from circulation of half of the paper currency paid into the Treasury. It also instructed the Treasury to hold a tenth of the gold coin it received in a fund to meet foreign payments. In 1884, a further law mandated that domestic creditors should be paid two-thirds in gold and one-third in paper. Brown estimated that this approximated to a 25 percent reduction in the nominal value of their claims. These efforts may have had some effect – the 1884 *Statesman's Yearbook* estimated an exchange rate of $5 in Liberian paper money to the pound sterling.[23] However, they were undermined by a further issue of paper money in 1893 to meet the costs of a renewed revolt by the Grebo, as a result of which, according to George Brown, the value of the paper currency fell 75 percent below par.[24]

Liberia's First "Dollarization"

The declining value of the Liberian dollar left many people in Liberia looking for an alternative. This was true not only of Americo-Liberian elites involved in trade but also of indigenous Africans involved in the commercial sector through trade or employment. McKinnon notes that in small areas with currencies that are not pegged to currencies of larger areas, the liquidity value of the small area's currency will be limited, and "domestic nationals will attempt to accumulate foreign bank balances."[25] Americo-Liberians and indigenous Africans involved in trade would have wanted to receive payment for their exports in a currency that could consistently be used to purchase imported goods, either for trade in the interior or for consumption. A large number of indigenous Liberians, particularly the Kru, were employed in the shipping trades along the West African coast. Working as sailors, boat-builders, warehousemen, interpreters, and so on, they would accumulate their wages over a period of several years and then use

---

[23] J. S. Keltie, *The Statesman's Yearbook: Statistical and Historical Annual of the States of the Civilised World* (London: 1884), 692.

[24] George W. Brown, *The Economic History of Liberia* (Washington, DC: The Associated Publishers, 1941), 259–63.

[25] R. I. McKinnon, "Optimum Currency Areas," *American Economic Review* 63 (1963): 722.

them to purchase European goods with which they would return home, acquire land, and marry.[26]

Just as the Liberian dollar was declining in value through the late nineteenth century, increasing quantities of British sterling currency were flowing into West Africa due to the expansion of trade and the establishment of British colonies in the region. The principal increase was in token silver coins, which had been introduced in Britain's colonial territories from 1825 and constituted the primary medium of exchange in the overseas trade of British West Africa despite not being backed by gold.[27] Figure 5.4 shows imports of British token silver coins into West Africa through the late nineteenth and early twentieth centuries. In 1906, Wallis reported that while Liberian dollars and cents were the "official coinage of the Republic," there was a "greater demand for pounds, shillings and pence, which is legal tender anywhere among the Americo-Liberian settlements."[28]

As Wallis was writing, the Liberian government's return to the capital market meant that the Liberian state had begun collecting its revenues in sterling. Liberia's default on the 1871 loan had left the government dependent on domestic borrowing – largely in the form of cash advances from merchants at interest rates on the order of 25 to 30 percent.[29] In 1899, after more than two decades in default, the Liberian government had negotiated a new agreement with its creditors from 1871.[30] This allowed the Liberian government to raise another loan of £100,000 at 6 percent interest. Like the 1871 loan, the purpose of the 1906 loan was to repay domestic debt, stabilize Liberia's fiscal position, and fund an expansion of public works.[31] British officials were placed in charge of customs collections as security for

---

[26] Foreign Office to Colonial Office, January 24, 1914, TNA, T1/11612. For more on the Kru, see William E. Allen, "Liberia and the Atlantic World in the Nineteenth Century: Convergence and Effects," *History in Africa* 37 (2010): 24; George E. Brooks, *The Kru Mariner in the Nineteenth Century: An Historical Compendium* (Newark: Liberian Studies Association, 1972), 5–7.

[27] Richard Fry, *Bankers in West Africa: The Story of the Bank of British West Africa Limited* (London: Hutchinson, 1976), 7–8; West African Currency Committee, *Minutes of Evidence* (London: HMSO, 1912), 1.

[28] UK Foreign Office, *Report for the Year 1906*, 15.

[29] Charles S. Johnson, *Bitter Canaan: The Story of the Negro Republic* (London: Transaction Publishers, 1992), 102.

[30] *Annual General Report of the Council of the Corporation of Foreign Bondholders* (London: CFB, 1898–9), 238–47.

[31] Brown, *Economic History of Liberia*, 164

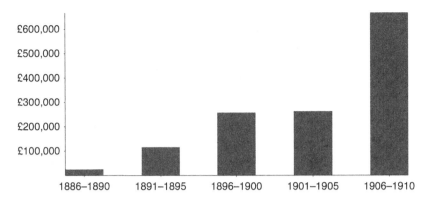

Figure 5.4 Imports of sterling coins into West Africa
Source: West African Currency Committee, *Report* (London: HMSO, 1912), 6.

the second loan.[32] Wallis noted a substantial increase in customs collections following the requirement that collections be made in gold, and further observed that "previous returns showed the value principally in paper currency as against gold under the new arrangement."[33]

Like the 1871 loan, however, the 1906 loan failed to deliver on its promised purposes. In search of assistance from outside Britain, the Liberian government sent a commission to the United States. It arrived in Washington DC in 1909, at the height of American enthusiasm for "dollar diplomacy." During the trip, the Liberian commission was told about the great success of the "fiscal protectorate" established in the Dominican Republic in 1905, in which private financiers refinanced the Republic's debt, in exchange for which US officials were placed in charge of customs collection and a share of customs revenue was devoted to debt service.[34] A return commission appointed by the US government recommended a controlled loan based on the Dominican model be made to Liberia. The recommendation of the commission was largely put into place in a loan of $1,700,000 issued in 1912, known as the refunding loan. Both the British and French governments protested at the prospect of losing influence in West Africa, so the loan was raised internationally but managed by the National City Bank of New York. The international character of the 1912 loan was similar to a loan

[32] US Senate, *Affairs in Liberia* (Washington, DC: Government Printing Office, 1910), 20.
[33] UK Foreign Office, *Report for 1906*, 15
[34] Emily S. Rosenberg, *Financial Missionaries to the World: The Politics and Culture of Dollar Diplomacy 1900–1930* (Durham, NC: Duke University Press, 2007), 41–7.

proposed for China.[35] Unlike the previous two loans, the 1912 loan was denominated in US dollars.

As a condition of the loan, the Liberian government agreed to the establishment of a Customs Receivership comprised of representatives from the United Kingdom, France, and Germany under the leadership of a Receiver of Customs appointed by the US government. The Receivership was placed in charge of collecting and managing revenue earmarked for loan service payments. This included customs revenue (which remained the most important source of tax revenue), and the proceeds from the rubber export tax and the hut tax.[36] Revenue from other sources remained under the control of the Liberian government.[37] As soon as it was established, the Receivership issued a circular stating that "all customs dues upon imports and exports are payable solely in current gold, and no document or evidence of indebtedness of any kind whatsoever will be received in lieu thereof."[38] In practice, the medium of payment was principally British coin.[39] In 1919, it was reported to the Foreign Office that "although the Budget of the Republic is framed in Dollars the currency in use is almost entirely British Gold and Silver coin, which has displaced Liberian coin, the minting of which ceased some years ago."[40]

At the same time, the entry of the Bank of British West Africa (BBWA) into Liberia brought it into an effective currency union with the British West African territories surrounding it. The BBWA had originated as a department of the Elder Dempster shipping company and had taken over the business of the African Banking Corporation. Like other British banks operating in the Empire, it found opportunities in providing banking services to colonial governments. It became the government banker to the four British colonial administrations in West Africa and from 1894 enjoyed the sole right to import British token silver coin into West Africa from the Royal Mint free of charges for packing, freight, and insurance.[41] After the establishment of the West African Currency Board (WACB) in 1912, the Bank acted as its agent in British territories in West Africa.

[35] Rosenberg, *Financial Missionaries*, 75–6; US Senate, *Affairs in Liberia*.
[36] Couper to Harcourt, January 24, 1915, TNA T1/12212.
[37] Bank of British West Africa (BBWA) to Foreign Office, February 12, 1918, TNA T1/12212.
[38] Administrative Circular no. 1 of the Customs Receivership, November 26, 1912, in US Department of State, *Papers Relating to the Foreign Relations of the United States for 1912* (Washington, DC: Government Printing Office), 694
[39] Couper to Langley, January 22, 1914, in TNA T1/11612.
[40] BBWA to Foreign Office, in TNA, T160/887.
[41] Richard Fry, *Bankers in West Africa*, 23–26; Geoffrey Jones, *British Multinational Banking* (Oxford: Oxford University Press, 1995), 114; Chibuike Uche, "Foreign Banks, Africans and Credit in Colonial Nigeria, c. 1890–1912," *Economic History Review* LII (1999): 673.

It also expanded into a number of non-British and sovereign territories in Africa, including Morocco and German Togo, as well as Liberia. The BBWA's first extension into Liberia was in 1905, when it hired W. D. Woodin & Co. as its agents in Monrovia. Five years later, the bank opened its first Liberian branch in the same city.[42] Agency agreements were signed with trading companies, such as the Oost Afrikaansche Compagnie in Grand Bassa (a major trading port) for operations outside the capital city.[43]

The BBWA became increasingly important in Liberian finances in the turbulent years which followed the outbreak of World War I. When Liberia joined the Allied cause and severed its relations with Germany, which had been a major trading partner, its finances suffered greatly.[44] Revenues declined with the shock to trade, and internal debt burdens expanded. In 1915, an official with the American legation in Monrovia noted that "the Government is undoubtedly very hard pressed. How far it can drag along, in its present manner of going, drawing behind it a burden that increases rapidly as the weeks go by, is an indeterminate question."[45] By the end of 1916, the Liberian government had asked the BBWA to lend it $9,000 on the first day of each month. All government revenue was to be collected by the Bank in repayment, but given the depressed state of Liberia's revenue, the Bank anticipated a monthly deficit of $5,000.[46] The Bank, anxious about the potentially unlimited liability which could be generated by this arrangement, asked the British government to guarantee the loan. When the British government refused, a cap of $100,000 (or £20,000) was imposed on the debt.[47] The BBWA was not the only British bank to engage in such lending – in Greece, the government looked to the Ionian bank to "assist the perennially chaotic state of Greece's finances."[48]

---

[42] "Notes on a Company History"; "Chronology of Events" and "Branches," in LMA CLC/B/207/MS28816/001.

[43] For the full text of the Grand Bassa agency agreement, see LMA, CLC/B/207/MS28536.

[44] Sperling (Foreign Office) to McFadyean (Treasury), January 26, 1919, TNA T1/12212; Gus Liebenow, *Liberia: the Evolution of Privilege* (Ithaca: Cornell University Press, 1969), 17.

[45] US Legation, Monrovia, to Secretary of State, May 11, 1915, in US Department of State, *Papers Relating to the Foreign Relations of the United States for 1915* (Washington, DC: Government Printing Office, 1924), 639.

[46] Couper to Langley, December 13, 1916, TNA T1/12212.

[47] BBWA to Foreign Office, October 29, 1917, in TNA T1/12212 . See also Memorandum of agreement between the Government of the Republic of Liberia and the BBWA, February 21, 1917, in US Department of State, *Papers Relating to the Foreign Relations of the United States for 1917* (Washington, DC: Government Printing Office, 1926), 889.

[48] Jones, *British Multinational Banking*, 106.

Liberia fits many of the characteristics which are today thought likely to lead to dollarization.[49] The Liberian dollar's history of depreciation relative to gold standard currencies combined with dependence on British imports provided key actors – including not only the Americo-Liberian elite but also indigenous Liberians – with a strong incentive to deal in sterling rather than local currency. The government had similar incentives, mandating the payment of taxes in sterling so that it could service its debts, denominated in foreign currency. Further, the expanding involvement of the BBWA in Liberia's public finances provided additional reasons for this transition. The next section examines the costs and benefits to Liberia of adopting sterling, focusing particularly on the changes that led to its eventual adoption of the US dollar in 1943.

Super-Fixed Regimes in a Changing World

It is difficult to measure the benefit to Liberia of convertibility relative to the costs of losing its monetary sovereignty. In their study of Mexico in the late twentieth century, Cooley and Quadrini conclude that "the cost of losing the ability to react to shocks is much smaller than the potential losses or gains deriving from the reduction of the long-term inflation and interest rate."[50] The Liberian Treasury's difficulties in managing its currency suggest that the same would be true there. However, "dollarization" also came with costs.

One was that Liberia's supply of circulating currency depended on the continued export of silver coins to West Africa, and it had no control over decisions about the monetary arrangements of British West Africa made in Britain. By 1910, the scale of exports of silver coins had become a matter of some concern for the British government. While it was the dominant circulating medium in West Africa, the silver coin was a token currency in Britain, and not backed by gold. Its value was managed by a careful judgment of supply and demand, which could be undermined if an economic crisis in West Africa led to substantial quantities of British silver flowing back to Britain.[51] To avoid this possibility, a separate West African currency was introduced in 1912, managed by the newly established WACB. The board was allowed to repatriate substantial quantities of British coinage as it increased the quantity of West African issues. The introduction of the new WACB currency prompted efforts in Liberia to

---

[49] Alberto Alesina and Robert J. Barro, "Dollarization," *American Economic Review* 91 (2001): 384.

[50] T. F. Cooley and V. Quadrini, "The costs of losing monetary independence: the case of Mexico," *Journal of Money, Credit and Banking* 33 (2001): 372.

[51] Armitage-Smith to Blacket, September 27, 1919, in TNA T160/887.

demonetize foreign currency and return to the Liberian dollar. A bill imposing heavy penalties on anyone caught importing foreign currency, and authorizing a new issue of Liberian coinage, was put before the Liberian legislature and passed in 1914. The bill was originally intended to target only the British West African coinage, but the final version included all foreign currency.[52]

Objections to British West African currency were two-pronged. First, there was limited confidence in the value of WACB currencies relative to sterling, not only in Liberia but among trading firms in the region.[53] This concern prompted Liberian President Daniel Howard (1912–20) to ask the British consul general "what good a pocketful of this new money would be to anybody landing in Liverpool or London." Further, the president was concerned about rumors that banks would only receive British West African currency at a substantial discount. At the president's request, the consul produced a letter from the manager of the BBWA's Monrovia branch, stating that the currency could be changed into British sterling in London or Liverpool and that the Bank would receive it at par value.[54] Second, they perceived a threat to Liberian sovereignty in the new currency. Howard wrote to the manager of the BBWA's Monrovia branch that "the people did not want any coins bearing the description 'British West Africa' in Liberia. They did not mind the imperial coins so much, but they strongly objected to the colonial coins, and fancy that an attempt is being made to gradually 'British-ise' Liberia."[55] Ultimately, the bill was suspended under British and American pressure.[56] The objections of the British government were based on the fact that the refusal of Liberians to accept the new WACB currency might interfere with its acceptance in British West Africa, and that the passage of the bill might hinder British trading interests in the Republic.[57] By the end of the war, WACB coins were accepted in payment of customs duties, alongside imperial silver.[58]

---

[52] British Consul General, Monrovia, to Foreign Office, February 9, 1914, in TNA T1/11612.

[53] Jeffrey Herbst, *States and Power in Africa: Comparative Lessons in Authority and Control* (Princeton: Princeton University Press, 2000), 206–7. See also Helleiner, *Making of National Money*, 184–85.

[54] A record of the meeting between the British Consul General and President Howard is provided in British Consul General, Monrovia, to Foreign Office, February 9, 1914, TNA T1/11612.

[55] Monrovia Branch to Head Office, January 19, 1914, in TNA T1/11612.

[56] British Embassy, Washington DC, to Foreign Office, January 12, 1914; Couper to Langley, January 22, 1914; Board of Trade to Foreign Office, January 19, 1914, in TNA T1/11612.

[57] Treasury to Foreign Office, January 31, 1914, in TNA T1/11612.

[58] BBWA to Foreign Office, November 3, 1919, in TNA T160/887.

How far the introduction of WACB currency affected Africans in Liberia's interior (and the extent to which indigenous people raised any objection) remains uncertain. Export industries were slow to develop and surviving records indicate that there were limits to the degree of monetization, particularly in rural areas. The 1916 agreement with the BBWA also included instructions on how to account for the payment of taxes in goods rather than cash.[59] As late as 1937 the US financial adviser to the Liberian government reported that WACB coins were used alongside "native 'iron' money."[60] The level of monetization in the interior may have increased with the establishment of the Firestone Rubber plantation, which not only employed a large labor force of 30,000 by the 1940s but also encouraged the independent production of rubber by African smallholders.[61]

The Firestone concession was also part of a major change in Liberia's banking sector. The BBWA, which had functioned as the state bank of Liberia since 1916, closed its Liberian branches in September 1930.[62] The Bank's stated reason for closing was that the limited sanitation facilities in Monrovia presented a danger to the Bank's staff.[63] However, officials in the British government suspected that the real reason was limited profitability. The Liberian branches were among a number of branches closed by the Bank during the 1930s – from a prewar peak of fifty-five branches in 1929, the number had decreased to thirty-nine by 1941.[64] A Firestone subsidiary, known as the United States Trading Company (Banking Department), stepped into the breach left in the management of state finances. The new bank was an ad hoc arrangement, designed to make sure the Liberian government did not have to go without banking services after the departure of the BBWA. The USTC already operated in Liberia, selling provisions to Firestone staff. Its banking branch was intended to serve primarily as a depository for government revenue, in order to safeguard payments servicing the Firestone loan. Its sole branch was in Monrovia, in the same building that had been occupied by the BBWA.[65] In 1935, the USTC (Banking

[59] Memorandum of Agreement, February 4, 1916, in TNA T1/12212.
[60] Extract of a report enclosed in letter from the Colonial Office to the Treasury, January 27, 1937, in TNA T160/887.
[61] Raymond Leslie Buell, *Liberia: A Century of Survival, 1847–1947* (Philadelphia: University of Pennsylvania Press, 1947), 49.
[62] Foreign Office memorandum, June 14, 1930, in TNA, CO 267/630/8.
[63] BBWA Monrovia Branch to Head Office, June 20, 1930, in LMA CLC B/207/MS28698; BBWA to Foreign Office, January 22, 1930, in TNA CO 267/630/8.
[64] "Number of branches open at 31st March," in LMA CLC/B/207/MS28816/001
[65] Department of Overseas Trade (Board of Trade) to Bank of England, 26 November 1930, December 19, 1930, and May 7, 1931, in Bank of England Archive, London, OV 67/1.

Department) became the Bank of Monrovia but remained a Firestone subsidiary. In his study of the overseas expansion of American banking, Phelps notes that one source of such expansion involved commercial firms not actually classified as banks that nevertheless provided banking services abroad. The Bank of Monrovia fitted into this category until 1955 when it was acquired by the First National Bank of New York, which had opened branches through Latin America and Europe following the passage of the Federal Reserve Act of 1914.[66] The Bank of Monrovia served as the fiscal depository to the Liberian government until the establishment of the National Bank of Liberia in 1974.[67]

This shift from British to American dominance did not present problems for Liberia so long as the pound-dollar exchange rate remained stable. When the rate changed, however, it raised the cost of servicing Liberia's debt and exacerbated the country's fiscal difficulties. After World War I, for example, sterling was received in Liberia at a rate of $4.80, but remittances to the United States in payment of interest on the 1912 refunding loan were received at the London/New York rate of around $4.15. The devaluation of the early 1930s also made it difficult for Liberia to service its debts and affected the purchasing power of Liberians. The annual message of President Edwin Barclay (1930–44) to the legislature for 1932 reported that "the difference in the rate at which we receive sterling for government taxes and other income and the rate at which the government is credited when it has to pay its foreign claims represents a loss of a little over 26 per cent."[68] Liberian revenues were already suffering owing to a falling off of trade during the Depression. An uprising among the Kru also required rapid increases in public spending.

The outbreak of World War II resulted in further difficulties relating to the devaluation of the pound. In 1939 Firestone commissioned Edwin Kemmerer, Princeton economist and "money doctor," to write a plan for monetary reform in Liberia. In his report, he noted that "the advisability of Liberia's continuing with its present currency system is extremely

---

[66] C. W. Phelps, *The Foreign Expansion of American Banks: American Branch Banking Broad* (New York: Ronald Press, 1927), 11, 142–47.

[67] International Monetary Fund, *Surveys of African Economies, Volume 6: The Gambia, Ghana, Liberia, Nigeria and Sierra Leone* (Washington, DC: International Monetary Fund, 1975), 262–63; Geoffrey Maynard, "The Economic Irrelevance of Monetary Independence: The Case of Liberia," *Journal of Development Studies* 6, no. 2 (2007): 113.

[68] Edwin James Barclay annual message, October 24, 1932 in *The Annual Messages of the Presidents of Liberia 1848–2010: State of the Nation Addresses to the National Legislature from Joseph Jenkins Roberts to Ellen Johnson Sirleaf*, edited by D. Elwood Dunn (Berlin: De Gruyter, 2011), 842.

doubtful."[69] As in the 1930s, the declining dollar value of sterling made it increasingly difficult for the Liberian government to satisfy its obligations. The burden of both the salaries of US officials and external debt payments was increased by the decline of sterling from $4.80 to approximately $4.00. This change did not merely affect state finances. With the establishment of the Firestone plantation as well as the outbreak of war, Liberian trade had become increasingly oriented toward the United States, at the expense of Britain.

After the turmoil of the early 1930s, there was increasing pressure for Liberia to move from British sterling to the US dollar. That included advice from Kemmerer, who recommended that Liberia shift to a currency system based on the US dollar. Local circumstances provide much of the explanation for this, but contemporaries also saw it as a symptom of the global rise of the dollar at the expense of sterling.[70] In December 1942, the Federal Reserve Bank of New York Press Summary noted that Liberia's currency change "is believed to foreshadow the emergence of the dollar as an international currency ... Dollar exchange is steadily replacing the pound sterling as an international currency exchange."[71]

Despite pressure coming from several sources, the implementation of the change was slow. In 1935, a law was passed establishing a gold dollar equivalent to the US dollar as Liberia's monetary unit and empowering the Treasury to demonetize British silver. In practice, the law did not take effect until eight years later, when sterling was replaced by the dollar in 1943, and shipments of British sterling were made as late as 1942, when £20,000 in British silver coins were shipped to Monrovia. The next section examines the challenges of changing currency in a dollarized economy.[72]

From Sterling to the Dollar

Dollarization is effective in limiting expectations of inflation precisely because it is difficult to reverse. Eichengreen describes dollarization as

---

[69] Edwin Kemmerer, Plan for Monetary Reform in Liberia (1939), Seeley G. Mudd Manuscript Library, Princeton. For more on "money doctors" in historical context, see Marc Flandreau, ed., *Money Doctors: The Experience of International Financial Advising 1850–2000* (London: Routledge, 2003).

[70] For background, see Barry Eichengreen, *Globalizing Capital: A History of the International Monetary System* (Princeton: Princeton University Press, 2008), 78–85; Catherine Schenk, *The Decline of Sterling: Managing the Retreat of an International Currency 1945–1992* (Cambridge: Cambridge University Press, 2010), 13–21.

[71] Federal Reserve Bank of New York Press Summary, December 14, 1942, in Bank of England OV135/1.

[72] Treasury to Bank of England, January 31, 1942, in TNA MINT 20/1590.

"not just locking the door to the central bank (the currency board solution) but effectively throwing away the key."[73] The transitional costs of
switching from one currency to another are one reason for the additional
credibility of dollarization as compared with a fixed exchange rate.[74] In
Liberia's case, the cost of physically replacing the circulating currency was
a major obstacle to moving from sterling to the US dollar. According to
US officials in Liberia, these costs were estimated to be $100,000–
150,000, "which Liberia does not have available for this purpose."[75]
Further, the cooperation of the British Treasury was needed to dispose
of large quantities of token silver coin, as it was only legal tender up to £2.

In the end, the needs of the war effort prevailed over both obstacles.
From 1942 an extensive US military establishment was based in Liberia.
A letter sent from the State Department in Washington DC to the US
legation in Liberia noted that "the appearance of American forces in
Liberia will immediately present an important commissary and paymaster
problem. The War Department has expressed a desire to introduce, if
possible, American currency for local expenditures and salary
payments."[76] This was the option preferred by the Bank of Monrovia,
which was trying to limit its exchange rate risk.[77]

In addition to the costs of physically changing one currency for
another, such a currency change has considerable information costs.
Goodhart argues that "in many historical, and current examples, of
currency-area dissolution, separation has occurred when some event
has already diminished the information value of the shared currency
within the separating region or state."[78] The information costs of the
change would have been mitigated by the fluctuations in the pound–
dollar exchange rate, which had complicated past efforts to plan
future expenditure. A League of Nations report from 1932 noted
that "it was clear that in view of the changing currencies and the
varying economic conditions it was impossible to fix a budget here

---

[73] Barry Eichengreen, "When to dollarize," *Journal of Money, Credit and Banking* 34 (2001):
3. See also S. Fischer, "Seigniorage and the case for a national money," *Journal of Political
Economy* 90 (1982): 300.
[74] Goodhart, "Political Economy," 485.
[75] US Charge d'Affaires, Monrovia, to Secretary of State, March 8, 1942, in US
Department of State, *Foreign Relations of the United States: Diplomatic papers 1942, vol. 4*
(Washington, DC: Government Printing Office, 1963): 431. For more on the costs of
physically changing currency, see Goodhart, "Political Economy," 485–86.
[76] Acting Secretary of State to the Charge d'Affaires, Monrovia, March 4, 1942, in US
Department of State, *Foreign relations 1942*, p. 430.
[77] British Supply Councils in North America to Treasury, September 10, 1942, in TNA
MINT20/1590.
[78] Goodhart, "Political Economy," 485.

and now."[79] The devaluation of the late 1930s is likely to have produced similar confusion. However, many private contracts were denominated in sterling. The League of Nations recorded a range of pawnship contracts, in which people were used as collateral for debt, the vast majority of which were denominated in sterling. For example, one Jadgua, a headman from Kanga, living near Royesville, fined £18 0s 2d for road delinquencies, pawned his wife and child for £7 to one Kankawah.[80] This suggests that not only credit contracts but also state fines were denominated in sterling, and would need to be changed on the switch to the dollar.

After negotiations with the British government, token silver coin and WACB coinage were collected in Liberia and shipped to the West Indies (where there was a shortage of British currency) and Sierra Leone, respectively.[81] A public notice of December 7, 1942, by President Barclay announced that it was the "intention of the Government to withdraw British coins and to adopt US currency as a circulating medium." British coins would be redeemed in US dollars at the rate of $4.00 to the pound. They could also be used to pay 'taxes and other public obligations' up to June 30, 1943.[82]

The question of Liberia's monetary independence continued to be discussed in subsequent decades. While some viewed the use of the US dollar as necessary to attract investment under the open door policies pursued after the war, others saw it as unnecessarily exposing Liberia to volatility in the global economy and subjecting it to weaknesses in US monetary policy.[83] An effort to reintroduce higher denomination Liberian currency in the form of $5 coins by the government of Samuel Doe following the 1980 coup initially drove US dollar notes out of circulation, as people hoarded the higher-value currency. "Doe dollars" were initially used at par with the US dollar, but eventually depreciated to half or less of their original value.[84] Even after the establishment of the Central Bank of Liberia in 1999, the ratio of foreign currency deposits to local currency deposits has remained high.[85] The Central Bank of Liberia

[79] Cuthbert Christy, *Report of the Commission of Enquiry into the Existence of Slavery and Forced Labour in the Republic of Liberia* (Geneva: League of Nations), 5.

[80] Christy, *Report*, 15.

[81] Royal Mint to Treasury, March 1, 1943, in TNA MINT 20/1590.

[82] Public notice by Edwin Barclay, December 7, 1912, in TNA, MINT 20/1590.

[83] Liebenow, *Liberia*, 244–45; Robert E. Miller and Peter R. Carter, "The Modern Dual Economy: A Cost-Benefit Analysis of Liberia," *Journal of Modern African Studies* 10, no. 1 (1972): 114.

[84] Liebenow, *Liberia*, 307

[85] L. Erasmus, J. Leichter, and J. Menkulasi, "Dedollarization in Liberia: Lessons from Cross-Country Experience," *International Monetary Fund Working Paper* WP/09/37 (2009): 21–2.

reported that 73.5 percent of broad money (M2) was comprised of US$ in the first quarter of 2013, indicating the "highly dollarized nature of the economy."[86]

An Illusion of Monetary Independence?

President Roberts wanted to create the Liberian dollar in part as a symbol of Liberia's sovereignty. Fiscal realities, however, stripped that symbol of much of its meaning. Coins had to be minted in Britain, with the subsidy of a British banker, and their value diminished as more notes were printed. Studies of colonial currency regimes often argue that the super-fixed regimes which linked colonial currencies to metropolitan ones stripped colonial governments of a valuable tool of economic management. However, the Liberian case suggests that in contexts of low state capacity, such tools were difficult to use.

It also shows that super-fixed regimes served the interests of African elites, who relied on access to global markets, as much as it did colonial government. As Bordo and Flandreau's analysis suggests, there are parallels with sovereign countries in Asia and Latin America where some degree of monetary sovereignty was abandoned in exchange for the economic benefits of exchange rate stability. Borrowing to meet the costs of military expansion was central to Japan's adoption of the gold standard, for example.[87] The continuing restrictions on the actions of African central banks after independence suggest that, as in Liberia, key constituencies in many former British colonies also gained from the monetary stability offered by the currency board system. In a context in which multiple currencies often circulate, such an approach also implies investigating why actors choose one currency over another.[88]

The second is whether monetary independence in colonial Africa would, in fact, have benefited colonial economies.[89] The structural factors that undermined the Liberian dollar were also present elsewhere. Budget crises were common in African colonies which, like Liberia, were vulnerable to changes in external demand for their exports.[90] It seems likely that other African territories would also have succumbed to the

---

[86] Central Bank of Liberia, *Financial and Economic Bulletin January–March 2013* (Monrovia: Central Bank of Liberia, 2013), 24.

[87] Michael Shiltz, "Money on the Road to Empire: Japan's Adoption of Gold Monometallism, 1873-97," *Economic History Review* 65 (2012): 1147–68.

[88] These issues are explored in Jean-Paul Azam, *Trade, Exchange Rates and Growth in Sub-Saharan Africa* (Cambridge: Cambridge University Press, 2007), 69–104.

[89] This remains a matter for debate, even today. See Herbst, *States and Power*, 226.

[90] Leigh Gardner, *Taxing Colonial Africa: The Political Economy of British Imperialism* (Oxford: Oxford University Press, 2012), 64.

temptation to print money in order to fund emergency expenditure or development efforts if they had not been limited by a super-fixed regime. The fear that colonial administrations would do just that was one key motivation for the establishment of currency boards in British colonial Africa.[91] The other independent country in Africa, Ethiopia, also used a foreign currency (the Maria Theresa dollar) despite having a history of coin production dating from the third century.[92]

Many of Liberia's challenges in maintaining the value of its own currency or using a foreign currency stemmed from debt, either domestic or foreign. Frequent deficits led to the use of the printing press to cover government liabilities. However, this undermined the value of the Liberian dollar relative to other currencies in the region. This became a particular problem once Liberia began to borrow abroad, and revenue in depreciated currency made it difficult to service its debt. The next chapter tells the history of Liberian debt in greater detail, focusing on the challenges faced by the Liberian government in raising loans abroad, and the sacrifices in sovereignty it needed to make to do so.

---

[91] Herbst, *States and Power*, 206.

[92] H. G. Marcus, *A History of Ethiopia* (Berkeley: University of California Press, 2002), 6–7, 63–90; Akinobu Kuroda, "The Maria Theresa Dollar in the Early Twentieth-Century Red Sea Region: A Complementary Interface between Multiple Markets," *Financial History Review* 14 (2007): 92.

6 The Costs of Foreign Capital

They will tell you in Anchuria, that President Miraflores, of that volatile republic, died by his own hand in the coast town of Coralio; that he had reached thus far in flight from the inconveniences of an imminent revolution; and that one hundred thousand dollars, government funds, which he carried with him in an American leather valise as a souvenir of his tempestuous administration, was never afterward recovered.

O'Henry, *Cabbages and Kings* (1904)

This instance of the Liberian seven per cent loan is not unique – similar cases occur with other nations – the smaller states. And the same principle, or rather non-principle, underlies them all: the money is squandered or consumed by the so-called foreign friends of these smaller states under the pretense of developing their alleged untold and inexhaustible resources.

Annual Message of President Hilary R. W. Johnson, December 15, 1890

On August 15, 1871, a garden in Kent was decked out in the red, white, and blue of the Liberian flag to celebrate the successful issue of the Republic of Liberia's first public loan. The guests of honor were William Anderson, Speaker of the Liberian House of Representatives, Secretary of the Interior Henry Johnson, and a British merchant named David Chinery, who also acted as the Liberian charge d'affaires in London. These three had formed a commission appointed by President Edward Roye to negotiate the loan. The account of the party published in the *Daily News* the next day noted that "the majority of the company were said to be subscribers to the loan." Also in attendance were Joseph Jenkins Roberts, Liberia's first president, the Consul General of the United States, and members of Holderness, Nott and Company, which underwrote the loan. The group "drank with equal enthusiasm the healths of the Presidents (Grant and E. J. Roy[sic]) of the United States of America and of Liberia, coupling with the latter, 'Prosperity to Monrovia, the capital of Liberia'."[1]

In Monrovia itself, just over two months later, a group of self-described "leading citizens" voted in a public meeting to depose President Roye. One of the reasons they gave for overthrowing him was the loan celebrated at the Kent garden party. The manifesto adopted by the meeting declared: "he has contracted a foreign loan, contrary to the law made and provided; and without an act of appropriation by the Legislature he has, with his officers, been receiving the proceeds of that loan."[2] By the end of the year, Roberts had resumed his former role as president of the Republic, and the disgraced President Roye had died trying to escape from prison. One account claimed that he drowned trying to reach a merchant ship while carrying a bag of gold sovereigns. The circumstances of his death bear a strange and striking resemblance to the end met by President Miraflores in O'Henry's novel *Cabbages and Kings*, published more than thirty years later. Anderson, Johnson, and Chinery were among a number of defendants named in a lawsuit in the Court of Chancery in London filed by the Government of Liberia over the disposition of the loan proceeds. When the first coupon came due in 1874, the Liberian government defaulted and remained in default for more than twenty-five years.

Roye's intentions in raising the loan were the subject of mixed opinions by later Liberian politicians. Hilary R. W. Johnson, quoted at the beginning of this chapter, ridiculed the project in an 1882 address on "The independence of Liberia: the causes that contributed to it, the dangers that threaten it, and some of the means to be employed for perpetuating it." He argued that the loan's ostensible purpose "was to set on foot about five times as many enterprises as that amount would legitimately support."[3] However, under William V. S. Tubman's administration, famous for its enthusiasm for foreign capital, Roye's tenure was viewed more charitably. In 1954, Tubman renamed the headquarters of the True Whig Party in Roye's honor. In his speech opening the building, Tubman proclaimed that Roye "pursued liberal policies with the intent to develop trade, expand commerce and improve the economic conditions of our people and country, for which purposes he negotiated a loan with British businessmen." He was overthrown, Tubman said, by "old Republican die-hards."[4]

---

[1] "The Republic of Liberia," *Daily News*, August 16, 1871, 3.

[2] "Affairs in Liberia," *African Repository* 1872, 45.

[3] Extract in Box 54, IULC, Svend Holsoe Collection.

[4] "On the Occasion of the Laying of the Cornerstone of the Edward T. Roye Memorial Headquarters of the True Whig Party," January 8, 1964, in IULC, Svend Holsoe Collection, Box 56.

Almost a century and a half later, at the time of writing, the 1871 loan is still discussed by both Liberian government officials and private citizens as one source of the country's later financial and economic troubles. The loan and its successors were not repaid until 1951. In an unpublished biography of Roye, historian Svend Holsoe writes that, because of the loan, "Roye had left a legacy."[5] This legacy went beyond financial liabilities to include debates about the need for foreign capital and the price Liberians were willing to pay – in money, land, and concessions of their sovereignty – to get it.

In promoting economic growth, the Liberian government had to cope with the same "catch-22" that faced other governments of poor countries at the time. David Sunderland describes this as follows: "funds were required to build infrastructure, but the very lack of transportation networks and economic activity reduced the likelihood that they would be forthcoming" at an affordable price.[6] Sunderland wrote this in reference to colonies in the British Empire, but the same challenges faced independent governments. In addition, they had to contend with the fact that creditors lending to poor countries tended to demand some sacrifice of sovereignty, from the hypothecation of certain revenue sources to outright control over important areas of policy.[7] This made the choice to access capital a difficult one for governments that saw nation-building as closely linked to economic development, which in turn depended on foreign capital. Siam (later Thailand), for example, "was wary of borrowing from abroad because debt to foreign powers – Britain and France in particular – may have put it at risk of outright colonization."[8] This chapter focuses on the Liberian government's efforts to access foreign capital from the 1871 loan through 1951, when the obligations created by the 1871 loan were repaid. Throughout this period, the Liberian government struggled to find a balance between internal and external threats, between the demands of lenders and the tolerance of the people it governed.

---

[5] Box 56, Svend Holsoe Collection, IULC.
[6] David Sunderland, *Managing the British Empire: the Crown Agents, 1833–1914* (Woodbridge: Royal Historical Society, 2004), 149.
[7] Adam Tooze and Martin Ivanov, "Disciplining the 'Black Sheep of the Balkans': Financial Supervision and Sovereignty in Bulgaria, 1902–1938," *Economic History Review* 64, no. 1 (2011): 32. See also Kris James Mitchener and Marc D. Weidenmier, "Supersanctions and Sovereign Debt Repayment," *Journal of International Money and Finance* 29, no. 1 (2010): 19–36.
[8] Christopher Paik and Jessica Vechbanyongratana, "Path to Centralization and Development: Evidence from Siam," *World Politics* 71, no. 2 (2019): 301.

The 1871 Loan: Liberia's Original Sin?

In January 1870, one of Roye's first tasks after his election was signing into law legislation authorizing a loan of "not more than $500,000 in gold and silver coin, for which shall be issued Liberian government bonds, bearing interest, payable in gold at a rate not exceeding seven per cent per annum."[9] The proceeds of the loan were to serve several purposes related to the economic progress of Liberia. First, the loan was intended to consolidate internal floating debt and stabilize Liberia's currency system. The legislation specified that "not less than $100,000 of the loan be solely applied to the purpose of purchasing at auction by the Secretary of the Treasury at the lowest bid (and canceling) all the checks, scrip, currency, debentures and government paper of whatever denomination." A further $100,000 would act as reserve fund for a new issue of paper currency. The remaining funds were to be deposited for use in emergencies as well as to "further develop the agricultural and other rich resources of Liberia."

The loan was a centerpiece of the policy agenda that Roye laid out at his inauguration, which linked economic development to a wider project of nation-building. He called for the establishment of a national bank to manage Liberia's depreciated currency, and legislation to encourage the investment of foreign capital in a railway.

I do not deem it necessary to demonstrate to you the utility of railroads. We have numerous examples of their beneficial effects all over the civilized world. And we should endeavor to follow such examples as far as they can be adopted, in our circumstances, to promote intercourse between distant portions of the country, and to facilitate the interchange of commodities, commercial rarities, and indigenous productions, between Liberia and foreign countries.[10]

The need for development was not just for Liberia itself, according to Roye. He saw it as a wider project of demonstrating racial equality to a skeptical world. "It is our duty," he said, "to prove that the mental and other disabilities under which the Negro labors as a result of his servile antecedents are not inherent, as our adversaries would say, but that they are solely the result of circumstances, to be altogether removed when those circumstances are altered, or their influence counteracted." The "odious and damaging epithets" under which the race suffered, he claimed, would be undermined "if we assiduously devote ourselves to

---

[9] "An Act Authorizing the Negotiation of a Loan," January 26, 1870, Acts of the Legislature, 1867–1870, IULC.

[10] Edward J. Roye Inaugural Address, January 3, 1870, reprinted in Joseph Saye Guannu, ed. *The Inaugural Addresses of the Presidents of Liberia: From Joseph Jenkins Roberts to William Richard Tolbert Jr., 1848 to 1976* (Hicksville, NY: Exposition Press, 1980), 76–85.

this work of reconstructing the reputation of the race by successfully prosecuting the work before us in this land." It would be "a great dishonor" if they were unable to develop Liberia.

Roye's statements about race had a double meaning in Liberia at that time. In a community intended to remove the barriers of racial prejudice, racial divisions had still crept into the political landscape. Through the nineteenth-century political tensions grew between an elite group of largely mixed-race Americo-Liberians, who had been among the earliest migrants, and the majority of later migrants who had been born into slavery. Roye's election was a victory for the latter, many of whom harbored deep suspicions about the loyalties of the mulatto elite.[11]

There was thus a lot riding on the success of the 1871 loan, for both the Liberian government and for Roye personally. How to ensure that it achieved its goals was an uncertain prospect. At this point few African countries had raised loans on the growing London market: only the Cape Colony, Natal, Egypt, and Tunisia had done so previously, but most of these were British colonies and Tunisia had defaulted in 1868.[12] Neighboring Sierra Leone raised a small loan of £50,000 in the same year, albeit with assistance from colonial institutions to be discussed later in this chapter. Investors also had little knowledge of African countries. In 1871, the *Statesman's Yearbook*, a key reference for investors, recorded with regard to Liberia that "there are no statistics regarding the extent of the commercial relations of the republic with the United Kingdom," and used a figure for "Western Africa" instead.

This level of ignorance was not necessarily unusual in this period of financial globalization, when investors were sending increasing amounts of money to ever-more-distant destinations. Financial intermediaries played a potentially important role in providing a stamp of credibility on bond issues and overcoming information asymmetries.[13] In the financial history literature on sovereign debt in the period, most of the focus is on the impact of effective intermediaries; little work has been done on the price paid for employing incompetent ones. One explanation for the outcome of the loan issue was that the Liberian government had been forced to make use of financial institutions described later as "not perhaps of the first rank."[14]

---

[11] Charles S. Johnson, *Bitter Canaan: The Story of the Negro Republic* (London: Transaction Publishers, 1992), 97–98; James Ciment, *Another America: The Story of Liberia and the Former Slaves Who Ruled It* (New York: Hill and Wang, 2013), ch. 5.

[12] Ali Coskun Tuncer, *Sovereign Debt and International Financial Control: The Middle East and the Balkans, 1870–1914* (Basingstoke: Palgrave Macmillan, 2015), 2.

[13] See Marc Flandreau and Juan H. Flores, "'Bonds and Brands': Foundations of Sovereign Debt Markets, 1820–1830," *Journal of Economic History* 69, no. 3 (2009): 646–84.

[14] H. H. Johnston, *Liberia* (London: Hutchinson, 1906), 259.

This was particularly the case with regard to Chinery, whose competence was later questioned by the Liberian government after Roye's overthrow. Chinery became the Liberian Consul General at the recommendation of his predecessor, an abolitionist named Gerard Ralston. Ralston was a financial backer of the ACS and an honorary Board member, who was appointed as Consul General when Liberia declared independence in 1847.[15] Chinery was a merchant who in 1864 published a pamphlet on the importance of commerce in suppressing the slave trade which claimed he had "twelve years' intimate connection" with Africa.[16] From what can be reconstructed about his career in business, the connection does not appear to have been a successful one for him. He was sued for bankruptcy in 1859 by creditors from West African centers including Sierra Leone, Cape Coast, and Badagry as well as Liverpool, Manchester, and London.[17] In 1863, he became one of the founders of the London and African Trading Company.[18] Less than four years later, however, the company was being wound up after it had "endeavored to transfer its business to a new undertaking, which did not succeed and has since succumbed through total want of capital."[19] His own financial future was not far from his mind in making the loan arrangements. At the time the loan was issued, he had set up a new venture called the African Barter Company. Apparently, he hoped that organizing the loan would generate Liberian government support for the new company. In a letter to Roye in June 1871, he wrote that "another matter of grand importance to Liberia is the success of the African Barter Company and we recommend the Government of Liberia to invest £5000 or say £7500 in the company with the undertaking that we open trade at once in Liberia."[20]

In April, Chinery had written to Roye that "some first-class firms will have to be appointed in London to issue the loan," and that "having a personal knowledge of these matters it is only feasible that I should be the better judge of the parties most desirable with whom to negotiate."[21] According to the bill of complaint filed in the Court of Chancery by the Liberian government, the parties he chose turned out to be "Edward

---

[15] "Gerard Ralston (c. 1800–ca. 1880)," in *Encyclopedia of Emancipation and Abolition in the Transatlantic World*, edited by Junius P. Rodriguez (London: Routledge, 2007), 446.

[16] David Chinery, *The African Slave Trade and the Real and Practicable Means for Its Suppression* (London: M. Lownds, 1864).

[17] David Chinery, African Merchant, filing in the Court of Bankruptcy, 1859, in TNA B9/230.

[18] *The Times*, July 6, 1863, 7.   [19] *The Times*, January 9, 1867, 5.

[20] Chinery to Roye, June 17, 1871, in TNA C/16/731/L168.

[21] Bill of Complaint in the Court of Chancery between the Republic of Liberia and David Chinery, July 11, 1872, in TNA C/16/731/L168.

Williams (a wine merchant and personal friend . . .) and Henry Stavely King (a medical gentlemen) to the intent and understanding that a commission should be paid" to Stavely and King and shared with Chinery. Williams and King were willing to pay only £70,000 for £100,000 in 7 percent bonds. Williams and King sold the bonds to Holderness, Nott and Company, who marketed them at 85 percent and paid part of the proceeds to Chinery. Three years' interest was deducted from this amount, leaving less than half of the £100,000 that the Liberian government had anticipated raising.

The interest rate and the size of the discount were the subject of bitter lament by the Liberian government, but these terms were not necessarily unusual for independent borrowers during this period. A number of countries issuing loans in 1871 had similar (or sometimes even higher) discount rates, including Costa Rica, Egypt, Mexico, Paraguay, Peru, and the Ottoman Empire. Liberia did not have £7,000 per year to spend on servicing the debt, let alone repaying the principal across the comparatively short term of the loan. In 1870 nominal revenue was approximately £28,000, meaning that interest payments alone would have absorbed a quarter of the total. As trade and revenue declined during the 1870s, this percentage rose to close to half of total government revenue. The high costs of debt service, along with the lack of a revenue return from the proceeds, almost guaranteed that Liberia would default on the loan during the great depression of the 1870s. It was not alone. By 1876 some fourteen countries were in default, including the Ottoman Empire, Egypt, and Spain, along with Liberia.

Creditors could do little to prevent the default, or to force Liberia and other defaulters to come to the table. The Corporation of Foreign Bondholders, which represented holders of the Liberian bonds, was the most effective of the various creditor organizations which emerged during the late nineteenth and early twentieth centuries. As a permanent body representing creditor interests, it was able to obtain better terms for creditors after default than other, more ad hoc groups.[22] However, its annual reports on the Liberian loan showed that its efforts had little effect in this case. In 1894, a letter from the CFB chairman to the Liberian president stated with some exasperation that "this is the twentieth year during which the loan has remained in absolute default," and referenced letters sent in 1874, 1875, 1877, 1878, and 1890. In 1881, the Council

[22] Rui Esteves, "The Bondholder, the Sovereign, and the Banker: Sovereign Debt and Bondholders' Protections before 1914," *European Review of Economic History* 17, no. 4 (2013): 389–407; Paulo Mauro, Nathan Sussman and Yishay Yafeh, *Emerging Markets and Financial Globalization: Sovereign Bond Spreads in 1870–1913 and Today* (Oxford: Oxford University Press, 2006).

concluded that "the absence of a resident representative of Great Britain in that Republic, and the brief and infrequent sojourns in this country of a Minister from its government, render remonstrance difficult, if not impossible, against the determination of Liberia to ignore the engagement of the state."[23]

Financial constraints were not the only explanation for Liberia's protracted default. The overthrow of Roye gave some political legitimacy to later claims that the loan itself was illegitimate. On taking over the office of the president, Joseph Jenkins Roberts said to the Legislature that "it becomes our painful duty to inform you that we have abundant evidence in our possession to show that there has been an unwarrantable interference on the part of the deposed President and the heads of his departments." In 1874, the year of the default, Roberts referred to the "great fraud and peculation" with regard to the loan. In fairness, Roberts still asserted that Liberia needed to meet its obligations, and even negotiated a compromise with Holderness, Nott and Company, during a trip to England in 1873. However, the deal failed to be ratified by the Legislature, partly because, as Holsoe writes, popular attitudes in Liberia "had shifted from an earlier one of honoring the debt to one of little concern, since so little of the funds had been received."[24]

Liberia remained in default for nearly a quarter of a century after missing its first payment in 1874. This was by no means record setting; Honduras was in default for 91 of the 118 years between independence and World War II.[25] Still, it was long enough that the accumulation of interest arrears added considerably to Liberia's overall debt burden. Investor confidence, or lack thereof, in the Liberian government was reflected in the spreads over British consols (see Figure 6.1). This is a standard measure in financial history which gives the difference between interest rates on the safest possible instrument – in this period, long-term British government debt – and those of the country in question. Figure 6.1 shows that the spreads on Liberia's bonds were broadly in line with other independent countries which had a similar history of default, but much higher than those of British colonies, which appear in panel B.

The Liberian government finally agreed to renegotiate terms with the Corporation in 1898, by which point interest arrears had accumulated to a point far exceeding the principal of the loan. The new agreement reduced the interest rate to 3 percent for three years, rising half a percent every three years to a maximum of 5 percent. Certificates were issued for

---

[23] Corporation of Foreign Bondholders, *Annual Report* (London: CFB, 1881).

[24] Svend Holsoe, "Roye," in IULC Holsoe Collection Box 56.

[25] Christian Suter, *Debt Cycles in the World-Economy: Foreign Loans, Financial Crises and Debt Settlements, 1820–1990* (Boulder: Westview Press, 1992), 2.

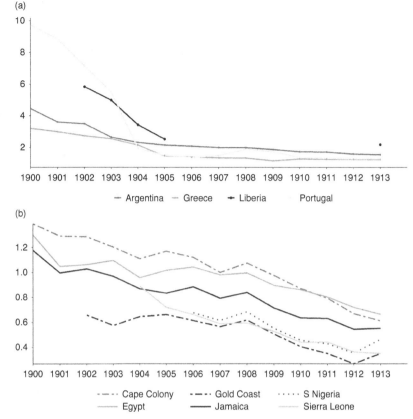

Figure 6.1 Liberian bond spreads in comparative view
A. Liberia in comparison
B. Colonies
Source: Gardner, "Colonialism or Supersanctions."

the interest arrears, increasing Liberia's overall debt burden.[26] Given this heavy cost, it is worth asking why the Liberian government did not simply remain in default. The prevailing political context in the region provides some clues. The final decades of the nineteenth century saw the carving up of much of Africa by European colonial conquest, including in territories neighboring Liberia. Correspondence between ACS officials at the time makes clear that the Liberian government's greatest fear from the default may have been that the British government, or perhaps even the French or German governments, would use the debt as an excuse to take

[26] Corporation of Foreign Bondholders, *Annual Report* (London: CFB, 1899), 239.

over Liberian territory or make Liberia a protectorate. As early as 1876, an article in the *African Repository*, the newsletter of the ACS, remarked that Liberia "lies at the mercy of her bondholders. England, with her lion's paw on the trade of the world, would, and perhaps will eventually, assume the debt for the trifling consideration of possession."[27] The ACS continued to articulate these fears when the Liberian government approached the ACS for guidance on how the loan question could be resolved. One letter from John Latrobe, a prominent member of the Maryland Colonization Society, to William Coppinger, secretary of the ACS, speculated that "England would be willing, I have no doubt, to assume the debt *for consideration* – and the only question would be as to the amount to be paid to her in the only article that Liberia has to pay with – land." He added that "if Liberia did not apply for aid to England, English creditors, I am very sure will, before long ask their government to do what she has done, again and again, in the enforcement of the claims of her subjects on foreign nations."[28] Such a move would not have been unprecedented; as Noel Maurer documents with regard to US policy, imperial interventions were often motivated by efforts to protect the property rights of metropolitan actors.[29]

Gunboats, by Invitation

How real were the fears articulated by the ACS? Histories of sovereign debt once argued that compulsion was a relatively unusual method of bringing defaulters to the table. However, more recent work has stressed that "super-sanctions," or instances in which "default was met with gunboat diplomacy or a loss of fiscal sovereignty" were commonly used in the period from 1870 to 1913, and could be effective in reducing perceived default risk among borrowers.[30] Such interventions were not always imposed by force but were often presented as conditions for negotiating settlements with creditors or returning to the market. This section reviews the introduction of super-sanctions in Liberia, at the invitation of the Liberian government.

During the twenty-four years of Liberia's default, there were various proposals for ways of disposing of the debt. As predicted by Latrobe, most involved concessions of one kind or another to foreign interests. Several proposed concessions failed to be ratified by the Legislature in the 1880s

---

[27] "Liberia and the American Flag," *African Repository* 1876, 109.
[28] John H. B. Latrobe to William Coppinger, June 28, 1884, in IULC, Holsoe Roye Materials, box 135.
[29] Noel Maurer, *The Empire Trap: The Rise and Fall of US Intervention to Protect American Property Overseas, 1893–2013* (Princeton: Princeton University Press, 2013).
[30] Mitchener and Weidenmier, "Supersanctions."

because they viewed the terms – usually monopoly rights over particular exports – as too onerous. In 1890, a proposal was made by a group of bondholders aiming to export rubber from Liberia. One was granted to Ellis Parr and associates from London, doing business as Liberian Concessions and Explorations Company, which was sold to a new company called the India Rubber Estates Company, of which a number of 1871 bondholders held shares. However, the concession failed to raise enough capital and the company ceased trading in 1894.[31]

Despite the failure of the 1890 deal, rubber was the vehicle by which the Liberian government returned to the capital market in 1906, when Liberia raised another loan of £100,000 at 6 percent interest. In this instance, the 1906 bonds were purchased by Emile Erlanger & Co., who advanced the money. The loan was secured by the revenue from customs tariffs and an export duty on rubber.[32] Enforcement of the terms of the loan was made by means of two British officials placed in charge of customs collection.[33]

Erlanger was acting at the behest of a concession company, the Liberian Development Company (LDC), which was placed in charge of spending the loan proceeds. The LDC was managed by the same Sir Harry Johnston quoted earlier as writing disparagingly of the financial agents who managed the 1871 issue.[34] After the repayment of the domestic floating debt, most of the remaining funds were handed over to Johnston's company, which was to use them for road construction and the establishment of a national bank.[35] The scheme unfortunately ended in failure. After two years and $200,000, the Company had funded what a later observer described as "fifteen miles of dirt road, a small launch and two automobiles" before announcing that "all the funds were exhausted."[36] The proposed bank, meanwhile, existed only on paper. The relationship between the LDC and the Liberian government was terminated in 1908, and the latter took control of the roughly $150,000 that remained of the loan proceeds.[37]

---

[31] Holsoe, "Roy," IULC, Holsoe Roye Materials, Box 56.
[32] Corporation of Foreign Bondholders, *Annual Report* (London: CFB, 1911), 211.
[33] George W. Brown, *The Economic History of Liberia* (Washington, DC: The Associated Publishers, 1941), 164.
[34] He had been the first commissioner of British Nyasaland in the 1890s and was a widely published naturalist and explorer. Just before the loan was issued, Johnston published what remained for many years a widely cited study of the country. See J. M. Lyon, "The Education of Sir Harry Johnston in Liberia, 1900–1910," *The Historian* 51 (1989): 627–43; Johnston, *Liberia*.
[35] Brown, *Economic History of Liberia*, 165–66.   [36] Johnson, *Bitter Canaan*, 103.
[37] "Plan of Settlement for the Liberian Development Company, 1907," in IULC, Holsoe Papers, Box 2.

Liberia's forays in the British capital market had left it with nothing except, as George Brown put it, "more debts and humiliation."[38] The fear that its unpaid debts would trigger invasion by Britain or France prompted the Liberian government to turn next to the United States for support.[39] In 1909, the American government appointed a commission to investigate conditions in Liberia. One recommendation of this commission was "the establishment of some system of collection and control of the revenues of the country for the benefit alike of the Government and its creditors, modeled in some respect upon the plan which has been of such practical success in Santo Domingo."[40] This diagnosis was standard orthodoxy for the early twentieth century, when American officials, at least, believed that "political instability, insecure property rights, poor infrastructure, and what today would be called 'underdevelopment' all stemmed from a single, common root: poor revenue collection caused by internal corruption."[41] The report also noted, however, the potentially tricky international politics of the Liberian situation. Liberia could not, it reported, "call to her aid either Great Britain, France or Germany. Two of these powers she deeply distrusts, and each of them distrusts the other two."[42]

Two years later, bonds up to a value of $1,700,000 at 5 percent, maturing in forty years, were authorized. A total of $1,400,000 in bonds were issued and the proceeds were used to repay existing debt, including the 1871 and 1906 bonds as well as the interest arrears from the former, and domestic debt. The distribution of the bonds was as follows: $225,000 in Germany, $460,000 in Amsterdam, $715,000 in London, and $158,000 in New York.[43] Reflecting this distribution, the customs receivership included one official each from Britain, France, and Germany under the leadership of an American Receiver General.[44]

The loan agreement also placed an American army officer as an adviser to the Frontier Force.[45] The initial appointee to this position, Benjamin

---

[38] Brown, *Economic History of Liberia*, 166.

[39] Emily S. Rosenberg, *Financial Missionaries to the World: The Politics and Culture of Dollar Diplomacy 1900–1930* (Chapel Hill: Duke University Press, 2007), 70.

[40] US Senate, *Affairs in Liberia* (Washington, DC: Government Printing Office, 1910), 11.

[41] Maurer, *The Empire Trap*, 5.   [42] US Senate, *Affairs in Liberia*, 28.

[43] National City Bank to the Secretary of State, November 30, 1917, in US Department of State, *Papers Relating to the Foreign Relations of the United States* (Washington, DC: Government Printing Office, 1917), 896–900.

[44] There remained disputes about the placement and relative influence of European members of the receivership. See correspondence in US Department of State, *Papers Relating to the Foreign Relations of the United States* (Washington, DC: Government Printing Office, 1912), 672–91.

[45] Rosenberg, *Financial Missionaries*, 86; Corporation of Foreign Bondholders, *Annual Report* (London: CFB, 1913), 221.

Davis, would later become the first African-American general in the US armed forces. With his appointment in 1910 he had joined a small group of black officers serving as attaches in Liberia and Haiti before World War I.[46] However, his role was merely advisory, rather than any kind of command position, and neither the Liberian nor the American governments seem to have taken it very seriously.[47] Davis, with his wife and daughter, spent around a year and a half in Liberia before he requested reassignment due to both health problems linked to the tropical climate and his frustration with the unwillingness of both governments to invest in improving the efficiency of the Frontier Force.[48] This in many ways reflected the limited goals of such "supersanction" regimes.

The involvement of Germany and the other two European countries in the receivership effectively ended with the outbreak of World War I. Owing to its financial links to the United States and Britain, Liberia was forced to declare war on Germany, which had devastating consequences for Liberian trade and government revenue, discussed in the next chapter. By the end of the war, both the US State Department and US Treasury concurred that it was in the interests of the US government to provide further assistance to Liberia to avoid the expansion of British interests in the region. President Wilson approved a credit of $5,000,000 at the end of August 1918. This was authorized under the Liberty Bond Acts during the war, and some Liberian officials proposed in particular that African-American subscribers could support the loan.[49] However, the agreement faced a number of obstacles in both Washington and Monrovia. One problem was the proposed terms of the loan agreement which, according to one US government assessment, "would establish American control by American officers in practically every important department of the Liberian Government – a control which is more extensive and intimate than the control of the United States in Caribbean countries."[50] This raised the objections of the British and French governments, both of which argued that the agreement amounted to the establishment of a protectorate over Liberia. As a result, a number of American officials argued that as a treaty was unlikely to be approved by Congress, it would

---

[46] Marvin E. Fletcher, *America's First Black General: Benjamin O. Davis, R., 1880–1970* (Lawrence, KS: University of Kansas Press, 1989), 40.

[47] Ciment, *Another America*, 144.   [48] Fletcher, *America's First Black General*, 43–44.

[49] Liberian Consul to Secretary of State, March 31, 1918, *Papers Relating to the Foreign Relations of the United States* (Washington, DC: Government Printing Office, 1918), 514–16.

[50] Acting Secretary of State to the Commission to Negotiate Peace, April 24, 1919, in *Papers Relating to the Foreign Relations of the United States* (Washington, DC: Government Printing Office, 1919), 473–74.

be better to proceed without a formal treaty at all. In the end, Congress refused to ratify the loan in 1922.[51]

Enter Firestone

The State Department then turned to the Firestone Rubber Company, and a new loan became part of the concession agreement of 1926. Much as it had twenty years earlier, a rubber concession provided access to foreign capital. However, the presence of Firestone would be much more extensive and durable than that of Harry Johnston's LDC. Accordingly, the conditions imposed by Firestone were also more onerous, making the agreement a source of lasting controversy both within and outside Liberia.

The year 1922 was fortuitous timing in terms of attracting the interest of Firestone. In the same year a British government committee published a report, known as the Stevenson Plan, on rubber production in the British Empire in the context of falling prices after the end of the postwar boom, recommending export quotas in Malaya and Ceylon. Coming after a British embargo on rubber exports during World War I, the report exacerbated fears in the United States that Britain and other imperial powers would adopt policies that would restrict American access to raw materials from their colonial territories.[52] Harvey Firestone saw the Stevenson plan as "a threat to the industry's supply of rubber," and took steps to secure alternative supplies.[53] In 1925, the Liberian government concluded an agreement with Firestone which gave the company a ninety-nine-year lease on an experimental rubber plantation near Monrovia, and on a million acres to be used for rubber production.

The Firestone concession was linked to an agreement with the Finance Corporation of America, a subsidiary of Firestone, for a new loan of $5,000,000 to be managed by the National City Bank of New York. Ultimately, the conditions of the loan agreement followed those of the proposed US government loan from 1922, but this outcome was not reached without considerable debate. Both the concession and the loan agreement were controversial in Liberia. A 1925 editorial in the *Liberian News* described the agreement as "the handing over of the country to a commercial group, whose officials operating the loan would be immune

---

[51] Rosenberg, *Financial Missionaries*, 120; Maurer, *Empire Trap*, 153.

[52] Michael J. French, "The Emergence of US Multinational Enterprise: The Goodyear Tire and Rubber Company, 1910–1939," *Economic History Review* XL (1987): 66–67.

[53] Frank Chalk, "The Anatomy of an Investment: Firestone's 1927 Loan to Liberia," *Canadian Journal of African Studies* 1, no. 1 (1967): 14–6.

to Liberian law no matter what they did. Does not this indicate the bartering away of our sovereign rights for 'a mess of potage'?"[54]

Such controversies were only enhanced by the fact that the agreements were, at least initially, negotiated away from the gaze of the public so that "even the Legislature knew nothing of the loan proposal prior to January."[55] Unhappiness about this lack of transparency was expressed in a local newspaper in 1930 when the full text of a revision to the loan agreement was also kept under wraps. "The Loan agreement should be the property of the public. It is no longer a diplomatic question to be hid from the people. If it is a loan, it is the people that will have to pay it through their taxes; why then keep them in ignorance concerning the terms?" The main questions asked related to the concessions in sovereignty. "Does the loan effect in any way the autonomy of the country? Are the powers of our President limited to any extent by this agreement? Is the office of the Secretary of the Treasury only on honorary one now? Is the Financial Adviser Secretary of the Treasury de facto under the terms of the Agreement?"[56]

The scope of this "bartering away" was the subject of disagreements which nearly scuppered the whole agreement. After signing an initial set of agreements with Firestone during a rushed trip to New York, the Liberian government then tried to amend them in ways that would preserve some of the sovereign rights initially granted away. A key objection was the share of government revenue hypothecated for loan payments. In one letter to the Secretary of State in Washington, the American representative in Liberia noted that

for the Department's information it should be known that the President had made no secret of his position with reference to the loan agreement which was that he could not be in favor of a loan for $2,500,000 or even $5,000,000 which pledged all the revenues of the country. He at all times has considered the customs revenues alone sufficient security but would be willing to make provision should the customs be insufficient.[57]

Other points of disagreement included the right of the Liberian government to raise further loans and jurisdiction over disagreements between the company and the government.

---

[54] "The Firestone Deadlock," *Liberian News*, May 1925, Holsoe Collection, Liberian Newspapers, Box 49, IULC.

[55] Wharton to Secretary of State, February 24, 1926, *Papers Relating to the Foreign Relations of the United States* (Washington, DC: Government Printing Office, 1926), 531.

[56] "Loan agreement not yet made public," *Crozierville Observer*, February 1930, from Daily Observer Library.

[57] Wharton to Secretary of State, February 24, 1926, *Foreign Relations of the United States 1926*, 531.

Harvey Firestone's initial response to these changes was to threaten to withdraw from Liberia entirely. In February 1926, he wrote a testy letter to the Chief of Division of Western European Affairs in the State Department, stating that he had ordered all equipment then en route to Liberia to be returned. "I note tenor of your cables. I am not in humor to negotiate as we did before. They must accept agreements without single change if we go into Liberia, and that they probably will not do; therefore, our only alternative is to withdraw with exception of agreement number 1, Mount Barclay, with as little embarrassment and expense as possible."[58]

The two parties eventually reached a compromise on all of these points. On arbitration, initial jurisdiction was granted to Liberian courts but with a clause allowing for external intervention. On revenue, however, the concession made by Firestone was more cosmetic than real. Formally, only customs revenue and headmoneys were officially claimed for loan repayments. However, the agreement stated that if these were insufficient, other revenues could be claimed. Furthermore, the financial adviser was to manage all central government revenue collections. This was billed as part of an effort to "modernize" Liberian revenue collections, improving their efficiency and transparency.

One of the conditions of the loan agreement was that the Liberian government pay the salaries of a growing number of American officials. This included a financial adviser, to be designated by the US president, five officials to organize the customs and internal revenue departments, and four American army officers to advise the Liberian Frontier Force. A foreign auditor had the right to monitor government expenditures, and the government budget was to be prepared in consultation with the financial adviser.[59] The salaries of these officials added considerably to the already high costs of servicing the loan, and were one of the more controversial parts of the agreement with Firestone. In 1930, an article in the *Crozierville Observer* recounted that "the first thing that happened after the loan agreement became effective was to raise the salary of the President, not because the cost of living was so high as to necessitate this, but so as to make it a trifle higher than the salary of the Financial Adviser, the highest salaried financial officer under the loan."[60] Beyond the salaries which were stipulated in the loan agreement there were additional costs imposed by the high turnover amongst the foreign advisers, many of whom struggled in Liberia's tropical climate. Illness, alcoholism, and nervous breakdowns all contributed to their lack of

[58] Letter from H. S. Firestone, February 18, 1926, in *Foreign Relations of the United States 1926*, 530.
[59] Chalk, "The Anatomy of an Investment," 30.   [60] *Crozierville Observer*, 1930.

effectiveness. Rosenberg writes that "the succession of US advisers who came and went, all at the Liberian government's expense, hardly could have convinced the Liberians of the usefulness of such supervision."[61]

As shown in Chapter 1, it took a long time for the Firestone plantation to improve Liberia's financial position owing to both the slow growth of rubber trees and to the volatile price of rubber in the interwar period. Eventually, renegotiations in the 1930s reduced the financial burden of the loan, and it was repaid some fifteen years later.[62] However, controversies about the scope of foreign intervention and the impacts on Liberia's fiscal system remained, and are the subject of Chapter 7. The final section of this chapter compares Liberia's experience under foreign financial control to that of formally colonized West African territories.

Not Sovereign, but Not a Colony?

Did investors view the imposition of ever-expanding foreign control over Liberia's finances as equivalent to colonial status? Parallels are frequently drawn between financial control and colonial rule. Sevket Pamuk describes European financial control of the Ottoman Empire as "one of the most striking forms of imperialist penetration short of de jure colonialism."[63] In his history of Liberia, Azikiwe similarly argues that "the control of the finance of one nation by another is one of the latest phases of imperialism."

The evidence from West African bond spreads, although fragmentary, suggests that investors did not see financial control and colonialism as equivalents.[64] Figure 6.1 shows that while Liberia's bond spread began to converge on those of colonized territories, they were still considerably higher. Furthermore, anecdotal evidence suggests wariness even after the establishment of the customs receivership. Of the 1912 loan, the *Financial Times* stated that "under the international control now established the bonds seem fairly well secured, though they can hardly be described as a gilt-edged investment."[65] The verdict of the *Economist* was even less enthusiastic, noting that "the revenue depends very largely on Customs duties and the conditions of trade and the stability of the State administration are not satisfactory enough to make the present offer attractive."[66]

[61] Rosenberg, *Financial Missionaries*, 227.   [62] Suter, *Debt Cycles*, 151–52.
[63] Sevket Pamuk, *The Ottoman Empire and European capitalism, 1820–1913* (Cambridge: Cambridge University Press, 1987), 56.
[64] This section derived from Leigh Gardner, "Colonialism or Supersanctions: Sovereignty and Debt in West Africa, 1871–1914," *European Review of Economic History* 21 (2017): 236–57.
[65] "Liberia Five Per Cent Bonds," *The Financial Times*, January 4, 1913, 6.
[66] "New capital issues," *The Economist*, January 4, 1913, 28.

Why was control over Liberia's finances and military insufficient to replicate the "empire effect" visible in the low spreads on bonds issued by West African colonies? To answer this requires looking more closely at how the process of raising loans differed between Liberia and its colonized neighbors. While both issued bonds in the same market, the intermediaries differed considerably. From the 1860s, the Crown Agents for the Colonies were responsible for approving, advertising, and issuing colonial loans.[67] The Crown Agents were a semi-autonomous body which acted as a general commissary service for colonial administrations, managing their finances as well as government purchasing.[68] They had an interest in protecting the creditworthiness of all colonies, and were therefore active in trying to ensure the marketability of colonial loan issues, particularly those for which there was likely to be limited demand. Owing to this encompassing interest in all colonial bond issues, they shared many features with the prestige underwriters described earlier.

The archival records surrounding African colonial loan issues suggest that the Agents faced a challenge in overcoming investor prejudice against the bond issues of little-known colonies in West Africa.[69] A letter from Scrimgoers, which underwrote many colonial bond issues for the Crown Agents, noted in regards to an issue of Nigerian bonds in 1911 that "many of the general public regard the West African colonies on their own merits alone, and for this reason they have never been a popular investment amongst the outside public."[70] Even after the passage of the Colonial Stock Act of 1900, West African issues were met with skepticism. The first of the West African colonies to borrow under the new system was the Gold Coast, which issued £1,035,000 in 3 percent bonds in 1902. In response to the loan's announcement, the *Financial Times* pronounced: "how times have changed of late is well exemplified by the appearance of a new Trustee stock in the form of Gold Coast Government Three per cents. A few years ago investors would have thrown up their hands in horror at the suggestion." Though the bonds were priced at ninety-one

---

[67] Before 1883, the Crown Agents commissioned loan issues for all colonies. After that date, they no longer handled the loans of territories with responsible government. They continued, however, to manage loan issues for the crown colonies such as the three West African territories. See T. Suzuki, *Japanese Government Loan Issues on the London Market, 1870–1913* (London: Athlone Press, 1994), 32 and Sunderland, *Managing the British Empire*, 152–53.

[68] A. W. Abbott, *A Short History of the Crown Agents and Their Office* (Portsmouth: The Grosvenor Press, 1971), 2; R. M. Kesner, *Economic Control and Colonial Development: Crown Colony Financial Management in the Age of Joseph Chamberlain* (Oxford: Clio Press, 1981), 61; Sunderland, *Managing the British Empire*, 284.

[69] This discussion relies primarily on the papers of the Crown Agents for the Colonies held in the UK National Archives, as well as the records of the Colonial Office and Treasury.

[70] A Scrimgoer to Crown Agents, November 16, 1911, TNA CAOG 9/37.

rather than at par, the *Financial Times* writer argued that "in view of the whole circumstances we should have thought a lower price would have been fixed for this first appearance on the loan market."[71] Faced with such responses, the Agents employed a range of methods to make African bond issues more attractive both in primary and secondary markets, often in coordination with private sector actors and other parts of the British government.

One obstacle to be overcome was the state of the finances of the West African colonies in the early years of colonial rule. Figure 6.2 gives the budget balance of Liberia next to that of the British colonies. Liberia was not unique, and colonial administrations were similarly in deficit more often than not, especially during the period when they raised their first loans. Fiscal stability was elusive in the early years of colonial administration, owing to both the volatility in revenue and the military and political uncertainties of colonial conquest.

At the same time, the most important initial criterion used by the Agents to determine whether a colony could borrow was whether the state of the colony's finances would allow it to service the loan – a test the Liberian government surely would have failed in regards to the 1871 loan. In Sierra Leone's 1871 issue, the timing was driven by "the improved and yearly improving condition of the revenue."[72] Fiscal solvency was also a key factor in the marketing of loans. The announcement in the *Financial Times* of a Sierra Leone issue in 1904 noted that the revenue had increased considerably between 1898 and 1902, from £117,700 to £205,800.[73] In a letter from the Colonial Office to the Crown Agents ahead of the 1911 Nigeria issue, they wrote: "the governor desires that in the advertisement of the contemplated issue of £2,000,000 stock you will give prominence to the large revenue and surplus in 1910, and also to satisfactory railway returns for the same period."[74]

Despite these positive headlines, West African colonies remained vulnerable to fiscal crises. In Sierra Leone, the revenue declined in 1873 and 1874. The effects of this decline were compounded by unrest at Sherbro, which demanded new expenditure on military excursions. As a result, the amount that Sierra Leone could borrow was limited to £50,000 instead of the £60,000 which had initially been authorized, and the program of expenditure was cut.[75] In future years, the imperial government often

---

[71] "The Gold Coast Loan," *Financial Times*, March 29, 1902, 8.
[72] Sierra Leone Ordinance 1 of 1871.
[73] "A Sierra Leone Issue," *Financial Times* June 3, 1904.
[74] Colonial Office to Crown Agents, May 10, 1911, in TNA CAOG 9/37.
[75] House of Commons, *Correspondence Respecting the Financial Condition of the Colonies of Sierra Leone, Gambia and St Helena* (London: HMSO, 1877), 16.

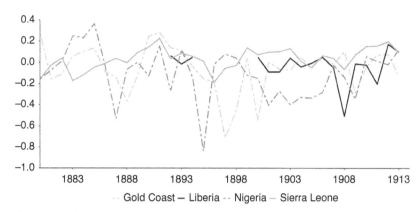

Figure 6.2 Budget balance of West African governments, 1880–1913
Source: Gardner, "Colonialism or supersanctions," p. 240.

intervened to mitigate the effects of such crises by offering contingency financing of various kinds, usually on concessionary terms. Loans from the British Treasury and advances from the Crown Agents were granted to compensate for severe revenue shortfalls or when emergencies required increased spending, and prevented the colonies from accumulating a domestic floating debt the way Liberia had. The colonial administration of Lagos, for example, received an interest-free loan of £20,000 in 1873 to repay several loans advanced from local merchants to "meet the current expenses of the government."[76] In 1879, Sierra Leone received a loan of £38,000 at zero interest from the imperial government "in aid of the local revenue of the settlement."[77] This was repaid in uneven installments by 1890. A further concessionary loan was issued to assist with the costs of the 1898 Hut Tax War, an uprising against the extension of British Authority over the interior.[78] These funds – a total of £45,000 – were advanced from the Treasury Chest, described as "a fund of several hundred thousand pounds spread through the Empire for public services and emergencies."[79] The colonial administration of the Gold Coast received several concessionary loans through the 1890s to cope with the

---

[76] Lagos, *Blue Book* (Lagos: Government Printer, 1873).
[77] Sierra Leone, *Blue Book* (Freetown: Government Printer, 1879).
[78] John Hargreaves, "The Establishment of the Sierra Leone Protectorate and the Insurrection of 1898," *Cambridge Historical Journal* 12 (1956): 56–80.
[79] L. Davis and R. Huttenback, *Mammon and the Pursuit of Empire: The Political Economy of British Imperialism, 1860–1912* (Cambridge: Cambridge University Press, 1986), 149.

costs of the Ashanti Wars.[80] As a share of total British spending, these loans and grants were very small, but relative to the much smaller budgets of individual colonies they could be substantial. In terms of the primary market for colonial bond issues, such interventions also had the effect of making colonial finances appear perhaps more stable than was actually the case. It also meant that colonies would not have to resort to higher cost methods of budget support like Liberia did.

Another form of financial assistance provided by imperial institutions was advances for the construction of the infrastructure to be funded by the loan proceeds. Though the first railway loan issued by a West African colony was not until 1902, when the Gold Coast 3 percent bonds described earlier were issued, railway construction had actually begun in the 1890s. Over the next decade, it proceeded sporadically, with frequent interruptions due to conflicts with the African population, the difficulty of continuing surveys and construction during the wet season, insufficient labor supplies, and high turnover amongst the European staff.[81] In some cases, for example Sierra Leone, the advances came from the Crown Agents, who later recovered the money with the proceeds of the loan issue.[82] In Lagos, £725,000 of the £2,000,000 raised through the issue of 3.5 percent inscribed stock in 1906 was used to repay the Treasury for earlier railway loans.[83]

These means of financing infrastructure construction had several advantages. They ensured that loan proceeds would not be diverted to other purposes, as had been the case in Sierra Leone in 1871, when half of the proceeds of the loan were used to support the "general service" of the colony, instead of expanding Freetown Harbour.[84] They also ensured that the revenue returns of spending on railways would at the very least follow the issue of the loan without much delay, if not perhaps even precede it. The system of advances also allowed the Crown Agents some flexibility in terms of the timing of loan issues, meaning they could delay an issue if market conditions were not favorable.[85] In the case of the West African loans, the Sierra Leone issue in particular was postponed until the end of the South African War. A Crown Agents memorandum on the loan noted that

---

[80] Kesner, *Economic Control*; Gold Coast, *Blue Book 1901*.
[81] House of Commons, *Papers Relating to the Construction of Railways in Sierra Leone, Lagos and the Gold Coast* (London: HMSO, 1904).
[82] Sierra Leone, *Blue Book* (Freetown: Government Printer, 1903).
[83] Lagos, *Blue Book* (Lagos: Government Printer, 1905).
[84] House of Commons, *Correspondence Respecting the Financial Condition of the Colonies of Sierra Leone, Gambia and St Helena*, 16.
[85] Sunderland, *Managing the British Empire*, 156.

preliminary consideration of the prospects of raising a loan began in 1901. ... Some time elapsed while these points were settled, during which time the program was financed by temporary advances. Before the market had returned to normal (after the South African War) it became necessary to liquidate the advances and a short-term issue of 4 percent 10-year convertible debentures was made in 1904 at 98.[86]

Even with these measures to make bonds more attractive to investors, further intervention was necessary to maintain high prices after the bonds were sold. Several West African bond issues were poorly received among investors. An article in the *Financial Times* on the 1908 Southern Nigeria issue of £3,000,000 observed that "80 per cent of the Southern Nigeria scrip has been left in the hands of the underwriters."[87] To avoid this, the Crown Agents and their affiliates negotiated with other financial institutions to arrange the informal underwriting of the bonds. For the 1911 Nigeria issue, for example, Scrimgoers noted that half of the bonds were purchased by "certain of the larger underwriters with our active cooperation, in order to strengthen the position."[88] They particularly approached Leslie Couper of the Bank of British West Africa. In response, he wrote to the Crown Agents that "we are taking at least £100,000."[89] Finally, the Crown Agents themselves also purchased West African bonds, using the reserve funds which they held on behalf of other colonies. In their 1911 letter, Scrimgoers also noted that, "as you are doubtless aware in ordinary times there is very little market in the stocks of Southern Nigeria, Gold Coast and Sierra Leone, and it is only the heavy purchases made from time to time by your good selves which has kept the prices of these stocks at their comparatively high levels."

In terms of public borrowing, colonial status was not merely a matter of external control over government finance and other functions. Investor discrimination against the bond issues of West African colonies, as well as their reactions to Liberian bonds after the imposition of foreign financial control, suggests that this was not enough to bring the terms of lending in line with other borrowers. Nevertheless, British colonies in Africa were able to borrow on terms close to those of older, larger colonies with more stable fiscal systems. They were able to do so because of a linked system of intermediaries with an interest in maintaining access to capital at low cost for colonial governments. This interest was not at all philanthropic. Colonies faced the same development "catch-22" as Liberia. In order for colonial governments to achieve financial self-sufficiency, they needed

[86] Undated. TNA CAOG 9/63.
[87] "Stock Markets and Money," *Financial Times*, May 7, 1908.
[88] A Scrimgoer to Crown Agents, November 16, 1911, TNA CAOG 9/37.
[89] Couper to Antrobus, November 7, 1911, in TNA COAG 9/37.

to access foreign capital to invest in infrastructure. The Crown Agents, colonial banks, and export companies all had their own interests in the promotion of export production. For Liberia, foreign financial control failed to replicate this network of support. Perhaps the central irony of Liberia's history of public debt in comparison to that of its neighbors was that strategic concessions of sovereignty, intended to prevent a full takeover, were actually worse for borrowing than the full takeover would have been. In the end, however, the Liberian government deemed that too high a price.

Sovereignty and Debt in Liberia

The era of financial globalization during the late nineteenth and early twentieth centuries offered both opportunities and risks for countries like Liberia. On the one hand, easier and cheaper access to capital from Britain and other industrialized countries made it possible to overcome the constraints of local capital markets, which were often underdeveloped. Almost a century after Roye made his speech in favor of the 1871 loan, Walt Rostow would argue that the transfer of capital and technology from rich countries to poor ones could speed the process of economic development.[90] Chapter 8 illustrates the ways in which these ideas influenced the use of foreign aid after 1945. It was similar logic which motivated Roye to look abroad for the resources that would allow what was then still a relatively new state to cement its place on the world stage, not only economically but also politically. On the other hand, even in a rapidly expanding market, capital was not available to everyone on the same terms. For governments which lacked resources and access to the right networks, the price of that capital went beyond higher interest rates to include existential threats to their sovereignty.

Whether to borrow or not was therefore a finely balanced decision across much of the world. Few governments took the view of Siam and avoided it entirely. Like Roye's government, many were overly optimistic about what capital borrowed from abroad could accomplish, particularly in contexts of limited state capacity as existed in Liberia and other places. While there is a robust literature on how features of borrowing states influenced investor attitudes and the terms on which they could borrow, understanding of what shaped the use of borrowed funds is more limited. Countries which had issued loans in the hopes that economic growth would enable them to service the debt were frequently disappointed and

---

[90] Walt Rostow, *The Stages of Economic Growth: A Non-Communist Manifesto* (Cambridge: Cambridge University Press, 1960).

wound up in default. They then faced many of the same dilemmas that the Liberian government did about how best to escape from default without losing control of the state entirely, as elites and government officials feared would happen in Liberia and as did happen in countries like Egypt, for example.[91] International financial control (IFC) regimes like the Customs Receivership provided something of a middle ground. By parceling out specific areas of sovereign control between lenders, they allowed borrowing governments to retain at least their formal recognition as sovereign states while at the same time reassuring investors, at least to some extent.

Such arrangements had their own costs – financial and otherwise. Paying foreign officials associated with IFCs could add considerably to the fiscal burden of foreign debt, and as in Liberia the number of these officials tended to increase over time. Beyond that, however, the histories of Liberia and other borrowing countries suggest that foreign control had sometimes unpredictable political consequences. In the short term, such arrangements were often controversial and could result in political upheaval. Adam Tooze and Martin Ivanov document the political upheaval that accompanied the imposition of IFCs in Bulgaria, concluding that this case "suggests the need for a more complex understanding of the relationship between foreign debt and national sovereignty."[92]

The same argument could be made with regard to Liberia. The overthrow of Roye was the most immediate sign of "nationalist rejection," but it was not the only one. Objections to the Firestone loan and its successors, discussed further in Chapter 9, helped motivate opposition to the Liberian government through the interwar period and beyond. In his study of Liberian debt, Suter links Liberia's next coup d'état, in 1980, at least partly to conditions agreed on by William Tolbert in his negotiations with the IMF.[93] It is possible to draw wider parallels to controversies around the conditional loans by international financial institutions later in the twentieth century, and in many ways, Liberia's history foreshadowed later challenges faced by African governments with the politics of structural adjustment.[94] The next chapter examines the impact of foreign financial controls on domestic governance, and the subsequent strategies adopted by the Liberian government to sustain its authority.

[91] Tuncer, *Sovereign Debt*, ch. 3.
[92] Tooze and Ivanov, "Disciplining the 'Black Sheep of the Balkans'," 49.
[93] Suter, *Debt Cycles in the World-Economy*, 155.
[94] See, for example, Jeffrey Herbst, "The Structural Adjustment of Politics in Africa," *World Development* 18, no. 7 (1990): 949–958.

7   Financial Controls and Forced Labor

The Government lives on us but does no good for us, and will not hear our complaints. It takes all our food and as much rice as we can grow. Soldiers came in the night and catch us by force for F. Poo or elsewhere. This happened in March last year. They make slaves of us.

Paramount Chief Kleyea of Wadaka, May 30, 1930, in
testimony before the Christy Commission.

We were here when trouble come to our people;
For this trouble Jeh was imprisoned and fined.
For this reason Yancy came to our country –
He caught our husbands and our brothers,
Sail them to 'Nana Poo
And there they die!
And there they die!

"The sad song of the Wedabo woman," reprinted in Charles S. Johnson,
Bitter Canaan: The Story of the Negro Republic

Foreign financial controls and other external interventions often claimed to do more than improve the creditworthiness of recipient countries. In the process, proponents argued, they could help build fairer, less corrupt, and more representative institutions. The improvement of domestic institutions remains the stated intention of many foreign interventions, whether by governments or international organizations, to this day. Stephen Krasner proposes that "shared sovereignty can offer hope for moving countries closer to democracy and decent governance," and gives the example of foreign financial controls in the Ottoman Empire as a case of the historical success of such interventions.[1] However, whether such aims can actually be fulfilled remains debatable, both then and now.

---

[1] Stephen D. Krasner, "Building Democracy after Conflict: The Case for Shared Sovereignty," *Journal of Democracy* 16, no. 1 (2005): 76–77. See also Stephen Krasner and Jeremy M. Weinstein, "Improving Governance from the Outside In," *Annual Review of Political Science* 17 (2014): 123–45 and Alia M. Matanock, "Governance Delegation Agreements: Shared Sovereignty as a Substitute for Limited Statehood," *Governance* 27, no. 4 (2014): 589–612.

Numerous studies of forced regime change, often inspired by the apparent failure of US ventures in Iraq and Afghanistan, find little improvement in institutions or democratization.[2] Looking beyond the use of force, skeptics point to the often unintended consequences of efforts to improve institutions from the outside.[3]

In Liberia, foreign financial controls began to influence the development of its institutions in the period when the government in Monrovia was, for the first time, extending its jurisdiction into the interior. The costs of foreign advisers and servicing the debt absorbed a large and growing share of total revenue, and in bad years the government struggled to pay its administrative and military personnel. This chapter argues that one response to the loss of control over cash revenue by the central government was the decentralization of domestic revenue collection to local officials who relied increasingly on in-kind exactions of labor and food. In making this argument, the chapter offers a new interpretation of one of the more infamous incidents in Liberian history: the 1930 League of Nations investigation into forced labor, which found that the Liberian government along with many of its senior officials had supported and profited from forced labor, in contravention of the 1926 convention on slavery, which the Liberian government had signed.[4] The investigation and its findings were controversial at the time and have been extensively debated since.[5]

In explaining the prevalence of forced labor found by the Commission, both historians and people at the time have made reference to the financial struggles of the Liberian government in framing this period of the

---

[2] Bruce Bueno de Mesquita and George W. Downs, "Intervention and Democracy," *International Organization* 60 (2006): 627–49; Alexander B. Downes and Jonathan Monten, "Forced to Be Free? Why Foreign-Imposed Regime Change Rarely Leads to Democratization," *International Security* 37, no. 4 (2013): 91–31; John M. Owen, *The Clash of Ideas in World Politics: Transnational Networks, States and Regime Change, 1510–2010* (Princeton: Princeton University Press, 2010); Mark Peceny, *Democracy at the Point of Bayonets* (University Park, PA: Pennsylvania State University Press, 1999).

[3] Noel Maurer and Leticia Arroyo Abad, "Can Europe Run Greece? Lessons from US Fiscal Receiverships in Latin America, 1904–1931," SSRN Working Paper (2017); Deborah A. Brautigam and Stephen Knack, "Foreign Aid, Institutions and Governance in Sub-Saharan Africa," *Economic Development and Cultural Change* 52, no. 2 (2004): 255–85.

[4] Cuthbert Christy, *Report of the International Commission of Inquiry into the Existence of Slavery and Forced Labor in the Republic of Liberia* (Geneva: League of Nations, 1932), henceforth *Christy Report*.

[5] See, for example: James Ciment, *Another America: The Story of Liberia and the Former Slaves Who Ruled It* (New York: Hill and Wang, 2013), ch. 8; Charles S. Johnson, *Bitter Canaan: The Story of the Negro Republic*; Ibrahim Sundiata, *Black Scandal: America and the Liberian Labor Crisis, 1929–1936* (Philadelphia: Institute for the Study of Human Issues, 1980); Charles Morrow Wilson, *Liberia: Black Africa in Microcosm* (New York: Harper and Row, 1971), ch. 9.

country's history. The Liberian government defended itself from the charges by arguing that it had insufficient resources to stamp out indigenous labor practices. Ibrahim Sundiata, arguably the leading historian of the period, stresses instead that labor was "one of the few available sources of revenue for a government apparently plunging towards a financial nadir."[6] This chapter attempts to link these arguments more concretely to Liberia's government finances by arguing that the specific forms of forced labor identified by the Commission were, at least in part, a response to creeping foreign controls over central government revenue. In its place, Liberian officials turned to the decentralized collection of in-kind revenue, including not only labor but also agricultural produce, as well as cash through the levying of fines. This effort to preserve a source of income for an expanding group of government officials ultimately resulted in international condemnation which came close to ending Liberia's history as an independent nation.

"The Government Is Undoubtedly Very Hard Pressed"

Creating a more effective system of revenue collection was one of the explicit aims of IFC regimes, not only in Liberia but also around the world. "With Americans in charge," ran the argument, "revenues would increase, borrowing costs would go down, and political stability would result."[7] President Arthur Barclay, in his annual message to the legislature of 1911, reiterated this point, explicitly linking sound public finances to national sovereignty: "The government of the United States evidently impressed that the chief danger to the stability of the Republic will lie in an unsound financial administration. It is through bad finance that many states have come, in the last 25 years, to be controlled by the Great Powers of the European continent." In the 1926 Firestone agreement, the management of all of Liberia's cash revenue by the financial adviser and other foreign officials was, at least according to the American consul, "desired as a means of increasing their efficiency and bettering their system."[8]

The fall in bond spreads which occurred in Liberia and in other countries after the imposition of foreign financial controls suggests that

---

[6] Ibrahim K. Sundiata, "Prelude to a Scandal: Liberia and Fernando Po, 1880–1930," *Journal of African History* 15, no. 1 (1974): 107.

[7] Noel Maurer, *The Empire Trap: The Rise and Fall of US Intervention to Protect American Property Overseas, 1893–2013* (Princeton: Princeton University Press, 2013), 92.

[8] Wharton to Secretary of State, February 24, 1926, in US Department of State, *Papers Relating for the Foreign Relations of the United States, 1926, Volume II* (Washington, DC: US Government Printing Office, 1941), 531.

investors believed such controls would make it more likely that their debts would be serviced on time. However, this did not always mean that there was any improvement in revenue collections, and research on other countries has shown that foreign controls were only rarely associated with any gains in fiscal performance. In the Ottoman Empire, which Krasner cites as a successful example of "shared sovereignty," the establishment of the Public Debt Administration in 1881, and corresponding transfer of important revenue sources to foreign control, did not prevent a return to substantial government deficits from 1900.[9] In Latin America, most foreign financial control resulted in worse fiscal performance. The only exception was the Dominican Republic, but even there the increase in revenue did not translate into greater political stability.[10] In Bulgaria, foreign interventions prompted the government to diversify their revenue base, but this also came at a cost of political instability.[11]

In Liberia, nominal revenue did indeed increase in the first decade or so of the twentieth century, which some credited to foreign control. In 1907, after British officials had taken over collection of customs revenue, Arthur Barclay observed that "under the careful supervision of Mr. W. J. Lamont, the Chief Inspector, this source of revenue has manifested signs of gratifying expansion."[12] His successor, Daniel Howard, gave similar plaudits in 1912, observing that "our revenue has steadily increased for the past six years, and a great measure of the credit for this splendid showing is due to the British inspectors who have organized and supervised our customs since 1906. It is hoped that this rate of progress will be fully maintained by the new Receivership."[13] A year later Howard was optimistic enough to declare that "the net results of the operation of the Receivership for this first year are indeed satisfactory and indicate that the financial embarrassments and make-shifts hitherto experienced by the Government are a closed chapter in Liberian history."

His optimism did not last long. Figure 7.1 shows total revenue and expenditure in constant prices from 1900 to 1937. While revenue more than doubled across the period from 1900 to 1912, these gains were erased

---

[9] Sevket Pamuk, *The Ottoman Empire and European Capitalism, 1820–1913* (Cambridge: Cambridge University Press, 1987), 62.

[10] Maurer, *Empire Trap*, 92.

[11] Adam Tooze and Martin Ivanov, "Disciplining the 'Black Sheep of the Balkans': Financial Supervision and Sovereignty in Bulgaria, 1902–1938," *Economic History Review* 64, no. 1 (2011): 44–45.

[12] Annual message of Arthur Barclay to the Legislature, December 12, 1907, in *The Annual Messages of the Presidents of Liberia 1848–2010: State of the Nation Addresses to the National Legislature from Joseph Jenkins Roberts to Ellen Johnson Sirleaf*, edited by D. Elwood Dunn (Berlin: De Gruyter, 2011), 455.

[13] Annual message of Daniel Howard, December 12, 1912, in Dunn, *Annual Messages*, 514.

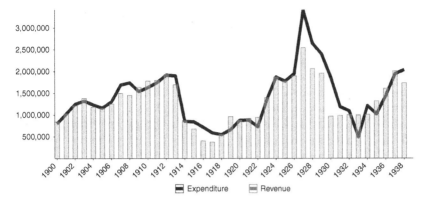

Figure 7.1 Revenue and expenditure (constant 1950$)
Source: See Chapter 1.

with the outbreak of World War I. By 1919 revenues had fallen to a low previously seen during the global depression of the 1870s. They did not reach prewar levels until 1927, but by 1930 they had been cut in half again with the onset of the Great Depression. While there was some fluctuation during the 1930s, it was more than ten years before 1927 levels were regained. The figure also shows that despite the increase in revenue, Liberia was far from fiscally solvent during the period before 1914. Rather, higher revenue was largely offset by growing expenditures. Though there were some good years in which the Liberian government was in surplus, these were outweighed in both number and scale by years with substantial deficits.

During much of the nineteenth century, the Liberian government had spent little in terms of money or effort on governing much of the territory it claimed in the interior. In the closing decades of the century, however, Liberia came under pressure from colonial expansion by Britain and France along its boundaries, ultimately suffering considerable territorial losses on the frontier.[14] As Arthur Barclay put it,

while West Africa remained outside the circle of political life of the world, we could afford to jog along quietly and conservatively, to follow lines laid down more than fifty years ago by the founders of Liberia and their advisers. But now that phase has passed and we are confronted with new problems growing out of the new conditions around us.[15]

[14] J. Gus Liebenow, *Liberia: The Evolution of Privilege* (Ithaca: Cornell University Press, 1969), 22–23. Other independent states faced similar pressures. See Christopher Paik and Jessica Vechbanyongratana, "Path to Centralization and Development: Evidence from Siam," *World Politics* 71, no. 2 (2019): 289–331.
[15] Annual message of Arthur Barclay to the Legislature, December 12, 1907, in Dunn, *Annual Messages*, 449.

The Berlin Act of 1885 had made "effective administration" a requirement for territorial claims in Africa, and Liberia had to expand its administrative presence to counter claims by the British and French governments. The fact that Liberia's claims predated those of Britain and France was less relevant, according to Barclay, than its limited power and influence. "It is a fact," he observed to the legislature in 1906, "that the great powers really settle the principles of international law. Small states must conform. It results, therefore, that we are compelled to occupy our frontiers with a frontier guard, suitable officials, and customs stations, and to give the frontier District an organized government on civilized lines."[16]

There had been attempts to extend the authority of the Liberian government into the interior through the nineteenth century, and debates on the topic had divided "proponents of an 'outreach' approach and advocates of integration" between Americo-Liberian and indigenous communities.[17] One strategy proposed by the latter group was the creation of a network of settler communities in the interior which would, proponents like Edward Blyden hoped, establish new channels of communication and trade. During the late 1860s, Blyden sought funds from the ACS and Pennsylvania Colonization societies for the establishment of interior settlements, but progress was limited due to the declining number of emigrants after the end of the US Civil War. By the 1880s, a combination of economic decline and external pressure began to direct efforts instead toward a system of administration frequently compared to indirect rule in neighboring colonized territories. In 1900, President G. W. Gibson proposed to make influential chiefs government officials who would each be assigned a clerk and made responsible for the collection of taxes. Gibson's successor in office was Arthur Barclay, who built on this plan to develop what would become the system of administration in Liberia's interior. Under Barclay's plan, the interior was divided into administrative districts overseen by a commissioner who reported to the Secretary of the Interior. District commissioners came from one of four groups: Americo-Liberians who had been active in the then-declining trade between interior and the coast, members of the elite who had failed to gain positions in central government, migrants from British colonies who were unable to hold professional positions there, and indigenous elites who had been educated in mission schools.

---

[16] Annual message of Arthur Barclay to the Legislature, December 11, 1906, in Dunn, *Annual Messages*, 445.

[17] The best history of the administrative expansion Amos Sawyer, *The Emergence of Autocracy in Liberia: Tragedy and Challenge* (San Francisco: Institute for Contemporary Studies Press, 1992), ch. 8. For an official account, see *Handbook of the Interior Department* (Monrovia: Government Printer, 1953), 2–3, in Svend Holsoe Papers, IULC.

Within each district, indigenous chiefs were tasked with maintaining order, collecting hut taxes (on which they received a 10 percent commission), and providing labor for public works. Though, as discussed in Chapter 2, many of Liberia's indigenous groups were governed by comparatively decentralized institutions through village heads and other local officials, the Interior Department regulations specified that there should be "one Paramount Chief for the whole Tribe."[18] This same naming of an individual "chief" also occurred at times in African countries under colonial rule. Mahmood Mamdani argues that this practice created a system of "decentralized despotism" by which indigenous elites were stripped of constraints by their association with the national government. Other studies of African institutions under colonial rule have, however, shown that there was significant variation in the structure of those institutions.[19]

The expansion of government staff required by Barclay's administrative reforms, including district commissioners and their clerks, absorbed most if not all of the increase in revenue. The Barclay reforms included a Frontier Force of 600 soldiers, along with some 20 district and assistant commissioners distributed through the interior.[20] As a result, the first decade of the twentieth century was one of nearly constant fiscal crisis despite the improvement in customs collections. In 1909, an exasperated Barclay said to the legislature: "[I]t is to be hoped that at the present sessions some real financial help be given to the Administration by way of additional resources. The Secretary of the Treasury cannot make three dollars do the work of five."[21]

These existing difficulties were exacerbated by the sharp decrease in revenue following the outbreak of the war. By December 1914, Howard's optimism of the previous year had disappeared. After observing that collections of "assigned revenues," or those allocated to the Receivership for debt service, had declined from just over $40,000 in July to $16,000 in August, he noted that "the financial outlook is now nothing short of desperate. . . . Liberia is without a reserve of any kind to fall back upon: her very existence is dependent upon the continuance of trade, and trade is paralyzed."[22] As the war continued over the next four

[18] Department of the Interior, *Regulation for the Government of the Hinterland* (Monrovia, 1929), from IULC Liberian Government collections.

[19] Mahmood Mamdani, *Citizen and Subject: Contemporary Africa and the Legacy of Late Colonialism* (Princeton: Princeton University Press, 1996). Jutta Bolt and Leigh Gardner, "How Africans Shaped British Colonial Institutions: Evidence from Local Taxation," Journal of Economic History 80, no. 4 (2020): 1189–1223.

[20] Annual message of Arthur Barclay to the Legislature, December 12, 1907, in Dunn, *Annual Messages*, 448–56.

[21] Annual message of Arthur Barclay to the Legislature, December 13, 1909, in Dunn, *Annual Messages*, 480.

[22] Annual message of Daniel Howard to the Legislature, September 23, 1914, in Dunn, *Annual Messages*, 541.

years, things would only get worse. While Liberia initially declared neutrality, its financial ties to Britain and the United States led to pressure from the Allies, and Britain in particular, to cut its extensive commercial ties with Germany. In April 1916, the British government prohibited the export of goods to Liberia. According to James Curtis, the American consul at the time, the proclamation "fell like a pall on the populace here, officials alike, and many express the fear that suffering for the want of actual necessities of life is sure to follow."[23] The Liberian government eventually succumbed to this pressure, and by August 1917 all German subjects were deported and their property liquidated by the state.[24] Contrary to the promises made by the British government, however, this action was not followed by any resumption of shipping from Britain, and as a result the financial situation of the Liberian government grew increasingly dire.[25]

Improvements in both trade and revenue after the war allowed the government to retain some semblance of financial stability, if only temporarily. Interest arrears from the war years were repaid. As noted in Chapter 6, fluctuations in the dollar–pound exchange rate occasionally made this more difficult. Nonetheless, the late 1920s were a period of considerable fiscal optimism for Liberian officials. In October 1929, President King made much of the fact that in the previous fiscal year nominal revenues had "exceeded the one and a quarter million mark" for the first time. "This is indeed a most gratifying fact, and testifies to the substantial financial progress Liberia is making. We're getting out of the 'woods', the woods of financial chaos, and are beginning to see, through [sic] yet at a great distance, bright lights along the richly paved road which leads to national prosperity, happiness and greatness."[26]

Much as for Daniel Howard, King's sunny predictions would be misplaced. The global economic crisis of the 1930s also created serious fiscal problems and reversed many of the gains of the 1920s, and in the 1929–30 fiscal year revenue declined by nearly 23 percent. King initially downplayed the decline as being in part due to revenue from the hinterland not arriving in time for the closing of accounts, and reassured the legislature

---

[23] Curtis to Secretary of State, June 13, 1916, in US Department of State, *Papers Relating to the Foreign Relations of the United States 1916* (Washington, DC: US Government Printing Office, 1925), 459.

[24] Annual message of Daniel Howard to the legislature, December 20, 1917, in Dunn, *Annual Messages*, 550–56.

[25] Johnson to Secretary of State, November 20, 1917, US Department of State, *Papers Relating to the Foreign Relations of the United States, 1917* (Washington, DC: US Government Printing Office, 1926), 895–96.

[26] Annual message of Charles D. B. King to the legislature, October 18, 1928, in Dunn, *Annual Messages*, 742.

"that the basic economic conditions of Liberia are no worse now than in other periods." However, in the next year revenue fell to less than half of what it had been in the late 1920s, and even King had to admit to the seriousness of the situation.

The consequences of these periods of financial crisis for Liberian institutions were severe. During both World War I and the Great Depression, the government kept itself afloat in part by temporarily suspending payment on all of its liabilities. This included, in 1916 and 1932, the servicing of foreign debt. However, the rules of the Receivership and the Firestone agreement which followed it made debt service a first charge on all cash revenues. The first payments to cease, therefore, were not to foreign bankers but rather to Liberian government employees. As early as January 1915, the American minister reported to the Secretary that the Receiver "can shortly transmit November interest. American officers and Frontier Force unpaid three months ... Impossible to pay their arrears or future maintenance; disintegration force certain if unpaid."[27] While in this instance the bankers agreed that the payment of the Frontier Force should be made ahead of interest, employees of the rest of the government went largely unpaid through much of the duration of the war. In March 1915, Daniel Howard said pointedly that government employees, who at that point were due six months' salary, "cannot much longer endure this financial inhibition, nor can the Government reasonably expect efficiency in service or discipline from employees whose spirits are broken and demoralized by continual lack of payments."[28] In October, the government suspended many of the interior commissioners, resulting in "a state of unrest" due to the "absence of the force of Government authority."[29] Nor was the situation any better during the 1930s, when salaries for government employees and pensioners were not paid for periods as long as nine months in 1932.[30]

Diversification of Revenue

The fact that the government had again in 1932 been forced to cease paying its employees suggests that its financial position continued to be

---

[27] Received January 2, 1915, in US Department of State, *Papers relating to the Foreign Relations of the United States 1915* (Washington, DC: US Government Printing Office, 1924), 635.

[28] Special message of Daniel Howard to the Legislature, March 10, 1915, in Dunn, *Annual Messages*, 543.

[29] Annual message of Daniel Howard to the Legislature, September 9, 1916, in Dunn, *Annual Messages*, 548.

[30] Annual report of the Treasury Department for 1933, IULC Liberian government Records; Treasury; General Records 1916–33.

tenuous, despite deepening controls. However, officials had learned something from the crisis of World War I, namely: that they needed to diversify the sources of government revenue. Before the Firestone agreement, the only taxes hypothecated to the Receivership were customs revenues, headmoneys, and a rubber tax. In practice, customs revenue represented the vast majority of Liberian government revenue. However, in the years following World War I, the government sought to introduce new forms of taxation in order to ensure that it would have some revenue even if the Receivership failed to make any payments to it, as had been the case during the war. However, the implementation of these new taxes was hindered by the limited administrative capacity of the Liberian state, and in particular its inability to enforce tax policies in an even-handed way.

In terms of generating revenue, its efforts in this direction were successful – as Frank Chalk noted:

[T]he share of the Liberian government's income which came under the jurisdiction of the receivership had declined from at least ninety-one per cent of total revenue when the loan of 1912 was negotiated to about forty-eight per cent in 1925. While intensifying the collection of hut taxes in the hinterland, the Liberian government had significantly reduced the Receivership's sphere of financial control.[31]

Figure 7.2 gives customs revenue as a share of total through this period, and shows that it fell in favor of what was collectively referred to as "internal" revenue. Internal revenue was comprised primarily of a range of direct taxes, from the hut tax to real estate taxes and a stamp duty known as the "emergency relief fund." Increasing internal revenue was a key priority for the Liberian government from 1906, when British administrators first took control of customs collection under the terms of the loan agreement with Harry Johnston's Liberian Development Company. In his annual message of that year, Arthur Barclay noted that "the internal revenue needs looking after. For the last ten years it totals only $122,091, something more than $12,000 per annum, not including Kru boys tax." At that point there were a variety of taxes on the books, including poll taxes, real estate taxes, fines, taxes on Kru laborers, school taxes, taxes on distilleries, and so on. However, according to Barclay, they "are not regularly or properly collected. The taxes are exacted from some, others escape. Some officers are honest, others do not faithfully account owing to a want of a proper system, and strict oversight."[32]

---

[31] Frank Chalk, "The Anatomy of an Investment: Firestone's 1927 Loan to Liberia," *Canadian Journal of African Studies* 1, no. 1 (1967): 19.
[32] Annual message of Arthur Barclay to the legislature, December 11, 1906, in Dunn, *Annual Messages*, 447.

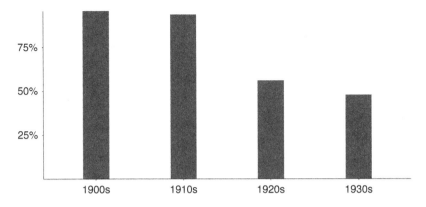

Figure 7.2 Customs revenue as a share of total
Source: See Chapter 1.

In 1907, a Bureau of Internal Revenue was established in an effort to improve and regularize collections, along with the Frontier Force, which was intended in part to help enforce tax collection. In 1909, President Barclay justified the expansion of taxation to the legislature in part as a means of reducing corruption in local administration.

If for the purpose of supporting the State formed for our benefit, we refuse to tax the population, the people will not thereby be helped for the same money or more will be paid in a thousand indirect ways for the protection and security which the authorities are to furnish. The trader, after paying his license to the state, will have to give further and larger sums to the local, and often self-created authority for some protection.[33]

World War I provided the first real spur to expanding the collection of a variety of new taxes. The most important of these was the hut tax. It had been introduced in law in 1910 but was not collected until 1915.[34] The same year saw the introduction of the emergency relief tax. Its aim, according to President Howard, was to "properly provide for the present officials." Revenue from these sources did help compensate for the sharp decline in customs revenue and the lack of payments from the Receivership, and the increase in internal revenue was a frequent bright spot in presidential annual addresses. "Within a period of thirteen years," Charles King reported in 1924, "these revenues, under absolute Liberian management and control, have exceeded a quarter of million [sic]

[33] Annual message of Arthur Barclay to the legislature, December 13, 1909, in Dunn, *Annual Messages*, 481.
[34] Augustine Konneh, "The Hut Tax in Liberia: The High Costs of Integration," *Journal of the GAH* XVI (1996): 48.

dollars." He went on to say that "all impartial observers must give some credit to Liberian financial initiative, ability and management."

From the beginning, however, the Liberian government struggled to collect these taxes, owing to resistance from taxpayers. In 1918, the fear of organized opposition to the hut tax among the "chiefs and tribes" of the interior prompted the Financial Adviser and the Secretary of the Treasury to discuss abolishing the tax, "in view of the fact that the Government has no ammunition to enforce its demands if it meets with active resistance." This proposal was blocked by the manager of the Bank of British West Africa, which was at that point subsidizing the Liberian government through a monthly loan.[35]

Resistance was not only from indigenous taxpayers. One of the biggest disappointments of the fiscal expansion undertaken during this period was the real estate tax, levied on Americo-Liberian property owners in cities and towns. It generated relatively little revenue throughout this period, in part due to resistance from taxpayers and irregularities in the assessment of real estate values. In 1914, Daniel Howard noted in his annual message that "there being no definite law laid down" with regard to assessment of real estate value for the purposes of taxation,

the assessors too often act in a most arbitrary manner in making these valuations. A case in point is fresh in my mind when, years ago, a certain person from Barnesville was appointed one of the assessors and who had a pique against a citizen of that settlement. When the assessment list came out, this poor individual's property was taxed far in excess of everyone else in the place.

A surviving set of letters from one of these assessors suggests that taxpayer cooperation was also a problem. T. W. Duignei-Leigh wrote to several higher government officials, including the Commissioner of Internal Revenue and the Superintendent of Grand Bassa County, where he was working, to complain about the failure of taxpayers to register their properties for taxation.[36]

You'll be very surprised, that after being here for the past two months in Lower Buchanan, having filed over 26 public notices to the different settlements for the registration of their properties, we have been able to receive 52% of deeds as compared with the old Registration. I have mentioned this, to confirm my repeated letters, in the lack of travelling facilities and expenses which were withheld us, in order to expedite the work.

[35] Financial adviser to Bundy, May 29, 1918, in US Department of State, *Papers Relating to the Foreign Relations of the United States, 1918* (Washington, DC: US Government Printing Office, 1930), 527–29.
[36] Internal Revenue Department, IULC Liberia Govt Papers.

He continued on to claim that "the government has been loosing [sic] over 75% of their real estate taxes."

In part as an effort to address these problems, the Liberian government began to decentralize the collection and expenditure of some internal revenue, giving over more power to district commissioners and chiefs. Daniel Howard noted in 1913 that "by appointing chiefs as collectors of taxes due by their subjects, paying them the same commission as is paid other tax collectors ... several hundred dollars have been collected as less cost to the Government and more satisfaction to the taxpayers than in previous years." In 1922, this was extended to allocating "5 per cent of from the hut tax collections from each native district towards the maintenance of schools in such districts."[37]

The decentralization of tax collection extended beyond cash revenue to include in-kind collections of various kinds. In 1911, Edwin Barclay reported that

the interior and district commissioners especially in Montserrado County, have done good work; many of them have remained at their post for terms of over two years at one time, and have manifested much diplomatic tact and adaptability in the management of their district within which they have raised the food necessary for feeding the police force stationed there to support their authority. The saving to the Treasury has amounted to about $30,000 yearly.

This method of decentralization provided an important foundation for the ways in which the Liberian government would seek to circumvent foreign financial controls in later years.

By 1927, therefore, the Liberian government had succeeded in developing new sources of revenue and increasing its financial independence from the Customs Receivership. However, the collection of these new taxes continued to suffer from the limited capacity of the Liberian government and its lack of control over officials working in the interior. In 1927, it lost control over even these sources of revenue to the foreign financial advisers. After that point, the government had limited options for retaining any sort of independence from foreign administration. The Liberian government's response to these constraints remained the same as in the pre-1927 period, namely: decentralization and the development of new revenue sources. However, given increasing foreign claims on tax revenues, this meant a turn toward in-kind revenue taxes at a local level, particularly in the form of labor taxes. This, then, was the backdrop to the League of Nations investigation of 1930.

[37] Annual message of Charles D. B. King to the legislature, December 19, 1922, in Dunn, *Annual Messages*, 614.

League of Nations Investigation

The immediate origin of the investigation was a letter from the American Secretary of State to his Liberian counterpart in 1929. It raised accusations of forced labor in the Republic which had been rumbling through diplomatic channels and the popular press through the 1920s. "There have come to the attention of the government of the United States from several sources reports bearing reliable evidence of authenticity which definitely indicate that existing conditions incident to the so-called 'export' of labor from Liberia to Fernando Po have resulted in the development of a system which seems hardly distinguishable from organized slave trade" and further that "in the enforcement of this system the services of the Liberian Frontier Force and the services and influence of certain high government officials are constantly and systematically used." The message added, rather ominously, that "it might not be possible to withhold the governments of the world from considering that some effective affirmative action should, if necessary, be invoked by them to terminate" the situation.[38]

The Liberian government responded to the allegations in the letter from the US Secretary of State by issuing a "solemn and categorical denial" of the charges, declaring that "the Government of the Republic will have no objection to this question being investigated on the spot by a competent, impartial and unprejudiced commission."[39] The 1926 Convention placed the question in the jurisdiction of the League of Nations, and the League duly established a Commission to investigate.

It was an invitation the Liberian government would come to regret. From the beginning, the composition and mission of the Commission were the subject of debate between the Liberian government and the League, rooted in wider political implications. This began with the appointment of the chair of the Commission. The League proposed Cuthbert Christy, who had wide experience in British colonial Africa as well as other regions of the world. Antoine Sottile, Liberia's representative to the League, said that "he felt sure that his Government would strongly object to the appointment of a British national, because of the fact that Liberia was surrounded by British possessions and British political influences gave rise to great suspicion."[40] These objections were

---

[38] Secretary of State to the Minister in Liberia, June 5, 1929, in US Department of State, *Papers Relating to the Foreign Relations of the United States, 1929, Volume I* (Washington, DC: US Government Printing Office, 1943), 274–75.

[39] Minister in Liberia to Secretary of State, June 13, 1929, in US Department of State, *Papers Relating to Foreign Relations of the United States 1929* (Washington, DC: US Government Printing Office, 1944), 277–78.

[40] 'Record of conversation', February 18, 1930, in LON 6B/14697/14352.

ignored by the League, and Christy joined two others in forming the Commission. The American appointee was Charles Spurgeon Johnson, an African-American sociologist. The third member of the Commission was former Liberian president Arthur Barclay, who Johnson described as "the sole ex-public official whose record invited international confidence."[41]

The members of the Commission met for the first time in Monrovia in March 1930.[42] From the beginning, they faced resistance from the government that had invited them. Just after his arrival in Monrovia, Christy wrote in his diary that "until they actually heard that I was on the way and that the Commission was unavoidable the Govt seems to have schemed its level best to prevent the Commission eventuating even after its arrival."[43] Johnson also noted this, describing Barclay's attitude as one of "cheerful noncooperation."[44]

While in Monrovia, the Commission met with a number of Liberian officials, including President King and his cabinet and representatives of the Firestone Rubber Plantations. Christy in particular kept a detailed diary of these encounters. In one entry shortly after his arrival in Liberia, Christy described being caught off guard by the formality of Liberian politics. He described his first meeting with President King as "the most trying occasion I have ever gone through. The President and all the Cabinet were elaborately and correctly dressed in black morning coats, striped trousers and patent-leather boots. I was only in a blue sere suit and Dr J[ohnson] in a dark grey one, the best we can do. No one had advised us as to dress."[45] In addition, they had casual meetings with various other members of the religious, economic, and political elite, described in great detail in Christy's diaries. Former Senator Twe provided "many useful details of districts, tribes, boundaries, habits, routes, etc, etc for an hour." The Bishop of Monrovia, Robert Campbell, "drank three glasses of whiskey and soda as if he liked it and had not had such a chance in years. Knows the whole country apparently and the people." Christy stayed for a time in a "hospitable and quite delightful Firestone bungalo [sic]" while recuperating from an illness in May, and both met with Firestone officials several times.

---

[41] Johnson, *Bitter Canaan*, 167.
[42] Cuthbert Christy diary, Christy papers volume 1, Cambridge University Library RCMS 124/8.
[43] Cuthbert Christy diary, Christy papers volume 1, Cambridge University Library, RCMS 124/8.
[44] Johnson, *Bitter Canaan*, 168.
[45] Diary of Cuthbert Christy, April 7, 1930, in Cambridge University Library, RCMS 124/8/1.

At the end of April, Christy and Johnson began their travels into the interior, while the elderly Barclay remained in Monrovia. They traveled first together to Kakata and Cape Palmas, then separated. Along the way they took testimony from local officials, chiefs, and others about the prevalence of forced labor. Most of the evidence in the report came from witness testimonies taken at hearings in Monrovia and various points in the interior. The number of people attending the hearings could be substantial, despite what both Christy and Johnson thought were government attempts to prevent people from coming. Two Frontier Force guards who initially attended the first hearings in Monrovia were removed early on as "a possible intimidation to native witnesses."[46] Furthermore, the coincidence of the Commission's investigation with the rainy season made travel difficult for both the commissioners and the witnesses. Still, the Commission managed to gather a considerable amount of evidence. The final report claimed that more than 3,000 had come to meetings in Maryland County alone. Overall, the committee drew on a total of 264 depositions in composing its report, along with both private and public documents, though the report observed that "the state of records in many of the bureaus made it very difficult to confirm or amplify testimony, and the virtual absence of records and statistics for any of the towns made it difficult to carry out any study of native social conditions."[47]

Some of what has subsequently been written on the Commission has drawn on this evidence to paint a more human picture of the kinds of abuses inflicted on Liberia's indigenous population.[48] Other work has looked beyond the report itself to focus on the international politics behind the Commission. What was sometimes seen as the unfair targeting Liberia sparked fierce debates among African Americans in the United States, in particular, as well as around the world.[49] No less than W. E. B. Du Bois wrote in defense of Liberia, in an article in *Foreign Affairs* in 1933, which argued that the condemnation of Liberia merely served the interests of Firestone. "Liberia is not faultless," he argued, "but her chief crime is to be black and poor in a rich, white world; and in precisely that portion of the world is ruthlessly exploited as a foundation for American and European wealth."[50] Nnamdi Azikiwe, who would later

[46] *Christy Report*, 8.   [47] *Christy Report*, 10.

[48] Monday B. Akpan, "Black Imperialism: Americo-Liberian Rule Over the African Peoples of Liberia, 1841–1964," *Canadian Journal of African Studies* 7 (1973): 217–36; Sundiata, *Black Scandal*.

[49] See Ibrahim K. Sundiata, *Brothers and Strangers: Black Zion, Black Slavery, 1914–1940* (Durham: Duke University Press, 2003).

[50] W. E. B. Du Bois, "Liberia, the League and the United States," *Foreign Affairs* 11, no. 4 (1933): 682–95.

become the first president of independent Nigeria in 1963, wrote while studying in the United States in the early 1930s that Liberia was being made a scapegoat for the forced labor practices suborned by all colonial governments as well as the United States.[51]

This chapter is interested less in the origins and effects of the investigation and more in what the investigation can reveal about how Liberian institutions reacted to the expansion of foreign financial controls. Owing to the type of evidence collected, the findings of the report were anecdotal rather than quantitative. However, the testimonies can serve to illustrate the structure and organization of forced labor requisitions, allowing subsequent sections to place them within the wider fiscal system of Liberia.

Liberian Systems of Forced Labor

The report acknowledged that systems of "domestic servitude" were "not confined to Liberia" but rather were "more or less prevalent throughout West Africa." The issue was "one of degree," and that policies had varied between countries. "While it is realized that in tropical African states and dependencies, where advanced and backward cultures are in contact, there is a certain educative advantage in compulsory labor, it is, at the same time, recognized that these ends are defeated and may degenerate into conditions analogous to slavery."[52] President King, in defending his government against the accusations of the US Secretary of State, noted that the 1926 Convention on Slavery signed by members of the League included a clause which explicitly permitted the use of forced labor for public purposes.[53] According to Suzanne Miers, the 1926 convention was watered down after pressure from metropolitan governments afraid of any proposals which might infringe on their own policies.[54]

There is now an extensive literature on the history of forced labor in sub-Saharan Africa, both before, during and after the colonial periods.[55] While colonial conquest was justified in part as a way of stopping the domestic trade in slaves, colonial governments had little capacity or

---

[51] Ben Nnamdi Azikiwe, "In defense of Liberia," *Journal of Negro History* 17, no. 1 (1932): 30–50.
[52] *Christy Report*, 16, 72.
[53] Annual message of Charles D. B. King to the legislature, October 30, 1929, in Dunn, *Annual Messages*, 759–86.
[54] Suzanne Miers, "Slavery and the Slave Trade as International Issues, 1890–1939," *Slavery and Abolition* 19, no. 2 (1998): 28.
[55] For a survey, see Richard Roberts, "Coerced Labor in Twentieth-Century Africa," in *Cambridge World History of Slavery, Volume 4: 1804–2016*, edited by David Eltis, Stanley Engerman, Seymore Drescher and David Richardson (Cambridge: Cambridge University Press, 2017), 583–609.

inclination to interfere with existing systems. Colonial officials were anxious to avoid the risk of resistance from African slave owners, or of any disruption in the production of export crops which might result. In addition to turning a blind eye to existing systems of forced labor, colonial governments added their own. Crawford Young describes forced labor as "of enormous importance" to colonial budgets.[56] Similarly, Marlous van Waijenburg argues that recent efforts to understand colonial fiscal systems have neglected the fact that "virtually all African colonial governments raised revenue through various in-kind levies, such as cattle, grains, and rubber, and through a broad spectrum of labor obligations."[57] She goes further in offering a tentative calculation of the value of such labor obligations to colonial budgets. Using a unique data source on French colonial corvée labor, she calculates an approximate implied contribution to colonial budgets, which fell from 70–100 percent of cash revenue in the early 1900s to around 20 percent in the interwar period. Nor was it only in West Africa that states turned to forced labor as a revenue generator. In his history of prison labor in the United States after emancipation, Douglas Blackmon notes that the leasing of prison labor to industrial and agricultural concerns was an important source of funds for Alabama and other southern states during the late nineteenth and early twentieth centuries.[58]

The anecdotal nature of the evidence presented in the League of Nations report, along with the fragmentary nature of Liberia's own records, means that it is impossible to calculate any similar statistics for Liberia. However, the League's report does show the development of systems of forced labor and local seizures of money and goods linked to the Liberian government's efforts to both diversify revenue sources and ensure the compensation of government employees even in the absence of sufficient cash revenue. The report focused particularly on three forms of forced labor: the coerced "export" of workers to other parts of West Africa; labor requisitions for road construction; and the pawning of relatives, particularly children, to pay for fines and fees levied by the Liberian government. While each of these systems had its own genesis in Liberia's particular economic and political history, it is argued here that they fit into a wider pattern by which the Liberian government hoped to

---

[56] Crawford Young, *The African Colonial State in Comparative Perspective* (New Haven: Yale University Press, 1994), 173, 131–32.

[57] Marlous van Waijenburg, "Financing the African Colonial State: The Revenue Imperative and Forced Labor," *Journal of Economic History* 78, no. 1 (2018): 44.

[58] Douglas Blackmon, *Slavery by Another Name: The Re-Enslavement of Black Americans from the Civil War to World War II* (London: Icon, 2012), 95. For an assessment of the wider economic impact of prison labor, see Michael Poyker. "Economic Consequences of the U.S. Convict Labor System." INET Working Paper No. 91 (2019).

diversify its tax system, particularly through the decentralization of revenue collections.

Of the three, most attention in both the report and in historical research on the League's investigation has been paid to the shipping of coerced laborers to work outside Liberia, most prominently though not exclusively to the cocoa plantations on Fernando Po. Labor migration to the island was nothing new in 1930, nor were attempts by the Liberian government to regulate and tax it.[59] Cocoa had revived the economic fortunes of the island when it was introduced in the 1850s, but planters struggled to overcome labor shortages created by the decline of the indigenous population.[60] Migrant workers initially came from across West Africa, and sometimes carried cocoa plants back to their home regions. However, as Sundiata writes, "Fernando Po's demand for workers coincided with other colonial regimes' attempts to organize labor for European use." Migration from British West Africa was cut off in 1900. By comparison, the slow development of export industries in Liberia meant there was limited domestic competition for labor. At the same time, the taxation of migrant workers provided a potential source of revenue.

From the 1890s, the Liberian government began to regulate labor recruitment, issuing licenses and requiring recruiters to post bonds for each worker, though such requirements were often waived in agreements with individual firms. Instead, companies like Woermann would pay a license fee and a $5 per worker to the Liberian government. In 1905, and then again in 1914, the Liberian government signed direct agreements with the Spanish administration of Fernando Po. The Commission estimated that "between 1919 and 1926 a total of 4,268 had been so recruited. Averaging 600 a year, the total number from 1914 to 1927, the period of the termination of the convention, would be at least 7,268."[61]

Though there had been previous efforts to restrict the shipment of laborers from Montserrado and Grand Bassa counties, home to the farms of many prominent Liberian officials, it was not until the coming of Firestone that the Liberian government ended its direct coordination with Spanish authorities. Instead, plantation interests from the island, represented by the Syndicato Agricola de Guinea, negotiated a private agreement with "a group of Liberian citizens," many of whom nevertheless had government ties. Under the agreement, the Syndicato paid Liberian recruiters a flat rate of £9.0.0 per laborer to cover the costs of

[59] See Sundiata, "Prelude to a Scandal."
[60] William G. Clarence-Smith, "African and European cocoa producers on Fernando Poo, 1880s to 1910s," *Journal of African History* 25, no. 2 (1994): 179–99.
[61] *Christy Report*, 53.

taxes, advances, and food, plus a bonus of £1,000 per 1,500 laborers.[62] It was this private arrangement that generated the most criticism from the Commission. "While the arrangement under Government supervision was regarded as a serious economic error, involving hazards of discomfort, death from disease, encouragement to slave methods, the private recruiting with such liberal sums paid for each labourer must certainly prove worse."[63]

The export of workers to Fernando Po was concentrated in spatial terms on the county of Maryland. The Commission's report argued that one consequence of heavy recruitment in this region was the depopulation of previously prosperous settlements. In Soloken,

the once fairly populous town now has a total of 651 inhabitants with thirty per cent more females than males. ... Most important, it seems, of the families remaining there 91 of their men and boys had either died at Fernando Po, or for some other reason failed to return or communicate with the tribe. ... The town Kordor, which is about two hours' walk from Soloken, was visited and photographed. Forty-one huts were inhabited at the time of the Fernando Po demands. All are deserted now, the town site overgrown with weeds and tough vines, the thatched roofs and mud covered sides crumbling in.

More widely distributed through the country was a road-building program that relied almost entirely on coerced labor. The government had begun a major campaign to construct roads from coastal centers into the interior during the 1920s. The stated goals of the program were "to recover the loss of produce and revenue vital to the Liberian market by diverting the course of the market from the British and French border which has been due to lack of routes of transportation to Liberian ports" and "to provide a network of roads, through the more populous and developed areas, thus facilitating the transportation of raw materials."[64] The road program was initially praised by American officials. In 1925, the American charge d'affaires wrote that "the Liberian government should be commended on the progress of its road building program. Though there are no statistics available on the number of automotive vehicles in Liberia, it is safe to state that in all Liberia there are over 100."[65]

The use of forced labor for road construction was hardly unique to Liberia, which the report acknowledged. The report thus focused on what the Commission saw as the problematic implementation of the policy which increased the hardships it caused. First, recruited workers were rarely if ever paid by the Liberian government, unlike what was at least

---

[62] *Christy Report*, 36.   [63] *Christy Report*, 37.   [64] *Christy Report*, 48.
[65] Liberia Commerce and Industries report, 1925, 61, in NARA RG 84, UD 584, Volume 43.

claimed by other governments. "The purport of the universally reiterated complaints of the chiefs and people is not that they object to taxes but to the fact that in addition to finding the men they have to pay for their food, pay for their tools, pay numerous fines, and are subjected to ill-treatment; all in the face of no remuneration whatever."[66]

Second, poor planning of the road network relative to the distribution of population meant that roads were often built in areas where workers had to travel far from their homes for road work. The report noted that "the lack of census returns, the lack of interest on the part of the district commissioners, and the self-interest of the chiefs makes an equable arrangement difficult." Furthermore, practices were inconsistent. According to the report, "between sections, the number of laborers required, the length of time spent on roads, the fines for delinquencies, as well as the method of imposing and collecting them, very considerably. This in itself reflected a weak and often ineffectual central supervision and control over policies."[67]

Another feature of this system was the levying of seemingly arbitrary fines by members of the Frontier Force and other local officials. If any of the aforementioned conditions were not met, witnesses claimed, they could be fined by district commissioners. A town chief testified that "if you do not send the boys on the road they fine you; they tie you with a long stick on your back." Another chief said that the district commissioner

fines people for the smallest things. One day he say my people had killed a chicken of his and he made me pay for it. One of my boys found a pig belonging to him dead in the bush. He made me pay £1.10/- apparently on the pretext that the boy had killed it and sent the boy the work on the road.[68]

It was most often the payment of these fines that led to the third form of forced labor that was the focus of the report, namely: pawning, or the use of people as collateral for debts. As a general practice, pawning was widespread in West Africa during the precolonial period, perhaps a natural outgrowth of a system of property rights focused on scarce labor.[69] It was used extensively during the Atlantic slave trade, when both people and gold could be pawned. Like many forms of domestic forced labor, pawning continued to be used during the colonial period, in particular as a means of coping with economic hardship and the pressures of colonial taxation.[70]

---

[66] *Christy Report*, 76.   [67] *Christy Report*, 80.   [68] *Christy Report*, 84–85.
[69] Paul Lovejoy, "Pawnship, Debt and 'Freedom' in Atlantic Africa during the Era of the Slave Trade: A Reassessment," *Journal of African History* 55 (2014): 66–67.
[70] Martin A. Klein and Richard Roberts, "The Resurgence of Pawning in French West Africa during the Depression of the 1930s," *African Economic History* 15 (1987): 23–37.

In Liberia, according to Martin Ford, pawnship became part of the reward structure of the expanding interior administration.[71] The Commission collected numerous accounts from people who had been involved in pawning in some way. Many of the witnesses were chiefs or headmen and testified that pawning their relatives was a means of repaying fines levied for failing to recruit sufficient labor. Most commonly the pawns were their own children. This was the case for Jadgua, a headman from Kanga, who was fined £18.0.2 for road delinquencies and pawned his wife and child for £7.0.0. Johnny Carr, town chief of Bengonow, pawned his son for an undisclosed sum after being fined £17.12.6 for road delinquencies. Varnai Quai, a headman from Baimeh, was fined a similar amount for failure to provide carriers and road labor, and pawned his two sons for £8 and £7, respectively. Varney pawned his sister for £3 to help repay £14.0.0. For those who were not chiefs, taxes were the impetus for pawning. One witness at Kakata testified that he had pawned his children for tax money. A town chief of the same area said that his people had placed their children in pawn to Vais to get money for food and fines. As Ford puts it, "one way for town chiefs to avoid mistreatment or incarceration was to give livestock and children in pledge to their administrative superiors in return for cash."[72]

Like the coercion of workers for Fernando Po, labor requisitions for the road program and the related fines and seizures had the effect of impoverishing the interior. According to the report,

they tried to make clear their position by comparing themselves now with times not so far past, when they possessed little herds of cattle and goats, sheep and chickens, and their wants were reasonably supplied. Now, they assert, most of them have nothing, not even chickens. Their chickens and live stock are required by soldiers, messengers, and officials whom they dare not refuse.

Forced Labor and Foreign Financial Controls

In the aftermath of the report's publication, the Liberian government attempted to lay the blame on individual officials. If this were a court of law, a defense attorney for the Liberian government in this period might describe the evidence presented here as circumstantial. Owing to the limited survival of internal government records from the period, it is

---

[71] Martin Ford, "Indirect Rule and the Brief Apogee of Pawnship in Nimba, Liberia, 1918–1930," in *Pawnship, Slavery and Colonialism in Africa*, edited by Paul E. Lovejoy and Toyin Falola (Trenton, NJ: Africa World Press, 2003), 283–98.
[72] Ibid, 287.

difficult to provide direct proof of a policy shift which decentralized revenue to local officials in the ways described earlier. However, there are two further pieces of evidence on the prosecution's side. The first is that the revenue, in cash and in kind, generated through these systems was retained locally. The second is that state involvement in the recruitment of labor and collection of fines appears to have gone well beyond a small number of corrupt officials

It is clear from both the revenue statistics given earlier that the revenues raised through labor requisitions and related fines were not accounted for in central government revenues. The report also makes it clear that the revenues were retained locally. The Commission's report noted that "at all events, if accounts before the commission are to be in any way relied upon, the government exchequer derives no benefit whatever from these fines. The practice permits of infinite abuse and requires further and deliberate investigation through the Department of Internal Revenue. Without question, fines are levied. And yet the Secretary of Public Works asserts that these do not come officially into the Department."[73]

It might be argued, as the Liberian representative to the League did, that this was not so much Liberian government policy as reflective of its lack of capacity and inability to enforce the law. However, based on the witness testimonies, the Commission was clear that the system relied heavily on public resources and officials to operate. On the recruitment of labor to Fernando Po, the report noted that "public officials, messengers and soldiers are used systematically and mandatorily to assist in the recruiting of these laborers." Furthermore, it added that "no private citizen without the implied authority of high Government office could command such a monopoly unrestricted, or with impunity employ the channels of Government so completely to his private ends."[74]

Witness testimonies suggest that not only did the government not act to prevent such low-level corruption, it seemed to punish those raising complaints. Statements of those affected by the Fernando Po traffic noted the use of political intimidation against those who protested. P. C. Lemandine, who had served as Commissioner of Sinoe District in 1924, testified:

During my term of service many boys were sent from the interior by Capt. Howard to Mr. Ross for shipment to Fernando Po. They were sent down under military escort with rice and were detained by Mr. Ross, who placed an armed guard over them till the steamer arrived. . . . I made a complaint to the President

---

[73] *Christy Report*, 94.   [74] *Christy Report*, 57.

and to the Secretary of the Interior. To those communications I never got any reply, and was shortly afterwards relieved of my post.[75]

In his deposition, Chief Sodokeh said:

Since last year Vice President Yancy has been making demands on me for boys for Fernando Po. I have refused to comply with his request, and the Vice President Yancy has openly stated that he will oppress me for this refusal. He sent Commissioner Frederick Proud to arrest me, and I was tied up and taken down to Cape Palmas.[76]

While the money and in-kind revenue generated by fines, pawning, and seizures of crops may not have come directly into the Liberian Treasury, it did provide an alternative form of compensation for government officials during a period of fiscal crisis for the central government. With cash revenue largely hypothecated to debt service, the Liberian government relied on such means to support local officials and retain its alliances with local elites. According to Martin Ford, "military and civilian officials went without pay for many months and turned to living off the local population by extracting labor, materials and cash."[77] Efforts by the government to shield this system from view suggest this was by design not neglect.

The Christy Commission's findings meant that Liberia entered the 1930s as an international pariah. Governments around the world, no matter their own labor practices, reacted harshly in public. On January 7, 1931, Liberia made a rare appearance on the front page of the *New York Times*. "In one of the most scathing notes handed a foreign government since war days," the paper reported, "the State Department has threatened what comes close to a break with Liberia unless that country makes some move to abolish slavery and clean out the high officials responsible for it." The article speculated that it was this threat which prompted the resignations of both President King and Vice President Yancey even as the Liberian delegate to the League of Nations denounced the findings of the report.

The internal reaction was no easier, and the Liberian government's handling of the situation contributed to the international pressure. The Kru Coast, which had been the site of rebellions during World War I, erupted again in 1931. This prompted a brutal response from Monrovia, which was condemned by the League and by the British

---

[75] Mr. P. C. Lemandine deposition, Cuthbert Christy papers, vol. 6, Cambridge University Library, RCMS 124/8.
[76] Chief Sodokeh deposition, Cuthbert Christy papers, vol. 6, Cambridge University Library, RCMS 124/8.
[77] Ford, "Indirect Rule and the Brief Apogee of Pawnship in Nimba," 285.

and American governments.[78] Together, the scale of the international scandal and the continued economic and financial effects of the Great Depression represented a grave threat to Liberian sovereignty, as both League officials and foreign governments speculated that Liberia had no choice but to become a protectorate.[79]

If the intent of foreign financial controls was indeed to improve the efficiency and equity of the Liberian fiscal system, they were not successful in doing so. Such failure was not unique to Liberia, and even to this day there remain debates about the extent to which foreign interventions are capable of improving institutions in poor countries. The controversies surrounding the publication of the League's report meant that the system it documented was not a sustainable solution to the problem. The next three chapters show that from the 1940s onward, the Liberian government proved increasingly adept at exploiting what comparative advantages existed for small, independent states in a rapidly changing world. However, Liberian elites still struggled to distribute the gains from those strategies widely enough to build a stable social order.

---

[78] D. C. Dorward, "British West Africa and Liberia," in *The Cambridge History of Africa, Volume 7: From 1905 to 1940*, edited by A. D. Roberts (Cambridge: Cambridge University Press, 1986), 459.

[79] Liebenow, *Liberia*, 65; "Strategic Survey of Liberia," July 10, 1942, in NARA Military Intelligence Division regional files RG 165, Entry 77, Box 2395. Declass NND745020.

Part III

Sovereignty for Sale?

8   An African Marshall Plan

In July 1947, Liberia celebrated its centenary as an independent nation. The festivities included a play, church services, and a series of speeches by Liberian and foreign politicians. One of the speeches was delivered by Brigadier General Benjamin Davis, at the time the highest-ranking African American in the United States armed forces, who had been a military adviser to Liberia before World War I. In his speech he made it clear that the granting of American aid would be conditional on reforms in Liberian governance. "I feel sure that there is a very clear ratio between the total of American capital which will be available to Liberia, and the wisdom and vision with which the Liberian Republic manages its own affairs," he said. He compared American efforts in Liberia to the Marshall Plan in Europe, noting that "Secretary of State Marshall, in a recent address at Harvard University, pointed out to the nations of Europe that it was precisely these terms of measurement" – including the degree of cooperation of the recipient governments – "which would determine the ability of the United States to aid these countries in recovering from the ravages of war."[1]

The speech irritated Liberian officials, according to subsequent diplomatic correspondence. A telegram from the Monrovia Legation to the American Secretary of State noted that "Liberians also object to the fact that no mention made of Liberia's contributions and cooperation with US and its policy towards this country." Other attendees also picked up on the theme. According to the telegram, the British minister characterized the main message as, "you be a good boy and we will continue to help you."[2] Despite this irritation, foreign aid became an important source of foreign capital for the Liberian government in the decades after the war.

The four chapters in Part II examined the difficulties the Liberian government faced in exercising economic sovereignty with limited

---

[1] Address by Brigadier General Benjamin O. Davis, in NARA RG 59 882.6351/12–3149, Box 7146.
[2] Telegram from Monrovia Legation, August 22, 1947, in NARA RG 59 882.6351/12–3149, Box 7146.

resources, and argued that policies regarding trade, money, and debt reflected difficult dilemmas about the terms of Liberia's engagement with the global economy. In Part III, the book explores three ways in which Liberian elites leveraged the external recognition of the state to raise resources for their own survival. In so doing, they presaged the strategies adopted by many African states after independence to use that recognition to compensate for limited domestic authority. Historians and political scientists have offered various labels for such strategies. Frederick Cooper describes African states as "gatekeeper states," which sat "astride the interface between a territory and the rest of the world, collecting and distributing resources that derived from that point itself."[3] Jean-Francois Bayart outlines the "strategies of extraversion" by which African elites over the centuries have used resources derived from unequal relationship to the global economy "to compensate for their difficulties in the autonomization of their power."[4]

In the decades following 1945, foreign aid became an important part of such strategy. During the Cold War, foreign financial assistance was one of a number of diplomatic tools used by the United States, the USSR, and other governments. Though ostensibly intended to promote development or democratization, geopolitical priorities meant that aid was often not contingent on outcomes.[5] It therefore became one tool used by African elites to sustain what became increasingly autocratic governments. As Cooper observes, "even a modest amount of economic or military aid could be a major patronage resource to a leader, or to an insurgency trying to topple or evade the gatekeeping state."[6] The Liberian government was one such example. Other such resources came from foreign concessions (Chapter 9) and the Liberian shipping registry (Chapter 10).

General Davis's comparison with the Marshall Plan in Europe was apt, as it generated many of the same debates and questions which would apply to aid programs in countries like Liberia. Europe also enjoyed a period of rapid economic growth during the postwar "golden age."[7] Contemporaries, and some later historians, credited Marshall aid with playing a major role in that growth. According to Michael Latham,

---

[3] Frederick Cooper, *Africa since 1940: The Past of the Present* (Cambridge: Cambridge University Press, 2019), 235.

[4] Jean-Francois Bayart, *The State in Africa: The Politics of the Belly* (Harlow: Longman, 1993), 21–24.

[5] Crawford Young, *The Postcolonial State in Africa: Fifty Years of Independence, 1960–2010* (Madison: University of Wisconsin Press, 2012), 15.

[6] Cooper, *Africa since 1940*, 239.

[7] N. F. R. Crafts, "The Golden Age of Economic Growth in Western Europe, 1950–1973," *Economic History Review* 48, no. 3 (1995): 429–47.

"American optimism about the potential for engineering sweeping transformations abroad was raised by the occupation of Japan and the reconstruction of Western Europe. ... Both appeared to prove that US interventions in foreign societies could produce impressive economic growth and lasting reforms."[8] However, later work has challenged the link between European growth and Marshall Plan interventions. In a preview of later debates on aid effectiveness, critics argued that the resources devoted to Marshall were insufficient to promote the kind of economic recovery seen in Europe, and that by flooding European markets with American goods might have actually restricted growth.[9] European governments also chafed at the policy prescriptions of American technical advisers, and opposition to Marshall aid often influenced domestic politics of recipient countries.[10]

The same ideas about modernization which underpinned the Marshall Plan, including the "firm expectation that expert planning could make the United States' own historical experience a kind of universal template," also influenced American policy toward Liberia.[11] By 1947, Liberia's fortunes had taken a dramatic turn, both economically and geopolitically. Diplomatic relations with the United States had resumed in 1935, and by the early 1940s, Liberia was home to thousands of American troops as well as the Allied military planes that helped bring victory in the North Africa campaign. Over the course of the 1940s and 1950s, Liberia became one of the biggest per capita recipients of American foreign assistance in the world (see Figure 8.1).

---

[8] Michael Latham, *The Right Kind of Revolution: Modernization, Development and US Foreign Policy from the Cold War to the Present* (Ithaca: Cornell University Press, 2011), 30.

[9] See, for example, Susan Collins and Dani Rodrik, *Eastern Europe and the Soviet Union in the World Economy* (Washington, DC: Institute for International Economics, 1991); Alan S. Milward, *The Reconstruction of Western Europe, 1945–51* (London: Methuen, 1987) and Chiarella Esposito, *America's Feeble Weapon: Funding the Marshall Plan in France and Italy* (Westport, CT: Greenwood Press, 1994). For a more positive take, see Barry Eichengreen, Marc Uzan, Nicholas Crafts, and Martin Hellwig, "The Marshall Plan: Economic Effects and Implications for Eastern Europe and the Former USSR," *Economic Policy* 7, no. 14 (1992): 130–75; Timothy Besley and Torsten Persson, *Pillars of Prosperity: The Political Economics of Development Clusters* (Princeton: Princeton University Press, 2011). For a thoughtful review taking broader political considerations into account, see Ben Steil, *The Marshall Plan: Dawn of the Cold War* (New York: Simon and Schuster, 2018), ch. 13.

[10] Michael J. Hogan, *The Marshall Plan: America, Britain and the Reconstruction of Western Europe, 1947–52* (Cambridge: Cambridge University Press, 1987), ch. 2; Tony Judt, *Postwar: A History of Europe Since 1945* (London: Vintage, 2010), 96.

[11] Latham, *The Right Kind of Revolution*, 31.

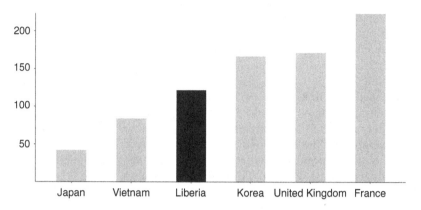

Figure 8.1 Per capita US aid, 1946–1961 Total US$ per capita
Source: US Agency for International Development, *US Foreign Assistance from International Organizations* (Washington, DC, 1962).

From 1946 to 1961, it received more aid per capita from the United States than Japan or Vietnam and only slightly less than Korea or the United Kingdom under the Marshall Plan. In his history of American aid and economic diplomacy, Ekbladh stresses the importance of Asia, which he describes as seeing "the largest and most intense application of these ideas." South Korea, in particular became a "proving ground" for American ideas about modernization.[12] As Liberia's population was substantially smaller, the total amount of aid received by Liberia was also much lower. However, contemporaries placed Liberia in the same category. A 1951 State Department policy paper described it as "a proving ground for President Truman's Point IV program to show that underdeveloped areas are capable of rapid economic progress."[13] At the same time, Liberian officials also objected to the conditions attached to aid which they saw as infringements on their sovereignty, and there were frequent tensions between the two governments over the setting of priorities and control over development projects.

[12] David Ekbladh, *The Great American Mission: Modernization and the Construction of an American World Order* (Princeton: Princeton University Press, 2011), 7–9.
[13] US Department of State Policy Statement, January 10, 1951, in US Department of State, *Papers Relating to the Foreign Relations of the United States 1951, Volume V* (Washington, DC: Government Printing Office, 1982), 1276.

Foreign Assistance in Liberia, 1942–1970

From the 1940s, foreign assistance – and in particular American foreign assistance – became an important source of funds for the Liberian government. Measuring the precise scale of these transfers is not necessarily straightforward. In the 1960s, the OECD's Development Assistance Committee, comprised of leading donor countries, defined net overseas development assistance as "financial flows to developing countries from the official sector (essentially, government and multilateral institutions) that have the promotion of economic development and welfare as their main objectives, and that are on concessional financial terms: either grants, or loans at interest rates substantially below a reference rate."[14] There remain debates about how to count technical assistance or other in-kind transfers, and spending commitments often differ from actual expenditures. However, no such standard definitions existed in the 1940s when these flows first began. During and after the war, aid came from various institutional sources and definitions of categories remained flexible.[15]

As a result of these confusions, available series of data on Liberian foreign aid do not all agree with each other precisely in terms of the allocation of aid to different financial years. However, the three sets of data presented in Figure 8.2 tell the same basic story. Aid began at a high level in the 1940s. In 1943, the Liberian government received a $12.5 million loan under the Lend–Lease program for the construction of the Port of Monrovia. This was more than ten times government expenditure of around $1 million at the time. It was also more than double the amount of Colonial Development and Welfare funds devoted by the British government to the whole of British West Africa (Nigeria, the Gold Coast, Sierra Leone, and the Gambia) during the period from 1940 to 1943, the three years following the passage of the Colonial Development and Welfare Act, which summed to £1.3 ($5.2) million.[16] In 1946, the USAID data reported aid equivalent to nearly 300 percent of the Liberian government's expenditure in that year.

At the end of the 1940s, aid flows declined in nominal terms before increasing again in the early 1960s. This reflected, in part, a shift in

---

[14] Some critics argue that this definition can be misleading. For example, loans are counted at face value, net of principal repayments but not of interest. See Jonathan R. W. Temple, "Aid and Conditionality," in *Handbook of Development Economics Volume 5*, edited by Dani Rodrik and Mark Rosenzweig (Amsterdam: North-Holland, 2010), 4425.

[15] Ekbladh, *Great American Mission*, 11–13.

[16] Michael Havinden and David Meredith, *Colonialism and Development: Britain and Its Tropical Colonies, 1850–1950* (London: Routledge, 1993), Table 10.9.

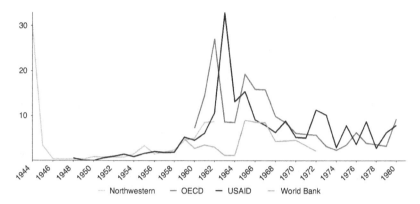

Figure 8.2 US foreign development assistance to Liberia, 1946–1970 (current US$ millions)
Source: USAID; Clower et al., *Growth without Development*; OECD.

American government policy.[17] Enthusiasm for aid under President Truman gave way to skepticism and cuts under Dwight Eisenhower when he took office in 1953. The Truman Doctrine itself, articulated on Truman's second inauguration in 1949, had stressed the provision of technical assistance rather than financial transfers. Eisenhower was a noted skeptic of aid programs, and overall American aid flows fell in the early 1950s, as the Eisenhower administration made the case for "trade not aid." During this period the power of the Export–Import Bank expanded even as the aid budget shrank. Competition with Russia, which began providing extensive aid to India and other strategically important countries, prompted Eisenhower to rethink this strategy. Overall funds devoted to foreign aid increased gradually in the late 1950s, in Liberia as well as other African countries – Libya, Morocco, Tunisia, and Ethiopia also received substantial sums, though in all cases except Libya they were smaller than Liberia in per capita terms.[18] US foreign aid expenditures then expanded dramatically in the 1960s under the administrations of John F. Kennedy and Lyndon Johnson. What Kennedy declared the "decade of development" saw the establishment of the US Agency for International Development and an aggressive policy of economic diplomacy shaped by the theories of Walt Rostow, who argued that foreign

[17] For an overview, see Jeffrey F. Taffet, "Foreign Economic Aid," in *Oxford Research Encyclopedia of American History*, edited by John Butler (Oxford: Oxford University Press, 2013).
[18] US AID, *US Foreign Assistance*.

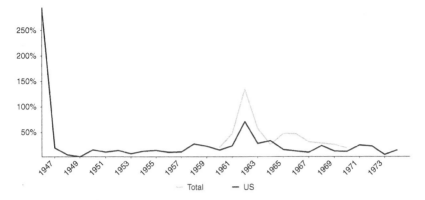

Figure 8.3 US and total foreign aid as a share of Liberian government expenditure
Source: As for Figure 8.2.

aid might facilitate the movement of economies through the various "stages" of economic development.

Rapid growth in Liberian government revenue and expenditure across the postwar decades meant that as a share of expenditure this aid was less substantial than it had been in the 1940s, but in years when large flows of aid were received, they could still be larger than total government expenditure (see Figure 8.3). "For a country whose national income is less than $200 million," wrote Robert Clower and his co-authors in 1962, "the tens of millions in grants and loans provided over the years represent very substantial amounts."[19]

During the 1940s and 1950s, the US government was virtually the sole source of foreign aid, but it was soon joined by other countries. Germany became a major donor in the 1950s, beginning with a $3.5 million credit extended in December 1951. In January 1962, the German government made a further grant of $675,000 to construct a vocational school. Further long-term loans followed. Swedish programs of technical assistance also began in 1961. During the 1960s, Britain, France, Italy, and Israel also joined the list of donors to Liberia.

The grants and loans of donor countries were intended to address a wide range of issues. For example, in 1962, US aid was spread across the areas of agriculture, transportation, health and sanitation, education, public administration, and natural resources, among others. Education

[19] Robert W. Clower, George Dalton, Mitchell Harwitz and A. A. Walters, *Growth Without Development: An Economic Survey of Liberia* (Evanston: Northwestern University Press, 1966), 361.

was the most important of these in terms of the share of total funding (45.7 percent), followed by transportation and public health. German and Swedish programs also emphasized education and training, alongside health and sanitation. A significant contributor to the spike in US foreign assistance in the early 1960s was the creation of a large Peace Corps program in 1962 that saw 100 Americans arrive to serve as teachers in Liberia.

Flows of foreign aid in the postwar period were thus important, but also uneven in their intensity and varied in their targets. The provision of aid was the product of complex negotiation between the Liberian government and its donors, whose positions were shaped by domestic and international political agendas. Officials at the time were occasionally clear-eyed about their limitations. The recently retired US Ambassador to Liberia wrote to the US Secretary of State Dean Acheson in 1946, "on the basis of accomplishment, there may be little or no justification for the maintenance of an economic mission in Liberia." However, he argued, the potential future benefits of both countries – economic and strategic – meant that, at least in his opinion, "it would not be to the best interests of the two countries to abandon altogether these activities."[20] Adding to the complexity were difficulties in implementation due to both agency problems among American staff posted to Liberia as well as a lack of technical, administrative, and financial capacity in Liberia itself.

Past as Prologue: Tuskegee in Liberia

Histories of American aid and economic diplomacy during and after World War II are quick to point out that the ideas behind them were not new. As Latham puts it, "modernization was grounded in older imperial assumptions about the United States's ability to transform a foreign world, the legacies of Wilsonian thinking about the meaning of modernity, and shifting understandings of race, culture and the perils of revolutionary change." Such ideas had shaped US government policies ranging from the colonization of the Philippines to dollar diplomacy in Liberia, the Caribbean, and Central America.[21] Nor was the US government the only proponent. Private sector institutions, from corporations to universities to charitable foundations, also took up the cause and their experiences often informed subsequent aid efforts.[22] In Liberia, the

---

[20] Walton to Acheson, April 16, 1946, in NARA RG 59 882.63A.
[21] Latham, *The Right Kind of Revolution*, 11–16.
[22] Ekbladh, *Great American Mission*, 23.

establishment of the Booker T. Washington institute in Kakata provides a useful prologue to the history of foreign aid programs.

The institute had its origins in 1909, when American philanthropist Olivia Egerton Phelps-Stokes wrote to Booker T. Washington and proposed the creation of an agricultural and industrial school in Liberia. The school was to be modeled after Washington's Tuskegee Institute in Alabama, and in future years the project would often be referred to as "Tuskegee in Liberia."[23] Stokes was a benefactor of Tuskegee, along with numerous other causes in the United States related to the African-American and Native American populations. However, as her nephew Anson observed later, "there were few matters in which Miss Stokes was so deeply interested as in Liberia," due to her family's long involvement with the ACS and Liberia. Her grandfather, Anson Green Phelps, had been a founder of the New York Colonization Society and a benefactor of Liberia College through $50,000 left to the institution in his will in 1858.[24] Anson even claimed that "the first flag of the Republic of Liberia was made at her grandfather's home."[25]

For his part, Washington was enthusiastic, but wary. It was not his first venture into Africa; in 1900, he had sent three Tuskegee graduates and a faculty member to German Togo to establish an experimental cotton farm.[26] That project had originated in an approach not from any American interest but rather from the German government, via Baron Beno von Herman auf Wain, appointed agricultural attaché to the United States in 1895. According to Zimmerman, the position of agricultural attaché and the partnership with Tuskegee were motivated by the desire to transplant American methods of cotton growing using black labor to its colony in West Africa. Booker T. Washington's support for a colonial development project in Africa reflected the "ambivalent politics" of both Tuskegee and its founder toward the supposed "civilizing mission" of colonialism, an ambivalence also reflected in what became the complicated domestic politics of the Liberia project.

In his initial response to Stokes's proposal in October 1909, Washington suggested that it might be better to start with bringing Liberians to Tuskegee to study. "To start an industrial school at present might not be a successful thing," he wrote, "taking for the reason that they

---

[23] Booker T. Washington to Olivia E. P. Stokes, October 27, 1909, Phelps-Stokes Fund papers, NYPL Sc MG 162, Box 113, Folder 10.
[24] Gregg Mitman, *Empire of Rubber: Firestone's Scramble for Land and Power in Liberia* (New York: The New Press, 2021), 141.
[25] Draft announcement, July 20, 1928, NYPL Sc MG 162, Box 113, Folder 10.
[26] Andrew Zimmerman, *Alabama in Africa: Booker T. Washington, the German Empire, and the Globalization of the New South* (Princeton: Princeton University Press, 2010).

would not have proper backing in the way of teachers who understand the methods and policies to be pursued at an industrial school thoroughly enough to make a success."[27] Eventually, however, he seemed to warm to the idea, and drew parallels with Yale University's establishment of a college in China, writing: "I believe that through our influence and work at Tuskegee we could develop a school in Liberia that would prove most helpful to the civilization and Christianization of that part of Africa."[28]

Washington's death in 1915 led to these plans being momentarily shelved, as Washington's colleagues at Tuskegee were less optimistic about the plan than he had been.[29] Interest in the project was, however, revived later in the 1920s by James L. Sibley, author of a report on education in Liberia and eventually the Liberian Institute's first principal. Olivia Phelps-Stokes herself died in December 1927, but left the project $50,000 in her will. Under the authority of her nephew, the Phelps-Stokes Trust gave an additional $25,000, as did the Methodist Church, giving Tuskegee in Liberia an initial endowment of $100,000.[30] The sitting president of Liberia, Charles King, was enthusiastic and pledged another $5,000 a year in government funds, along with land in Kakata. An act to charter the Booker Washington Industrial and Agricultural Institute of Liberia was passed by the Liberian legislature in December 1928, and a ceremonial Founders Day celebration was held in Kakata.

After this apparently auspicious beginning, however, the Institute got off to a difficult start. In June 1929, Sibley died of yellow fever in Monrovia, an event which no doubt reminded Tuskegee staff of similar tragedies associated with the Togo project. In 1902, two out of a group of five Tuskegee students drowned when their landing boat capsized on arrival in Togo, and later that summer a Tuskegee staff member died of fever. The deaths of their colleagues made it impossible to recruit any further Tuskegee students or staff to make the journey, and by 1908 the colonial government had taken over the model farms established at Tove and Notse.[31]

Similarly, Sibley's death halted progress on the Kakata school, at least temporarily. At a special meeting of the Advisory Committee on

---

[27] Booker T. Washington to Olivia E. P. Stokes, October 27, 1909, Phelps-Stokes Fund papers, NYPL Sc MG 162, Box 113, Folder 10.

[28] Booker T Washington to Olivia E. P. Stokes, December 3, 1909, in Phelps-Stokes Fund papers, NYPL Sc MG 162, Box 113, Folder 10.

[29] R. R. Moton to Olivia Stokes, September 26, 1916, Phelps-Stokes Fund papers, NYPL Sc MG 162, Box 113, Folder 10.

[30] Minutes of meeting of Advisory Committee on Education in Liberia, June 6, 1929, in Phelps-Stokes Fund papers, NYPL Sc MG 162, Box 114, Folder 8.

[31] Zimmerman, *Alabama in Africa*, 7–8.

Education in Liberia, the body which managed the funds raised in the United States, "the Committee was clearly of the opinion that before any plans could be made for the continuation of the work, every possible effort should be made to work out some scheme for cleaning up Monrovia and establishing on a permanent basis in Liberia such sanitary methods as are known to be effective in controlling or eliminating yellow fever." The Committee gave $7,500 to a "Yellow Fever Fund" intended to support such efforts, though through both lack of local capacity and the resistance of the Liberian government, the funds were never spent.[32] By November 1930, the Committee was deliberating whether to abandon the project altogether. It decided to continue, and the school soon came into operation.[33] Its progress was again interrupted by both the fiscal crisis caused by the Great Depression and the political crisis that came after the League of Nations report. The promised $5,000 a year from the Liberian government did not appear, and as late as 1935 there were few signs that it ever would. Jackson Davis, a member of the committee, reported after a visit in April of that year that it would need to await "further improvement" in the revenue.[34]

It was perhaps due to these financial difficulties that observers at the time reported poor conditions at the school. In July 1938, the Supervisor of Schools for the Liberian government sent a scathing letter to the Institute complaining about the state of accommodation for students. Among other issues, she noted: "there seems to be no accommodation for the sick students. I saw a sick boy, suffering with pneumonia, I was told, lying on his cot in the same room that housed all of the other students." The coverings of the cots and beds "were badly in need of soap and water," and the dining hall was also dirty. The "water closet" was merely "an open place dug into the ground with no covering of any sort," which the inspector described as "a menace to health."[35]

The Institute promised to resolve these problems by building a new dormitory, among other improvements (on which they received assistance from a Firestone engineer). However, they remained restricted in the number of students they could accept due to lack of both funds and teaching staff. In his 1942 report, Embree wrote:

---

[32] Minutes of meeting of Advisory Committee on Education in Liberia, July 2, 1929, in Phelps-Stokes Fund papers, NYPL Sc MG 162, Box 114, Folder 8.

[33] Minutes of meeting of Advisory Committee on Education in Liberia, November 25, 1930, in Phelps-Stokes Fund papers, NYPL Sc MG 162, Box 114, Folder 8.

[34] Jackson Davis, "Impressions of Liberia, March 31-April 12, 1935," in Phelps-Stokes Fund papers, NYPL Sc MG 162, Box 116, Folder 1.

[35] Report of the Supervisor of Schools, Republic of Liberia, July 14, 1938, in Phelps-Stokes Fund papers, NYPL Sc MG 162, Box 116, Folder 7.

[O]ne of the most encouraging, yet heartbreaking conditions in this respect is the flood of new students who desire each year to enter BWI, but for whom we have only a strictly limited amount of space or money. We opened registration of applications for new students for 1942 on December 1st. Before the day was over we had interviewed over thirty applicants for the places left vacant by nine graduates. The list is now over fifty and many have been turned away.[36]

Adding to the Institute's difficulties, but also part of the patchwork of support networks that allowed it to continue functioning, were its continued entanglements with other American interventions, both political and economic. In 1932, the Advisory Committee dispatched Harry L. West on a trip to Geneva and Liberia to assess what the Institute's response should be to the scandal surrounding the League of Nations investigation. "In a conference with Mr. Grimes, the Liberian representative at Geneva," he learned "that the Liberian government has no goodwill toward the Firestone Company; that they distrust the United States State Department and are generally anti-American." West encountered further difficulties when he arrived in Monrovia. At a reception held in his honor by President Barclay he "learned of rumors that were circulating to the effect that he was coming to Liberia to take charge of the country, and that, as President of the American Colonization Society, he intended to claim about half of the territory of the country under an old deed given to the Society in the early days of Liberian settlement." The BWI enjoyed a close relationship to the Firestone Plantations Company, in two respects. First, it was heavily dependent on the staff and infrastructure of the Firestone operation, which had arrived not long before the BWI was founded. As the funds with which the Institute had been founded dwindled in terms of their annual return, Firestone became a key source of funding for the Institute.

From the early 1940s, the US government itself became an important source of funds. Its support for the BWI was part of a rapid escalation of American interventions in Liberia which began during the war. Initially, it was strategic concerns related to the war effort that overrode American resistance to foreign involvement in general, and military intervention in Liberia in particular. The Advisory Committee and Firestone may have been tangentially involved in attracting the attention of US defense interests to Liberia. Jones wrote a confidential, personal letter to Harvey Firestone Jr. in July 1941, noting that "American organizations interested in Liberia should appeal to our government for military and naval protection for Liberia." The next section examines the process by which

---

[36] Principal's Report to the Annual Meeting of the Local Board of Managers for 1941, in Phelps-Stokes Fund papers, NYPL Sc MG 162, Box 118, Folder 4.

wartime investments in strategic infrastructure paved the way for a broader development program.

Lend–Lease in Liberia

"We shall have invested much in victory. It would be foolish to practice false 'economy' on the relatively small additional amounts necessary to hasten the rebuilding of production and trade and the establishment of economic and political stability, without which the victory will be hollow and temporary."

Eugene Staley, "The Economic Implications of Lend-Lease"

Central to Liberia's change of fortunes was its strategic position along the Atlantic narrows as well as its production of natural rubber. A 1942 survey by American military intelligence noted that,

when the first World War removed her markets and the services of foreign shipping, Liberia suffered a major economic crisis. In the present conflict, her position is much more fortunate than it was in the preceding one. Two factors account for this change: (1) the large increase in rubber exports to America, and (2) the development of Liberia as an African cornerstone for Pan American Airways – Africa and the Ferry Command.[37]

However, these two features by themselves do not necessarily explain the scope of American involvement in Liberia in the 1940s and its continuation after the war. Correspondence from the time shows that American officials encountered a broader constellation of problems when attempting to build and maintain military facilities. This justified a more expansive agenda during the war, which was continued after the war on the basis that such investments would have a likely economic payoff for US interests.

The prospect that the US government would send troops to Liberia, let alone begin extensive aid programs, would have looked remote through much of the 1930s, despite the activity of organizations like the Phelps-Stokes Fund and even as diplomatic relations thawed and the US government recognized the Barclay government in 1935. In 1937, a State Department official named Hugh Cumming wrote to the Minister of Liberia in response to a hypothetical question by President Barclay about whether the United States would come to Liberia's defense against any foreign invasion. Cumming's career up to that point was in many ways typical of the agents of American economic diplomacy at the time; after law school, he had gone to work for the international division

---

[37] "Strategic Survey of Liberia," July 10, 1942, in NARA Military Intelligence Division regional files RG 165, Entry 77, Box 2395. Declass NND745020.

National City Bank of New York – the same bank which had issued Liberia's 1912 loan – before he joined the State Department where he would ultimately establish the Bureau of Intelligence and Research in 1957.[38] The query he was answering arose after reports in the press that the Polish government had requested the League of Nations to make Liberia a Polish mandate.[39]

It is, of course, not possible for us to answer President Barclay's hypothetical question as to what our attitude would be in the event of a foreign aggression against Liberia. Moreover the question is a particularly awkward one to answer because of our neutrality policy and the widespread opposition among our people to participation in any activities abroad which might in any way involve us in hostilities.

He concluded that "there is little or no likelihood of our ever undertaking military measures" in Liberia's aid.[40]

Just two years later, the situation began to change as conflict loomed. In 1939, a British politician and military officer named Jack Macnamara published an article in the *United Services Review* which argued that Liberia would become strategically important in the growing conflict with Germany. "Perhaps some of us have never given Liberia a thought before," the article began. However, it noted that "a hostile power based in Liberia could play havoc, until successfully bottled up, with the shipping that passes down the West Coast of Africa, either to South Africa, Australia and New Zealand, or the East, and most probably would be able also to hamper the shipping of the South Atlantic in general."[41]

British and French interests in Liberia's position were driven in part by fears that Liberia's close economic relationships with Germany made it vulnerable to becoming a German stronghold. In April 1939, the French Ambassador in Washington said in a conversation with a State Department official that while the French could not spare any resources to protect the Liberian coast that "in case of war both the British and French Governments would be obliged to take all necessary steps to prevent the establishment of hostile submarine or air bases in

---

[38] "Hugh Cumming, Jr, Dies," *The Washington Post*, November 26, 1986.

[39] Piotr Puchalski, "Polish Mission to Liberia, 1934–1938: Constructing Poland's Colonial Identity," *Historical Journal* 60, no. 4 (2017): 1071–96.

[40] Cumming to Walton, February 4, 1937, in US Department of State, *Foreign Relations of the United States Diplomatic Papers, 1937, Volume II* (Washington, DC: US Government Printing Office, 1954): 824.

[41] Lieut.-Col J. R. J. Macnamara, "The Question of Liberia," *The United Services Review*, June 22, 1939, in NARA RG 165 NM 84 77 Box 2393, Declassification NND 754020.

Liberia."[42] After some negotiation with the Liberian government, the French government proposed an agreement by which Liberia would agree to raise a force of 5,000 troops who would be trained by twelve French officers. Suspicious of French motives, American officials tried to discourage the Liberian government from signing the agreement, noting that the Liberian government did not have the means to support such a force, which would represent a significant expansion of its current 600-strong Frontier Force, and further that there was not enough time to train and equip these soldiers well enough to stand up to any determined Axis attack. Still in extensive correspondence between the State Department and Liberian, French, and British officials, the US government continued to reiterate that it was unlikely to be directly involved in Liberia's defense. By 1940, such fears were compounded for the British by Vichy control of French West Africa, where the Tirailleurs Senegalais were being expanded in preparation for an invasion of British territories, and the Italian–German presence threatening the Suez Canal.[43]

The first move toward American military intervention in Liberia was the signing of the Air Navigation Agreement of 1939, which gave Pan-American Airways permission to operate an airfield in Liberia.[44] Roberts Field, the main Liberian airfield outside Monrovia, became one of the main hubs in an "American-pioneered, American-supplied and American-maintained trans-Atlantic 'air bridge' between North America and the African continent," hosting planes that flew from the United States to Brazil then to North Africa, the Middle East and even as far as East Asia.[45] Liberia's role in the "air bridge" brought it under increasing pressure from the German Reich, which argued that this violated Liberia's professed neutrality. In 1942, the Liberian and American governments signed the Defense Areas Agreement, which allowed the US government to use Liberian territory for defense purposes. In return, the American

---

[42] Memorandum of Conversation by the Chief of Division of Near Eastern Affairs (Murray), April 18, 1939, in US Department of State, *Foreign Relations of the United States,1939, The Far East, The Near East and Africa, Volume IV* (Washington, DC: US Government Printing Office, 1955), 566.

[43] Harrison Akingbade, "US Liberian Relations during World War II," *Phylon* 46, no. 1 (1985): 26–27; Timothy Parsons, "The Military Experiences of Ordinary Africans in World War II," in *Africa and World War II*, edited by Judith A. Byfield, Carolyn A. Brown, Timothy Parsons and Ahmad Alawad Sikainga (Cambridge: Cambridge University Press, 2015), 4–5; William R. Stanley, "Trans-South Atlantic Air Link in World War II," *GeoJournal* 33, no. 4 (1994): 459.

[44] Akingbade, "US Liberian Relations," 28.

[45] Stanley, "Trans-South Atlantic Air Link," 459–60.

government agreed to provide protection to Liberia. The agreement was based on a similar one between the United States and Greenland.[46]

American officials planning for the implementation of the agreement were immediately confronted with the problem of Liberia's lack of infrastructure. In some ways, this served as an advantage, making facilities in Liberia less vulnerable to ground attack from neighboring territories. One intelligence report noted that "there are no roads through Liberia from the coast to the adjoining Vichy French territory or to Sierra Leone, and there is very little road mileage of any kind. The movement of troops through the interior would be extremely difficult."[47] In the area of shipping, however, it presented what American officials considered to be a grave disadvantage.

There are now in Liberia no protected anchorages or port facilities for ocean-going vessels; all cargo must be lightered. This makes shipments to and from Liberia slow and difficult, and lengthens greatly the time consumed per voyage by vessels engaged in that service, causes such vessels to be unduly exposed to enemy attack while unloading and loading in Liberia, and causes the naval graft needed to give such vessels some degree of protection while unloading and loading to be diverted during those period from other duties.

An agreement to use Lend–Lease funds for the construction of a port followed in September 1943, providing for the first large influx of American funds into Liberia during the war.

With hindsight, it is easy to see Lend–Lease as "a precursor of the worldwide foreign aid commitment" undertaken by the US government after the war, but that was not its initial intention when the first Lend–Lease Act was passed in 1941. Rather, it was "an ingenious solution to a major problem facing Franklin D. Roosevelt" at the beginning of the war in Europe, namely: how to aid Britain in the war effort while getting around the restrictions of the Neutrality Act and the Johnson Act which forbade lending to countries in default to the United States.[48] As one Roosevelt biographer put it, the program was sold to a reluctant Congress on the basis that, "providing weapons would help ensure that American soldiers not go into battle."[49] As the war progressed, however, there were

---

[46] Wharton to Secretary of State, March 3, 1942, in US Department of State, *Foreign Relations of the United States 1942, volume I* (Washington, DC: US Government Printing Office, 1960), 361.

[47] Report by Joint US Intelligence Committee on Port Facilities in Liberia, October 14, 1942, in RG 218, Geographic File on Liberia, Box 144, Declass NND943011.

[48] Leon Martel, *Lend-Lease, Loans and the Coming of the Cold War* (New York: Routledge, 1979), ch. 1.

[49] Henry W. Brands, *Traitor to His Class: The Privileged Life and Radical Presidency of Franklin Delano Roosevelt* (New York: Doubleday, 2008), 577.

increasingly fraught debates over when Lend–Lease should end and to what extent it should support economic reconstruction as well as combat.

These debates were visible in the ways in which the aid program in Liberia progressed over the 1940s. Military intelligence surveys conducted during the early 1940s pointed to a number of problems beyond the lack of infrastructure which would need to be addressed in the implementation of any defense project. These assessments are largely anecdotal impressions. Such commentary, according to Ekbladh, "should not be taken as a statement of what conditions actually were in all situations. American observers were prone to statements colored by their own bias, racisms, ignorance, enthusiasm and cynicism." Rather, he says, they should be used "to describe what US perceptions motivated and then shaped actual modernization policy and activity."[50] In this case, they help explain why US programs in Liberia moved so quickly from airfields, ports, and roads required by the armed forces to wider investments in public health and education.

Descriptions of Liberia by American officials were universally unflattering and highlighted the range of problems American forces might face in trying to use Liberia as a base in the war effort, which included everything from housing to roads to food supplies. Lt. H. D. B. Claiborne wrote that "all churches, stores, government buildings, etc., are shabby, dirty, and unkempt. None of these places are suitable to house a large number of men."[51] A 1942 strategic survey also noted the high cost of living in Liberia owing to the need to import food for both the Americo-Liberian and indigenous populations.[52] "Good living in Liberia is expensive," the report noted, "as even food must be imported for both the native and the foreign populations. Housing and sanitation are primitive, except for limited facilities in the few larger towns. Water must be boiled and filtered everywhere."

Education and public health were also the subject of comments by American officials. In 1942, the Acting Secretary of State wrote to the American Charge d'Affaires in Liberia that "the War Department deems it essential that adequate sanitary and health precautions should be taken before American forces are sent to Liberia."[53] A 1943 memorandum noted that "only one street in Monrovia is paved. The gutters on the

[50] Ekbladh, *Great American Mission*, 11.
[51] Reports from October 10, 1940, in NARA RG 165 Entry NM84 77, Box 2393, Declassification NND745020.
[52] "Strategic survey of Liberia," July 10, 1942, in NARA RG 165 Entry 77 Box 2395 NND745020.
[53] Welles and Wharton, February 26, 1942, in US Department of State, *Foreign Relations 1942*, 360.

street serve as breeding places for mosquitoes, which transmit malaria. There is not a general water supply, no system of sewage disposal, nor modern plumbing. The Government spends almost nothing on the improvement of the condition of the people."[54] As the final Lend–Lease agreement was being negotiated, the American Minister wrote to the Liberian Secretary of State that "as the health of the American troops is of paramount importance greater collaboration between the medical services of USAFIL and those of Liberia in conducting anti-malarial surveys and the adoption of other preventative measures in areas to be agreed upon beyond the limits of the defense areas it is thought should prove high [highly] beneficial to all concerned."[55] In the same year, a report by E. A. Bayne, Assistant Special Representative to the Office of Economic Warfare (OEW) in Accra argued that "if development of dormant Liberian economic potentialities is to be a policy of OEW, or subsequently of the United States government as a whole, labor training must be the prerequisite to any development, just as public health must be."[56] A later official reported that "we found that many of the people employed could neither read nor write, tell where they were born, sign their name, complete applications or oaths of office."[57]

Resolving these problems involved the expansion of American efforts beyond the construction of the port and roads, and beyond the territorial boundaries of the areas occupied by American forces. In 1944, the US government established a Health Mission under the leadership of Dr. John West, and dispatched several agricultural advisers as part of a wider Economic Mission operating under the OEW.[58] The OEW and the Foreign Economic Administration were among the US government agencies tasked with supplying the US war effort with strategic materials, and oversaw a rapid rise in the US trade with the West African region as a whole, generated by demand for raw materials like rubber, palm oil, tin, and manganese.[59] Coincidentally, or not, one of those advisers had

---

[54] NARA RG 169 Entry P40 Box 1, Declassification NND30379.

[55] Walton to Simson, June 28, 1943, in US Department of State, *Foreign Relations of the United States: Diplomatic Papers, 1943, The New East and Africa, Volume IV* (Washington, DC: US Government Printing Office, 1964), 668.

[56] "First Liberia Report," August 1–20, by E. A. Bayne, Assistant Special Representative, Accra, Gold Coast, West Africa, September 11, 1943, in NARA RG 169 Entry P40 Box 1, Declassification NND30379.

[57] Memorandum from Powell and Hanson, Foreign Economic Administration, January 14, 1945, NARA RG 160, Entry P40, Box 2, Declassification NND30379.

[58] M. Teah Wulah, *Back to Africa: A Liberian Tragedy* (Bloomington, IN: AuthorHouse, 2009), 471–72.

[59] Adebayo Oyebade, "Feeding America's War Machine: The United States and Economic Expansion in West Africa during World War II," *African Economic History* 26 (1998): 119–40.

previously taught agricultural subjects at the Tuskegee Institute in Alabama responsible for the founding of the BWI.[60] The link between the presence of military forces and the construction of infrastructure was not new. During World War I, American forces occupying Haiti resurrected systems of corvée labor to build roads and schools and string telegraph lines.[61] Nor was the unanticipated expansion of Lend–Lease programs unique to Liberia. In a number of countries, the remit of Lend–Lease soon expanded to include investments in infrastructure and economic reconstruction, as economic prosperity was increasingly linked with political stability and security. One quarterly report from the Lend–Lease program noted that "Lend–lease aid to China in 1941 consisted principally in improvements on the Burma Road that doubled its previous capacity and in building a new railroad line from Burma into China."[62] The history of lend–lease in France suggests that "believing that economic rivalries led to war, American foreign-policy planning for the postwar period had sought both security and prosperity through economic instruments."[63]

There were clear economic motivations behind US interventions in Liberia. Frank Knox, the Secretary of the Navy, wrote to Secretary of State Cordell Hull in March 1943 that "the Navy Department is unable to certify that the development of harbors and port facilities in Liberia, or elsewhere on the West Coast of Africa, during the war would measurably aid our war efforts." The port was not likely to be finished for some time, and by May 1943 the Germans had surrendered North Africa to the allies. Knox did see some future commercial advantage in the program but did not believe the project should be allocated American machinery or manpower needed elsewhere.[64] Roosevelt himself intervened to ask the Board of the Navy to reconsider this decision.[65] This intervention followed a personal visit to Liberia by the US president in January 1943, which included a review of Roberts Field and the Firestone Plantation as well as lunch with President Barclay.[66]

---

[60] US Department of State, *Point Four Pioneers: Reports from a New Frontier* (Washington, DC: US Government Printing Office, 1951), 4.

[61] Lester D. Langley, *The Banana Wars: United States Intervention in the Caribbean, 1898–1934* (Lanham, MD: SR Books, 2002), 153–34.

[62] US House of Representatives, *Eighth Quarterly Report to Congress on Lend-Lease Operations For the Period Ended March 11, 1943*, House Document No. 129.

[63] John S. Hill, "American Efforts to Aid French Reconstruction between Lend-Lease and the Marshall Plan," *Journal of Modern History* 64 (1992): 502.

[64] Knox to Hull, March 16, 1943, RG218 Geographical File 1942–1945, Liberia, Box 144.

[65] Memorandum from FDR for the Secretary of the Navy, June 23, 1943, in RG218 Box 144.

[66] Hibbard to Secretary of State, January 28, 1943, in US Department of State, *Foreign Relations of the United States 1943*, 656–57.

Commercial justifications were also used to justify the continued construction of the port and maintenance of the airfield after the war ended. A 1945 Pan-American Airways handbook for employees being sent to its Fisherman's Lake airfield noted that "because of its strategic position on the supply routes to the battle front of the war, Liberia has assumed a position of great value to the United Nations. In years to come it may well play an important part in Pan American's air routes of post-war travel and commerce."[67] The next year, the army announced its plan to disestablish the army base at Roberts Field. This was met with protest from the State Department. In a letter to the Secretary of War, Truman's Secretary of State Dean Acheson argued that "it would be in the national interest of the United States for the War Department to maintain the present base at Roberts Field until such time as arrangements can be made for maintenance on a permanent basis."[68]

Acheson did not immediately get his way. The US delegation in Liberia for the centenary celebrations the following year visited the airfield and observed a steep decline in its condition, just as Acheson had predicted. The debate about Roberts Field reflected wider discussions about the purpose and extent of American aid to Liberia after the war. Proponents of continued grants, loans, and technical assistance stressed the potential economic and political benefits which would accrue to the United States if the human and physical infrastructure built during the war was maintained. In 1966, an internal State Department memorandum described these goals as follows: "The basic US objectives in Liberia are to help ensure Liberia's continued commitment to the US and alignment with other free nations, and to safeguard US economic, information and military interests in that country, and maximize the moderating influence of Liberia in Africa."[69] That moderating influence had been particularly visible during the early 1960s, when Liberia helped lead a group of countries, known unofficially as the "Monrovia bloc" after a meeting in Monrovia in 1961, which pushed back against what were seen as the more radical positions of the "Casablanca group" which sought a more confrontational relationship with Europe following decolonization. The two groups eventually joined to form the Organization of African Unity in 1963.[70]

---

[67] "Handbook for Pan American Employees going to Fisherman's Lake," University of Miami Library, Special Collections, Technical Operations, Manuals, Box 1, Folder 23.

[68] Acheson to Secretary of War, 10/30/46, in RG 59 Dec 882.7962.

[69] RG Entry A1 5713 Declass NND37720.

[70] Paul Nugent, *Africa since Independence: A Comparative History* (Basingstoke: Palgrave Macmillan, 2004), 101–105.

Aid, Institutions, and Sovereignty

"Before the turkey was roasted it would like to have a chance to say a few words about the manner in which it would be carved up" (Memorandum of conversation between President Barclay and Mr. Villard, June 19, 1943).

It was these expansions in American intervention that General Benjamin O. Davis compared to the Marshall Plan in Europe in his speech in 1947. As the response to his speech suggests, what might have appeared to be an arrangement of mutual benefit between the Tubman regime and the US government still had significant tensions. The aims pursued by each government were often sufficiently different to create difficulties in the planning and implementation of specific programs, and the Liberian government struggled to retain some control over American-funded facilities. At the same time, American complaints about the quality of Liberian governance were often overtaken by other strategic and geopolitical priorities, and they settled for no more than nominal reforms, even while increased US involvement helped legitimize and support the Liberian government.

From the beginning of negotiations with the United States, Barclay insisted that any US programs must serve Liberian interests as well as American. This was the upshot of President Barclay's comments to Mr. Villard, quoted earlier in this section. In a conversation with Villard on a visit to Washington, Barclay said that

the only condition he attached to the development of a port in his country was that it should be economically beneficial to Liberia. He said he fully realized the strategic purposes to which it would be placed by the United States government. ... Nevertheless, any port which did not take into account the economic possibilities of Liberia and their systematic development could not meet with Liberia's approval.

During and after the war, frequent complaints about the actions of American officials in Liberia appear in diplomatic communications from the Liberian government. At a dinner in Washington in May 1943, Barclay raised a number of such complaints with a State Department official, including a claim that American military police had gone outside their jurisdiction to seize a Liberian customs official. In this conversation, "the President said that the commanding general should remember that the American military forces did not constitute an army of occupation, as General Sadler seemed to think."[71] Such

---

[71] Memorandum of conversation by Villard, June 1, 1943, in US Department of State, *Foreign Relations of the United States 1943*, 661.

complaints did not stop after the war. During the visit of the American delegation to the Liberian centenary, a close adviser to Tubman raised several issues about Dr. John West, Chief of the Public Health Mission, including that he operated a drug store for personal profit in Monrovia selling drugs imported duty free for the use of the Mission, and that he and his staff engaged too much in local politics.[72]

Control over the facilities built by American government programs was another point of discontent. The final signing of the Lend–Lease agreement in 1943 was delayed for several months while the Liberian government tried to press for equal Liberian and American representation in the governance of the port. The US government swiftly rejected this request. "Considering the probable cost of the port and the fact that this project is not to be paid from the revenues of the Liberian government but from the port itself, this Government feels that operating control must, in the final analysis rest with the American company. It is not certain that this could be accomplished under joint control."[73]

Hull's decision on the governance of the port reflected long-standing American criticisms of the quality of Liberian institutions. The topic was raised frequently in the intelligence reports cited earlier in the chapter. Berger stated bluntly that "the administration is characterized by its inefficiency, unreliability, graft, oppression and exploitation of the natives."[74] In 1943, E. A. Bayne wrote to State Department that "the government is a personification of incompetence and empty pomp. It is unreliable in virtually all respects, shot through with graft, and dominated by the True Whig Party which is the personal following of Edwin Barclay."[75] Similar observations can be found in American correspondence through the rest of the period, and not just from government sources. Robert Clower, leading the Northwestern University economic survey in the early 1960s, wrote to a colleague that "we do, of course, avoid agitating among the locals for things in which we happen to believe; and this is sometimes not easy to do, since the similarity between the Tubman regime and that of the Third Reich from the years 1933 and 1939 are sometimes quite striking."[76]

---

[72] Memorandum, Special Report of the State Department members of the United States Delegation to Liberia, July 24–31, in RG 59 882.6351/12–3149 Bo 7146.

[73] Cordell Hull to Lester Walton, December 29, 1943, US Department of State, *Foreign Relations of the United States 1943*, 690.

[74] NARA RG 169 Entry P40 Box 1, Declassification NND30379.

[75] "First Liberia Report," August 1–20, by E. A. Bayne, Assistant Special Representative, Accra, Gold Coast, West Africa, September 11, 1943, in NARA RG 169 Entry P40 Box 1, Declassification NND30379.

[76] Robert Clower to P. J. D. Wiles, September 28, 1961, in Economic Survey of Liberia Box 1, Folder 9.

Despite these observations, American officials did little to press the Barclay and Tubman regimes toward more democratic policies during this period, although the American government had few illusions about the nature of their governments. Barclay had been elected in 1935 by a vote of 344,569 to 7,784, despite the fact that the electorate was only about 15,000.[77] Nevertheless, the United States recognized Barclay's presidency and resumed diplomatic relations. Not all US officials were happy with this. The American charge d'affaires in Monrovia noted after Roosevelt's visit in January 1943 that "unquestionably the President's visit at this time will be interpreted as strengthening Barclay's hand and it is for this reason particularly that I regret the current problems were not more thoroughly discussed."[78]

The US government did push back when funds were seen as being used for political purposes or when the excesses of the Tubman regime drew too much international attention. In the early 1950s, the Liberian government applied to the US Export–Import Bank for funds to undertake an expansion of its roadwork, build a hydroelectric plant, and a water and sewage system for Monrovia. While the Export–Import Bank was willing to loan money for the expansion of the road network, its initial response was that the other two projects needed more detailed engineering data before they could be considered viable. Tubman's immediate response was to put the application on hold, telling American officials that he was not willing to undertake the road expansion without funding for the water and sewage system for Monrovia. This, he argued, was top priority for political reasons. In their own internal correspondence, American officials characterized Tubman's attitude as one of seeking to placate a few around Monrovia rather than promoting wider development. For Tubman, it seemed as though the American government was forcing him into an undesirable plan to serve American economic interests. This tension was ultimately resolved when the Export–Import Bank agreed to fund all three programs. However, when Tubman's government in 1951 imprisoned several opposition leaders on sedition charges, it raised questions from both the American media and prominent Americans like Eleanor Roosevelt. While the State Department initially defended many of Tubman's policies, the sedition charges made them particularly nervous, and they pressed the US Ambassador to Liberia to convey this anxiety to Tubman.[79]

---

[77] Ibrahim K. Sundiata, *Brothers and Strangers: Black Zion, Black Slavery, 1914–1940* (Durham: Duke University Press, 2003), 252.

[78] Hibbard to Hull, January 28, 1943, in US Department of State, *Foreign Relations of the United States 1943*, 657.

[79] Secretary of State to the Embassy in Liberia, October 18, 1951, in US Department of State, *Foreign Relations of the United States, 1951, The Near East and Africa, Volume V* (Washington, DC: US Government Printing Office, 1982), 1307–8.

In response to both external and internal pressures, Tubman made a number of reforms to Liberia's institutions during his tenure, under his signature "Unification" policy. This included the expansion of the franchise as well as the representation of the indigenous population in the interior. These were significant changes to a political system that had long disenfranchised the interior and segregated its governance from that of the coast. However, Gus Liebenow argues that these changes reflected the "formalism" that characterized much of Liberian politics. "The tendency towards formalism is readily apparent in the constant emphasis upon constitutionalism, adherence to legal technicalities in the courts, and the charade of conducting elaborate electoral campaigns when there are no opponents to the True Whig Party candidates."[80] Tubman's reforms did little to change the actual balance of power, and they were accompanied by the intensification of other efforts to undermine his political opponents through the 1950s and 1960s. Put simply, newly enfranchised Liberians had the right to vote in elections for which the outcome was increasingly a foregone conclusion.

The impact of aid on the institutions of recipient countries is now the subject of an extensive literature. According to one survey, "attempting to use aid to stabilize a fragile state might effectively mean funding internal repression."[81] Aid may cause government expenditure to be displaced to other activities, and the expectations of future aid may increase competition over resources within recipient governments.[82] While it is not clear how fragile the Tubman government really was, it is clear that its close association with the US government added to its legitimacy in a period when it was struggling with increasingly organized indigenous resistance to one-party rule. As the next chapter will show, aid was also closely linked to another source of funds and patronage for the Tubman government, namely foreign concessions.

An African Marshall Plan?

By the 1970s, Liberia was seen abroad as "the epitome of a stable, pro-US client in a world dominated by the Cold War."[83] This was certainly not the case in the 1930s. While there were significant US interests in Liberia

---

[80] J. Gus Liebenow, *Liberia: The Evolution of Privilege* (Ithaca: Cornell University Press, 1969), 81–82.
[81] Temple, "Aid and Conditionality," 4462–63.
[82] Jakob Svensson, "Foreign Aid and Rent Seeking," *Journal of International Economics* 51 (2000): 437–61.
[83] Stephen Ellis, *The Mask of Anarchy: The Destruction of Liberia and the Religious Dimension of an African Civil War* (New York: New York University Press, 2007), xxv.

at that time, principally Firestone and its affiliates, Liberia was neither stable nor a predictably reliable US ally. Firestone officials were powerless to stop Liberia from defaulting on its loans in 1932, and one of the only significant US philanthropic efforts in the country was debating whether to abandon its project owing to poor public health conditions and a lack of support from the Liberian government. The forced labor scandal added to calls for the governance of Liberia to be taken over by a foreign power in some way or another.

What changed all of this was Liberia's strategic value during World War II. Being a producer of natural rubber and within flying range of the Americas placed Liberia unexpectedly, and for the first time, at the heart of European and American strategic considerations. In part as a result of the flows of aid and foreign investment which followed, Stephen Ellis noted in 2007, "Liberians today generally view the mid-twentieth century as a golden age." It was a period when the Liberian economy was growing faster than almost any other economy in the world. And despite the political repression of the Tubman regime, it was also a period in which the living standards of the indigenous majority increased, as will be shown in the next chapter. However, this stability came at a cost. "In reality," Ellis continues, "the country was run by an elite that was at best patronizing, at worst brutal, arrogant, and insouciant." Tubman's reforms of Liberian institutions, which reassured foreign donors, were often nominal, and did little to shift the balance of power away from him and his allies. Correspondence from the time shows that donor countries, and particularly US officials, were aware of Tubman's crackdowns on the opposition and the limiting of political freedom. However, their concerns were not only with the institutions of Liberia itself but also with the appearance of Liberia as a "stable, pro-US client" in the region.

This was not the last time that the American and other governments would support leaders in Liberia and elsewhere in Africa whose domestic policies did not fit with their proclaimed values. During the 1980s, Samuel Doe played Cold War politics as effectively as Tubman had and attracted considerable aid from abroad, particularly from the United States.[84] Subsequent studies of aid have shown this is not just a feature of Liberian history. Examples from elsewhere in Africa suggest that aid might be used to keep leaders in power, as was the case for Mobutu in Zaire.[85]

---

[84] D. Elwood Dunn, *Liberia and the United States during the Cold War* (Basingstoke: Palgrave Macmillan, 2009), Chapter 4.

[85] Deron Acemoglu, Thierry Verdier and James A. Robinson, "Kleptocracy and Divide-and-Rule: A Model of Personal Rule," *Journal of European Economic Association* 2, no. 2–3 (2004): 162–92.

Geopolitics was not the only reason for foreign interest in Liberia. The United States and other donors had economic interests in mind, too. Robert Clower and his co-authors pointed out in 1962 that the principal donors of foreign aid to Liberia were also countries that held concessions there. "In great measure the scale of loans and gifts reflect the economic stake of the donor nations in Liberian enterprises. This is immediately evident, for example, in the cases of recent grants and loans from the governments of Sweden and Germany; in both cases their nationals now have large investments in Liberian ore mines."[86] Such investments were the other part of the lifeline that sustained the Tubman administration. However, the generous terms on which those concessions were agreed undermined the development of fiscal capacity that might otherwise have accompanied the rapid economic growth Liberia enjoyed in its "golden age."

---

[86] Clower et al., *Growth Without Development.*

9   Concessions and Growth

> If a country is to be truly independent, a large proportion of its citizens
> must be so economically. Mexico under the dictatorship of Diaz is a case
> in point. Diaz, supported by a clique of self-centered autocrats bent on
> enriching themselves, gave away to foreign concessionaires the land and
> mineral resources of the Mexican people, reducing them to a state of
> peonage in the land from which their fathers had driven the Spaniards at
> the cost of so much blood and suffering, and thereby vitiating their
> political autonomy.
>
> George S. Best, "The economic aspects of political
> independence," *Crozierville Observer*, May 1931

The *Crozierville Observer* was established during the turmoil of the League
of Nations investigation. In the years to follow, it fought against increasing government pressure – including a sedition law passed in 1933 – to
publish stinging critiques of Liberia's leaders and their economic policies.
Its editor, a descendent of the Barbadian migrants named Albert Porte,
and its contributors often paid dearly for their frank assessments of the
Liberian government. In his long career, Porte was jailed and fined for
libel as a result of claims made in the press, and ultimately took to self-
publishing when printers in Monrovia were no longer willing to accept his
work for fear of invoking official retaliation. George Best, author of the
piece quoted above, was Porte's brother-in-law.[1]

The subject of the article was a concession granted to Firestone Rubber
Company in 1926. It gave Firestone, an American company, a ninety-
nine-year lease on up to a million acres of land for the production of
natural rubber. The company was to pay rent of six cents an acre for each
acre selected for production for the first six years, and ten cents per acre
thereafter. All imported machinery and materials were exempt from
customs but after the first six years the company agreed to pay a revenue
tax of 1 percent of the value of rubber or other products exported from the

---

[1] Carl Patrick Burrowes, *Power and Press Freedom, 1830–1970: The Impact of Globalization
and Civil Society on Media-Government Relations* (Africa: World Press, 2004).

plantation.[2] Alongside the planting agreement was a contract for a loan of up to $5 million, discussed in detail in Chapter 6, which expanded American control over Liberia's government finances and its military. Though the Firestone agreement attracted considerable protest from people like George Best and Albert Porte, it was to be the first of many. In the decades following World War II, the granting of concessions to foreign companies accelerated dramatically under the "open-door" policies of Presidents Tubman (1944–71) and Tolbert (1971–80). This influx of foreign investment resulted in the dramatic increases in the production and export of rubber, iron ore, and other export commodities which underpinned Liberia's rapid economic growth during the postwar decades.

George Best's comparison of Liberia with Mexico under Porfirio Diaz – a period frequently described by Mexican historians as the Porifiriato – would be more accurately applied to Tubman than to Barclay. Like Tubman, Diaz governed Mexico for a period of several decades, from 1876 to 1911, with only a brief interruption from 1880 to 1884. During this period the Mexican economy, which had not grown much since it achieved independence from Spain in 1821, expanded rapidly through foreign investment in railways, mines, oilfields, and agriculture. In both countries, decades of economic growth ended in violence. In Mexico, the beginning of the Mexican Revolution in 1910 forced Diaz from power the following year. Over the next thirty years, war and institutional upheaval reshaped modern Mexico.[3] Liberia's postwar growth stalled in the late 1970s before being reversed when Tolbert was overthrown and killed by Samuel Doe in 1980. Political instability turned to civil war when Doe himself was killed in 1989, and did not end fully until 2003. This long period of conflict erased all of the economic gains made in preceding decades, leaving hundreds of thousands dead or displaced. Historians of both countries often claim that it was the inequities of economic change in the decades prior which led directly to the conflicts which followed. Despite this, there remains a certain degree of nostalgia for the past. In 2019, Liberian President George Weah declared November 29 a national holiday, marking the anniversary of Tubman's birth. Among the reasons he gave was the "open-door" policy and economic success associated with it.

[2] Frank Chalk, "The Anatomy of an Investment: Firestone's 1972 Loan to Liberia," *Canadian Journal of African Studies* 1, no. 1 (1967): 12–32. For full text of the agreement, see US Department of State, *Foreign Relations of the United States, 1926, Volume I* (Washington, DC: US Government Printing Office, 1941), 561–67.
[3] Alan Knight, *The Mexican Revolution: A Very Short Introduction* (Oxford: Oxford University Press, 2016), 1–3.

The cases of Liberia and Mexico challenge common narratives about institutions and growth. While both social scientists and policy-makers have emphasized the importance of limited government to economic development, history provides many examples of economic growth and even structural change under regimes which lack the inclusive institutions of many developed economies, prompting speculation that there may be multiple institutional equilibria that can support economic expansion, from Mancur Olson's "stationary bandits" to the developmental dictatorships of Ethiopia and Rwanda in the twenty-first century. In the introduction to a collection of case studies of "natural states" or "limited access orders," North, Wallis, Webb, and Weingast point out that such states encompass a range of different political structures and levels of economic development. "Although all low- and middle-income countries today are limited access orders," they write, "they have per capita income levels that differ by a factor of twenty or more, reflecting wide differences in the quality of institutions."[4] While certainly not unique to Africa, such debates are particularly pertinent in a region which, in 2019, was home to half of the world's longest-serving leaders.[5]

The Tubman era is one of the most extensively studied periods of Liberia's economic history, but as in other cases discussed in this book, its origins and impacts are generally situated within the specific context of Liberian history rather than in comparison with other countries. The comparison with Mexico in this chapter offers a new interpretation of the postwar decades. It argues that many of the policies adopted by Tubman, Tolbert, and even Doe should be understood within a context of institutional weakness. One implication was that the only way of achieving the levels of growth seen during that period was through a system of elite coordination and rent-seeking, which was insufficiently flexible to cope with either external economic fluctuations or pressure from below for entry into the elite group.

Institutions, Foreign Investment, and Growth: The Story of the Porfiriato

Economic performance is often linked to the quality of institutions. What is now a significant body of research in both economics and economic

---

[4] Douglass C. North, John Joseph Wallis, Steven B. Webb, and Barry R. Weingast (eds), "Limited Access Orders: An Introduction to the Conceptual Framework," in *In the Shadow of Violence: Politics, Economics and the Problems of Development* (Cambridge: Cambridge University Press, 2013), 10.
[5] Nic Cheeseman and Jonathan Fisher, *Authoritarian Africa: Repression, Resistance and the Power of Ideas* (Oxford: Oxford University Press, 2020), xxi.

history argues that the shift to modern economic growth in the industrializing economies of Europe and North America depended in part on the development of institutions which were both capable of protecting property rights but also restricted from abusing that power.[6] Since at least the emergence of the Washington Consensus of the 1990s, this research has been the backbone of development policies promoting limited government.[7] As discussed in the previous chapter, such policy changes are often part of the price of receiving foreign aid. However, as the previous chapter also showed, the lack of such institutions was no barrier to the receipt of aid. Nor, as more recent work on institutions has shown, are corrupt or weak institutions always a barrier to economic growth. This section examines the theory of growth under autocratic institutions, and provides a brief history of the Porfiriato, a period of Mexican economic history in which coalitions of elites and the selective enforcement of property rights formed an effective (if ultimately temporary) substitute for the limited government prescribed by economic theory.

New institutional economics (NIE) emerged initially as a critique of neoclassical theory which, according to early proponents like Ronald Coase and Douglass North, neglected the impact of information asymmetries and agency problems on economic decision-making. It has since, however, become part of mainstream economics.[8] Definitions of institutions can be quite broad, including everything from the structure of governments to informal cultural norms, but in all cases they serve the function of helping resolve problems that might otherwise inhibit exchange – the enforcement of contracts and land rights, the ability to predict what counterparties will do in a transaction. Today, according to Besley and Persson, "almost all economic analyses presume the existence of an effective state. Specifically, economists invoke the existence of an authority that can tax, enforce contracts, and organize public spending for a wide range of activities." However, as they point out, "many of the major developments in world history have been about creating this starting point."[9]

[6] Noel D. Johnson and Mark Koyama, "States and Economic Growth: Capacity and Constraints," *Explorations in Economic History* 64 (2017): 1–20; Philip T. Hoffman, "What Do States Do? Politics and Economic History," *Journal of Economic History* 75, no. 2 (2014): 303–32.

[7] Pranab Bardhan, "State and Development: The Need for a Reappraisal of the Current Literature," *Journal of Economic Literature* 54, no. 3 (2016): 862–92.

[8] Daron Acemoglu, Simon Johnson and James A. Robinson, "Institutions as a Fundamental Cause of Long-Run Growth," in *Handbook of Economic Growth, Volume 1A*, edited by Philippe Aghion and Steven Durlauf (Amsterdam: North-Holland, 2005), 385–472; Thrainn Eggertsson, *Economic Behavior and Institutions* (Cambridge: Cambridge University Press, 1990), ch. 1; Oliver E. Williamson, *The Economic Institutions of Capitalism* (New York: The Free Press, 1985).

[9] Timothy Besley and Torsten Persson, *Pillars and Prosperity: The Political Economics of Development Clusters* (Princeton: Princeton University Press, 2011), 1.

Economic history has provided rich fodder for debates about the origins of modern states and their links to economic growth, in particular by exploring the links between emerging national governments of the early modern period and the process of industrialization during the eighteenth and nineteenth centuries. Britain has been a key focus of these debates, with a number of prominent economists and economic historians arguing that the British state had the right combination of high administrative capacity and constraints on the executive to facilitate its early shift to sustained economic growth.[10] These arguments have been influential not only in history but also in subsequent development policy, with the quality of institutions becoming a key method for judging the economic prospects of a country by both providers of aid and the private sector. One explanation for the boom in foreign investment during the 1990s was democratization and improvement in macroeconomic management by many developing countries. In his theory of foreign investment, John Dunning noted that levels of investment depend on "the extent to which the country is able to create a satisfactory legal system, commercial infrastructure and business culture, and to provide the business sector with the transport and communications facilities and human resources they need."[11]

There remain, however, fierce arguments about the nature of "good" institutions and the extent to which these have existed during periods of rapid economic growth. According to NIE, one of the main purposes of government is the protection of property rights. However, during the crucial period from the late seventeenth to the early nineteenth centuries when Britain's industrialization began, it was actually government policies that weakened feudal systems of property rights which helped reduce transaction costs.[12] The global shift in the field of economic history over the past several decades has raised further questions about the ways in which state institutions have influenced economic growth. First, new data on long-run economic growth has shown that growth itself was not only a product of industrialization. Rather, preindustrial economies experienced frequent periods of growth, sometimes lasting several decades. It

[10] Daron Acemoglu, Simon Johnson and James Robinson, "The Rise of Europe: Atlantic Trade, Institutional Change and Economic Growth," *American Economic Review* 95, no. 3 (2005): 546–79; Douglass C. North and Barry R. Weingast, "Constitutions and Commitment: The Evolution of Institutions Governing Public Choice in Seventeenth-Century England," *Journal of Economic History* 49, no. 4 (1989): 803–32.

[11] John H. Dunning, "The Eclectic (OLI) Paradigm of International Production: Past, Present and Future," *International Journal of Economics of Business* 8, no. 2 (2001): 181.

[12] Dan Bogart and Gary Richardson, "Making Property Productive: Reorganizing Rights to Real and Equitable Estates in Britain, 1660–1830," *European Review of Economic History* 13, no. 1 (2009): 3–30.

was only subsequent periods of shrinking that led to long-run stagnation in per capita incomes.[13] Periods of shrinking are often due to the fracturing of coalitions following economic shocks or disputes about the distribution of rents when conditions change. In the worst-case scenario, such fracturing can lead to violence and war. However, limited access orders have varied in the strength or fragility of those coalitions: North, Wallis, and Weingast distinguish between fragile, basic, and mature limited access orders, with the last category best able to sustain economic growth over longer periods and even potentially shift toward the establishment of limited government (what they refer to as an open-access government). The so-called Asian Tigers are examples of countries where growth begun under autocratic regimes has been sustained to generate significant improvements in standards of living.[14] North, Wallis, and Weingast stress that these three categories are points on a spectrum. There is no natural linear progression from one category to another, but it suggests that not all limited access orders are equally vulnerable to shrinking.

There are numerous cases of economic expansion under what Robert Allen, in his study of economic expansion in the Soviet Union, refers to as "substitutes" for inclusive institutions.[15] One such case was Mexico under the government of Porfirio Diaz. Stephen Haber, Noel Maurer, and Armando Razo draw on the same theories of NIE that inspired North, Wallis, and Weingast to explain Mexico's success in attracting foreign capital. The Mexican state in the 1870s was incapable of providing limited government, and protecting property rights for all, much like the Liberian state was in the 1940s. Before Diaz came to power, authority was held by local elites in a system described as "crumbling, peripheralized feudalism."[16] Diaz did not have the means to undermine these local elites either by force or by offering universal protection of property rights. Instead, he increased the credibility of commitments to investors by creating a "rent-seeking coalition" of elites whose interests were aligned with those of concession holders. This system, which Haber and his co-authors refer to as "vertical political integration," made Mexico

[13] Stephen Broadberry and John Wallis, "Growing, Shrinking and Long-Run Economic Performance: Historical Perspectives on Economic Development," NBER Working Paper 23343 (2017).

[14] See, for example, Jong-Sung You, "Transition from a Limited Access Order to an Open Access Order: The Case of South Korea," in *In the Shadow of Violence*, edited by Wallis, Webb, and Weingast (Cambridge: Cambridge University Press, 2013), 293–327.

[15] Robert C. Allen, *Farm to Factory: A Reinterpretation of the Soviet Industrial Revolution* (Princeton: Princeton University Press, 2003), 16.

[16] Stephen H. Haber, Noel Maurer and Armando Razo, *The Politics of Property Rights: Political Instability, Credible Commitments and Economic Growth in Mexico, 1876–1929* (Cambridge: Cambridge University Press, 2003), 42.

attractive to foreign investors even in a context of limited state capacity and authority.

Concessions provided an ideal vehicle for such a system of selectively enforced rights. While there is no single agreed definition, concessions can be defined broadly as "a contractual arrangement between the Government and foreign investor."[17] Historically, they have taken many forms, from territorial concessions which came closer to treaties between countries to smaller-scale mining and agricultural ventures. The individual nature of concession agreements meant that land rights, tax liabilities, and other privileges could be specified for each concession holder. One survey describes them as "an institutional foundation of modern capitalism about which we have virtually no systematic, comparative knowledge."[18] The inequality in relationships between foreign firms, sometimes backed by their home governments, and the weaker institutions of developing countries made concessions controversial the world over, and in the interwar period they were the subject of high-profile debates in newspapers and in literature by such writers as Evelyn Waugh and Joseph Conrad.

Diaz granted concessions across a range of sectors, from railroads to public sanitation to mining and oil drilling.[19] From the 1880s, foreign concessions to companies under American, French, and British ownership increased the amount of railway track in Mexico from 400 miles in 1876 to 15,000 in 1911. Mining concessions similarly led to steep expansion in the output of silver and gold, reviving the industry after a long period of decline following Mexican independence. Holders of mining concessions ranged from large conglomerates like the Guggenheims to individual proprietors like Colonel William Greene, whose concession in Sonora soon became one of the largest copper mining companies in the world. American and British concessions opened up Mexico to oil drilling. There were also industrial concessions, with companies producing steel, beer, cement, textiles, and a number of other goods.

One problem Diaz had was how to convince the holders of concessions that his government would honor its agreements. He did this partly by bringing members of the Mexican elite – and particularly the political elite – into a system of patronage fed by the profits of concession agreements. In a

---

[17] L. Michael Hager, "Taxation of Foreign Investment in Liberia," *Liberian Law Journal* 1, no. 2 (1965): 151.

[18] Cyrus Veeser, "A Forgotten Instrument of Global Capitalism? International Concessions, 1870–1930," *International History Review* 35, no. 5 (2013): 1139.

[19] See Michael C. Meyer and William L. Sherman, *The Course of Mexican History* (Oxford: Oxford University Press, 1991), ch. 27.

study of business networks in Mexico and Brazil, Aldo Musaccio and Ian Read show that connections between firms, banks, and the government were more important in Mexico than in Brazil. "Perhaps the best example of the union of politics and business in Mexico was Porfirio Diaz Jr, the son of the long-ruling dictator," they write. "Diaz Jr served on the boards of many important companies, including two banks, El Buen Tono, the Mexican Eagle Oil Company, one railroad company, and the biggest utility company in Mexico."[20]

Concessions brought this elite coalition into conflict with the majority, in particular over the enforcement of land rights. Prior to the late nineteenth century, land rights in Mexico were poorly defined, and contained a mix of legal titles, deeds from the Spanish crown, and traditional claims for which there was no written proof. Even before Diaz, large landowners ensured the selective enforcement of their rights over and above those of other claimants through relationships with regional and local political elites, held together through business or kinship ties. Under Diaz, the center of gravity shifted toward the federal rather than regional governments, but programs intended to privatize federal and municipal lands helped concentrate landholdings in the hands of a small number of very large landholders who could be integrated into the rent-seeking coalition.

Under the Porfirian regime, Mexico experienced rapid growth. There remain debates, however, on how far the benefits were distributed. Many argue that only the elite gained, an argument reflected in the titles of key works on the period, such as John Coatsworth's 1981 study of Mexican railroads during the Porfiriato (*Growth Against Development*). Unfortunately, there is not much systematic evidence with which to measure trends in living standards in Mexico. What evidence there is paints a mixed picture. By some metrics living standards did increase, but at the same time inequality between people and regions increased. Over the long run, increases in GDP per capita are associated with a wide range of other metrics, including health and education, but these do not always move together in the short run. Industrialization in Britain and the United States was accompanied by stagnating or even declining standards of living for some groups, particularly the urban working classes.[21] Similar divergences can be found for Mexico.

---

[20] Aldo Musaccio and Ian Read, "Bankers, Industrialists and Their Cliques: Elite Networks in Mexico and Brazil during Early Industrialization," *Enterprise and Society* 8, no. 4 (2007): 865.

[21] Michael R. Haines, Lee A. Craig and Thomas Wiess, "The Short and the Dead: Nutrition, Mortality, and the Antebellum Puzzle in the United States," *Journal of Economic History* 63 (2003): 382–413; Roderick Floud, Robert W. Fogel, Bernard Harris and Sok Chul Hong, *The Changing Body: Health, Nutrition and Human Development in the Western World since 1700* (Cambridge: Cambridge University Press, 2011).

Data on military recruits during the Porfiriato showed that the heights of men from the lower classes stagnated or declined, while those of elites increased steadily.[22]

Concessions and Elite Coalitions in Liberia

In 1971, just six months before Tubman's death, leaders of the True Whig Party issued a statement commemorating the opening of the new party headquarters, named in honor of Edward Roye, the president who negotiated the 1871 loan discussed in Chapter 6 but was ousted from power shortly thereafter. In it, they compared Roye's policies to those of Tubman. "Both had emphasized the need for encouraging the investment of foreign capital," the statement read.

President Tubman has been the only President in the almost seventy-five intervening years between 1870 and 1944, who was brave enough to risk the implementation of the policy which allowed the application of foreign capital to the development needs of the Nation. Only he, out of eighteen Presidents, was bold enough to openly invite foreign capital, and make it work to improve the living conditions of his people, and to modernize and industrialize the country by exploiting its natural resources.[23]

The singling out of Tubman reflects what Stephen Ellis describes as a "personality cult," which emerged around him during the post-war decades, but is not quite justified.[24] Earlier presidents had also sought foreign investment in their efforts to promote economic expansion and increase revenues. Arthur Barclay signed one of the earliest rubber concession agreements with Sir Harry Johnston in 1906. Though that concession was short-lived, it provided the foundation for the Firestone plantation established under C. D. B. King in 1926. Edwin Barclay, nephew of Arthur, who became president after King resigned in the aftermath of the League of Nations investigation, signed several concession agreements during the 1930s. In 1935, a group of Polish nationals was granted a concession for growing castor beans, an intervention which prompted the questions about a Polish mandate discussed in the previous chapter. In 1937, a Dutch firm agreed a concession for the mining of iron ore at Bomi Hills, but this was cancelled in 1938 due to pressure from American

[22] Moramay Lopez-Alonso, "Growth with Inequality: Living Standards in Mexico 1850–1950," *Journal of Latin American Studies* 39 (2007): 81–105.

[23] Box 56, Sven Holsoe Roye papers, IULC.

[24] Stephen Ellis, *The Mask of Anarchy: The Destruction of Liberia and the Religious Dimension of an African Civil War* (New York: New York University Press, 2007), 47.

officials who believed the effort was funded by Axis interests.[25] Other presidents had issued plenty of invitations, as did the leaders of other countries. However, few were as successful in getting foreign investors to accept, even though the decades following the end of World War II were not a period of expansion in terms of foreign investment, particularly compared with the first era of globalization in the late nineteenth and early twentieth centuries. From the 1950s to the 1970s, Liberia was one of the leading recipients of foreign investment in sub-Saharan Africa, outstripping even South Africa from the 1960s.[26]

The number of concession agreements expanded rapidly from the 1940s. The first postwar concessions emerged from connections forged during the war between Liberia and American officials and entrepreneurs. In 1945, the Liberian government granted a concession to Lansdell Christie to prospect for iron ore in the Bomi Hills. Christie had served in Liberia in the US Army during the war. The concession gave Christie exclusive rights to explore a region of about three million acres for three and a half years. Within that area he could select areas to mine of up to 25,000 acres, on which he would pay 5 cents per acre on mined lots in addition to a monthly exploration tax of $100 and a royalty of 5 cents per ton on any iron ore shipped. Albert Porte circulated a petition protesting the terms of this agreement, in response to which he was jailed for a month under Emergency Powers legislation maintained by the Tubman regime.[27]

One of the investors in Christie's mining effort was a company founded by Edward Stettinius Jr., who had been administrator of the Lend–Lease program during the years the Liberian port project was being negotiated. In 1947, the Liberian government signed an agreement with Stettinius Associates-Liberia, Inc. According to the agreement, the company was to serve as "an instrument of the government for carrying out overall development and for expanding Liberian production, employment and trade by appropriate international domestic measures." The role of the Company would be "to provide necessary finances, specialized knowledge, and all senior business management."

---

[25] F. P. M. van der Kraaij, *The Open Door Policy of Liberia: An Economic History of Modern Liberia* (Bremen: Bremer Afrika Archiv, 1983), and "History of economic and financial development in Liberia," February 7, 1949, in NARA RG 59 Entry A1 1423 Box 1, Declassification NND933006.

[26] Michael J. Twomey, *A Century of Foreign Investment in the Third World* (Abingdon: Routledge, 2000).

[27] Burrowes, *Power and Press Freedom*, 230.

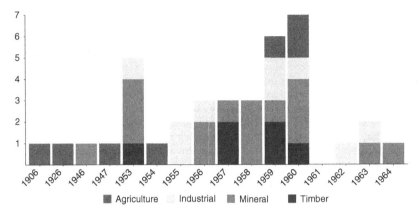

Figure 9.1 Concessions by industry
Source: Clower et al., *Growth without development*; van der Kraaij, *Open door.*

From the 1950s onward, the Liberian government expanded its granting of concession to a variety of industries. Figure 9.1 gives an overview of
the number and industrial focus of concessions. A full list of known
concessions, on which these data are based, appears in Appendix 1. It
may be not be comprehensive, as there was no definitive list maintained
even by the Liberian government at the time.[28] Some companies with
formal concession agreements did not survive long. A 1952 concession
agreement granted Latourneau of Liberia, a company owned by a
preacher from Texas, rights to 500,000 acres for eighty years. It was to
pay an annual rental of 5 cents per acre on a minimum of 50,000 acres. By
the end of the decade, however, the company had only a small poultry
enterprise and twenty churches. It folded by the early 1960s. There were
also companies that operated but never had a formal concession agreement approved by the Liberian legislature. One example was the African
Fruit Company, started by a German firm which had previously exported
bananas from Cameroon. Its concession agreement, for 600,000 acres
over eighty years, was never formally ratified. Despite this, it began
production of bananas, at first, then coffee and rubber, and in 1975 was
purchased by the Liberian Minister of Finance.

As in Mexico, Liberian government officials and their relatives were
frequently appointed to board positions on concession companies, and
received shares of those companies as part of the negotiation process. One

[28] van der Kraaij, *The Open Door Policy.*

record of a conversation at the US Embassy in Monrovia documented how such exchanges might have worked.

Mr. Khalifa said that, before signing the concession agreement with CEMENCO in March 1966, the President had made clear that his signature would depend upon Shad Tubman Junior's receiving a 5 per cent interest in the company. As a result, Shad Jr owns one third of the stock which was to have been sold to the Liberian public, and he is on the company's board of directors as representative of the private Liberian investors. Khalifa had been informed by other concessionaires that they also had to donate stock in their companies to Shad Tubman Jr. (He would not be more specific but said that this apparently constituted a current requirement for doing business in Liberia).[29]

Surveys of companies at the time illustrate that this practice extended beyond Tubman's son. In his listing of timber concessions, van der Kraaij also names Liberian lawyers/advisers employed by each concession. Shad Tubman, Jr., was one of these but not the only one. The list included a range of current and former officials and other members of the Liberian elite. George Padmore, lawyer for the Liberian Industrial Forestry Corporation, a joint Spanish and Liberian concession of 364,000 acres in Lofa County, was a grandson of former president Arthur Barclay and Tubman's son-in-law. He had acted as ambassador to the United States. Richard Henries, acting for the French-owned Lofa Timber Company, was the speaker of the House of Representatives and a representative for Montserrado County. He also acted as legal adviser for the LAMCO concession, the Liberian Mineral Company, and the Firestone plantation. Other advisers included an Associate Justice of the Supreme Court, an Assistant Minister of Agriculture, senators and members of the House of Representatives, party officials, and various relatives.[30] A survey of 386 companies registered in Monrovia in 1961 by Gus Liebenow showed that "of the firms largely financed by Swiss, Swedish and other European investors, the more successful ones included prominent Liberian officials on their boards of directors or retained lawyer-legislators to represent them in their negotiations with the government."[31]

Such connections between political elites and concession companies provided the system of third-party enforcement which Haber, Maurer, and Razo theorize was important in establishing the credible protection of the selective set of property rights granted to concessionaires. By giving an

[29] Memorandum of conversation, US Embassy Monrovia, August 11, 1967, RG59 Entry A1 (5713, Declass NND37720).
[30] van der Kraaij, *The Open Door Policy*, Annex 19.
[31] J. Gus Liebenow, *Liberia: The Evolution of Privilege* (Ithaca: Cornell University Press, 1969), 92–93.

existing political elite an interest in the concession system, it made it less likely that the Liberian government would expropriate the capital of concession companies. The system of selective property rights can be illustrated particularly through land rights and taxation, examined in the next two sections.

Creating Queezahn (Or "White People Took Us from There")

Concession agreements often granted companies at least theoretical rights to put large swathes of the country into production, with little regard for indigenous claims to the same territory. The selective enforcement of land rights already had a long history in Liberia even before the concession era, but the scale of the concessions generated increasing conflicts between the government and people dispossessed of land and capital.

Historically, the abundance of land in much of West Africa meant that systems of property rights were generally not oriented around individual ownership of specific plots of land.[32] Instead, land was held communally, and the distribution and enforcement of land rights was managed through local elites. However, the investment of labor in a particular plot or the planting of tree crops could secure rights to that land for its produce.[33] Rights were sufficiently secure for people to use long fallowing periods in order to restore the productivity of the soil.[34] In Kru villages, for example, fallow periods extended from four to fifteen years.[35]

As the Liberian government extended its jurisdiction into the interior, all lands acquired from indigenous communities, whether voluntarily or by force, were declared public land which could only be purchased or acquired through the government. The government then granted that land to new settlers, churches, or private companies, or as a reward for

---

[32] Gareth Austin, "Resources, Techniques and Strategies South of the Sahara: Revising the Factor Endowments Perspective on African Economic Development, 1500–2000," *Economic History Review* 61 (2008): 587–624.

[33] Carl Burrowes, *Between the Kola Forest and the Salty Sea: A History of the Liberian People before 1800* (Bomi County: Know Your Self Press, 2016), 261; Gregg Mitman and Emmanuel King Urey, "'Sitting on Old Mats to Plait New': The Gendered Struggle over Land and Livelihood in Liberia," in *The Social Life of Land*, edited by Michael Goldman, Nancy Peluso and Wendo Wolford (Ithaca: Cornell University Press, 2023), 10.

[34] Fallowing has been defined as an investment in other studies of West African land rights. See Markus Goldstein and Christopher Udry, "The Profits of Power: Land Rights and Agricultural Investment in Ghana," *Journal of Political Economy* 116, no. 6 (2008): 981–1022.

[35] Zetterstrom, "Preliminary Report on the Kru," in Bai T. Moore papers, IULC, 15.

public or military service.[36] Such grants were sometimes speculative as to their locations, much like the land grants to concession companies later on. In his will, Joseph Jenkins Roberts, the first president of independent Liberia, bequeathed to each of his three nieces government certificates for twenty-five acres of land. The certificates allowed the recipients to select the location of these acres before a deed was granted.[37] Land commissioners in each county managed the sale of public lands to settlers who wished to purchase more, although due to a combination of fraud and poor record-keeping such sales were often subject to disputes.[38]

The classification of public land retained considerable ambiguity through much of Liberian history, and did not represent the wholesale seizure of land from the indigenous population. In 1931, the administrative regulations of the Department of Interior stated "the primary title to all lands in the Republic is in the Government. The Government, however, recognizes the usufructuary interest of a tribe in the lands upon which it is settled."[39] However, the precise implications of this regulation were never defined very clearly. Stevens argued that this ambiguity may have been deliberate, balancing two conflicting imperatives faced by the Liberian government. To recognize indigenous rights would have been in effect a cession of sovereignty, since through much of Liberia's history indigenous groups did not recognize themselves as under the jurisdiction of the Liberian government. The Liberian government could not therefore offer general enforcement of these rights and still maintain its claims to territory. At the same time, however, it did not have the military might necessary to abrogate those rights entirely.

The scale of grants to concessions made the question more pressing. Firestone could claim up to a million acres as part of its concession, and Lansdell Christie three million. The scale of notional claims declined over time but they remained substantial. In its 1954 concession agreement, B. F. Goodrich was granted rights to 600,000 acres. The same amount was granted to the Liberian Agricultural Company, a Dutch concern, in 1959 and the African Fruit Company in 1952. Timber concessions could be equally large. Per the terms of its 1960 concession, the Maryland

---

[36] Caleb J. Stevens, "The Legal History of Public Land in Liberia," *Journal of African Law* 58, no. 2 (2014): 251; Tom W. Shick, *Behold the Promised Land: A History of Afro-American Settler Society in Nineteenth-Century Liberia* (Baltimore: The Johns Hopkins University Press, 1980), 78. See also example of land grant in return for military service by Stephen Bens on to Thomas Howland, September 3, 1863, in Joseph Jenkins Roberts family papers, Library of Congress.

[37] Joseph Jenkins Roberts, Last will and testiment, March 5, 1876, in Joseph Jenkins Roberts family papers, Library of Congress.

[38] Shick, *Behold the Promised Land*, 79–82.

[39] Quoted in Stevens, "The Legal History of Public Land in Liberia," 256.

Logging Company, a German firm, held rights to an area of 750,000 acres. The Liberian Timber Industries, backed by American capital, was granted 450,000 acres the year before.

None of these firms ever managed to put such large acreages into production. A 1949 memo by the US State Department pointed out that "Liberia's concession history shows that rarely have concessionaires been able to establish operations in as many fields and on as large a scale as was first contemplated."[40] By the early 1960s, almost forty years after its first arrival in the country, Firestone had just under 70,000 acres in production with another 18,200 acres in immature rubber trees, out of the million it was originally granted. B. F. Goodrich had 10,000 acres planted, out of the 600,000 to which it was entitled. Still, even these limited plantings involved sometimes significant disruption of indigenous land use, and the potential for claims to the rest generated uncertainty for indigenous producers. Through concessions, Stevens writes that "much of Liberia's littoral land and even some of its land in the interior was transferred from public to private tenure arrangements."[41]

These seizures of land met with protest from the beginning. In 1924, as the prospect of the Firestone concession was first being discussed, a letter from the British Consul, MacDonnel, in Monrovia to the Foreign Office in London noted that "my attention has been called to the fact that the Liberian government apparently intend to expropriate the tribes on whose land the rubber is to be grown, without compensation, and it has been suggested to me that this is a singular proceeding on the part of a member of the League of Nations."[42] For his part, MacDonnel did not share this outrage, and wrote:

I feel that the Liberian authorities would be acting in the best interests of the republic and probably of the dispossessed natives, by expropriating them. The scheme certainly offers a prospect of developing and enriching the country, and the tribesmen whose land is taken over will no doubt be employed by the firm at better wages than they could enjoy as the fruit of their labour on their farms.

Those being dispossessed did not agree, and land seizures were a constant source of criticism and protest. F. W. M. Morias, a member of the Liberian legislature from Maryland County, wrote in a piece published in the *Tribune de Geneve* in September 1931, "from every corner of the land rises the same cry of lamentation, 'we are despoiled of our patrimony, our fields and villages.'" The piece noted particularly "the

[40] Memo on the "History of economic and financial development in Liberia," February 7, 1949, in NARA RG 59 Entry A1 1423 Box 1, Declassification NND933006.
[41] Stevens, "The legal history of public land in Liberia," 251.
[42] MacDonnel to Lansdowne, October 21, FO 458/70.

destruction of plantations of coffee, bananas, and sugar cane."[43] He wrote this piece while he was attending a League of Nations meeting. When he returned to Liberia in 1932, he was arrested for sedition and imprisoned.[44] Forty years later, Charles Morrow Wilson, a former US diplomat who spent four years in Liberia employed by Firestone, wrote in 1971 that one of the "socially consequential shortcomings" of the concessions policies was "the displacement of tribes or tribespeople from lands that were being leased by foreign investors and their less than satisfactory resettlement in less desirable forest land or bush sites."[45]

One such dispossessed village is called Queezahn, which translates from Bassa as "white or Civilized people took us from there."[46] According to Gregg Mitman and Emmanuel King Urey, who conducted extensive oral history interviews in Queezahn, "this Bassa place name memorializes the displacement of rural people that took place in Liberia first major land concession." Such removals were not merely bureaucratic transfers of ownership, but often involved considerable violence, with the burning of existing crops and villages and the intervention of the Frontier Force. Like others similarly dispossessed, the people of Queezahn were promised compensation for their removal. "When a Queezahn elder remarks that the community is still waiting for Firestone to rebuild their village, more than ninety years after the company took their land and destroyed their ancestor's homes, the large group, young and old, gathered together on a rainy afternoon, erupts in laughter."

It was not only concession holders responsible for land claims in the interior. Both Firestone and B. F. Goodrich promoted the independent production of rubber alongside their own plantings, handing out seeds and purchasing rubber grown by Liberian farms. According to surveys by Gus Leibenow in the 1960s, those who gained most from this were members of the same group of political elites discussed in the previous section. "Of the eleven leading independent producers, all but two of the farms were owned by families of previous Presidents of Liberia or by individuals who had served in the Tubman administration at one stage or another. Prominent in the top twenty-five producers were members of the cabinet, leading legislators, and even district commissioners."[47]

How widespread the impact of land claims by concessions was remains the subject of debate. In their history of Mexico, Michael Meyer and

---

[43] Extract from the *Tribune de Geneve*, September 5, 1931, in FO 458/115.
[44] Burrowes, *Power and Press Freedom*, 191.
[45] Charles Morrow Wilson, *Liberia: Black Africa in Microcosm* (New York: Harper and Row, 1971), 201.
[46] Mitman and Urey, "Sitting on Old Mats to Plait New," 2.
[47] Liebenow, *Liberia*, 93–4.

William Sherman emphasize both the scale of the land transfers, in which they claim that "some 134 million acres of the best land had passed into the hands of a few hundred fantastically wealthy families," and the wide gap that opened up between the wealthy hacendados and the peones who actually worked the land.[48] Their conclusions concur with standard Marxist accounts of the Mexican Revolution as resulting, in part, from the proletarianization of the peasantry. However, Riguzzi challenges this claim, arguing that the process of land consolidation was restricted to marginal lands in a small number of states, giving the standard Marxist account "an extremely flimsy empirical basis."[49] Similarly, in Liberia, it is unclear how far land dispossession impacted subsistence production more broadly, even as some communities (like the occupants of Queezahn) were clearly stripped of valuable assets. In one unpublished report, Northwestern economist Robert Clower claimed that "land is still a free good in most of the hinterland of Liberia, and dispossession of tribal people has not so far imposed operative limits to land areas available for tribal cultivation."[50] However, he did observe inequalities in who got access to which land. "Large tracts of public land along newly constructed roads have been sold to nontribal individuals for business, farming, or speculative purposes."

As private contracts between government and corporations, concession agreements could establish specific rights to land, minerals, and other resources which governments could enforce even at the expense of other claims to the same resources. In neither Liberia nor Mexico was such selective enforcement purely an invention of the concession era. Rather, concession agreements built on and consolidated existing systems in which the strength of property rights was not universal but rather depended upon connections to a network of political elites.

Not One Tax System, but Several

The selective granting and enforcement of rights over land were not the only ways in which governments could favor specific asset holders. As the case of Mexico illustrates, they can do so through "a broad range of policies or regulations that affect the ability of those who hold property rights to earn returns from that property. These include tax regimes, labor laws, monetary policy, exchange rates and a whole host of other

---

[48] Meyer and Sherman, *Course of Mexican History*, 458–64.
[49] Paulo Riguzzi, "From Globalization to Revolution? The Porfirian Political Economy: An Essay on Issues and Interpretation," *Journal of Latin American Studies* 41 (2009): 347–68.
[50] Clower, "Liberian Agriculture and Economic Development," Northwestern University Economic Survey of Liberia Staff Paper No 14, Herskovits Library.

regulations."[51] In Liberia, tax privileges were an important feature of many concession agreements. In his study of the Liberian tax system, Michael Hager points out several loopholes that allowed the government to negotiate individual deals with foreign companies. Section 151 of the Revenue and Finance Law, for example, exempted from income tax liability any business having "contractual agreements with the Republic of Liberia which ... explicitly cover taxation." Since concession agreements were approved by the legislature, they carried the force of law, which meant that any agreement with specific tax exemptions constituted, in effect, a bespoke tax law for that company.

Most concession agreements contained some kind of tax exemption. Exemptions from all import and export duties were common.[52] After the imposition of the income tax of 1951, personal incomes and corporate profits should have been taxed at a progressive rate of up to 35 percent for incomes or profits over $100,000. However, few concession companies paid that rate, at least not initially. Agricultural concessions agreements generally contained a tax holiday determined in part by how long particular crops took to mature. For tree crops like coffee, cocoa, and rubber, exemptions were between twelve and sixteen years.[53] Even after the end of the exemption period, however, rates were often lower than 35 percent. B. F. Goodrich, for example, had a 16.5-year period of exemption, after which it was to be 25 percent of net profits for the next ten years. The Liberian Agricultural Company's concession agreement had similar terms.

In mineral concession agreements, a more common method than the taxation of profits was a profit-sharing arrangement in which the government took part ownership of the concession company. In such agreements, the government generally received 50 percent of the authorized capital stock of the concession then up to 50 percent of the net profits. There were, however, numerous ways for companies to underreport their net profits or otherwise manipulate their tax liabilities. There was no association of accountants in Liberia at that stage to certify acceptable principles, and thus practices and terms differed per agreement. As a result of these variations, Hager concludes that "Liberia has not one tax system but several. The general law and the various concession agreements provide a mélange of tax policy governing foreign investment."[54]

[51] Haber, Maurer and Razo, *Politics of Property Rights*, 23.
[52] International Monetary Fund, *The Economy of Liberia* (Washington, DC: IMF, 1963), 8.
[53] Robert W. Clower, George Dalton, Mitchell Harwitz and A. A. Walters, *Growth without Development: An Economic Survey of Liberia* (Evanston: Northwestern University Press, 1966), 161.
[54] Hager, "Taxation of Foreign Investment," 176.

Such tax concessions did not stop the Liberian government from increasing its revenue collections during this period. Revenue as a share of GDP more than doubled during the 1950s with the introduction of the income tax, and hovered around 20 percent of GDP through subsequent decades. This is the target level considered to be a minimum for meeting development spending needs, and was comparatively high for African countries during that period. Data on revenue as a share of GDP are not widely available before the 1990s, but at that point the average revenue/GDP ratio was 16 percent.[55] The taxation of income and profits was responsible for much of this increase; according to calculations by van der Kraaij, Firestone was the largest single source of government revenue during the 1950s after it began to pay taxes for the first time (albeit at a rate of 12.5 percent rather than 35). By the 1960s, iron ore profit-sharing arrangements had become more important.

Despite Liberia's comparatively successful system of tax collection, the rapid growth of government spending meant that it was an almost constant state of fiscal crisis from the 1950s onward. In 1950, Byron Larabee of Firestone reported to the State Department that the Liberian government had just requested to borrow $1,000,000 from Firestone, on top of the $400,000 that the Company had already loaned the government.[56] Through the 1926 loan agreement, Firestone in this period occupied a position similar to Bancamex in Mexico. Larabee blamed Liberia's fiscal difficulties on spending commitments "far in excess of its ability to pay" and asked the State Department to warn that in future it would be "necessary for President Tubman to exercise a tighter rein over government expenditures." The State Department duly provided such warnings. However, government outlays continued to grow.

Much like Diaz's government had done decades earlier, the Liberian government invested significant sums in the expansion of administration, roads, and in particular Liberia's diplomatic presence abroad.[57] The expansion in spending combined with a drop in commodity prices in the early 1960s culminated in a fiscal crisis in 1963. The government sought help from the IMF, which Liberia had just joined the year before, and Liberia's short-term debts were restructured. In return, the government committed to significant austerity measures, including a

[55] Mick Moore, Wilson Prichard and Odd-Helge Fjeldstad, *Taxing Africa: Coercion, Reform and Development* (London: Zed Books, 2018), 12, 33.

[56] Memorandum of conversation, "Financial situation in Liberia," June 29, 1950, in NARA RG 59 Entry A1 1423, Box 1. Declass NND933006.

[57] van der Kraaij, *Open Door*, 316–18; IMF, *The Economy of Liberia*, 16.

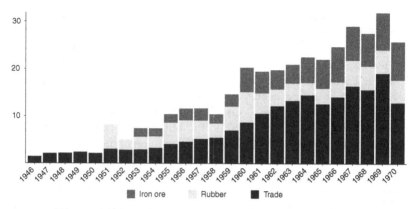

Figure 9.2 Revenue by source, 1946–1970 (constant 1950 US$)
Source: Republic of Liberia, *Economic Survey of Liberia* (Monrovia: Ministry of Planning and Economic Affairs, various years); Robert F Steadman, *Report on the Fiscal System of the Republic of Liberia* (Monrovia: Executive Manion, 1952).

new austerity tax targeting lower-income Liberians and spending cuts.[58] Despite these commitments, Liberia struggled to maintain its expenditure through subsequent decades.

Both contemporary observers and historians have argued that the Liberian government should have gotten more revenue from the concession companies than it did.[59] By the late 1960s, the IMF was pressuring the Liberian government to increase the taxation of concession companies by renegotiating agreements. However, "Liberian Treasury Secretary Weeks stated that neither he nor President Tubman would agree to 'hit' the concessions as the IMF officials advised."[60] By that point, as previous sections have shown, the concession companies were part of an extensive "patronage machine," as Ellis describes it.[61] This "rent-seeking coalition" provided the foundation for Liberia's economic growth and political stability during this period, and Tubman and Tolbert may have been unwilling to risk "hitting" the concessions and undermining what remained a fragile institutional equilibrium.

---

[58] van der Kraaij, *Open Door*, 319–20.
[59] Robert E. Miller and Peter R. Carter, "The Modern Dual Economy: A Cost-Benefit Analysis of Liberia," *Journal of Modern African Studies* 10, no. 1 (1972): 113–21; van der Kraaij, *Open Door*.
[60] Draft position paper: Liberian debt stretch out, 5/9/68, NARA RG59 Entry A1 (5713) Declass NND37720.
[61] Ellis, *The Mask of Anarchy*, 48.

Growth without Development?

Assessments of the Tubman regime have generated debates very similar to those about the Diaz regime. Critics of the regime make the same case as critics of Diaz: that while their policies generated growth, that growth benefitted only the few, sometimes at the expense of the many. The title of the final published report of the Northwestern economists who surveyed Liberia in 1962, *Growth without Development* is similar to that of Coatsworth's *Growth against Development*. In a 1965 article in the *Journal of Economic History*, one member of the Northwestern team wrote:

[T]he few new production lines initiated by foreigners since the Second World War make for short-run growth but not long-run development: they do not induce complementary activities so as progressively to enmesh wider sectors of the economy in new skills, new technology, and higher productivity. There is no reason to believe that Liberia will be appreciably more developed in 1970 than it was in 1960.[62]

As in Mexico, however, the empirical basis by which to test such claims is thin. Unlike for Mexico, there are no height data for Liberia from the period in question. The only systematic source of such data are from the 2007 Demographic and Health Survey, which collected data on the heights of women aged fifteen to forty-nine. This would mean that the oldest women in the sample were not born until 1958, halfway through Tubman's period in office and after much of the period of rapid economic growth. There is limited data on the incidence of child stunting caused by poor living conditions, which in 1976 was measured at 43.1 percent of children under five.[63] Historically, such levels of stunting were not uncommon in West Africa and in developing countries more broadly.[64] Japan, for example, had rates of stunting above 60 percent during the early twentieth century.[65] However, stunting was nearly eradicated during its period of rapid economic growth after World War II, with levels falling to less than 6 percent by 1986. While no earlier data are available to show the impact of Liberia's postwar economic growth on stunting over

[62] George Dalton, "History, Politics and Economic Development in Liberia," *Journal of Economic History* 25, no. 4 (1965): 571.
[63] World Bank, World Development Indicators, April 2018 version.
[64] For comparative data on stunting across space and time, see UNICEF, WHO and World Bank Group, *Joint Child Malnutrition Estimates – Levels and Trends in Child Malnutrition: Key Findings for the 2019 Edition* (2019), https://apps.who.int/iris/bitstream/handle/10665/331097/WHO-NMH-NHD-19.20-eng.pdf?ua=1 and Eric B. Schneider, *Stunting: Past, Present and Future* (2018) http://doi.org/10.21953/lse.9teyst78nhxh.
[65] Eric B. Schneider and Kota Ogasawara, "Disease and Child Growth in Industrializing Japan: Critical Windows and the Growth Pattern, 1917–1939," *Explorations in Economic History* 69 (2018): 64–80.

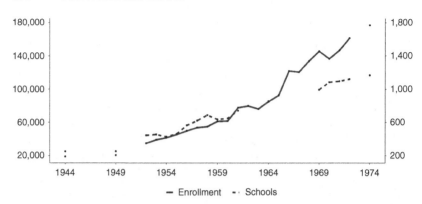

Figure 9.3 Number of schools and enrolled students, 1944–1974
Source: Liberia Department of Public Instruction, Annual Report
(1960); Republic of Liberia, Request to the World Bank Group
(1971); Ministry of Agriculture, Statistical Handbook (1975).

time, the fact that stunting remained at such a high level even after forty
years of economic growth suggests that the gains from that growth were
not always widely distributed.

At the same time, both the number of schools and the number of
enrolled students increased dramatically in this period, as shown in
Figure 9.3. Censuses taken from 1962 onward included questions
about both literacy and education. Using data on birth cohorts, it is
possible to observe changes in levels over time. As discussed in Chapter
3 with regard to migrants to Liberia during the nineteenth century, this is
not a perfect measure. It assumes that both literacy and educational
attainment depended only on the availability of services during childhood, which may not necessarily be the case. People also tend to overreport both literacy and educational attainment in contexts where
education is seen as prestigious. However, it is one of the few measures
available which can show the impact of this period on the majority of the
Liberian population.

Figure 9.4 shows literacy rates by birth cohort from 1974 to 2008
censuses, for which detailed microdata are available. It compares these
with similar data from Ghana and Sierra Leone, and shows that literacy
rates in Liberia were extremely low in the late nineteenth century, even
below the 10 percent estimated for enslaved African Americans in
Chapter 3. However, they increased rapidly from the 1920s and particularly for people born from the 1940s onward. During this period,
Liberia's literacy rates exceeded those of Sierra Leone, which had tracked

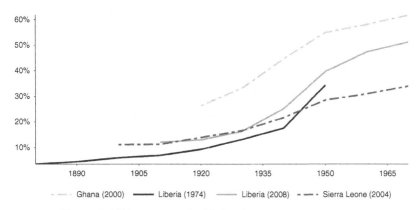

Figure 9.4 Literacy rates by birth cohort
Source: Census data from IPUMS International.

those of Liberia up to the 1940s and began to converge on those of Ghana which had been double those of Liberia in the 1920s.

Improvements in literacy rates and educational outcomes were not evenly distributed through the country. Figure 9.5 compares the outcomes for Montserrado County, where Monrovia is located, and areas outside it. The increase in literacy on Monrovia was both earlier and larger than in other areas. This gap would seem to fit narratives which would suggest that public spending and government services under Tubman and Tolbert were targeted to benefit elites in Monrovia rather than the wider population. However, it is worth noting that this pattern is not at all unique to Liberia. This was a period when education was expanding in Africa, but most countries saw considerable inequality in access at first.[66] Comparing those born in Greater Accra with people born in the rest of the country shows a similar gap of around 20 percentage points in the literacy rate in Ghana. Concession companies in Liberia contributed directly to some of these improvements. Oral histories taken by Mitman and Urey show that concession areas were important points of access for education and healthcare after World War II, attracting female employees in particular.[67]

[66] Rebecca Simson, "Ethnic (in)equality in the public services of Kenya and Uganda," *African Affairs* 118, no. 470 (2019): 75–100.
[67] Mitman and Urey, "Sitting on Old Mats to Plait New," 11.

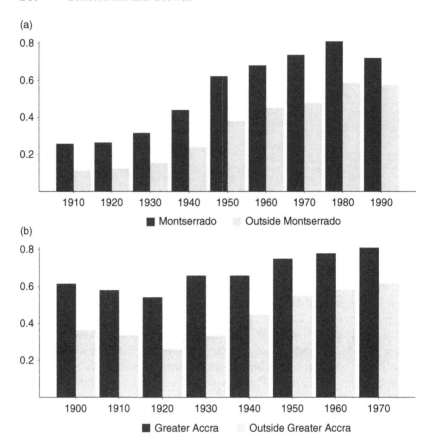

Figure 9.5 Urban and rural literacy rates by birth cohort
A. Liberia: Montserrado County compared to the rest of the country
Source: Liberia 2008 census, from IPUMS International.
B. Ghana: Greater Accra compared to the rest of the country
Source: Ghana 2000 census, from IPUMS International.

The movement of people from rural areas to work on concessions or in Monrovia presented a new challenge for the government, particularly in the aftermath of the fiscal crisis of the early 1960s, which may have impacted rural living standards. Through most of the twentieth century, and particularly after the establishment of the Firestone plantation, domestic agricultural production had struggled to supply sufficient food to urban areas. This was partly due to the lack of infrastructure, which made it difficult for domestic markets to integrate, and partly due to the negative incentives which faced farmers who from the 1930s had portions

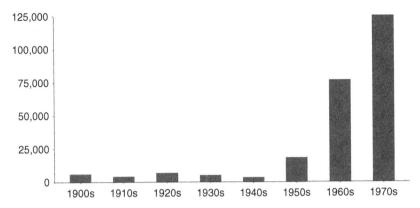

Figure 9.6 Average annual rice imports by decade, 1900–1980

of their crop seized by local officials, as discussed in Chapter 7.[68] As the export sector expanded, however, this problem became particularly acute. Rice imports expanded rapidly in the postwar period, as shown in Figure 9.6, rising from an annual average of around 5,000,000 pounds through the 1940s to 125,071,000 pounds in the 1970s. This was a significant quantity compared to local production, which rose from an estimate of 244,644 thousand pounds in 1960 to just over 500,000 thousand pounds in 1970 (see Figure 9.7).

Increasing rice production was a key political priority for Tubman, who initiated a government program called Operation Production in 1963, with the aim of tripling the domestic production of rice. As Cassandra Mark-Thiesen documents in her history of the program, what was marketed as a collective effort to bolster Liberia's sovereignty by reducing its dependence on rice imports actually relied on a number of coercive labor policies, including vagrancy laws which mandated that vagrants be returned to rural areas and put to work on farms. This was accompanied by a general tightening of labor regulations during the same period.[69]

Given the limitations in available evidence about how most people in Liberia lived during this period, it is difficult to say anything very definite about the impact of growth on living standards, and there remain debates in the cases of both Liberia and Mexico. Riguzzi argues against the notion

---

[68] Clower, "Liberian Agriculture and Economic Development," Northwestern University Economic Survey of Liberia Staff Paper No 14, Herskovitz Library.

[69] Cassandra Mark-Thiesen, "Of Vagrants and Volunteers during Liberia's Operation Production, 1963–1969," *African Economic History* 46 (2018): 154.

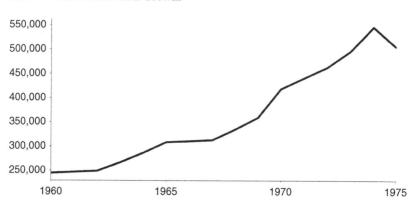

Figure 9.7 Estimated rice production, 1960–1975

that Mexico under Diaz was either predatory or subjugated to international finance, but instead points to empirical evidence of substantial
economic diversification.[70] Lawrence Marinelli, writing at around the
same time as Dalton, argued that it was true that "the economy is
dominated by foreign private capital and will be for several decades to
come. But the benefits have been tremendous for the country and its
citizens. Schools and hospitals are being built on an unprecedented scale.
New roads, airfields and railways are opening up the entire country; all
this will stimulate local agriculture, industry and trade."[71] Even Gus
Liebenow, otherwise a fierce critic of the Tubman regime, wrote that "it
must be recognized that development has in fact brought positive benefits
to many tribal areas ... New roads have made it possible for teachers,
medical technicians, agricultural instructors and others to reach the vast
interior of Liberia, where the majority of people live."[72]

Tubman's legacy has remained a lively area of public debate in Liberia
long after the end of the Liberian Civil War in 2003. In 2020, a Liberian
news website published a two-part editorial on the subject, written by
historian and former government official Samuel Toe.[73] In it, he identifies
two schools of thought regarding Tubman. One, dominant among people
writing during Tubman's presidency, "paints an almost saintly image" of a
great modernizer who transformed Liberia's economy. The second, which
has become more prominent since, "argues that Tubman exploited and

[70] Riguzzi, "From Globalization to Revolution."
[71] Lawrence A. Marinelli, "Liberia's Open-Door Policy," *Journal of Modern African Studies*
2, no. 1 (1964): 98.
[72] Liebenow, *Liberia*, 72–73.
[73] https://bushchicken.com/the-contested-legacy-of-liberias-19th-president-william-v-s-
tubman-part-1/

subjugated indigenous Liberians" to an American colonial project. "Broadly speaking," Toe writes, "it paints President Tubman as a grandstanding, cigar-smoking, pleasure-hugging, yacht-riding authoritarian dictator (a 'benevolent dictator') and American puppet." For his part, Toe offers a new interpretation somewhere between these two extremes.

The Collapse of the Coalition

Whatever the aggregate picture of living standards might have been, both countries saw evidence of growing disenchantment and anger in the shape of strikes and protests. In Liberia, these began on the Firestone plantation but appeared with greater frequency through the country from the 1950s onward. These were in part the reason for the tightening of labor regulations referred to in the previous section. It was one of these strikes which ultimately heralded the end of True Whig Party rule in Liberia. When Operation Production and similar initiatives failed to increase production as much as was hoped, the government increased the official price of rice in an effort to incentivize farmers to produce more. This raised the cost of living for a growing urban workforce. Over Easter weekend 1979, police in Monrovia fired into a peaceful demonstration, killing 40 and injuring 400.[74] Following the riots, there was serious looting throughout the city in which even some soldiers participated.[75]

Though President Tolbert attempted to blame the disorder on outside forces, American officials attributed the riots to the government's "neglect of the growing urban workers dilemma of a slow-growth economy and wildly inflationary food prices," along with "a very badly trained police and military." They saw Tolbert as being caught between the expectations of urban workers and a backlash by the Americo-Liberian elite.[76] Stephen Ellis describes the Tolbert regime as unable to cope with "the rise of a counter-elite" comprised of those educated through the expanded provision of schooling who began to establish opposition groups inspired by the radical politics of neighboring countries. This included the Movement for Justice in Africa (MOJA) established at the University of Liberia in 1973 and Progressive Alliance of Liberia (PAL) in 1975. Following the rice riots there were rumors of an impending coup, and MOJA and PAL began establishing relationships with members of

[74] Memorandum from Funk to Brzezinski, April 27, 1979, in US Department of State, *Foreign Relations of the United States, Volume XVII, Part 2, Sub-Saharan Africa* (Washington, DC: US Government Printing Office, 2018), 131.
[75] Ellis, *Mask of Anarchy*, 50.
[76] Memorandum from Funk to Brzezinski, March 21, 1980, in US Department of State, *Foreign Relations 1977–80, Volume XVII, Part 2*, 155–56.

the armed forces. In April 1980 and in response to a rumor that Tolbert was planning to assassinate a group of political prisoners on the anniversary of the riot, Tolbert was assassinated by twenty-eight-year-old Samuel K. Doe, one of a group of low-ranking soldiers of indigenous origin.[77]

The rent-seeking coalition created by Tubman and sustained by Tolbert provided sufficient order to attract foreign investment and generate rapid growth. This growth may have benefitted more of the population than previous work has suggested. However, as Haber and his co-authors point out with regard to the Porfiriato, maintaining the rent-seeking coalition created distortions within the economy and redistributed resources from those outside the coalition to those within it. Because stability is created through agreements between selected actors and government, it means that "government must be able to make deals in smoke-filled rooms without the necessity of public review and approval." As a result, such a system "is not consistent with high levels of political democracy."[78] Riguzzi attributes the ultimate collapse of the Porfiriato not to economic failings or inequality but rather to the inflexibility of the political system. "What distinguished Mexico from the rest of Latin America," he writes, "was not the excessive weakness of its economy or social inequality, but rather a frozen political regime, incapable of allowing political development to take place." He is keen to stress that this was not merely the result of Diaz's own preferences but rather something more systemic.

The 80-year-old president who continued to try to play the role of indispensable caudillo was only a reflection of that failed development. The issue did not boil down to the intransigence of the autocrat, but to the fact that the institutional links between voice (in Hirschman's meaning) and growth scarcely evolved during that period, and did not find outlets, in the form of parties or political movements.[79]

In Liberia, too, the structure of the political institutions which facilitated foreign investment and growth made it difficult for a more inclusive system to emerge. While it has been common for historians of Liberia to attribute this to the exclusivity of the Americo-Liberian elite, Ellis and others note that by the middle of the twentieth century the ruling elite extended beyond the descendants of migrants to include indigenous chiefs and others who were solidly integrated into patronage networks. "Even before the 1980 coup the Liberian elite was actually far less ethnically exclusive than has often been supposed."[80] But it remained difficult for those outside existing networks to find opportunities for social

---

[77] Ellis, *Mask of Anarchy*, 52–53.
[78] Haber, Maurer and Razo, *Politics of Property Rights*.
[79] Riguzzi, "From Globalization to Revolution," 367.   [80] Ellis, *Mask of Anarchy*, 285.

mobility or political voice in a system that increasingly quashed any competition or dissent, and the revenue raised through the granting of concessions and the expansion of exports was insufficient to meet the needs of an increasingly vocal urban workforce.

In his study of the Soviet Union under Stalin, Allen notes that any postmortem on the links between policies, institutions, and economic development requires an exploration of counterfactuals. "What institutions worked and which failed? Could the model have been modified to make it more attractive and to raise living standards more rapidly?"[81] Answering these questions is beyond the scope of this chapter, but they remain current in Liberia today. Despite the immediate political upheaval of Tolbert's assassination, little about the way in which Liberian government functioned changed under Doe, just as, in Mexico, Madero made use of many of the same elite networks to maintain his own position. Even after the Liberian civil war, the Poverty Reduction Strategy adopted by the elected government of Ellen Johnson Sirleaf emphasized the role of foreign direct investment, and concessions granted to foreign companies have remained controversial for appearing to bring benefits only to a ruling elite and not to the majority.[82]

Liberia and Mexico are hardly alone in sharing the histories outlined in this chapter. Historically, open-access institutions are the exception not the rule. However, the histories of places like Mexico and Liberia can help illustrate some the key obstacles to institutional change which developing countries face in trying to promote development and exercise their sovereignty on an unequal world stage. North, Wallis, and Weingast note that all limited access orders face problems of size; growth – whether in terms of territory, population, or economic output – has the potential to increase the rents absorbed by the elite, but at the same time can produce disputes about the redistribution of those rents which threaten the survival of the coalition.[83] The next chapter examines another plank in Tubman's "open-door" policy, in which the Liberian government attempted to commercialize its external sovereignty through the creation of liberal tax and corporation laws and, most durably, the flag of convenience. The Liberian shipping registry generated a new, and fungible, stream of revenue which became a contested resource during the period of conflict.

---

[81] Allen, *Farm to Factory*, 4.
[82] Agnieszka Paczynska, "Liberia Rising? Foreign Direct Investment, Persistent Inequalities and Political Tensions," *Peacebuilding* 4, no. 3 (2016): 297–316; Mitman and Urey, "Sitting on Old Mats to Plait New."
[83] North, Wallis and Weingast, *Violence and Social Orders*, 39–41.

10   Selling the Flag

> Sovereignty's erosion is as likely to occur by choice as by force. Today, many small countries voluntarily auction off their sovereignty to the highest bidder, reaping great rewards in the process.
>
> Daniel Drezner, "Sovereignty for sale," *Foreign Policy* (2009)

In the final weeks of 1976, the *New York Times* reported on a series of what it referred to as "maritime mishaps." On December 15th, a ship called the *Argo Merchant* ran aground near Nantucket, and less than a week later spilled 7.5 million gallons of oil into the Atlantic. Two days after the *Argo Merchant* had run around, another oil tanker, the *Sansinena*, exploded in Los Angeles harbor, killing four and causing extensive damage to the port facilities there. On the 27th, there were two more oil spills: one when a ship called the *Olympic Games* spilled 138,000 gallons of oil into the Delaware River and another when the *Oswego Peace* suffered a damaged hull in Connecticut. Three days later, another tanker, the *Daphne*, ran aground near Puerto Rico. All five ships were flying the Liberian flag at the time.[1]

The accumulation of five such incidents over the space of two weeks captured considerable media attention. By January 1977, the US Senate Commerce Committee had convened a two-day hearing on what the Chairman referred to as "the worst rash of tanker accidents ever."[2] So many people wanted to attend that they could not fit into the Committee's usual meeting room. During the hearings much anger was directed at what the Chairman referred to as "runaway flags," both for allowing "rust buckets like the *Argo Merchant*" to continue operating and for making it difficult to locate liability for damages.

---

[1] John Kifner, "Tankers' Use of Liberian Registry Aids Ship Concerns on Tax and Pay," *New York Times*, December 31, 1976, p. A1. Kifner authored a series of articles on the tanker spills that year.

[2] US Senate, *Hearings before the Committee on Commerce on Recent Tanker Accidents, Part 1* (Washington, DC: US Government Printing Office, 1977).

How the Liberian flag came to be attached to this collection of oil tankers, along with many others, is the subject of this chapter. The creation of the Liberian shipping registry was part of a package of policies adopted in 1948 with the intention of raising funds for the ambitious development program of the Liberian Company, a concession company founded by former American Secretary of State Edward Stettinius, Jr. They included the maritime registry, a corporation law intended to make it easier to set up corporations in Liberia not liable to Liberian taxation, and the creation of an International Trust Company. Of these three initiatives, the maritime registry had the biggest impact. Even through the civil wars of the 1990s and early 2000s, the Liberian fleet remained one of the largest in the world. In contrast, Liberia has made little mark on the world of offshore finance. The different trajectories of these two policies suggest that while small states may "voluntarily auction off their sovereignty," as Drezner puts it, the availability of willing buyers may depend on the form in which it is auctioned and on the structure of the state doing the auctioning.

Previous chapters have illustrated various ways that the Liberian government acted as a "gatekeeper," borrowing a phrase from Frederick Cooper, using its sovereign status to generate revenue and rents with which it could support the coalition of elites which sustained political stability.[3] The export of forced labor during the 1920s, for example, capitalized on unmet demand for labor in Fernando Po and elsewhere after neighboring countries began to tighten regulations. The granting of concessions, discussed in the previous chapter, created a selective system of property rights and tax privileges for foreign companies. Both of these provided important flows of revenue for the Liberian elite. However, all of these attempts ultimately faced constraints of one sort or another. The League of Nations investigation showed that there were limits to the extent to which a small country with few allies could deviate from international norms without facing pressure from more powerful states. There were physical limits to the number of concessions the Liberian government could grant within the country. At times, incomplete records led to the same exclusive rights being granted to more than one company. In 1973, for example, there was a conflict between LAMCO and LIBINC, a subsidiary of Getty Oil which had been granted a concession for palm oil production in 1965, over who had use of the port at Buchanan.[4] Generous concession agreements might draw foreign investors to Liberia's land and minerals, but these were finite resources.

[3] Frederick Cooper, *Africa since 1940: The Past of the Present* (Cambridge: Cambridge University Press, 2019), ch. 7.
[4] F. P. M. van der Kraaij, *The Open Door Policy of Liberia: An Economic History of Modern Liberia* (Bremen: Bremer Afrika Archiv, 1983), 112–13.

Sovereignty, however, was not a finite resource, and the 1948 corporation and shipping laws in effect allowed the Liberian government to create new channels by which to monetize its sovereignty. These policies have received less attention in histories of Liberia than the export of labor or the granting of concessions. Because the relevant activity occurred offshore, histories of Liberia itself rarely give the shipping registry or the corporation law more than a passing mention. Liberia's importance in the history of global shipping has generated significant work by scholars in the field of maritime history, most notably Rodney Carlisle.[5] However, this work is focused on the shipping registry and does not discuss the other laws of 1948 which were intended to turn Liberia into a center for offshore finance as well as shipping. This chapter compares the two efforts and asks why Liberia was able to achieve such dominance in shipping while at the same time having little impact as a tax haven. This contrast allows for a broader exploration of the "market" for sovereignty and its limits since the middle of the twentieth century.

Creating the Market for Sovereignty

In the article in *Foreign Policy* quoted earlier in the text, Daniel Drezner notes that while "history records many instances of countries treating sovereignty as a commodity," the period since the end of World War II had seen a rapid expansion in both supply and demand in this market for sovereignty. On the supply side, the number of sovereign states multiplied through the process of decolonization and the breakup of the Soviet Union. On the demand side, the increasing mobility of capital and the growing importance of international organizations made it easier for states to capitalize on their sovereign status through the exchange of votes for aid, for example, or the establishment of offshore financial centers. Within this market, however, there has been considerable specialization shaped by the preferences of both governments and firms.

Regulatory competition between states emerged in parallel with the expanding role of the state in regulating business. During the "Progressive Era," from the late nineteenth to the early twentieth century, regulation began to replace private litigation as the primary means of limiting the social externalities of commerce.[6] This then provided

---

[5] Rodney Carlisle, "The 'American Century' Implemented: Stettinius and the Liberian Flag of Convenience," *Business History Review* 54, no. 2 (1980): 175–91; *Sovereignty for Sale: The Origins and Evolution of the Panamanian and Liberian Flags of Convenience* (Annapolis, MD: Naval Institute Press, 1981).

[6] Edward L. Glaeser and Andrei Schliefer, "The Rise of the Regulatory State," *Journal of Economic Literature* XLI (2003): 401–25.

incentives for some states to impose lighter regulation than others in order to attract business or investment. Poorer jurisdictions within federal systems were often among the first to try this. During the 1880s, US corporations concentrated in New York and Massachusetts. When the governor of New Jersey asked a New York corporate lawyer named James Dill, who lived in East Orange, how the state could increase revenue, he suggested liberalizing the state's corporation law. This was done in a series of laws adopted during the 1890s. Delaware followed suit, and by 1902 there were 1,407 companies registered in the second-smallest state in the United States. Similarly, in Switzerland, innovations in the lenient banking regulations which would eventually establish the country as the world's leading tax haven first emerged in the poorer canton of Zug.[7]

The "Delaware model" suggests that, in theory, any state with international recognition or other recognized legal jurisdiction can adopt different or lower standards of regulation or taxation in order to attract capital. As a result, globalization is often thought to be incompatible with state regulation.[8] Historically, however, the picture seems to be more nuanced, and different regulatory equilibria are possible. According to Dale Murphy, "firms vary in their preferences for regulation" in terms of both levels and types.[9] Industrial structure and the degree of asset specificity are among the features that may shape firm preferences. Murphy identifies three distinct equilibria that might emerge as a result: (1) lowest common denominator (LCD), in which there is a "competition-in-laxity" (or race to the bottom) between states to attract capital through ever-lower levels of regulation; (2) conversely, highest common denominator, in which firms press for higher levels of regulation, and (3) heterogeneous regulation, in which states seek a comparative advantage by differentiating their regulatory regimes.

Both the theory and history of economic regulation point to numerous instances in which globalization is associated with higher levels of regulation rather than lower. For example, in one study of labor regulation in Europe before 1913, Michael Huberman and Wayne Lewchuk find that countries more open to trade were more likely to adopt labor regulations, rather than less. This, they argued, helped ensure political support for

---

[7] Ronen Palan, Richard Murphy, and Christian Chavagneux, *Tax Havens: How Globalization Really Works* (Ithaca: Cornell University Press, 2010), 108–12. See also Ronen Palan, *The Offshore World: Sovereign Markets, Virtual Places, and Nomad Millionaires* (Ithaca: Cornell University Press, 2003), 100–102.

[8] Kevin H. O'Rourke and Jeffrey G. Williamson, *Globalization and History: The Evolution of a Nineteenth-Century Atlantic Economy* (Cambridge: MIT Press, 2000).

[9] Dale D. Murphy, *The Structure of Regulatory Competition* (Oxford: Oxford University Press, 2004), 3.

globalization from among the working classes.[10] Dani Rodrik finds a similar pattern for the world after 1945.[11] In his classic paper on the economics of regulations, George Stigler argues that companies may actually seek regulation in order to restrict entry by potential competitors, but that the demand for such regulation and their ability to obtain it will depend on a range of factors specific to the industry and the political system.[12]

From the perspective of the state and political elites in a particular country, the question of what level and type of regulation to adopt is also a complicated one. Any change in regulation intended to benefit one group is likely to hurt another, and the relative influence of the two groups may vary depending on the nature of the benefits and costs and the extent to which the respective groups are able to act collectively. In addition, states may exert pressure on other states to adopt higher regulatory standards, for example, by restricting access to large domestic markets.[13] From the perspective of firms, a related literature on the location choices of foreign investment suggests that the regulatory environment is only one of several reasons why a firm may locate in a particular place.[14]

Much of the literature on regulation describes economic activities happening in the country in question. In the offshore world, this is largely not the case. Ronen Palan points out that

> if companies and individuals were required to completely relocate to tax havens, or if shipping companies had to relocate to flags of convenience states, then interest in taking advantage of tax havens would have remained relatively insignificant. In contrast to other forms of competitive deregulation, whether at municipal, national or international level, in the case of tax havens and flags of convenience often only a purely juridical residence is sought.[15]

Legal rather than physical residence reduces the degree of asset specificity, and as a result Murphy argues that both offshore shipping and finance

---

[10] Michael Huberman and Wayne Lewchuk, "European Economic Integration and the Labour Compact, 1850–1913," *European Review of Economic History* 7 (2003): 3–41.

[11] Dani Rodrik, "Why Do More Open Economies Have Bigger Governments?" *Journal of Political Economy* 106 (1998): 997–1033.

[12] George J. Stigler, "The Theory of Economic Regulation," *The Bell Journal of Economics and Management Science* 2, no. 1 (1971): 3–21.

[13] Murphy, *Structure of Regulatory Competition*, 13.

[14] John Dunning, "The Eclectic (OLI) Paradigm of International Production: Past, Present and Future," *International Journal of the Economics of Business* 8, no. 2 (2001): 173–90; Simona Iammarino and Philip McCanne, *Multinationals and Economic Geography: Location, Technology and Innovation* (Cheltenham: Edward Elgar, 2013), 34–37.

[15] Palan, *The Offshore World*, 83.

fall into the "competition-in-laxity" equilibrium, in which attempts by states to attract capital drives down overall levels of regulation.

However, the fact that location is juridical rather than physical does not necessarily mean that companies are entirely indiscriminate in their location choices, nor that the only movement will be toward less regulation rather than more. In their study of flags of convenience, Alderton and Winchester note that there are divisions in the "flag market." While new entrants will attempt to compete by offering environments with little regulation, older and more established flags of convenience are more likely to conform to international standards.[16] Similarly, different tax havens have specialized in different sectors of the offshore financial market, and comparative studies of the features of leading tax havens suggest that they are likely to be states with higher capacity.[17]

The political economy of why customers in offshore markets seek particular venues is little understood. The rest of the chapter examines the attempt by the Liberian government under Tubman to expand into two sectors of the offshore world – shipping and finance – and illustrates how differences in the demand for regulation and offshore services influenced its success in one area (shipping) and comparative failure in the other (finance).

The Three Laws of 1948

The legislation responsible for Liberia's entry into the world of offshore shipping and finance was linked to the concession granted the year before to Edward Stettinius's Liberia Company, described in one State Department memo as "undoubtedly Liberia's most ambitious concessionaire."[18] As noted in Chapter 9, this concession differed from many other major concessions in that it was not linked to a single industry, but rather gave the Liberia Company license to pursue a host of aims from agriculture to mining to services. So broad were its goals that a report on the operation of the US Economic Mission noted the "remarkable parallel" between the aims of the Mission and the Company. It added that "if a member of Congress were to ask the Department why the Economic Mission continued, at considerable expense to the Government of the United States, to carry out surveys

---

[16] Tony Alderton and Nick Winchester, "Globalisation and Deregulation in the Maritime Industry," *Marine Policy* 26 (2002): 35–43.
[17] Dhammika Dharmapala and James R. Hines, Jr., "Which Countries Become Tax Havens?" *Journal of Public Economics* 93 (2009): 1058–68.
[18] Memorandum on the history of economic and financial development of Liberia, February 7, 1949, in NARA RG 59 Entry A1 1423, Declass NND933006.

for the benefit of the Liberian Company, it might be difficult to make a convincing reply."[19]

To achieve these aims required significant capital. Initially, Stettinius intended to raise funds from either the US government or by inducing American companies to invest in Liberian projects. Stettinius was well connected, having been Chairman of the Board of United States Steel in the 1930s before Roosevelt brought him into government by making him Chairman of the War Resources Board in 1939. In 1941, Stettinius became Lend–Lease Administrator, in which capacity he had his first introduction to Liberia. In 1944, Stettinius became Secretary of State and a year later led the American delegation to Yalta. On his way back, he stopped in Liberia to open the Port of Monrovia.[20] Despite these connections, Stettinius found it difficult to generate interest in Liberia. In a meeting with the State Department, Liberian Company President Blackwell Smith described what he called the "Herculean task of lifting Liberia" out of its state of underdevelopment, and noted the difficulty of persuading American capital to invest in small, individual projects. "American capital was an easy conception originally but collapsed easily on testing," said Smith.[21] Instead, the company attempted to raise large-scale funds from the Export–Import Bank in the United States, but this also failed.

They proposed the three pieces of legislation passed in 1948 as a means of drawing capital to Liberia – in order, as Blackwell Smith said, to "supplement other forms of financing." One was the Liberian Corporation Law, which introduced the first uniform corporation law in Liberia. Prior to 1948, corporations were established by individual legislative charters. The new law allowed corporations to be established in Liberia without, crucially, being subject to Liberian taxation. A second pillar of this legal framework was the Maritime Law, which allowed ship-owners to sail under the Liberian flag with more limited regulation. The third pillar was a corporate charter establishing an International Trust Company which was intended to both administer the other two programs and to "make Liberia a financial center of Africa."[22] In his annual address to the Liberian legislature, President Tubman was even more ambitious,

[19] Quoted in Memorandum on Liberian Economic Mission, July 16, 1948, in NARA RG 59 Entry A1 1423, Declass NND933006.
[20] Carlisle, "The 'American Century' Implemented," 177.
[21] Memorandum of conversation on International Trust Company, October 19, 1948, in NARA RG 59 Lot 56D418, Box 2.
[22] For copies of legislation, see Philip A. Z Banks III and Seward Montgomery Cooper, *Liberia: World Corporate Domicile* (Monrovia: Liberian Law Experts, 1998).

stating that the intention of this package of legislation was to make Liberia "one of the financial centers of the world."[23]

This legislation was controversial for a number of reasons related to its conception and implementation. Within Liberia there were objections to the Statement of Understanding with Stettinius's company from the very beginning. One opponent of the measure described it as "a surrender of sovereignty." Tubman quoted this description in his annual address in 1948, and while he did not name its originator, he described the individual in colorful terms as a "spineless poltroon" and "flagitious bigot," and argued that the terms of the Stettinius concession were better than those of earlier concessions to Firestone and other companies. However, the extent to which the policies were designed in the interests of Liberia was potentially questionable. Drawing on the Stettinius papers, Rodney Carlisle shows that the creation of the Liberian shipping registry was a classic instance of regulatory capture, defined as "the process through which regulated monopolies end up manipulating the state agencies that are supposed to control them."[24] Stettinius and others held interests in ships registered in Panama. They, and others, complained about the growing demands of Panamanian officials. In composing the law, Stettinius's group sought the feedback of potential customers, including Standard Oil.

Officials in the US State Department voiced concerns about how the law was shaped and the potential impact it would have. One State Department official worried particularly about relationships with maritime unions. "The Department could not easily give its approval to such a proposal," he said of the Maritime Law, "since our government was striving to work harmoniously with the unions, and looked with disfavor upon the Panamanian registry service."[25] A review of the law was conducted, but under the sympathetic eye of Francis Adams Truslow. Like Stettinius, Truslow was a businessman and former government official. He served as president of the wartime Rubber Development Corporation during the war before becoming president of the New York Curb Exchange in March 1947. Truslow's review pointed out flaws and inconsistencies in the text but was otherwise uncritical of the concept. "It is not inconsistent with history," he wrote, "for less developed countries to [be]

---

[23] Willam V. S. Tubman, Annual Message to the Legislature, November 26, 1948, in D. Elwood Dunn, ed., *The Annual Messages of the Presidents of Liberia 1848–2010: From Joseph Jenkins Roberts to Ellen Johnson Sirleaf* (Berlin: Walter de Gruyter, 2011), 1068.

[24] Carlisle, "The 'American Century' Implemented"; E. Dal Bo, "Regulatory Capture: A Review," *Oxford Review of Economic Policy* 22, no. 2 (2006): 203.

[25] Memorandum of conversation on The Liberia Company, November 17, 1948, in NARA RG 59 Lot 56D418, Box 2.

aided in their development by people who want to escape the excessive regulation of more highly developed civilizations. I cannot advise Liberia to avoid this possible avenue of assistance."[26]

Despite Truslow's favorable ruling, others in the State Department had misgivings about the legislation. Some objections were driven more by the implications for American politics than anything to do with the impact on Liberia's development. There were concerns among State Department officials related to the impact on Liberia. Some questioned the link between the kinds of revenue the legislation was likely to attract, and the development aims of the Liberian Company. According to one official,

it was not clear whether the Trust Company was specifically designed to attract investment funds for these enterprises, or whether it was calculated merely to set up a haven for flight capital seeking relief from taxation, exchange regulations, political disturbance, etc., in other words a new Tangier or Lichtenstein which might be a very profitable business from the company whose basic mission in Liberia, according to the understanding, was to develop Liberian resources.[27]

In August 1948, Mr. Lynch of the US State Department called Sidney de la Rue, who represented the Liberia Company, to express those concerns.

I said to him that there was a good deal of question in my mind as to the desirability of the special session of the Liberian legislature which we understood had been called. I said that several pieces of legislation which The Liberia Company seemed to want to get through in a hurry were so important and far-reaching with regard to the whole financial structure of Liberia that it behooved the Liberian Government to make haste slowly.

In his memo on the call, Lynch recorded de la Rue as saying that "the company would be glad to consider any suggestions the Department might have to offer." However, he added "that they had some 40 ships lined up to be placed under the Liberian flag and that President Tubman was anxious to obtain the revenue from this deal at the earliest possible moment."[28]

The Rise of the Liberian Fleet

Sidney de la Rue's response to State Department concerns about the speed with which the 1948 legislation was drawn up and passed suggests

---

[26] "The Truslow report to the President of Liberia on the Liberian Corporation Law of 1948, the Maritime Code and the Act establishing the International Trust Company of Liberia," in Philip A. Z Banks and Seward Montgomery Cooper, *Liberia: World Corporate Domicile, vol 2,* 782.

[27] Memorandum of Conversation on the International Trust Company of Liberia, October 19, 1948, in NARA RG 59 Lot 56D418, Box 2.

[28] Memorandum of conversation on Activities of Liberia Company, August 12, 1948, in NARA RG 59 Lot 56D418, Box 2.

that there was a ready demand for a new "flag of convenience" among global shipowners. During the postwar period, the fleets of traditional maritime powers like the United Kingdom and the United States entered a period of decline as shipping moved abroad, often to so-called flags of convenience. Liberia's was among the fastest-growing of these new fleets.[29] However, this growth came with controversy and accusations like the one quoted in the introduction: that Liberia and other "flag of convenience" countries allowed unsafe ships to roam the seas. Shipowners countered that "flags of convenience" were actually "flags of necessity," which allowed them to maintain profitability in an increasingly competitive market. This section examines the growth and safety record of the Liberian fleet, arguing that its success was not necessarily due to competitive deregulation but rather to the early concentration of oil tankers, which, perhaps ironically, actually increased the degree of Liberian regulation compared to other flags.

The creation of flag states was a product of mercantilist trade policies of the early modern period. In 1660, the Navigation Act limited trade between England and its colonies to ships flying the English flag, with English masters and majority English crews. This formed the initial foundation for a body of international law which developed in subsequent centuries and located the responsibility and authority for regulating ships in the country whose flag the ships were flying. However, as Mansell notes, a state "can make the conscious economic decision not to exercise certain aspects of its authority as a flag state in order to attract tonnage that either does not, or cannot, conform to acceptable international standards."[30]

This space for sovereign discretion in the regulation of ships is the origin of what are often referred to as "flags of convenience." This phrase emerged in the second half of the twentieth century, but the practice of registering under foreign flags, or "flagging out," dates back to at least the nineteenth century, when some American merchant ships flew the Portuguese flag to evade British and American restrictions. After the abolition of the slave trade, slave ships often used the flags of countries that had not yet restricted the trade. In 1905, the Permanent Court of Arbitration in The Hague ruled that it was the flag and registry of the ship which determined its nationality rather than its ownership, setting the stage for the proliferation of new flags in the decades to follow.[31]

---

[29] Stephen Broadberry, *Market Services and the Productivity Race 1850–2000* (Cambridge: Cambridge University Press, 2006), 286.
[30] John N. K. Mansell, *Flag State Responsibility: Historical Development and Contemporary Issues* (Berlin: Springer, 2009), 3.
[31] Carlisle, *Sovereignty for Sale*, xiiv.

World War I and its aftermath ended Britain's long-standing domi-nance in the shipping industry, initially in favor of the United States.[32] However, tightening labor regulations imposed on American-flagged ships raised costs for shipowners. A small number of American ship-owners began to take advantage of a Panamanian law designed to encour-age Panamanian citizens to purchase ships abroad to build a local fleet. In 1916, the law was extended to Panamanian corporations, which, in turn, could be owned by foreigners. This legal framework was not unique to Panama. However, the political and commercial relationships created by the Panama Canal, and the role of American intervention in Panama's secession from Colombia, made Panama particularly attractive to American shipowners, as was the fact that the Panamanian currency was pegged to the dollar and transactions could be conducted in English.[33]

The Panamanian government faced conflicting incentives when it began to modify its shipping registry to attract more ships in the middle of the 1920s. Looser regulations quickly attracted smugglers, which in turn brought pressure from the American government. Panama's Maritime Code had to walk a fine line between the two, and as a result the expansion of the registry became closely associated with what Carlisle describes as "one of the central issues of Panamanian politics – defense of the country's sovereignty from affronts and incursions by the United States."[34] The two countries eventually reached an uneasy accord which allowed the Panamanian fleet to grow through the interwar period. European shipowners also began to register in Panama, fleeing the politi-cal and economic upheavals of the decade. By 1939, the Panamanian fleet consisted of 159 ships with a tonnage of 717,525, as yet a relatively small share of global tonnage. During World War II, registering in Panama became a way around the restrictions of American neutrality legislation. However, the expanding use of Panama's fleet drew opposition from both labor unions and from growing anti-American sentiment in Panama itself. For their part, shipowners objected to the sometimes arbitrary "fees" exacted by Panamanian consular officers when they registered their ships. As a result, after the war ended, shipowners were looking for an alternative registry.

[32] Broadberry, *Market Services*, 220–25.
[33] Carlisle, *Sovereignty for Sale*, ch. 1; Boleslaw Adam Boczek, *Flags of Convenience: An International Legal Study*, Introduction; Alderton and Winchester, "Globalisation and De-Regulation," 36; Francisco Piniella, Juan Ignacio Alcaide, and Emilio Rodriguez-Diaz, "The Panama Ship Registry, 1917–2017," *Marine Policy* 77 (2017): 13–22.
[34] Carlisle, *Sovereignty for Sale*, 19.

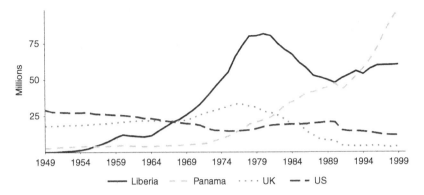

Figure 10.1 Major fleets by gross tonnage, 1949–1999
Source: Lloyd's World Fleet Statistics.

Liberia was the first, and most important, of what would become
a growing number of flag states in the postwar period. Figure 10.1 compares the tonnage of Liberia and Panama with that of two traditional
maritime powers: the United Kingdom and the United States. From the
late 1950s, there was a decisive shift away from the latter and toward the
former. The tonnage under the Liberian flag expanded rapidly, and by
1968, tiny Liberia had the largest shipping fleet in the world in terms of
registered tonnage. This did not mean that ships were owned by Liberians,
however. Comparing the decline of UK-registered tonnage to UK-owned
tonnage shows a much more muted decline in the latter as British-owned
ships were "flagged out" to other countries.[35] Instead, Liberia's fleet was
comprised of what John Forbes Munro calls "paper entries."[36]

If the size of fleets is measured instead by numbers of ships
(Figure 10.2), Liberia's position was less dominant although its growth
was still impressive. Its importance in terms of tonnage was due to the
widespread use of the Liberian flag by the ever-larger oil tankers being
constructed in the 1950s and 1960s. Average tonnages per ship for
Liberia were therefore much larger than for Panama. Stettinius's consultation with Standard Oil prior to the establishment of the registry suggests
that the targeting of this market was intentional.

---

[35] Broadberry, *Market Services*, 292.
[36] John Forbes Munro, "African Shipping: Reflections on the Maritime History of Africa
South of the Sahara, 1800–1914," *International Journal of Maritime History* II
(1990): 163.

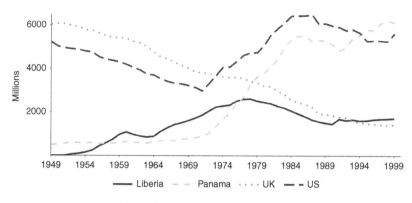

Figure 10.2 Major fleets by number of ships, 1949–1999
Source: Lloyd's World Fleet Statistics.

Who chose to register under the Liberian flag and why? According to Alan Cafruny,

> open registries confer four major types of benefits on shipowners. In descending order of importance, they are: (1) lower labor costs; (2) tax reduction; (3) ability to evade safety and environmental regulations; and (4) freedom from government intervention for political, economic and military purposes. At any given time, of course, any one of these benefits may be the predominating motive of a shipowner seeking open registry.[37]

The historical record suggests two primary factors: (1) the ability to evade restrictions on the manning of ships imposed by traditional maritime nations, and (2) the structure of government subsidies for shipping. Registering under the American flag, for example, required that a large share of the crew be American sailors with higher wages than sailors from elsewhere.[38] Ships registered under the UK flag faced similar requirements, and Broadberry observes that "it was extremely difficult for British shipping companies to obtain sufficient revenue to cover the high wage costs of British crews."[39] Registering with the Liberian flag reduced these costs considerably. Flags with more restrictive labor conditions were less successful, as Carlisle writes about the Honduran flag. "Because Honduras expected actual manning of its ships by Hondurans, organized in a government-recognized union, and also required ownership to be vested in a Honduran corporation, the system had drawn only a scattering of owners besides the United Fruit Company, which had considerable interests in Honduras."[40]

[37] Alan W. Cafruny, *Ruling the Waves: The Political Economy of International Shipping* (Berkeley: University of California Press, 1987), 92.
[38] Boczek, *Flags of Convenience*, 27.   [39] Broadberry, *Market Services*, 289.
[40] Carlisle, *Sovereignty for Sale*, 136

Another motivation was the level and structure of subsidies granted to particular kinds of ships by the governments of traditional maritime countries. The registration of Greek-owned ships, for example, helped spur the early growth of the Liberian flag. By the late 1950s, some 60 percent of Greek-owned ships were registered in Liberia. Greek-owned ships represented 80–90 percent of the Liberian fleet during its early years. Gelina Harlaftis attributes this flight of Greek ships to the Liberian flag to the inability of the Greek state to provide financial support to its merchant fleet like the governments of other maritime powers had done.[41] Similarly, Maritime Law in the United States discriminated against tankers before 1970. In his testimony before the 1977 hearings, Robert Blackwell, then the Assistant Secretary for Maritime Affairs, noted that "flag-of-convenience operations made some sense prior to 1970. The old 1936 act, which provided federal assistance to shipbuilding and ship operation prohibited operating subsidy to be paid for liquid bulk carriers, that is tankers. For Americans to participate in the international movement of cargo they had to go abroad."[42]

The many critiques of runaway flags voiced in the 1977 Senate hearing and other equivalent hearings through the postwar period did prompt efforts to impose tougher restrictions on the abilities of ships to register under foreign flags, or on the kinds of ships that could supply major markets. In 1974, for example, the US Congress passed the Energy Transportation and Security Act, which would have mandated that a minimum of 30 percent of oil imported into the United States be carried by American-flagged ships. This was vetoed by President Ford, however, on the basis that such restrictions would only increase the cost of oil to American consumers.[43] Such political conflicts ensured that, as Carlisle puts it, "the investigations served as platforms for the expression of conflicting ideas about the system," rather than as grounds for more rigorous regulation.[44] It was only in the 1990s that Port State Controls became an active counter to FOC regulatory standards.

In this context, one perhaps surprising feature of the Liberian fleet was its comparatively strong safety record. Claims that the ships under the Liberian flag were "rust buckets" are not borne out by the statistics on the fleet. Lloyd's provides data on both the age of the ships in each fleet and

---

[41] Gelina Harlaftis, "Greek Shipowners and State Intervention in the 1940s: A Formal Justification for the Resort to Flags-of-Convenience?" *International Journal of Maritime History* 1, no. 2 (1989): 37–63.
[42] US Senate, *Hearings before the Committee on Commerce on Recent Tanker Accidents, Part 1* (Washington, DC: US Government Printing Office, 1977), 78.
[43] US Senate, *Hearings on Recent Tanker Accidents*, 114.
[44] Carlisle, *Sovereignty for Sale*, 135.

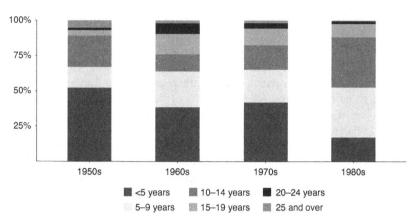

Figure 10.3 Age of tonnage in Liberian fleet by decade, 1950s–1990s
Source: Lloyd's World Fleet Statistics.

casualty statistics. Both show that the Liberian fleet was neither particularly old nor accident-prone. Figure 10.3 gives the share of Liberian
tonnage by age group, and shows that through the 1980s, the vast bulk
of Liberian tonnage was less than fifteen years old. Boczek writes that "as
a result of scrappings and the registration of a large number of newly
constructed vessels, mostly tankers, a lot of new ships are now flying the
colors of Liberia and Panama."[45]

The Lloyd's data were used by one witness at the 1977 Senate Commerce
Committee hearings – Arthur McKenzie, director of the Tanker advisory
Center – who noted that Panama and Liberia ranked tenth and eleventh in
terms of their casualty rates, while several traditional maritime nations had
higher casualty rates.[46] Even reports critical of the Liberian flag for other
reasons noted its relatively good safety record (Figure 10.4). In 2001, for
example, a report by the UN Committee of Experts on Liberia, which is
discussed in greater detail with regard to the misappropriation of registry
revenue later in the chapter, noted that the Liberian register "is generally
regarded as one of the quality open registries (called by some, flag of
convenience) with the fleet having a low average age and below average
PSC detention rate. The casualty figures are also low."

According to Murphy, the low casualty rate of the Liberian fleet was at
least in part linked to regulations demanded and adopted by the shipowners themselves. Ownership of oil tankers is concentrated in a small

---

[45] Boczek, *Flags of Convenience*, 17–22.
[46] US Senate, *Hearings on Recent Tanker Accidents*, 145.

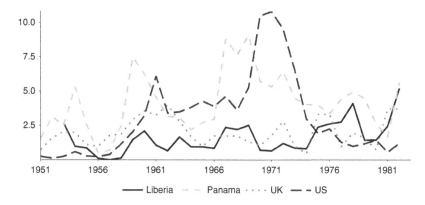

Figure 10.4 Tonnage lost by major fleet
Source: Lloyd's World Fleet Statistics.

number of very large firms. By the 1970s, the seven largest oil companies controlled around a fifth of world tanker tonnage. Exxon alone had 168 tankers.[47] From the 1960s, these large companies began to adopt regulatory innovations in ship safety which hurt independent shipowners and helped consolidate the market even further. These were compounded in the 1990s by the return of Port State Control measures which threatened to exclude poor-quality ships from major markets.

In 1980, Rodney Carlisle wrote that "with over 80 million tons of shipping registered under the Liberian flag, it is apparent that the ship-registry system is by far the most significant surviving part of the Stettinius activities."[48] The establishment of the Liberian fleet in 1948 coincided with both technological and economic developments, which increased the size of the world's tanker fleet. As a result, the Liberian registry was soon home to the largest fleet in the world in terms of gross tonnage. It has remained one of the largest fleets in the world even through two decades of civil war and political unrest, in part due to the external management of the registry, a topic dealt with later in the chapter. The comparative success of the shipping registry contrasts with the muted impact of Liberia's effort to join a growing group of offshore financial centers.

---

[47] Murphy, *Structure of Regulatory Competition*, 47.
[48] Carlisle, "The 'American Century' Implemented," 175.

Financial Center of the World?

The International Trust Company, which initially managed the Liberian ship registry, was also intended to attract flight capital of all kinds, turning Liberia into the "financial center of West Africa." While Liberia has appeared frequently on official lists of tax havens drawn up by the US Internal Revenue Service, the OECD, the IMF, and others since the 1970s, available measures of the size of tax havens – tentative though they are – show that it is at most a minor player in the world of offshore finance. This section explores why Liberia was not able to make the same impact in finance as it did in shipping.

While it is not certain how much wealth is held in tax havens, all available evidence suggests that it is large and growing. By the 1920s, the growing dominance of financial (rather than landed) wealth along with the more aggressive taxation of large fortunes created strong incentives for the wealthy to move their assets abroad. Based on the results of two investigative commissions in the 1990s, Zucman shows that the wealth managed by Swiss banks increased tenfold in real terms between 1920 and 1938.[49] In 2002, Ronen Palan wrote that "the combined effect of tax havens on the world economy is staggering: according to some estimates, as much as half the world's stock of money either resides in tax havens or passes through them" though he also admitted that "no one really knows how much money goes through offshore financial centers."[50] Neil Cummins compares predicted wealth with declared wealth for a group of Victorian elites with rare surnames and finds that, at least for this group, around 20–30 percent of their wealth is hidden.[51] He argues that this hidden wealth helps explain the "great compression" in wealth over the second half of the twentieth century.

Where does all of this wealth go? In theory, any country can become a tax haven, just as any country can establish a flag of convenience. As in the case of flag states, countries can opt not to exercise sovereign rights of taxation and banking regulation in order attract capital. As capital has become more mobile, such incentives have increased, and Murphy describes offshore finance as "the sine qua non of liberalization": like flags of convenience, a sector that tends toward a LCD of regulation through competition between states. According to some histories, this effect was exacerbated by the entry of a number of new competitors from the middle of the twentieth century. Vanessa Ogle, for example, has

[49] Gabrial Zucman, *The Hidden Wealth of Nations: The Scourge of Tax Havens* (Chicago: University of Chicago Press, 2015).

[50] Ronen Palan, "Tax Havens and the Commercialization of State Sovereignty," *International Organization* 56, no. 1 (2002): 151.

[51] Neil Cummins, "The Hidden Wealth of English Dynaisties, 1892–2016," *Economic History Review* 75, no. 3 (2022): 667–702.

argued that the collapse of the European empires led to a proliferation of tax havens in newly independent states. According to her account, "decolonization created a money panic of sorts" and it was as a result of "the influx of funds from the imperial and colonial world" that tax havens expanded in the postwar decades.[52] However, her evidence is based more on the intentions of states to attract capital than on measures of where private capital actually ended up.

More rigorous work has shown that, much like Liberia, these new tax havens failed to make much of a dent in the market until decades later, and even then the tax haven business remained fairly concentrated. Until the 1980s, Switzerland remained the dominant destination for hidden financial assets. US Treasury surveys of American securities held by non-American residents – a standard source of data on the size of tax havens – shows that in 1974, almost a third of such securities were held in Switzerland. Other major holders of such securities included Canada, France, and the Netherlands. Switzerland's percentage began to shrink from the 1980s, but remained over 10 percent in 2000. According to Zucman, "The hegemony of Switzerland over the international wealth-management market of the 1970s can be easily explained. Competition from other tax havens was still almost non-existent."[53]

With the 1948 Corporation Law, Liberia attempted to become one such competitor. However, the capital it managed to attract through such means remained small. According to the same Treasury surveys, Liberia has never held more than 0.5 percent of the American securities held abroad. In many periods this indeed made it a leader within Africa, though this may be more attributable to the concentration of American business there. Its holdings are dwarfed by those of Switzerland and the other leading tax havens, as shown in Table 10.1. Overall, the "micro-states" labeled as tax havens still only control a minority of US securities abroad. Larger shares are held in countries with leading financial markets, like the United Kingdom or the Netherlands.

Comparative studies of tax havens also emphasize the capacity of state institutions and political stability as one feature of successful centers of offshore finance. Palan notes that successful tax havens have "political and economic stability" and "are not tainted by scandals, money laundering or drug money."[54] Similarly, Dharmapala and Hines argue that the quality of governance is a key factor in determining the returns from tax havens.

---

[52] Vanessa Ogle, "'Funk Money': The End of Empires, the Expansion of Tax Havens, and Decolonization and Economic and Financial Event," *Past and Present* 249, no. 1 (2020): 213–49.
[53] Zucman, *The Hidden Wealth of Nations*.
[54] Palan, "Tax Havens and the Commercialization of State Sovereignty."

Table 10.1 *Percentage of US securities held by non-Americans*

	1974	1978	1984	1989	1994	2000
Liberia	0.09	0.11	0.16	0.29	0.39	0.04
Bahamas	0.87	0.67	1.29	2.07	3.5	1.3
Bermuda	1.13	1.91	3.10	2.94	6.77	6.37
Cayman Islands	–	–	–	–	–	7.4
Panama	0.74	0.84	1.53	0.87	0.99	0.97
Switzerland	28.5	28.03	21.37	12.68	14.24	10.96

Source: US Treasury.

Only better governed countries can credibly commit not to expropriate foreign investors (including indirectly through regulations or higher future taxes), or not to mismanage the economy in a way that prevents foreign investors from earning profits. Since this commitment is necessary for low taxes to induce high levels of foreign investments, the returns to being a tax haven would be sufficiently high only for better-governed countries.[55]

Political instability after 1980 was not the only hindrance Liberia faced. Even as the 1948 Corporation Act was passed, contemporaries noted that Liberia lacked the wider body of law and legal precedent needed to support its intended status as a financial center. In his report in 1949, Truslow noted that "no corporation code becomes wholly adequate until there grows up around it a body of supporting and supplemental law. I believe that in the jurisprudence of a country like Liberia such ancillary laws must in large part develop through the wise handling of cases as experience presents them and through supplemental legislation as gaps in the law become apparent."[56] However, a half century of experience as a tax haven was not sufficient to fill these gaps. In publishing a compendium of Liberian Corporation Law in 1998, Philip Banks, the Counselor-At-Law for the Liberian Supreme Court noted that Liberian "laws have not been readily available. Courts (including Liberian courts and lawyers) have had difficulty in disposing of matters before them and lawyers (including Liberian lawyers) have encountered like difficulty in providing advice, both to Liberian and foreign corporations and to persons and entities interacting with Liberia and Liberian corporations."[57]

Other factors no doubt also influenced Liberia's limited success as a tax haven. As shown in previous chapters, its financial sector was small, and

[55] Dharmapala and Hines, "Which Countries Become Tax Havens?," 1064.
[56] Truslow Report, in Banks and Cooper, *Liberia: World Corporate Domicile*, 742.
[57] Banks and Cooper, *Liberia: World Corporate Domicile, vol 1*, A–6.

even after the investments of the postwar period communications technology was hardly advanced. In contrast, tax havens are generally "equipped with sophisticated information-exchange facilities and are within easy reach of a major financial center."[58] Nor was it physically near any of the major markets it intended to serve. Still, even with greater proximity to markets and better communications technology, it seems likely that low state capacity and poor governance would have made it difficult for Liberia to attain the kind of prominence in offshore finance than it had in shipping. In contrast, the external management of the shipping registry meant that, as Murphy put it, "the civil war had less of an impact than one might expect, given that few transactions were conducted in Monrovia itself."[59]

The Registry and Liberia

Daniel Drezner, in the article quoted at the beginning of this chapter, referred to the "great rewards" countries could obtain by "auctioning off their sovereignty to the highest bidder." Previous sections have shown that Liberia's success in entering the market for sovereignty was restricted to its shipping registry – but this, arguably, was a significant success. This section addresses the rewards it received in return, and also attempts to explain how Liberia was able to retain its dominance in shipping even as the government collapsed and the country was overcome by civil war.

For all its global dominance, the registry was not, in fact, a very large revenue generator for the Liberian government during much of its history. Figure 10.5 shows maritime revenue as a percentage of total revenue from 1950 to 1980 and compares it with other sources such as tariffs and the income tax. Maritime revenue rose quickly to constitute around 10 percent of total revenue but never really became more important than that during the first three decades of its existence. Some observers at the time blamed the relatively limited contribution of revenue to the way in which the registry was organized. Like other flags of convenience, the Liberian government outsourced the direct management of its fleet to a private company.[60] In 1949, Stettinius's International Trust Company hired George Schaeffer to set up a contract with the Liberian government to operate the shipping registry. Schaeffer was a vice president of Chase National Bank and had previously worked in Panama. According to the terms of the contract, the registry would operate out of the International Trust Company office in New York, and the company would retain

---

[58] Palan, "Tax Havens and the Commercialization of State Sovereignty," 156.
[59] Murphy, *Structure of Regulatory Competition*, 67.
[60] Mansell, *Flag State Responsibility*, 5.

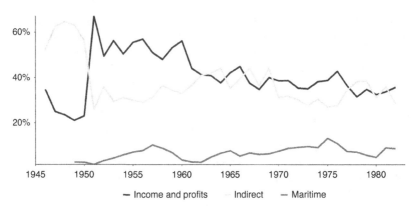

Figure 10.5 Maritime revenue compared with other sources, 1945–1983
Source: Liberia, *Economic Surveys.*

27 percent of the fees collected from shipowners as a service charge for acting as a "quasi-official" agent of the newly established Bureau of Maritime Affairs (BMA), which was initially part of the Treasury.[61] This first contract had a term of ten years and was followed by four renewals.[62]

This outsourcing of responsibilities for managing shipping registries was common practice for flag states without a coastline of their own, and has become even more widespread since. The Mongolia Ship Registry, for example, is based in Singapore. Though Liberia has a coastline, and a substantial maritime history of its own, Herbert attributes the adoption of the agency agreement with the ITC: (1) to a lack of specialized personnel in Liberia, (2) to the desire to avoid the problems of the Panamanian registry in using consular personnel, and (3) to "ensure that the interests of American shipowners were protected by exercising effective control over the vital aspects of the registry's operation."[63] The Liberian government paid a hefty price for these services, equivalent in the initial agreement to 27 percent of the overall revenue of the registry. A 1952 report on Liberia's fiscal system by Robert Steadman, the controller of the state of Michigan, recommended that "a less unfavorable arrangement" be worked out with the International Trust Company.[64]

[61] Carlisle, *Sovereignty for Sale*, 129.
[62] Christian Gbogboda Herbert, "The Liberian Shipping Registry: Strategies to Improve Flag State Implementation and Increase Market Competitiveness," MSc dissertation, World Maritime University (1999), 33.
[63] Herbert, "The Liberian Shipping Registry," 32.
[64] Robert F Steadman, *Report on the Fiscal System of the Republic of Liberia* (Monrovia: Executive Mansion, 1952), C37.

In addition, the agreement was also subject to principle-agent problems, and there were frequent disputes about whether the company was really serving the interests of the Liberian government. From the beginning, the Liberian government struggled to monitor the operations of the ITC. The relationship began to break down in in the 1980s, when rapid growth of the Liberian fleet was first checked and then reversed. While there were a number of exogenous factors which may have contributed to this decline, including the entrance of new flags, the Liberian government attributed it to the fact that the successor organization to the ITC, known as International Registries, Inc. (IRI) after several mergers and acquisitions, was by then managing not only the Liberian registry but also the shipping registry of the Marshall Islands. The Liberian government accused IRI of shifting registrations away from the Liberian flag and toward the Marshall Islands flag instead, and of using Liberian assets to build the Marshall Islands registry. The dispute eventually went to court in Virginia in 1998. In the meantime, the interim government of Amos Sawyer cancelled the agreement with IRI and established a new one with a new company called the Liberian International Ship and Corporate Registry (LISCR). This was subject to a countersuit by IRI, but both parties ultimately settled out of court in 2000.[65]

As other sources of revenue dried up during the early 1990s, revenue from the shipping registry remained one of the few, as Charles Taylor put it in 1999, "dependable sources of revenue."[66] In the late 1990s, it constituted up to 90 percent of the total state budget in some years.[67] It was also a source of revenue over which it was difficult for people in Liberia to exercise any real oversight. In 2001, the UN panel of experts on Liberia issued a report linking the registry to arms trades, which evaded UN sanctions against Liberia. LISCR's usual procedure was to make weekly deposits of the government's share of revenue into the bank account of the Embassy of Liberia at Riggs Bank in Washington, DC, from which it was then transferred to an account at the Ecobank in Monrovia. However, the LISCR received frequent requests for transfers to be made to nongovernmental accounts, including several to the account of a company called San Air General Trading at Standard

---

[65] Herbert, "The Liberian Shipping Registory," 52–6.

[66] Annual message by Charles Taylor to the legislature, January 25, 1999 (1998 message), in *The Annual Messages of the Presidents of Liberia 1848–2010: State of the Nation Addresses to the National Legislature from Joseph Jenkins Roberts to Ellen Johnson Sirleaf*, edited by D. Elwood Dunn (Berlin: De Gruyter, 2011), 1757.

[67] United Nations, *Report of the Panel of Exports pursuant to Security Council resolution 1343 (2001), paragraph 19, concerning Liberia* (Geneva: United Nations, 2015): 89–90; International Monetary Fund, *Liberia: Selected Issues and Statistical Appendix* (Washington, DC: IMF, 2000).

Bank, Sharjah, in the United Arab Emirates. The UN panel identified these particular payments as being for arms, which violated UN sanctions.

There were also ambiguities in accounting for the funds which reached Monrovia. These funds were supposed to be deposited into a government account operated by the Minister of Finance, with shares allocated to the Ministry of Foreign Affairs and the Ministry of Information. However, the UN panel determined that the account also had a third signatory from the Executive Mansion. In 1989, the Liberian legislature granted autonomy to the BMA, which meant that it reported directly to the president instead. In his address to the legislature that year, Samuel Doe reported that "this new status has given the Bureau the necessary flexibility required to effectively perform in a highly competitive commercial atmosphere of the international maritime industry."[68] This meant that the president's office could, in effect, access the maritime revenue at will. The scale of what the UN report termed "extrabudgetary use" of BMA revenue was such that it generated substantial discrepancies between the figures generated by the Ministry of Finance and those of the Central Bank. The UN panel also found that the Corporate Registry had been used by companies smuggling diamonds and arms during the 1990s.

The fungibility of maritime revenue no doubt served Charles Taylor well in terms of making illicit transactions, which helped fund his activities during the war. This carried the risk, however, of reputational damage to the registry. A survey conducted by a Liberian MSc student at the World Maritime University in 1999 pointed to political instability and worries about what the Liberian government did with the funds generated from the registry as sources of concern for shipowners.[69]

Sovereignty for Sale?

There remain fierce debates about the impact of offshore finance which echo many of the discussions surrounding the 1948 reforms. Can countries attract capital by reducing tax rates or regulatory standards? Will that capital contribute to their development or merely provide another source of patronage? How much can regulations be diluted before an international backlash undermines the prospects of success? Beyond this, there are also global questions. Does such a market undermine regulatory standards or threaten the tax bases of high-tax

---

[68] Annual message of Samuel Doe to the legislature February 1990 (1989 message), in Dunn, *Annual Messages*, 1736.
[69] Herbert, "The Liberian Shipping Registry."

countries? These questions are difficult to answer empirically given the inherent difficulty of collecting data on activities that people are trying to keep secret, and conclusions from research are mixed. However, Liberia's experience suggests that the barriers to entry into some parts of the "market for sovereignty" may be higher than previously considered. Not all countries can sell their sovereignty in the same way, and buyers may be fickle. It also suggests that, once sovereignty has been commodified, it can be difficult to reclaim it.

The case of Liberia provides a useful illustration of the market for sovereignty, and its limits. Liberia achieved great success as a flag state, dominating the global shipping industry in terms of gross tonnage within two decades. Despite the setbacks that have occurred, it remains one of the most important merchant fleets in the world. Perhaps surprisingly, it is also one of the open registries with the highest safety standards, as a result of the particular set of incentives facing the large corporations which own most oil tankers.

From the beginning the registry has been administered in the United States rather than Liberia, and while this has created numerous agency problems over the years, it also allowed the registry to continue operating during a time when it was not always clear which of the various combatants in the civil wars was the legitimate government. In contrast, Liberia failed to attract much business as a tax haven, a sector of the offshore market in which quality of governance appears to matter more than in the market for foreign flags. "Assets that float" are harder to seize than the financial assets which individuals and corporations use in tax haven transactions. In addition, the limited development of corporation law overall makes the Liberian government's commitment to honor its commitments as a tax haven less credible.

Collectively, the three chapters in Part III provide a detailed history of the precise mechanisms of "extraversion" or "gatekeeping" used by the government of one small state, namely Liberia. It was through these strategies that the Americo-Liberian elite managed to sustain its position at the center of Liberia's political and economic institutions for more than a century despite both internal and external threats. This did not mean there was internal consensus about the path chosen – far from it, and inequities generated by Liberia's engagement with the global economy were one important factor in setting the stage for the war.

The final chapter of the book considers what lessons can be drawn from Liberia's economic history for understanding the exercise of sovereignty by small states over the course of the nineteenth and twentieth centuries. During this period, many new states emerged, even as others were subsumed or amalgamated. It was this political realignment that facilitated the emergence of the offshore economy discussed in this chapter. However, our understanding of how states navigated this changing landscape focuses on the large and powerful – small states, as one recent contribution put it, "are usually referred to in footnotes."[70] The case of Liberia, and the many countries which shared its dilemmas, suggests there are important differences that deserve to be brought out of the footnotes and into the main text.

---

[70] Jari Eloranta, Peter Hedburg, Maria Cristina Moreira, and Eric Golson, "Introduction," in *Small and Medium Powers in Global History: Trade, Conflicts and Neutrality from the 19th to the 20th Centuries*, edited by Jari Eloranta, Eric Golson, and Peter Hedburg (London: Routledge, 2018), 1-27.

11   Sovereignty beyond the Age of Empires

> Liberia for many years has been an island of Independence, a relatively
> small one from the standpoint of the amount of land occupied and the
> number of people, but a very large one from the standpoint of the
> traditions which have been upheld and the principles for which you
> stand.
>
> US Vice President Richard Nixon, speaking at a state dinner
> in Monrovia, March 7, 1957

At midnight on March 6, 1957, Ghana celebrated the end of British
colonial rule. This was a symbolic moment for Africa, and for the
world, as Ghana, in Crawford Young's words, "traced a path along
which former British territories would soon follow, setting in turn
a precedent that other European colonial powers could not escape."[1]
Delegates from seventy-two countries came to Accra to mark the occasion, bringing with them journalists and photographers who would share
with the world images of the Union Jack being replaced by the Black Star.
They joined thousands of Ghanaians who traveled from across the country, by foot and ship and "mammy wagon," to their new national capital.[2]
"At long last the battle has ended," Kwame Nkrumah proclaimed at the
beginning of his speeches. That battle, in his words, was "the mighty task
of freeing this country from foreign rule and imperialism." By 1960, the
independence of seventeen African states had expanded the region's
international influence at the United Nations to such a degree that it
was described as the "year of Africa."[3] Liberia was no longer an island.

Even as Ghanaians cheered Nkrumah's speech in Accra, people in that
small "island of independence" were sounding a note of caution about the

---

[1] Crawford Young, *The Postcolonial State in Africa: Fifty Years of Independence, 1960–2010*
(Madison: University of Wisconsin Press, 2012), 3.
[2] Ghana Information Services, *Ghana is Born, March 6, 1957* (London: Newman Neame,
1958).
[3] Adom Getachew. *Worldmaking After Empire: The Rise and Fall of Self-Determination*
(Princeton: Princeton University Press, 2019), 14.

limits of sovereignty in an unequal world. Liberia celebrated the transfer of power in Ghana along with the rest of Africa. The government declared March 6 a national holiday and ordered a twenty-one-gun salute from Fort Norris at the top of Ducor Hill in Monrovia.[4] Vice President Tolbert and a delegation of Liberian officials traveled to Accra on a special Liberian Airways flight.[5] Meanwhile, President Tubman attended a ball in Monrovia described by an account published in *The Liberian Age* as "jammed to capacity with merry makers dressed both in the exotic formal style and the overflowing Ghana costume of Kente." Tubman, joining the dancing, was lifted up into the air on the arms of the other partygoers.[6] But even before the applause for the president's dance performance had subsided, Charles D. B. King, one of Tubman's predecessors in office, interrupted the festivities to give what one reporter described as a "long but interesting" speech in which he raised the possibility that "there was as much good as there was evil in colonization."

This was a striking statement to make at a time when much of the world was celebrating the end of colonization in Ghana, and anticipating its immediate demise in the rest of Africa. And King was not the only Liberian to make such a claim. When US Vice President Richard Nixon traveled to Monrovia after leading the US delegation to Accra, it prompted comparisons between Liberia and Ghana among the large press retinue that traveled with him. Ghana, they observed, had "better roads, better schools, better harbor facilities and more highly developed industry, agriculture and public revenue."[7] In his own discussions with Nixon, Tubman offered a simple explanation for those differences: colonialism. "There can be no doubt that the dependent people have a right to their own independence," he was reported to have said. "But they should be conscious of the advantages which their ties to Britain and France gave them in terms of developing their economies."[8] Other Liberians made similar points. Charles T. O. King, the Liberian representative to the United Nations (and the son of the former president who had interrupted the dancing at the ball in Monrovia) said in an interview with the *New York Times* that the difference between Liberia and Ghana was like "the difference between the home of a man who has had to accomplish

---

[4] "March 6, Declared a National Holiday," The Liberian Age, March 1, 1957, p. 1, Holsoe newspaper collection IULC.

[5] "Vice President and Thirteen Others Leave for Ghana Today," The Liberian Age, March 1, 1957, 1, Holsoe newspaper collection IULC.

[6] "Successful Ghana Independence Ball Held in Monrovia," The Liberian Age, March 11, 1957, 7, Holsoe newspaper collection IULC.

[7] Wayne Phillips, "Liberian Upholds Colonial Benefit," *New York Times*, March 23, 1957.

[8] Memorandum of conversation, US Embassy in Monrovia, March 8, 1957, in US Department of State, *Foreign Relations of the United States 1957*, 401.

everything by his own sweat and toil, and one who has enjoyed a large inheritance."[9] A letter submitted to *The Liberian Age* by one James Blunt made this same point even more starkly. Addressing Tolbert on the eve of his trip to Accra, the letter gave him a message for Ghanaians. "Tell them they are thrice blessed. If we had entered independence with a bank reserve of six hundred million dollars, as they are doing, no nation on this continent could equal us."[10]

How different were Ghana and Liberia in terms of their level of economic development in 1957? Chapter 1 shows that both countries had similar levels of GDP per capita during the 1950s. In 1957, Ghana's GDP per capita was $1,241 (1990 international dollars), while Liberia's was $1,203. This apparent equality masked differences in the patterns of long-run growth in the two countries. What Nixon and his entourage saw was the outcome of investments made during the first half of the twentieth century when Ghana (then the Gold Coast) was growing faster and Liberia was falling behind. In 1885, Liberia's GDP per capita was 87.8 percent of Ghana's. By 1929, it had fallen to a low of 45.3 percent. During the late nineteenth and early twentieth centuries, the rapid expansion of cocoa exports from Ghana made it one of the leading economies of the region. At the same time, the Liberian economy was at best stagnating, and sometimes even shrinking.

To what extent were these different paths the result of colonialism, as Tubman and others argued? This is difficult to say. Prior to the colonial period, the Gold Coast was arguably a more important commercial center in the Atlantic trade than the Grain Coast. It was home to the powerful Asante Kingdom, whose access to the gold which gave the region its name smoothed the transition between the end of the slave trade and the expansion of the commodity trade.[11] The introduction of cocoa production in West Africa came at the initiative of Africans, not Europeans.[12] However, the expansion of cocoa production was undoubtedly facilitated by the construction of infrastructure, particularly the railway. Remi Jedwab and Alexander Moradi find that Ghana's colonial railways played a major role in both the volume and the distribution of economic activity,

[9] Phillips, "Liberian Upholds Colonial Benefit."

[10] "Letters of Note," *The Liberian Age*, March 1, 1957, 2, Holsoe newspaper collection IULC.

[11] Gareth Austin. *Labour, Land and Capital in Ghana: From Slavery to Free Labour in Asante, 1807–1956* (Rochester: University of Rochester Press, 2005), ch. 3.

[12] A. G. Hopkins. "Innovation in a Colonial Context: African Origins of the Nigerian Cocoa Farming Industry, 1880–1920," in *The Imperial Impact: Studies in the Economic History of Africa and India*, edited by Clive Dewey and A. G. Hopkins (London: Athlone Press), 83–96.

which persisted even after the railways themselves ceased to operate.[13] The Asante kingdom had attempted to borrow to build a railway earlier in the nineteenth century, but struggled to raise sufficient capital in the face of British opposition.[14] Ethiopia also struggled in its efforts, constructing its railway only at the cost of considerable concessions to French financiers.[15] As Chapter 6 illustrates, the Gold Coast colonial government could only raise sufficient capital to construct the railway through coordination between imperial institutions like the Crown Agents for the Colonies and the Bank of British West Africa.

The economic expansion of the late nineteenth and early twentieth centuries was uneven, and impacted some areas more than others.[16] In those areas which gained, there were real improvements in living standards. Height data, which exists for Ghana if not for Liberia, show increasing heights particularly in areas of export production.[17] The expansion of mission schools in those same areas, driven largely by African demand for education, led to higher levels of school enrolment during the 1950s.[18] This helps explain the higher levels of literacy in Ghana compared to Liberia. And, as shown in Chapter 1, even minimal investment in public health infrastructure had a substantial impact on demographic change.

---

[13] Remi Jedwab and Alexander Moradi, "The Permanent Effects of Transportation Revolutions in Poor Countries: Evidence from Africa," *Review of Economics and Statistics* 98, no. 2 (2016): 268–84.

[14] Isaias Chaves, Stanley L. Engerman and James A. Robinson. "Reinventing the Wheel: The Economic Benefits of Wheeled Transportation in Early Colonial British West Africa," in *Africa's Development in Historical Perspective*, edited by Emmanuel Akyeampong, Robert H. Bates, Nathan Nunn and James Robinson (Cambridge: Cambridge University Press, 2014), 349–50. This account draws heavily on Ivor Wilks, *Asante in the Nineteenth Century* (Cambridge: Cambridge University Press, 1989).

[15] K. V. Ram. "British Government, Finance Capitalists and the French Jibuti-Addis Ababa Railway 1898–1913," *Journal of Imperial and Commonwealth History* 9 (1981): 146–68.

[16] Elise Huillery, "History Matters: The Long-Term Impact of Colonial Public Investments in West Africa," *American Economic Journal: Applied Economics* 1, no. 2 (2009): 176–215; Joan Ricart-Huguet. "The Origins of Colonial Investments in Former British and French Africa," *British Journal of Political Science* (published online 2021).

[17] Alexander Moradi, Gareth Austin and Joerg Baten, "Heights and Development in a Cash-Crop Colony: Living Standards in Ghana, 1870–1980," Working Paper (2013), https://alexandermoradi.org/research/Heights_Ghana_1870_1980.pdf.

[18] Remi Jedwab, Felix Meier zu Selhausen and Alexander Moradi, "The economics of missionary expansion: evidence from Africa and implications for development," *Journal of Economic Growth* 27 (2022): 149-92. Ewout Frankema, "The Origins of Formal Education in Sub-Saharan Africa: Was British Rule More Benign?" *European Review of Economic History* 16 (2012): 335–55.

Colonial investment should not be mistaken for benevolence. However, colonial rule created what Mancur Olson would have called an "encompassing interest," which gave imperial powers incentives to build up export industries in their colonies. In his *Rise and Decline of Nations*, Olson argued that "the members of the highly encompassing organization own so much of the society that they have an important incentive to be actively concerned about how productive it is."[19] He subsequently elaborated on this concept to explain the comparative popularity of a Chinese warlord, Feng Hu-hsiang, who extracted regular tribute from his subjects but also used his power to stop others from stealing from them. In Olson's words, "a bandit leader with sufficient strength to control and hold a territory has an incentive to settle down, to wear a crown, and to become a public good-providing autocrat."[20]

In the case of colonial governments in Africa, financial constraints added to the urgency of this incentive. Expanding electorates in metropolitan countries were making new demands of their treasuries at home, and imperial governments were reluctant to devote significant resources to running the colonies they had acquired. Colonial officials were under significant pressure to increase local tax collections to cover regular annual spending on their own salaries and the servicing of debt, while at the same time minimizing the risk of political instability. The most straightforward way to do this was to facilitate the expansion of export production and levy revenue tariffs on international trade. This was the path followed by the colonial government of the Gold Coast.

This encompassing interest was different from the more selective incentives of, for example, the Customs Receivership (Chapter 6) or concession holders like Firestone (Chapter 9). So long as interest payment were made on time, trade policies remained favorable, and property rights in plantations or mines enforced, they could remain relatively unconcerned by other domestic impacts. The expansion of forced labor during the tenure of foreign financial administrators, discussed in Chapter 7, provides a key example. These efforts were praised by the American financial adviser until international pressure grew sufficiently acute to prompt a change in policy by the American government. Similarly, the concession companies discussed in Chapter 9 had no interest in promoting a more efficient tax system that might strip them of their preferential tax arrangements. Most pointedly, perhaps, the remote management of the Liberian shipping registry examined in

---

[19] Mancur Olson, *The Rise and Decline of Nations: Economic Growth, Stagflation and Social Rigidities* (New Haven and London: Yale University Press, 1982), 48.
[20] Mancur Olson, *Power and Prosperity: Outgrowing Communist and Capitalist Dictatorships* (New York: Basic Books, 2000), 10.

Chapter 10 meant that ships continued to register under the Liberian flag even as the government that flag represented collapsed into civil war.

The two paths taken by Liberia and Ghana during the first half of the twentieth century suggest that the form of foreign intervention, which we might categorize as formal and informal colonial rule, played an important role in shaping economic development, but those roles were different. This runs counter to arguments frequently made by historians and contemporaries that the two were effectively equivalent. The phrase "informal empire" was first made famous by Robinson and Gallagher's "Imperialism of free trade" (1953), in which they argued that territorial conquest was just one method for extending Britain's economic and strategic interests abroad and, at least during the nineteenth century, not the preferred method.[21] Chapter 6 of this volume showed that comparisons are frequently drawn between IFCs, for example, and formal colonialism.

More recently, Adom Getachew has argued that studies of colonialism and decolonization should look beyond what she calls "alien rule" to include broader forms of "unequal integration," which also encompassed countries that were nominally independent. "From international relations to normative political theory," she writes, "the recurring emphasis on alien rule conceives of empire as a bilateral relationship between empire and colony." This tends to imply that countries not subject to alien rule were "sovereign equals," within the international system, when in fact their membership was often subordinated and constrained in various ways. "Unequal integration conceives of international society as an internally differentiated space that includes sovereign states, quasisovereigns and colonies, which are organized through relations of hierarchy."[22] The case of Liberia suggests that alien rule and unequal integration were overlapping but not equivalent, and it is only through the study of countries coping with different forms of foreign intervention that we can tease out the differences between the two, and fully understand the impact of both formal and informal interventions.

Sovereignty after Empire

While Ghana's economy may have grown faster during the late nineteenth and early twentieth centuries, the inheritance referred to by King

---

[21] John Gallagher and Ronald Robinson, "The Imperialism of Free Trade," *Economic History Review* 6, no. 1 (1953): 1–15.
[22] Getachew, *Worldmaking After Empire*, 18

and his son was not sufficient to generate sustained growth or overcome the hierarchies of the international system after independence. Ghana and other African countries soon discovered that external recognition of their sovereignty was not sufficient to guarantee economic convergence or geopolitical equality. After independence, African countries remained vulnerable to economic setbacks linked to shifts in the global economy, internal political instability, or often both.[23] One reason for this may have been that external recognition made it easier for weak or corrupt states to survive. Unequal integration still mattered, but so did formal recognition.

Newly independent governments faced a range of hurdles once one flag had been replaced by another. Where nationalist movements had managed a united front during the fight for independence, cracks began to emerge afterward. Richard Rathbone likens the photographs of smiling Ghanaian leaders at the celebration on March 6 to wedding pictures: "large numbers of people who loathe one another can be forced to smile when faced with a camera and the implications of a permanent record."[24] They had to decide how to manage new government functions which had previously been the province of imperial governments, from foreign policy to defense to the issuing of money. And they had to make good on promises made to newly enfranchised citizens about the restructuring of the economy and increasing living standards.[25]

Many of the dilemmas African states had to contend with were similar to those that Liberia had faced. One was whether to establish a national currency, or retain colonial-era currency arrangements.[26] The first option promised additional policy tools to be used for development purposes, as well as a powerful symbol of national independence, while the second ensured that exchange rate risk would not cause problems for trade or borrowing. African countries took a variety of decisions on this issue after independence. Many, though not all, Francophone countries retained the CFA franc first developed during the colonial period, exchanging control over national monetary policies for exchange rate stability. This favored elites and urban residents who consumed imported goods, but made

---

[23] Stephen Broadberry and Leigh Gardner "Economic Growth in Sub-Saharan Africa, 1885–2008," *Explorations in Economic History* 83 (2021): 101424.

[24] Richard Rathbone, "Casting 'the Kingdome into Another Mold': Ghana's Troubled Transition to Independence," *The Round Table* 97 (2008): 713.

[25] Leigh Gardner, *Taxing Colonial Africa: The Political Economy of British Imperialism* (Oxford: Oxford University Press, 2012), ch. 9

[26] Catherine R. Schenk, "Monetary Institutions in Newly Independent Countries: The Experience of Malaya, Ghana, and Nigeria in the 1950s," *Financial History Review* 4, no. 2 (1997): 181–98; David Stasavage, *The Political Economy of a Common Currency: The CFA Franc Zone since 1945* (Aldershot: Ashgate, 2003); Chibuike U. Uche, "Bank of England vs. the IBRD: Did the Nigerian Colony Deserve a Central Bank?" *Explorations in Economic History* 34 (1997): 220–41.

exports less competitive over time through the overvaluation of the franc. By contrast, most former British colonies established central banks which issued new national currencies, and could use intervention in exchange rates to reward particular constituencies. In practice, few used the new policy tools this offered right away, but eventually instability in the value of African currencies has led to full dollarization in some African economies, like Zimbabwe, and the widespread use of foreign currencies in others.

Access to foreign capital – whether through debt, aid, or investment – presented another set of decisions. "The blessings of new sovereignty included access to international financial institutions and external assistance from sources other than the imperial treasuries," writes Crawford Young. This included American aid, which flowed to a number of African countries beyond Liberia but has been understudied by economic historians. Cold War politics meant that external resources were plentiful and offered with little connection to outcomes.[27] That did not mean there were no strings attached, however, and independent African governments struggled to minimize the conditionality of that capital. Africa's nationalist leaders were aware of this risk and wary. On the occasion of Kenya's independence in 1963, Jomo Kenyatta declared in his address that "we want to befriend all, and we want aid from everyone. But we do not want assistance from any person or country who will say: Kenyatta if you want aid, you must agree to this or that." He continued by saying, "I believe, my brothers, and I tell you now, that it is better to be poor and remain free, than be technically free but still kept on a string." Across the continent nonalignment policies proliferated in an effort to free newly independent states to seek investment without ideological commitments. Tanganyika, under the leadership of avowedly socialist Julius Nyerere, became one of the biggest recipients of World Bank funding. The hope of loyalty was enough to keep donors giving even in the absence of ideological alignment or positive results. Flows of aid helped sustain the kleptocratic governments of Tolbert and Doe in Liberia, Mobutu in Zaire, and a range of others.

While research on African states tends to emphasize failure, there were some significant successes, particularly in the early decades of independence. Numbers of schools and teachers increased rapidly, and spread into parts of African countries previously neglected by colonial states. John Sender shows that along a number of different metrics, ranging from infant mortality to the number of radios and newspapers consumed, living

---

[27] Ralph Austen, *African Economic History: Internal Development and External Dependency* (Oxford: James Currey, 1994), 224.

standards for many Africans improved over that period.[28] However, the expansion of political voice that had accompanied independence did not last long in most places, and was replaced with what Crawford Young describes as "democratic erasure."[29] Some leaders, like Nkrumah, were overthrown, while others, like Tubman in Liberia, restricted political competition. Aid and other sources of external capital fed networks of patronage which kept increasingly autocratic states in power.

Despite this upheaval, the institutional structures and political geography inherited at independence have largely remained in place. This combination of weakness and persistence remains one of the central paradoxes of Africa's political history in the decades since 1960.[30] This was particularly true in the case of the Liberian government, which despite frequent threats from within and without survived for a century and a half in essentially the same form it took at independence in 1847, until it was overthrown in 1980. Even then, however, the basic structures of the state remained the same. Writing about African states more generally, Christopher Clapham writes that "the weaker the state, in terms of its size and capabilities, its level of physical control over its people and territory, and its ability to embody an idea of the state shared by its people, the greater the extent to which it will need to call on external recognition and support."[31]

One explanation is that external recognition of sovereignty provided access to resources that African governments could use to maintain fragile political coalitions. In Cooper's conceptualization of African states as "gatekeeper states," he argues that "what they could do best was sit astride the interface between a territory and the rest of the world, collecting and distributing resources derived from that point itself: customs revenue and foreign aid; permits to do business in the territory; entry and exit visas; and permission to move currency in and out." However, as in Liberia, the terms of integration with the global economy created winners and losers and it was easy for those coalitions to fragment if conditions changed. Cooper argues that "one of the origins of instability in Africa is the inability of gatekeepers to keep the gate."[32]

[28] John Sender, "Africa's Economic Performance: Limitations of the Current Consensus," *Journal of Economic Perspectives* 13, no. 3 (1999): 89–114.

[29] Young, *The Postcolonial State*, 16.

[30] Pierre Englebert, *Africa: Unity, Sovereignty and Sorrow* (London: Lynne Rienner, 2009), ch. 1.

[31] Christopher Clapham, *Africa and the International System: The Politics of State Survival* (Cambridge: Cambridge University Press, 1996), 11.

[32] Frederick Cooper, *Africa since 1940: The Past of the Present* (Cambridge: Cambridge University Press, 2019), 235–37.

What the story of Liberia, Ghana, and other African states makes clear is that the position of African economies in the international system has important domestic impacts. Neoclassical economics assumes perfect competition, and as a result economic historians have sometimes struggled to bring power into stories of economic convergence and divergence. In their study of globalization and trade policy, Findlay and O'Rourke argue that "international relations may in fact be a more relevant discipline for those wishing to understand what lies ahead for the world economy," pointing in particular to both the historical importance of dominant hegemons and the difficulty of integrating new powers into systems of hegemonic stability.[33] These shifts often had an outsize impact on the governments of small, poor countries that depended particularly on external recognition of their sovereignty. As Christopher Clapham notes, "international politics affects these states and people in ways that often differ appreciably from the ways in which it affects the people and governments of more powerful states."[34] And yet these are often the states and countries we know least about.

Historian Norman Davies notes that in political history, "smaller or weaker countries have difficulty in making their voices heard, and dead kingdoms have almost no advocates at all."[35] Owing in large part to the expansion of empires, the nineteenth century was a dynamic period of consolidation in the shape and nature of states. Some countries, like Ghana, were created through colonial boundary making. In the process, states like the Asante Kingdom lost their status as states recognized internationally, even if they remained influential as political units locally. Asante's downfall came through defeat by force of arms, but in other cases the collapse of state came through internal changes, and the inability of the existing political system to absorb new elites empowered through foreign trade. This, according to Sumner La Croix, was the primary cause of the overthrow of the Hawaiian government in 1893, for example.[36] Business historians have long worried about how survivor bias affects our understanding of corporations; Leslie Hannah argues, for example, that "our current knowledge of survivors dominates our impression of the typical experience, and their triumphs are lionized,

---

[33] Ronald Findlay and Kevin H. O'Rourke, *Power and Plenty: Trade, War and the World Economy in the Second Millennium* (Princeton: Princeton University Press, 2009), 539–40.
[34] Clapham, *Africa and the International System*, 3.
[35] Norman Davies, *Vanished Kingdoms: The History of Half-Forgotten Europe* (New York: Penguin, 2011), 4.
[36] Sumner La Croix, *Hawai'i: Eight Hundred Years of Political and Economic Change* (Chicago: University of Chicago Press, 2019), ch 6.

while the history of the failures is forgotten or considered untypical."[37] In questions about states and state capacity, the methods of survival to which small states turned are also important. Liberia survived along with other countries like Ethiopia and Thailand, which either obtained or retained external recognition. However, to do so they had to change their structure and shape to remain part of the international system. Government officials in many states would have related to Arthur Barclay's observation, quoted in Chapter 7, that "the great powers really settle the principles of international law. Small states must conform." What impact that need to conform had on the economic and political development of small states is one of the core questions of this book.

Lessons from Liberia

Readers might reasonably ask how much an economic history of Liberia can contribute to these wider debates. Liberia is only one small country, with its own particular history. Its long ties to the United States and the American origins of the ruling elite for much of its history are just two of the reasons it has been set apart from research on the economic history of West Africa. It provides no tidy counterfactual for what would have happened in the absence of colonialism, nor does it predict perfectly events after 1960. No two countries have had the same experience of colonialism or independence.

Liberia's economic history has been neglected in recent research, and there remain many questions to be answered which were beyond the scope of this book (or beyond the evidence available to the author at the time of writing). Hopefully in the future, additional material will become available from the reorganization and full cataloguing of Liberian government archives, or from the opening of archives which have thus far remained closed, notably those of the Firestone Corporation. If and when this material emerges, it will bring additional voices and perspectives to our understanding of Liberia's economic history which could not be included here as fully as was perhaps deserved. While Chapter 2, for example, attempted to address the neglect of indigenous economies in previous economic histories of Liberia, it remains the case that the documentary record is more comprehensive for government and the ruling elite, and there remain many questions about the impact of government policy on the majority of the population. Liberia's very recent past has

---

[37] Leslie Hannah, "Marshall's 'Trees' and the Global 'Forest': Were 'Giant Redwoods' Different?" in *Learning by Doing in Markets, Firms and Countries*, edited by Naomi R. Lamoreaux, Daniel M. G. Raff and Peter Temin (Chicago: University of Chicago Press, 1999), 255.

highlighted the importance of women in shaping its economic and political history, which this book does not address.[38]

This book has shown that Liberia's history paralleled that of other independent countries, within and outside Africa. The restructuring of a territorial state in response to colonial pressures closely resembled that of the Thai state. Liberia's struggle with trade policies during the nineteenth century was similar to those faced by Peru and other Latin American states over the same period. The ways in which William V. S. Tubman attracted concessions and other foreign investment through a selective system of property rights echoed Porfirio Diaz in Mexico. No doubt, experts in other regions and countries could add other examples. Divergences also raise interesting questions. Why was Japan able to develop its economy to the extent that it did while other independent countries were not?

Africa has often remained outside these more global debates in economic history. Owing to the dominance of formal colonial rule on the continent, the focus of the recent "renaissance" in African economic history, at least, has been on variations in the type colonial rule (based on the structure of colonial economies or the identity of the colonizer) and their impact on development outcomes. Such work has neglected outlier cases like Liberia, Ethiopia, South Africa, or countries in North Africa that had varying levels of autonomy which, in turn, had an impact on domestic institutions. By revisiting the economic history of the "small island of independence" in West Africa, this book hopes to inspire a broader and more comparative understanding of sovereignty without power. Such work will, in turn, help answer Jimmy Korkollie's question about why political independence didn't lead to better lives for most Liberians.

---

[38] Aili Marie Tripp, *Women and Power in Postconflict Africa* (Cambridge: Cambridge University Press, 2015), ch. 4.

Appendix 1: Data on Liberian Economic History

A key contribution of this book is to reconstruct the quantitative economic history of Liberia, allowing it to be compared to other countries both within and outside Africa. These data are explicitly a first step, and it is hoped that providing an initial set of annual data will prompt others to seek new resources to improve them. Accordingly, this appendix consolidates the annual data used in figures and tables elsewhere in the book so as to make it accessible to other scholars.

Population

Table A1.1 *Liberian population estimates, 1845–1979*

1845	370,041	1890	475,959	1935	662,248
1846	371,901	1891	479,314	1936	672,333
1847	373,770	1892	482,693	1937	682,572
1848	375,648	1893	486,095	1938	692,966
1849	377,536	1894	489,522	1939	703,519
1850	379,433	1895	492,973	1940	714,232
1851	381,339	1896	496,448	1941	725,109
1852	383,256	1897	499,948	1942	736,151
1853	385,182	1898	503,472	1943	746,604
1854	387,117	1899	507,021	1944	757,205
1855	389,062	1900	510,595	1945	767,956
1856	391,018	1901	514,194	1946	778,860
1857	392,982	1902	517,819	1947	789,919
1858	394,957	1903	521,470	1948	801,135
1859	396,942	1904	525,146	1949	812,510
1860	398,937	1905	528,847	1950	824,047
1861	400,941	1906	532,575	1951	835,747
1862	402,956	1907	536,330	1952	847,614
1863	404,981	1908	540,111	1953	863,150

Table A1.1 *(cont.)*

1864	407,016	1909	543,918	1954	878,972
1865	409,061	1910	547,752	1955	895,083
1866	411,117	1911	551,614	1956	911,490
1867	413,183	1912	555,502	1957	928,198
1868	415,259	1913	559,418	1958	945,211
1869	417,346	1914	563,362	1959	962,537
1870	419,443	1915	567,333	1960	980,180
1871	421,551	1916	571,332	1961	998,147
1872	423,669	1917	575,360	1962	1,016,443
1873	426,227	1918	579,416	1963	1,050,000
1874	428,799	1919	583,500	1964	1,084,000
1875	431,388	1920	587,613	1965	1,120,000
1876	433,992	1921	591,756	1966	1,157,000
1877	436,611	1922	595,927	1967	1,196,000
1878	439,247	1923	599,524	1968	1,235,000
1879	441,898	1924	603,143	1969	1,276,000
1880	444,566	1925	606,784	1970	1,318,000
1881	447,249	1926	610,447	1971	1,362,000
1882	449,949	1927	614,131	1972	1,407,000
1883	453,121	1928	617,838	1973	1,454,000
1884	456,315	1929	621,568	1974	1,503,000
1885	459,532	1930	625,320	1975	1,552,000
1886	462,771	1931	629,094	1976	1,603,000
1887	466,033	1932	632,892	1977	1,656,000
1888	469,318	1933	642,530	1978	1,711,000
1889	472,627	1934	652,314	1979	1,767,000

Source: Author's calculations to 1962, then Republic of Liberia, *Statistical Handbook* (Monrovia: Ministry of Agriculture, c. 1980).

Table A1.2 *Annual migration from the United States, 1820–1904*

1820	86	1847	88	1874	20
1821	33	1848	400	1875	2
1822	37	1849	417	1876	47
1823	65	1850	482	1878	151
1824	103	1851	844	1879	98
1825	65	1852	627	1880	145
1826	121	1853	861	1881	51
1827	234	1854	615	1882	27
1828	302	1855	217	1883	53
1829	147	1856	580	1884	43
1830	326	1857	424	1885	52
1831	196	1858	166	1886	112
1832	801	1859	231	1887	123

Table A1.2 *(cont.)*

1833	655	1860	317	1888	54
1834	293	1861	55	1889	98
1835	247	1862	79	1890	63
1836	284	1863	26	1891	152
1837	209	1864	24	1892	50
1838	295	1865	178	1893	4
1839	87	1866	611	1895	4
1840	115	1867	624	1897	2
1841	110	1868	451	1898	3
1842	363	1869	156	1899	11
1843	145	1870	194	1900	1
1844	205	1871	226	1901	1
1845	202	1872	142	1902	3
1846	107	1873	73	1903	3
				1904	4

Government Finance

Table A1.3 *Total public revenue (nominal US$)*

1845	8,853	1890	*173,808*	1935	632,386
1846	8,535	1891	151,941	1936	782,746
1847	*13,236*	1892	176,291	1937	1,009,433
1848	*17,937*	1893	185,345	1938	884,534
1849	*22,637*	1894	158,861	1939	827,802
1850	*27,338*	1895	164,357	1940	898,614
1851	32,039	1896	*175,247*	1941	1,166,693
1852	*33,566*	1897	*186,136*	1942	1,005,272
1853	35,093	1898	*197,025*	1943	1,429,936
1854	33,766	1899	*207,915*	1944	1,598,401
1855	*38,205*	1900	218,804	1945	1,933,706
1856	42,644	1901	*264,452*	1946	2,300,000
1857	47,048	1902	310,100	1947	3,200,000
1858	40,426	1903	353,104	1948	3,400,000
1859	46,612	1904	301,238	1949	3,800,000
1860	57,651	1905	296,662	1950	3,900,000
1861	138,016	1906	357,433	1951	12,800,000
1862	*129,970*	1907	*356,377*	1952	8,900,000
1863	*121,924*	1908	386,234	1953	11,200,000
1864	*113,877*	1909	*432,117*	1954	11,900,000
1865	*105,831*	1910	478,000	1955	15,300,000
1866	*97,784*	1911	483,255	1956	17,900,000
1867	*89,738*	1912	534,085	1957	19,400,000

Table A1.3 *(cont.)*

1868	81,691	1913	475,287	1958	18,100,000
1869	90,363	1914	270,978	1959	24,600,000
1870	*136,125*	1915	227,141	1960	32,400,000
1871	*163,341*	1916	151,646	1961	32,400,000
1872	190,558	1917	163,867	1962	35,600,000
1873	81,586	1918	273,016	1963	37,300,000
1874	95,663	1919	551,121	1964	40,100,000
1875	94,831	1920	489,844	1965	42,400,000
1876	113,026	1921	507,955	1966	46,700,000
1877	119,881	1922	493,889	1967	48,100,000
1878	*130,707*	1923	699,728	1968	51,800,000
1879	*141,534*	1924	943,208	1969	61,800,000
1880	*152,361*	1925	894,745	1970	66,000,000
1881	*163,187*	1926	959,474	1971	69,900,000
1882	174,014	1927	1,276,437	1972	78,100,000
1883	168,964	1928	1,028,123	1973	89,800,000
1884	184,300	1929	980,156	1974	108,600,000
1885	195,800	1930	482,029	1975	125,300,000
1886	*187,642*	1931	*479,199*	1976	149,800,000
1887	*179,483*	1932	476,368	1977	172,700,000
1888	171,325	1933	465,573	1978	190,600,000
1889	*172,567*	1934	479,206	1979	204,100,000

Source: See Chapter 1. Interpolated values in italics.

Table A1.4 *Total public spending (nominal US$)*

1845	7,536	1890	*163,987*	1935	489,865
1846	*11,953*	1891	165,213	1936	704,444
1847	*16,370*	1892	188,187	1937	976,863
1848	*20,788*	1893	151,975	1938	1,040,512
1849	*25,205*	1894	*159,969*	1939	834,570
1850	*29,622*	1895	*167,964*	1940	636,710
1851	34,039	1896	*175,958*	1941	691,511
1852	*33,056*	1897	*183,952*	1942	960,280
1853	32,072	1898	*191,946*	1943	1,044,657
1854	28,853	1899	*199,941*	1944	1,522,138
1855	*44,102*	1900	207,935	1945	2,042,000
1856	59,350	1901	*263,023*	1946	2,307,614
1857	47,556	1902	318,110	1947	3,533,323
1858	37,376	1903	338,481	1948	3,028,271
1859	46,166	1904	314,200	1949	4,013,202
1860	*92,333*	1905	298,800	1950	4,984,243
1861	138,499	1906	340,036	1951	10,261,209

Table A1.4 *(cont.)*

1862	145,783	1907	*401,233*	1952	*11,354,015*
1863	*130,293*	1908	462,430	1953	12,446,820
1864	*114,803*	1909	406,377	1954	14,006,150
1865	*99,313*	1910	*438,188*	1955	15,949,436
1866	*83,823*	1911	470,000	1956	19,623,000
1867	68,333	1912	529,548	1957	19,663,553
1868	106,745	1913	531,500	1958	23,100,000
1869	92,036	1914	266,861	1959	24,500,000
1870	60,095	1915	282,332	1960	47,830,000
1871	*122,317*	1916	*269,050*	1961	55,640,000
1872	184,539	1917	255,767	1962	58,650,000
1873	180,913	1918	273,017	1963	*58,825,000*
1874	*146,409*	1919	*381,323*	1964	59,000,000
1875	111,906	1920	489,629	1965	72,800,000
1876	120,000	1921	487,543	1966	79,500,000
1877	120,000	1922	381,358	1967	80,100,000
1878	120,000	1923	681,000	1968	55,239,933
1879	*129,366*	1924	943,208	1969	60,749,667
1880	*138,733*	1925	895,715	1970	65,200,000
1881	*148,099*	1926	984,285	1971	76,100,000
1882	157,465	1927	1,712,709	1972	79,700,000
1883	152,584	1928	1,319,768	1973	89,700,000
1884	157,625	1929	1,200,252	1974	108,900,000
1885	157,625	1930	927,111	1975	122,500,000
1886	*158,928*	1931	575,711	1976	136,000,000
1887	*160,232*	1932	517,397	1977	178,500,000
1888	161,535	1933	323,786	1978	236,300,000
1889	*162,761*	1934	572,243	1979	386,300,000

Interpolated values in italics

Table A1.5 *Foreign government debt (nominal US$)*

1871	484,440	1898	1,352,118	1925	1,224,800
1872	484,440	1899	1,377,570	1926	1,146,700
1873	484,440	1900	470,059	1927	2,500,000
1874	518,351	1901	472,860	1928	2,500,000
1875	552,262	1902	472,860	1929	2,500,000
1876	586,850	1903	470,920	1930	2,500,000
1877	620,800	1904	473,345	1931	2,500,000
1878	658,125	1905	467,133	1932	2,192,000
1879	687,990	1906	461,237	1933	2,192,000

Table A1.5 *(cont.)*

1880	721,905	1907	936,041	1934	2,192,000
1881	756,600	1908	921,091	1935	2,192,000
1882	790,550	1909	908,748	1936	1,846,000
1883	825,350	1910	900,497	1937	1,755,000
1884	858,450	1911	884,134	1938	1,632,000
1885	900,680	1912	1,700,000	1939	1,602,000
1886	926,350	1913	1,352,000	1940	1,486,000
1887	964,260	1914	1,510,000	1941	*1,392,875*
1888	1,003,475	1915	1,510,000	1942	*1,299,750*
1889	1,026,080	1916	1,458,000	1943	*1,205,625*
1890	1,061,055	1917	1,458,000	1944	1,113,500
1891	1,097,230	1918	1,458,000	1945	*1,153,250*
1892	1,138,205	1919	1,458,000	1946	1,193,000
1893	1,172,400	1920	1,458,000	1947	*906,000*
1894	1,209,065	1921	1,458,000	1948	619,000
1895	1,247,140	1922	1,458,000	1949	584,000
1896	1,290,760	1923	1,426,700	1950	*539,500*
1897	1,302,480	1924	1,365,200	1951	495,000

Interpolated values in italics. Debt denominated in sterling until 1912.

Trade and Investment

Table A1.6 *Total exports (nominal US$)*

1845	*77,025*	1890	*602,509*	1935	741,712
1846	*88,217*	1891	*609,764*	1936	1,312,365
1847	*99,409*	1892	*617,019*	1937	1,991,161
1848	*110,601*	1893	*648,708*	1938	1,937,093
1849	*121,792*	1894	*476,583*	1939	2,714,133
1850	*132,984*	1895	*482,026*	1940	3,330,000
1851	*144,176*	1896	*355,253*	1941	5,000,000
1852	*151,047*	1897	228,480	1942	6,800,000
1853	*157,919*	1898	238,476	1943	8,900,000
1854	*151,949*	1899	421,494	1944	10,300,000
1855	*175,939*	1900	396,032	1945	11,300,000
1856	199,930	1901	295,358	1946	12,300,000
1857	140,102	1902	363,902	1947	13,100,000
1858	141,590	1903	559,340	1948	15,800,000
1859	235,781	1904	547,023	1949	15,500,000
1860	400,000	1905	458,876	1950	27,600,000
1861	*417,040*	1906	769,491	1951	52,100,000

Table A1.6 *(cont.)*

1862	621,074	1907	786,667	1952	37,200,000
1863	578,830	1908	886,639	1953	31,000,000
1864	536,586	1909	956,566	1954	26,400,000
1865	494,342	1910	952,195	1955	42,800,000
1866	452,098	1911	1,001,332	1956	44,500,000
1867	409,854	1912	1,181,916	1957	40,500,000
1868	367,611	1913	1,288,915	1958	53,800,000
1869	490,086	1914	928,384	1959	66,900,000
1870	612,561	1915	567,853	1960	82,600,000
1871	735,036	1916	379,115	1961	61,900,000
1872	857,511	1917	618,536	1962	67,600,000
1873	367,138	1918	808,050	1963	81,100,000
1874	430,481	1919	997,563	1964	125,700,000
1875	426,742	1920	1,123,781	1965	135,400,000
1876	508,619	1921	819,594	1966	150,500,000
1877	539,503	1922	1,045,382	1967	158,500,000
1878	588,215	1923	1,166,735	1968	199,400,000
1879	636,927	1924	1,416,896	1969	232,800,000
1880	685,639	1925	1,916,053	1970	235,900,000
1881	734,351	1926	1,757,521	1971	246,600,000
1882	783,063	1927	1,614,671	1972	269,800,000
1883	960,000	1928	1,465,568	1973	324,000,000
1884	820,800	1929	1,475,356	1974	400,200,000
1885	864,000	1930	838,739	1975	394,400,000
1886	772,000	1931	679,885	1976	457,000,000
1887	680,000	1932	675,347	1977	447,400,000
1888	588,000	1933	616,415	1978	486,400,000
1889	592,255	1934	571,793	1979	536,600,000

Interpolated values in italics. Interpolation based on trend of revenue data.

Table A1.7 *Total imports (nominal US$)*

1845	79,677	1890	931,141	1935	1,294,941
1846	76,815	1891	960,232	1936	1,673,776
1847	98,152	1892	705,164	1937	1,958,268
1848	119,489	1893	1,250,824	1938	2,241,920
1849	140,826	1894	635,444	1939	2,002,864
1850	162,163	1895	675,406	1940	2,200,000
1851	221,567	1896	715,368	1941	3,300,000
1852	216,062	1897	755,330	1942	3,900,000
1853	210,558	1898	795,292	1943	4,000,000
1854	202,598	1899	835,254	1944	3,000,000

Table A1.7 *(cont.)*

1855	*229,232*	1900	*875,216*	1945	3,600,000
1856	*255,867*	1901	*915,178*	1946	4,700,000
1857	*282,291*	1902	*930,300*	1947	8,700,000
1858	*242,559*	1903	*1,059,312*	1948	8,800,000
1859	*279,672*	1904	537,846	1949	8,200,000
1860	*345,906*	1905	669,143	1950	10,600,000
1861	*828,099*	1906	737,546	1951	17,200,000
1862	*779,820*	1907	984,990	1952	18,100,000
1863	*731,541*	1908	965,626	1953	18,700,000
1864	*683,262*	1909	952,893	1954	22,700,000
1865	*634,984*	1910	1,048,772	1955	26,000,000
1866	*586,705*	1911	1,154,924	1956	26,800,000
1867	*538,426*	1912	1,667,857	1957	38,200,000
1868	*490,147*	1913	1,411,237	1958	38,500,000
1869	*542,176*	1914	*812,934*	1959	42,900,000
1870	*643,215*	1915	*681,423*	1960	69,200,000
1871	*744,253*	1916	*454,938*	1961	90,700,000
1872	845,292	1917	*491,601*	1962	131,600,000
1873	626,908	1918	*819,048*	1963	108,000,000
1874	*573,975*	1919	1,139,075	1964	111,200,000
1875	*568,989*	1920	1,922,292	1965	104,800,000
1876	*678,158*	1921	1,231,701	1966	113,700,000
1877	*719,284*	1922	1,501,515	1967	125,200,000
1878	*714,638*	1923	1,361,700	1968	108,500,000
1879	*709,993*	1924	1,433,185	1969	114,700,000
1880	*705,347*	1925	2,115,021	1970	149,700,000
1881	*700,702*	1926	2,251,597	1971	162,400,000
1882	*696,056*	1927	2,896,081	1972	178,700,000
1883	727,500	1928	4,029,506	1973	193,500,000
1884	*756,592*	1929	2,064,440	1974	288,400,000
1885	*785,683*	1930	1,228,102	1975	331,200,000
1886	*814,775*	1931	858,742	1976	399,200,000
1887	*843,866*	1932	641,212	1977	463,500,000
1888	*872,958*	1933	693,358	1978	480,800,000
1889	*902,049*	1934	1,180,601	1979	506,500,000

Interpolated values in italics. Interpolation based on trend of revenue data.

Table A1.8 *Estimates of US aid to Liberia*

Year	Northwestern	World Bank	OECD	USAID
1944	21.9			
1945	2.6			
1946	0.5			6.8
1947	0.5			
1948	0.5			0.7
1949	0.5			0.2
1950	1.0			0.1
1951	1.0			0.8
1952	1.0			1.2
1953	1.0			1.7
1954	1.8			1.1
1955	3.8			1.9
1956	1.8			2.4
1957	2.4			2.2
1958	3.0			2.4
1959	5.5	6.0		6.4
1960	6.3	3.5	9.0	5.7
1961	10.7	4.4	18.0	7.7
1962	11.0	3.9	34.0	13.4
1963		1.6	11.0	41.8
1964		1.7	11.0	16.9
1965		11.8	25.2	20.2
1966		11.7	21.5	12.3
1967		11.8	22.0	11.0
1968		6.3	14.3	9.2
1969		6.8	13.0	13.5
1970		7.5	10.0	8.5
1971		5.8	10.0	8.7
1972		3.9	10.0	19.7
1973			6.0	18.8
1974			5.0	6.1
1975			8.0	17.6
1976			15.0	8.8
1977			10.0	22.0
1978			10.0	7.9
1979			10.0	19.0
1980			32.0	27.2

Source: USAID; Clower et al., *Growth without Development*; OECD; World Bank.

Table A1.9 *Concessions granted by the Liberian government*

Company	Year	Industry
Liberia Rubber Company	1906	Agriculture
Firestone Rubber Company	1926	Agriculture
Liberia Mining Company	1946	Mineral
Liberia Company (Stettinius)	1947	Agriculture
African Fruit Company	1952	Agriculture
Munarriz Industrial Works	1952	Industrial
Industrial Trading Trust	1953	Mineral
United African-American Corporation	1953	Mineral
Industrial Trading Trust	1953	Timber
Limpex Palm Oil Co	1953	Industrial
Liberian American Swedish Minerals Company (LAMCO)	1953	Mineral
BF Goodrich Company	1954	Agriculture
Liberian Products and Manufactures Incorporated	1955	Industrial
Anglo-American Development Corporation	1955	Industrial
International African-American Corporation	1956	Mineral
Columbia-Southern Chemical Corporation	1956	Mineral
Monrovia Breweries, Inc.	1956	Industrial
J. J. Simons, Jr.	1957	Mineral
Morro River Lumber Company	1957	Timber
Liberia Industrial Forestry Company	1957	Timber
National Iron Ore Company	1958	Mineral
Gewerkschaft Exploration	1958	Mineral
German-Liberian Mining Company (DELIMCO)	1958	Mineral
Liberian Timber Industries Corporation	1959	Timber
Siga Lumber Company of Bassa, Incorporated	1959	Timber
Mafit Trust Corporation, Limited	1959	Industrial
Liberian Agricultural Company	1959	Agriculture
Consolidated Press	1959	Industrial
Liberian Development Company	1959	Mineral
Naamloze Vennoot Schap Rubber Cultur-Maatschappij	1960	Agriculture
Liberian American Swedish Minerals Company (LAMCO)	1960	Mineral
Bethlehem Steel Corporation	1960	Mineral
Maryland Logging Corporation	1960	Timber
Salala Rubber Corporation	1960	Agriculture
Providence Mining Company	1960	Mineral
Monrovia Storage (SAMCO)	1960	Industrial
Hunt International Petroleum Company	1962	Industrial
St. Andrews Securities, Ltd.	1963	Mineral
West African Explosives and Chemicals, Ltd.	1963	Industrial
Gwerkschaft Exploration	1964	Mineral
Liberian Operations Company (LIBINC)	1965	Agriculture
West African Agricultural Corporation	1967	Agriculture

Source: van der Kraaij, Clower et al.

Table A1.10 *Ships registered under the Liberian flag*

Year	Ships	Gross tonnage
1949	2	772
1950	5	47,314
1951	22	245,457
1952	69	595,198
1953	105	897,898
1954	158	1,434,085
1955	245	2,381,066
1956	436	3,996,904
1957	582	5,584,378
1958	743	7,466,429
1959	975	10,078,778
1960	1,085	11,936,250
1961	977	11,282,240
1962	903	10,929,551
1963	853	10,573,158
1964	893	11,391,210
1965	1,117	14,549,645
1966	1,287	17,539,462
1967	1,436	20,603,301
1968	1,513	22,597,808
1969	1,613	25,719,642
1970	1,731	29,215,151
1971	1,869	33,296,644
1972	2,060	38,552,240
1973	2,234	44,443,652
1974	2,289	49,904,744
1975	2,332	55,321,641
1976	2,520	65,820,414
1977	2,600	73,477,326
1978	2,617	79,982,968
1979	2,523	80,191,329
1980	2,466	81,528,175
1981	2,401	80,285,176
1982	2,281	74,906,390
1983	2,189	70,718,439
1984	2,062	67,564,201
1985	1,934	62,024,700
1986	1,808	58,178,717
1987	1,658	52,649,444
1988	1,574	51,412,019
1989	1,507	49,733,615
1990	1,455	47,892,529
1991	1,688	51,079,790
1992	1,627	53,289,569

Table A1.10 *(cont.)*

Year	Ships	Gross tonnage
1993	1,661	55,917,675
1994	1,611	53,918,534
1995	1,621	57,647,708
1996	1,666	59,800,742
1997	1,684	59,988,908
1998	1,697	60,058,368
1999	1,717	60,492,104

Source: Lloyd's of London.

Historical National Accounts

Table A1.11 *GDP per capita (1990 international dollars)*

1845	431	1890	522	1935	471
1846	433	1891	524	1936	504
1847	435	1892	524	1937	541
1848	437	1893	530	1938	533
1849	439	1894	502	1939	563
1850	441	1895	502	1940	578
1851	443	1896	481	1941	633
1852	444	1897	460	1942	683
1853	445	1898	460	1943	744
1854	444	1899	489	1944	786
1855	447	1900	482	1945	810
1856	451	1901	469	1946	806
1857	441	1902	480	1947	780
1858	443	1903	509	1948	812
1859	458	1904	505	1949	808
1860	482	1905	491	1950	1,084
1861	487	1906	533	1951	1,570
1862	517	1907	547	1952	1,227
1863	509	1908	547	1953	1,087
1864	502	1909	558	1954	989
1865	496	1910	555	1955	1,304
1866	488	1911	560	1956	1,320
1867	482	1912	579	1957	1,203
1868	475	1913	588	1958	1,406
1869	495	1914	526	1959	1,598
1870	536	1915	480	1960	1,885
1871	556	1916	455	1961	1,548

Table A1.11 *(cont.)*

1872	572	1917	468	1962	1,607
1873	481	1918	476	1963	1,753
1874	493	1919	482	1964	2,308
1875	493	1920	490	1965	2,381
1876	509	1921	472	1966	2,462
1877	514	1922	489	1967	2,436
1878	523	1923	501	1968	2,680
1879	535	1924	520	1969	2,835
1880	540	1925	550	1970	2,667
1881	549	1926	539	1971	2,611
1882	557	1927	535	1972	2,663
1883	587	1928	522	1973	2,865
1884	567	1929	521	1974	3,049
1885	574	1930	476	1975	2,736
1886	561	1931	467	1976	2,871
1887	543	1932	468	1977	2,619
1888	526	1933	464	1978	2,610
1889	526	1934	460	1979	2,522

Note: For more detail on the construction of these estimates, see Appendix 2.

Appendix 2: Calculating Liberian GDP Per Capita, 1845–1964

Appendix 2 documents the sources and methods used for calculating the estimates of Liberian GDP per capita from 1845 to 1965 which appear in Appendix 1. This is the first attempt to reconstruct Liberia's historical national accounts on an annual basis using directly observed data. The estimates presented here follow the method used by Broadberry and Gardner in calculating GDP per capita for eight other African countries.[1] The purpose of this appendix is to provide a clear and transparent accounting for the calculation of these figures, which can help facilitate refinements as more data become available.

Official GDP per capita data produced by the Liberian government begin in 1964.[2] Prior to that, there were two efforts to calculate Liberia's national income during the 1940s and 1950s. The first was an unpublished series compiled by a US government survey conducted in Liberia in 1959.[3] The second was from a more detailed study by a team of Northwestern University economists hired to complete a survey of the Liberian economy in the early 1960s.[4] Drawing on data collected from companies and government ministries in Monrovia, they provided estimates from 1950 to 1960, though they admitted that "the data underlying these estimates are very poor – especially for the years 1950–54."[5] Angus Maddison also provides data on Liberia dating back to 1950, though it is not clear what sources he used.[6] Thus far,

[1] Stephen Broadberry and Leigh Gardner, "Economic Growth in Sub-Saharan Africa, 1885–2008," *Explorations in Economic History* 83 (2021): 101424.

[2] Republic of Liberia, *Estimates of Domestic Product at Current and Constant 1971 Prices 1964–1973* (Monrovia: Ministry of Planning and Economic Affairs, 1975).

[3] Report of the United States Internal Security Survey Team to Liberia, November 16 to December 14, 1959, NARA RG 59, Entry A1 3107, Box 2.

[4] Robert Clower, George Dalton, Mitchell Harwitz and A. A. Walters, *Growth Without Development: An Economic Survey of Liberia* (Evanston, IL: Northwestern University Press, 1966).

[5] Clower et al., *Growth Without Development*, 47.

[6] Angus Maddison, "Statistics on World Population, GDP and Per Capita GDP, 1–2008 AD," Groningen Growth and Development Center (2010).

Leandro Prados de la Escosura has made the only attempt to estimate GDP per capita for Liberia before 1945. His figures, which cover the period from 1870 to 1950, are largely based on interpolated trade data from Banks (2010).

Collectively these series do not tell a consistent story about trends in Liberia's GDP per capita. For example, both the internal US government data and the Northwestern data show rapid economic growth through the late 1940s and early 1950s, which is consistent with the large influx of foreign investment and increase in export production during this period. In contrast, Maddison assumes slow growth through the 1950s and thus an implausibly high level of GDP per capita in 1950. Figure A2.1 compares the series presented in this book to other historical GDP per capita series. Here, Liberian GDP per capita is calculated from the output side. The economy is divided into three sectors: the traditional sector (which includes agriculture and domestic industry and services), the export sector, and government.

The appendix proceeds as follows. The next three sections derive output series for the three main sectors, and describe modifications that needed to be made to the method used by Broadberry and Gardner due to data constraints. The structure of the economy is then illustrated by data from previous national accounting efforts, so as to provide the weights used in the construction of the GDP series. Then the GDP series is derived and combined with the population series to estimate GDP per capita. The results are compared with existing alternative estimates and with other West African countries.

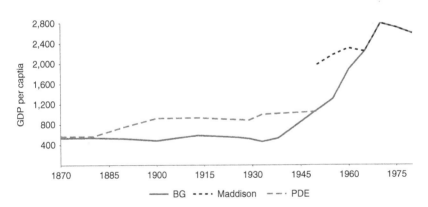

Figure A2.1 Alternative estimates of GDP per capita
Source: Angus Maddison, "Statistics on world population, GDP and per capita GDP, 1–2008 AD," Groningen Growth and Development Center (2010); Prados de la Escosura, "Output per head in pre-independence Africa."

The Traditional Sector

In Liberia, as in other African economies, the domestic production of food and other goods for home consumption is the least documented of the three sectors discussed here. It has been traditional to assume that output in this sector grows in line with population, as people produce only enough to maintain subsistence with no improvement in living standards over time. This is the approach used, for example, in estimates for Ghana for a set of benchmark years (1891, 1901, and 1911) by Szereszewski, and also in estimates for colonial Northern Rhodesia by Phyllis Deane.[7] Later, Deane also applied this same approach to her estimates of agricultural output in Britain in the eighteenth century.[8] The assumption that per capita consumption remains constant even as economies change and aggregate incomes rise has increasingly been challenged in work on Europe and Asia.[9] Instead, this work combines population data with an estimate of the income elasticity for food to derive the overall demand for food. Broadberry and Gardner apply this approach to other African economies, using real wage data compiled by Ewout Frankema and Marlous van Waijenburg.[10] Unfortunately, very little price and wage data survive for Liberia before 1945, and thus it is not possible to apply this same approach here. Instead, the traditional sector is assumed to move in line with population. Figure A2.2 gives the population data from Chapter 1 in index number form, showing a gradual upward trend in traditional sector demand.

With the recovery of additional data from Liberia and neighboring economies, it may be possible to improve on this and provide a more nuanced picture of demand in the traditional sector. One option, for example, might be to use real wages from Freetown for the nineteenth

[7] R. Szereszewski, *Structural Changes in the Economy of Ghana, 1891–1911* (London: Weidenfeld and Nicolson, 1965), Phyllis Deane, *Colonial Social Accounting* (Cambridge: Cambridge University Press, 1953).

[8] Phyllis Deane and W. A. Cole, *British Economic Growth, 1688–1959: Trends and Structure* (Cambridge: Cambridge University Press, 1962).

[9] N. F. R. Crafts, "English Economic Growth in the Eighteenth Century: A Re-Examination of Deane and Cole's Estimates," *Economic History Review* 29 (1976): 226–35; Paolo Malanima, "The Long Decline of a Leading Economy: GDP in Central and Northern Italy, 1300–1913," *European Review of Economic History* 15 (2011): 169–219; Carlos Alvarez-Nogal and Leandro Prados de la Escosura, "The Rise and Fall of Spain, 1270–1850," *Economic History Review* 66 (2013): 1–37; Stephen Broadberry, Johan Custodis, and Bishnupriya Gupta, "India and the Great Divergence: An Anglo-Indian Comparison of GDP per Capita, 1600–1871," *Explorations in Economic History* 56 (2015): 58–75.

[10] Ewout Frankema and Marlous van Waijenburg, "Structural Impediments to African Growth? New Evidence from Real Wages in British Africa, 1880–1965," *Journal of Economic History* 72, no. 4 (2012): 895–926.

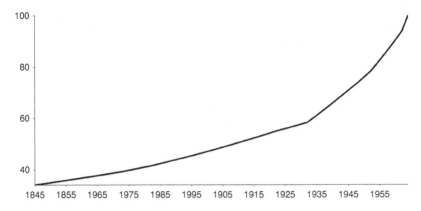

Figure A2.2 Population of Liberia (1964 = 100)

and early twentieth centuries when Liberian data are not available. Freetown is the closest city to Monrovia geographically, and the labor markets of the two cities were linked, particularly for maritime workers. During the early decades of Liberia's history, a substantial share of the wage-earning population were Kru mariners who would often work on British ships moving up and down the West African coast.[11] Frankema and van Waijenburg do include data on Freetown wages, but as they are relatively stagnant until the 1930s, this is unlikely to make a substantial difference in GDP calculations.

The Government Sector

Government finances are by far the best documented part of Liberia's economy, particularly during the nineteenth and early twentieth centuries. In this period, the main source of quantitative data is the annual messages of Liberian presidents to the legislature, which survive in various archival collections and have been reproduced in a volume edited by Elwood Dunn.[12] Annual messages covered a wide range of topics, from cultural and religious matters to financial and economic. They make frequent reference to tables and reports that were presented to the

---

[11] George E. Brooks, *The Kru Mariner in the Nineteenth Century: An Historical Compendium* (Newark: Liberian Studies Association, 1972).

[12] D. Elwood Dunn, ed., *The Annual Messages of the Presidents of Liberia 1848–2010* (Berlin: Walter de Gruyter, 2011). As the Dunn volume is not widely accessible, the annual messages accessed in this project were from IULC and CNDRA, supplemented by Dunn.

legislature in each year. While these supplementary reports have not survived for most years, the annual messages frequently report on government revenue and expenditure for the year. As discussed in Chapter 1, there remain some gaps in the annual series, which have been filled either by using data on revenue (on the occasions when figures for revenue but not expenditure appear) or failing that using linear interpolation.

For the purpose of calculating GDP, the output of the government sector is measured by nominal government spending deflated by a combination of two price indices: British pounds and US dollars. The deflation of nominal figures for Liberia is less straightforward than for British colonies because of the history of currency depreciation and substitutions, as discussed in Chapter 5. Reflecting this change in currencies, and as discussed in Chapter 1, Charles Feinstein's price series for UK public authorities' goods and services is spliced in 1943 to the US Federal Reserve price index for the US dollar.[13] The Feinstein series is frequently used to deflate nominal data for British Africa, and when compared to local prices in British Africa the two have similar trends, so the choice of deflators does not change the story. Similarly, the British and American series are very similar after 1943, so it makes little difference which is used.

Figure A2.3 shows real government expenditure and real government expenditure per capita, indexed to 1964. It shows that government

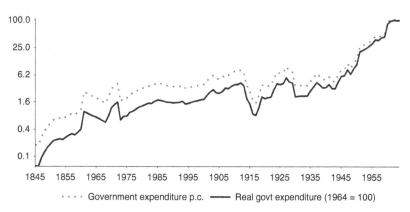

Figure A2.3 Real government expenditure and government expenditure per capita (1964 = 100)

[13] Charles H. Feinstein, *National Income, Expenditure, and Output of the United Kingdom, 1855–1965* (Cambridge: Cambridge University Press, 1972); Federal Reserve Board of Minneapolis, "Consumer Price Index 1913." www.minneapolisfed.org/about-us/monetary-policy/inflation-calculator/consumer-price-index-1913-.

spending grew rapidly in the first decades after Liberia's declaration of independence in 1847. Growth then slowed across the period from the middle of the 1870s until the early 1940s, when it accelerated again. As the next section will show, this follows the general pattern of the export sector, reflecting the importance of trade to Liberia's public finances.

The Export Sector

The output of the export sector is derived from the nominal value of exports, deflated in the same way as for government finances. Chapter 1 describes the reconstruction of the trade data. While no complete annual data could be found for the nineteenth century in particular, the current series relies less heavily on linear interpolation than the data presented by Banks, which contains little of the annual variations to be expected in export values. Instead, for periods when data are missing, interpolation is based on trends in revenue data which, given the importance of trade taxes as a source of revenue, are highly correlated with export values. Figure A2.4 shows real exports indexed to 1964. It shows an initial increase in exports during the middle of the nineteenth century, followed by a long period from the 1870s to the 1930s in which the gains from short-run periods of export growth were erased by declines during downturns. Real export values stagnated during this period, before rising dramatically from the early 1930s until the middle of the 1970s. Using the real value of exports represents a deviation from the method used by Broadberry and Gardner, who use the volume of goods exported as their primary indicator of output for the export sector. This is necessary due to

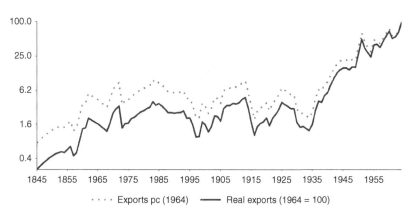

Figure A2.4 Real export values and export values per capita (1964 = 100)

the scarcity of data on the volume of Liberia's exports, particularly before 1930. After 1930, however, volume data are more readily available. Figure A2.5 shows an index of the volume of the four leading exports over this period, showing both the volatility of coffee and palm product exports and the rapid rise of rubber and iron ore. By 1964, iron ore represented 70 percent of the value of Liberia's exports.

Figure A2.6 compares an index of export volumes based on the relative values in 1964 to the index of real export values used in Figure A2.3. Though there are some short-term divergences between the two series, they follow the same long-run trend, suggesting that the use of real export

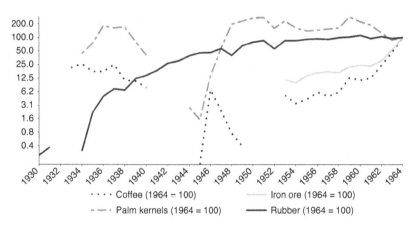

Figure A2.5 Liberia's major exports, 1930–1964 (1964 = 100)

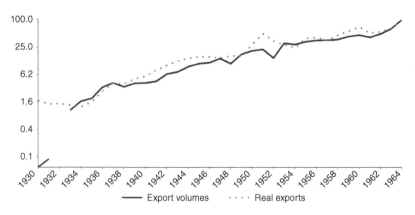

Figure A2.6 Export volumes compared to real values (1964 = 100)

values rather than volume indices in the calculation of Liberian GDP should not make much difference.

Calculating GDP and GDP Per Capita

To calculate GDP from the output figures of these three sectors, it is necessary to apply the appropriate weights for each sector. The earliest set of weights on a sectoral basis are from the US government series in 1941–3 then 1956–9. These are presented in Table A2.1A. At the beginning of this period almost half of GDP (49 percent) was generated by the traditional sector, while the export sector and government accounted for the other half. By the late 1950s, however, the share of the subsistence sector had declined to 20 percent, while both the government and export sectors had expanded considerably. The sectoral shares from the Northwestern series, presented in Table A2.1B, follow a similar track over the 1950s. Table A2.1C presents the weights from the official series in 1964. Differences in definition mean the levels vary between series but the overall trend of faster growth in the export and government sectors compared to the subsistence sector remains the same.

Table A2.1 *Sectoral weights*
A. *US government series*

	Traditional	Government	Export
1941–1943	49%	4%	47%
1956	20%	13%	66%
1957	20%	14%	65%
1958	19%	17%	64%
1959	17%	15%	68%

B. *Northwestern series*

	Traditional	Government	Export
1950	55%	8%	37%
1951	51%	11%	39%
1952	46%	16%	38%
1953	43%	16%	41%
1954	43%	19%	37%
1955	34%	19%	47%
1956	32%	20%	47%
1957	33%	24%	43%
1958	33%	27%	40%
1959	26%	25%	49%
1960	23%	27%	49%

C. *Official series 1964 weights*

	Traditional	Government	Export
1964	17%	7%	75%

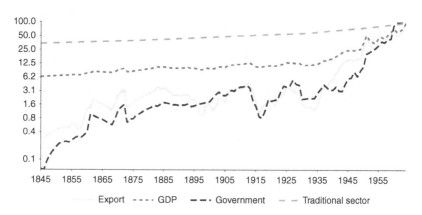

Figure A2.7 Liberia's real GDP by sector, 1845–1964 (1964 = 100, log scale)

Aggregate GDP is constructed by combining the output indices for the three main sectors using the 1964 weights from Table A2.1C. The time series for all three sectors are plotted together in Figure A2.7. It shows that growth was much faster in the export sector and government compared with traditional agriculture. The trend in aggregate GDP series is driven largely by the slower growing sectors, but in the short run fluctuations tend to be driven by the more volatile export sector.

The path of aggregate GDP reveals less about the pattern of economic development than GDP per capita. Figure A2.6 shows Liberian GDP, population, and GDP per capita together. It shows that while Liberian GDP per capita has grown, periods of shrinking have frequently erased many of the gains achieved during more prosperous times, so that overall improvements in per capita income have been limited (Figure A2.8).

These new estimates allow Liberia to be included in comparative work on long-run economic growth. Figure A2.9 compares Liberian GDP per capita to that of Ghana, Nigeria, and South Africa. It shows in particular that per capita incomes followed a different path than other African countries, stagnating during what was otherwise a period of growth and growing during more difficult periods. Figure A2.10 compares Liberia to

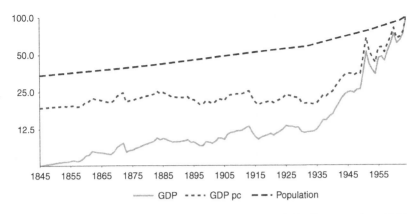

Figure A2.8 Liberian GDP, population and GDP per capita, 1845–1964 (1964 = 100, log scale)

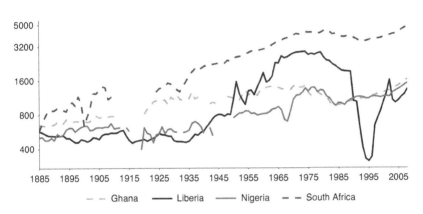

Figure A2.9 GDP per capita in Liberia and African economies

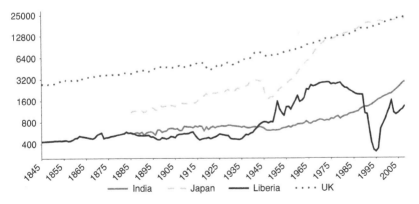

Figure A2.10 GDP per capita in Liberia and other global economies

the United Kingdom, Japan, and India. While Liberia enjoyed brief periods of catching up, the overall trend across this period was toward greater divergence.

References

Archives

Liberia

Center for National Documents and Records Agency (CNDRA)

Liberian Daily Observer (LDO)
   The Crozierville Observer archives

Other

Bank of England Archive (BEA)
   OV67 Overseas Department: West Africa
   OV135 Overseas Department: Liberia
British Library
   Maps C.46.f.12
Cambridge University Library
   RCMS 124 Cuthbert Christy papers
Herskovits Library, Northwestern University (HL)
   019 Records of the Economic Survey of Liberia
Indiana University Bloomington Liberia Collection (IULC)
   LCP2005/008 Bai T Moore papers
   LCP2008/004 Frederick Dean McEvoy Collection, 1956–1979
   LCP006 Liberian Government Archives I, 1828–1968
   LCP001 Liberian Newspaper Collection
   IULC035 Svend Holsoe Collection: Edward James Roye Materials, 1811–1986
   IULC039 Svend Holsoe Collection: Vai Materials, 1924–1995
   IULC036/IULC022 Svend Holsoe Newspaper Collection, 1830–1979
   LCP2001/001 Warren d'Azevedo Collection
   LCP2005/014 William V. S. Tubman Papers, 1904–1992

Library of Congress (LOC)
0630A American Colonization Society papers
MMC-3545 Joseph J Roberts family papers
Lloyd's Register Archive
Casualty Returns
World Fleet Statistics
London Metropolitan Archive (LMA)
CLC/B/207 Papers of Standard Chartered Bank
Maryland Historical Society
MS571 Maryland Colonization Society Papers, 1827–71
New York Public Library (NYPL)
Sc MG 162 Phelps-Stokes papers
Princeton University Library
MC146 Edwin W Kemmerer Papers
Smithsonian Museum of American History
National Numismatic Collection
United Kingdom National Archives (TNA)
B Records of the Commissioners of Bankrupts
C Court of Chancery
CAOG Crown Agents for the Colonies
CO Colonial Office
FO Foreign Office
MINT Royal Mint
T Treasury
United Nations Archives Geneva: League of Nations (LON)
1 Mandates
6B Slavery
United States National Archives and Records Administration (NARA)
RG 59 General Records of the Department of State
RG 84 Records of the Foreign Service Posts of the Department of State
RG 160 Headquarters Army Service Forces
RG 165 War Department General & Special Staffs
RG 169 Foreign Economic Administration
RG 178 US Maritime Commission
RG 218 US Joint Chiefs of Staff
RG 469 Foreign Assistance Agencies
RG Entry A1 5713
University of Miami Library
ASM0341 Pan American World Airways Records

Official Sources

Liberia

Central Bank of Liberia. *Financial and Economic Bulletin January-March 2013*. Monrovia: Central Bank of Liberia, 2013.

Department of Public Instruction. *Annual Report*. Monrovia: Republic of Liberia, 1961.

Grimes, L. A. *Report and Opinions of L.A. Grimes, Attorney General of Liberia*. Monrovia: Republic of Liberia, 1923.

National Bank of Liberia. *Annual Report*. Monrovia: Republic of Liberia, various.

National Investment Commission. *Annual Report*. Monrovia, 1980.

Republic of Liberia. *Acts*. Monrovia: Republic of Liberia, various.

  The Budget of the Government of Liberia. Monrovia: Bureau of the Budget, various.

  Economic Survey of Liberia. Monrovia: Ministry of Planning and Economic Affairs, various.

  External Trade of Liberia: Exports. Monrovia: Ministry of Planning and Economic Affairs, various.

  External Trade of Liberia: Imports. Monrovia: Ministry of Planning and Economic Affairs, various.

  The Population of Liberia. Monrovia: Ministry of Planning and Economic Affairs, 1974.

  Public Foreign Assistance to Liberia, 1965–1967. Monrovia: Department of Planning and Economic Affairs, 1968.

  Estimates of Domestic Product at Current and Constant 1971 Prices 1964–1973. Monrovia: Ministry of Planning and Economic Affairs, 1975.

  Statistical Handbook. Monrovia: Ministry of Agriculture, 1975.

  1971 Census of Agriculture: Final Report. Monrovia: Ministry of Planning and Economic Affairs, 1984.

Steadman, Robert F. *Report on the Fiscal System of the Republic of Liberia*. Monrovia: Executive Mansion, 1952.

Other

Christy, Cuthbert. *Report of the International Commission of Inquiry into the Existence of Slavery and Forced Labor in the Republic of Liberia*. Geneva: League of Nations, 1932.

Ghana Information Services. *Ghana is Born, 6th March 1957*. London: Newman Neame, 1958.

Gold Coast. *Blue Books*. Accra: Government Printer, various.

Lagos. *Blue Books*. Lagos: Government Printer, various.

Nigeria. *Blue Books*. Lagos: Government Printer, various.

Sierra Leone. *Blue Books*. Freetown: Government Printer, various.

UK Foreign Office. *Report on the Trade and Commerce of Liberia*. London: HMSO, various.

UK House of Commons. *Correspondence Respecting the Financial Condition of the Colonies of Sierra Leone, Gambia and St Helena.* London: HMSO, 1877.

Papers Relating to the Construction of Railways in Sierra Leone, Lagos and the Gold Coast. London: HMSO, 1904.

UNICEF, WHO, and World Bank Group, Joint Child Malnutrition Estimates – Levels and Trends in Child Malnutrition: Key Findings for the 2019 Edition (2019). https://apps.who.int/iris/bitstream/handle/10665/331097/WHO-NMH-NHD-19.20-eng.pdf?ua=1

United Nations. *Report of the Panel of Exports pursuant to Security Council resolution 1343.* Geneva: United Nations, 2015.

US Department of State. *Papers Relating to the Foreign Relations of the United States.* Washington, DC: Government Printing Office, various.

Point Four Pioneers: Reports from a New Frontier. Washington, DC: Government Printing Office, 1951.

US House of Representatives. *Eighth Quarterly Report to Congress on Lend-Lease Operations for the Period Ended March 11, 1943, House Document No. 129.* Washington, DC: Government Printing Office, 1943.

US Senate. *Affairs in Liberia.* Washington, DC: Government Printing Office, 1910.

Hearings before the Committee on Commerce on Recent Tanker Accidents, Part 1. Washington DC: US Government Printing Office, 1977.

West African Currency Committee. *Minutes of Evidence.* London: HMSO, 1912.

Other Serials

American Colonization Society. *African Repository.* Washington, DC: ACS, various.

Annual Reports. Washington, DC: ACS, various.

Corporation of Foreign Bondholders. *Annual Reports.* London: CFB, various.

Martin, Frederick, and Sir John Scott Keltie, eds. *Statesman's Yearbook.* London: Macmillan, various.

Secondary Sources

Abbott, A. W. *A Short History of the Crown Agents and Their Office.* Portsmouth: The Grosvenor Press, 1971.

Abramitzky, Ran, Leah Platt Boustan, and K. Eriksson. "Europe's Tired, Poor, Huddled Masses: Self-Selection and Economic Outcomes in the Age of Mass Migration." *American Economic Review* 102 (2012): 1823–56.

Abramitzky, Ran, and F. Braggion. "Migration and Human Capital: Self-Selection of Indentured Servants to the Americas." *Journal of Economic History* 66 (2006): 882–905.

Acemoglu, Deron, Simon Johnson, and James A. Robinson. "Reversal of Fortune: Geography and Institutions in the Making of the Modern World Income Distribution." *Quarterly Journal of Economics* 117 (2002): 1231–94.

"Institutions as a Fundamental Cause of Long-Run Growth." In *Handbook of Economic Growth, Volume 1a*, edited by Philippe Aghion and Steven Durlauf, 385–472. Amsterdam: North-Holland, 2005.

"The Rise of Europe: Atlantic Trade, Institutional Change and Economic Growth." *American Economic Review* 95, no. 3 (2005): 546–79.

Acemoglu, Deron, Thierry Verdier, and James A. Robinson. "Kleptocracy and Divide-and-Rule: A Model of Personal Rule." *Journal of the European Economic Association* 2, no. 2–3 (2004): 162–92.

Africa's Luminary. *Trial of the Suit Instituted by the Collector of Customs for the Port of Monrovia against the Superintendent of the Liberia Mission of the Missionary Society of the Methodist Episcopal Church before the Supreme Court of Liberia.* Monrovia: MPM Press, 1840.

Akingbade, Harrison. "US Liberian Relations During World War II." *Phylon* 46, no. 1 (1985): 25–36.

Akpan, Monday B. "Black Imperialism: Americo-Liberian Rule over the African Peoples of Liberia, 1841–1964." *Canadian Journal of African Studies* 7 (1973): 217–36.

Alderton, Tony, and Nick Winchester. "Globalisation and De-Regulation in the Maritime Industry." *Marine Policy* 26 (2002): 35–43.

Alesina, A., and R. J. Barro. "Dollarization." *American Economic Review* 91 (2001): 381–85.

Allen, Robert C. *Farm to Factory: A Reinterpretation of the Soviet Industrial Revolution.* Princeton: Princeton University Press, 2003.

Allen, William E. "Rethinking the History of Settler Agriculture in Nineteenth-Century Liberia." *International Journal of African Historical Studies* 37, no. 3 (2004): 435–62.

"Liberia and the Atlantic World in the Nineteenth Century: Convergence and Effects." *History in Africa* 37 (2010): 7–49.

Alvarez-Nogal, C., and Leandro Prados de la Escosura. "The Rise and Fall of Spain, 1270–1850." *Economic History Review* 66 (2013): 1–37.

American Colonization Society. *The Annual Reports of the American Society for Colonizing the Free People of Colour of the United States.* New York: Negro Universities Press, 1969.

Anderson, David M. "The Beginning of Time? Evidence for Catastrophic Drought in Baringo in the Early Nineteenth Century." *Journal of Eastern African Studies* 10, no. 10 (2016): 45–66.

Angelou, Maya. *All God's Children Need Travelling Shoes.* London: Virago Press, 2010.

Arndt, E. H. D. *Banking and Currency Development in South Africa 1652–1927.* Cape Town: Juta, 1928.

Atherton, John H. "Liberian Prehistory." *Liberian Studies Journal* 3, no. 1 (1971): 83–112.

Austen, Ralph. *African Economic History: Internal Development and External Dependency.* London: James Currey, 1997.

Austin, Gareth. *Labour, Land and Capital in Ghana: From Slavery to Free Labour in Asante, 1807–1956.* Rochester: University of Rochester Press, 2005.

"Resources, Techniques and Strategies South of the Sahara: Revising the Factor Endowments Perspective on African Economic Development, 1500–2000." *Economic History Review* 61 (2008): 587–624.

"Africa: Economic Change South of the Sahara since c. 1500." In *Global Economic History*, edited by Tirthankar Roy and Giorgio Riello, 241–70. London: Bloomsbury Academic, 2019.

Austin, Gareth, and Stephen Broadberry. "The Renaissance of African Economic History." *Economic History Review* 67 (2014): 893–906.

Azam, Jean-Paul. *Trade, Exchange Rate and Growth in Sub-Saharan Africa.* Cambridge: Cambridge University Press, 2007.

Azikiwe, Ben N. "In Defense of Liberia." *Journal of Negro History* 17, no. 1 (1932): 30–50.

Baines, Dudley. "European Emigration, 1815–1930: Looking at the Emigration Decision Again." *Economic History Review* XLVIII (1994): 525–44.

Bairoch, Paul. *Cities and Economic Development: From the Dawn of History to the Present.* Chicago: University of Chicago Press, 1988.

Bandyopadhyay, Sanghamitra, and Elliott Green. "Pre-Colonial Political Centralization and Contemporary Development in Uganda." *Economic Development and Cultural Change* 64 (2016): 471–508.

Banks III, Philip A. Z., and Seward Montgomery Cooper. *Liberia: World Corporate Domicile Treaties, Statutes, Cases and Legal Materials*, 3 Volumes. Monrovia: Liberia Law Experts, 1998.

Banton, Caree A. *More Auspicious Shores: Barbadian Migration to Liberia, Blackness and the Making of an African Republic.* Cambridge: Cambridge University Press, 2019.

Baptist, Edward E. *The Half Has Never Been Told: Slavery and the Making of American Capitalism.* New York: Basic Books, 2014.

Bardhan, Pranab. "State and Development: The Need for a Reappraisal of the Current Literature." *Journal of Economic Literature* 54, no. 3 (2016): 862–92.

Barnes, Kenneth C. *Journey of Hope: The Back-to-Africa Movement in Arkansas in the Late 1800s.* Durham: University of North Carolina Press, 2004.

Bassino, Jean-Pascal, Stephen Broadberry, Kyoji Fukau, Bishnupriya Gupta, and Masanori Takashima. "Japan and the Great Divergence, 730–1874." *Explorations in Economic History* 72 (2019): 1–22.

Bayart, Jean-Francois. *The State in Africa: The Politics of the Belly.* Harlow: Longman, 1993.

Bayly, C. A. *The Birth of the Modern World 1780–1914: Global Connections and Comparisons.* Malden: Blackwell, 2004.

"Indigenous and Colonial Origins of Comparative Economic Development." *World Bank Policy Working Paper* 4474 (2008).

Beleky, Louis P. "The Development of Liberia." *Journal of Modern African Studies* 11, no. 1 (1973): 43–60.

Berlin, Ira. *The Making of African America: The Four Great Migrations.* New York: Penguin Books, 2010.

Besley, Timothy, and Torsten Persson. *Pillars of Prosperity: The Political Economics of Development Clusters.* Princeton: Princeton University Press, 2011.

Beyan, Amos Jones. "Transatlantic Trade and the Coastal Area of Pre-Liberia." *The Historian* 57, no. 4 (1995): 757–68.

Blackmon, Douglas. *Slavery by Another Name: The Re-Enslavement of Black Americans from the Civil War to World War II*. London: Icon, 2012.

Blattman, C., Michael A. Clemens, and Jeffrey G. Williamson. "Who Protected and Why? Tariffs around the World 1870–1938." In *Conference on the Political Economy of Globalization*. Dublin, 2002.

Boczek, Boleslaw Adam. *Flags of Convenience: An International Legal Study*. Cambridge, MA: Harvard University Press, 1962.

Bogart, Dan, and Gary Richardson. "Making Property Productive: Reorganizing Rights to Real and Equitable Estates in Britain, 1660–1830." *European Review of Economic History* 13, no. 1 (2009): 3–30.

Bohannon, Paul. "The Impact of Money on an African Subsistence Economy." *Journal of Economic History* 19 (1959): 491–503.

Bohman, Anna. "The Presence of the Past: A Retrospective View of the Politics of Urban Water Management in Accra, Ghana." *Water History* 4 (2012): 137–54.

Bolt, Jutta, and Leigh Gardner. "How Africans Shaped British Colonial Institutions: Evidence from Local Taxation." *Journal of Economic History* 80, no. 4 (2020): 1189–223.

Boone, Catherine. *Merchant Capital and the Roots of State Power in Senegal, 1930–1985*. Cambridge: Cambridge University Press, 1992.

Booth, Anne. "Night Watchman, Extractive or Developmental States? Some Evidence from Late Colonial Southeast Asia." *Economic History Review* 60, no. 2 (2007): 241–66.

Bordo, Michael D., and Marc Flandreau. "Core, Periphery, Exchange Rate Regimes and Globalization." *NBER Working Paper* 8584 (2001).

Brands, H. W. *Traitor to His Class: The Privileged Life and Radical Presidency of Franklin Delano Roosevelt*. New York: Doubleday, 2008.

Brautigam, Deborah A., and Stephen Knack. "Foreign Aid, Institutions and Governance in Sub-Saharan Africa." *Economic Development and Cultural Change* 52, no. 2 (2004): 255–85.

Broadberry, Stephen. *Market Services and the Productivity Race 1850–2000*. Cambridge: Cambridge University Press, 2006.

Broadberry, Stephen, J. Custodis, and Bishnupriya Gupta. "India and the Great Divergence: An Anglo-Indian Comparison of GDP Per Capita, 1600–1871." *Explorations in Economic History* 56 (2015): 58–75.

Broadberry, Stephen, and Leigh Gardner. "Economic Growth in Sub-Saharan Africa, 1885–2008: Evidence from Eight Countries." *Explorations in Economic History* 83 (2021): 101424.

Broadberry, Stephen, and John Wallis. "Growing, Shrinking, and Long Run Economic Performance: Historical Perspectives on Economic Development." *NBER Working Paper* 23343 (2017).

Brooks, George E. *The Kru Mariner in the Nineteenth Century: An Historical Compendium*. Newark: Liberian Studies Association, 1972.

Climate and Periodisation – Western Africa to c. 1860 AD: A Provisional Historical Schema Based on Climatic Periods. Bloomington: Indiana University Press, 1985.

Brown, George S. *Brown's Abridged Journal Containing a Brief Account of the Life, Trials and Travels of Geo. S. Brown, Six Years a Missionary in Liberia, West Africa.* Troy: Prescott & Wilson, 1849.

Brown, George William. *The Economic History of Liberia.* Washington, DC:The Associated Publishers, 1941.

Brown, Robert T. "Immigrants to Liberia 1843 to 1865: An Alphabetical Listing." *Liberian Studies Research Working Paper* 7 (1980).

Buell, Raymond Leslie. *Liberia: A Century of Survival, 1847–1947.* Philadelphia: University of Pennsylvania Press, The University Museum, 1947.

Bueno de Mesquita, Bruce, and George W. Downs. "Intervention and Democracy." *International Organization* 60 (2006): 627–49.

Bulmer-Thomas, Victor. *The Economic History of the Caribbean since the Napoleonic Wars.* Cambridge: Cambridge University Press, 2012.

Burin, Eric. *Slavery and the Peculiar Solution: A History of the American Colonization Society.* Gainesville: University Press of Florida, 2005.

Burrowes, Carl Patrick. *Power and Press Freedom in Liberia, 1830-1970: The Impact of Globalization and Civil Society on Media-Government Relations.* Trenton: Africa World Press, 2004.

Between the Kola Forest & the Salty Sea: A History of the Liberian People before 1800. Bomi County: Know Your Self Press, 2016.

Cafruny, Alan W. *Ruling the Waves: The Political Economy of International Shipping.* Berkeley: University of California Press, 1987.

Calvo, G. A. *Money, Exchange Rates and Output.* Cambridge, MA: MIT Press, 1996.

Calvo, G. A., and F. S. Mishkin. "The Mirage of Exchange Rate Regimes for Emerging Market Countries." *Journal of Economic Perspectives* 17 (2003): 99–118.

Campbell, James. *Middle Passages: African American Journeys to Africa, 1787–2005.* New York: Penguin Press, 2006.

Cappelli, Gabriele, and Joerg Baten. "European Trade, Colonialism and Human Capital Accumulation in Senegal, Gambia and Western Mali, 1770–1900." *Journal of Economic History* 77, no. 3 (2017): 920–51.

Cardoso, Fernando Henrique, and Enzo Faletto. *Dependency and Development in Latin America.* Berkeley: University of California Press, 1979.

Carlisle, Rodney P. "The 'American Century' Implemented: Stettinius and the Liberian Flag of Convenience." *Business History Review* 52, no. 2 (1980): 175–91.

Sovereignty for Sale: The Origins and Evolution of the Panamanian and Liberian Flags of Convenience. Annapolis: Naval Institute Press, 1981.

Carson, Anne. *Autobiography of Red.* London: Jonathan Cape, 2010.

Chalk, Frank. "The Anatomy of an Investment: Firestone's 1927 Loan to Liberia." *Canadian Journal of African Studies* 1, no. 1 (1967): 12–32.

Chaves, Isaias, Stanley Engerman, and James A. Robinson. "Reinventing the Wheel: The Economic Benefits of Wheeled Transportation in Early Colonial British West Africa." In *Africa's Development in Historical Perspective*, edited by Emmanuel Akyeampong, Robert H. Bates,

Nathan Nunn and James A. Robinson, 321–65. Cambridge: Cambridge University Press, 2014.

Cheeseman, Nic, and Jonathan Fisher. *Authoritarian Africa: Repression, Resistance and the Power of Ideas.* Oxford: Oxford University Press, 2020.

Chinery, David. *The African Slave Trade and the Real and Practicable Means for Its Suppression.* London: M. Lownds, 1864.

Ciment, James. *Another America : The Story of Liberia and the Former Slaves Who Ruled It.* 1st ed. New York: Hill and Wang, 2013.

Clapham, Christopher. *Africa and the International System: The Politics of State Survival.* Cambridge: Cambridge University Press, 1996.

Clarence-Smith, W. G. "African and European Cocoa Producers on Fernando Poo, 1880s to 1910s." *Journal of African History* 35, no. 2 (1994): 179–99.

Clay, Karen, and Gavin Wright. "Order without Law? Property Rights During the California Gold Rush." *Explorations in Economic History* 42, no. 2 (2005): 155–83.

Clegg, Claude Andrew. *The Price of Liberty: African Americans and the Making of Liberia.* Chapel Hill: University of North Carolina Press, 2004.

Clemens, Michael A., and Jeffrey G. Williamson. "Why Did the Tariff-Growth Correlation Change after 1950?" *Journal of Economic Growth* 9, no. 1 (2004): 5–46.

Clower, Robert W., George Dalton, Mitchell Harwitz, and A. A. Walters. *Growth without Development: An Economic Survey of Liberia.* Evanston: Northwestern University Press, 1966.

Coatsworth, J. H., and J. G. Williamson. "Always Protectionist? Latin American Tariffs from Independence to the Great Depression." *Journal of Latin American Studies* 36, no. 2 (2004): 205–32.

Cogneau, Denis, and Yannick Dupraz. "Institutions Historiques Et Developpement Economique En Afrique: Une Revue Selective Et Critique De Traveau Recents." *Histoire et mesure* XXX, no. 1 (2015): 103–34.

Cohen, Benjamin. *The Geography of Money.* Ithaca: Cornell University Press, 1998.

Collins, S., and D. Rodrik. *Eastern Europe and the Soviet Union in the World Economy.* Washington, DC: Institute for International Economics, 1991.

Collins, William J., and Marianne H. Wanamaker. "The Great Migration in Black and White: New Evidence on the Selection and Sorting of Southern Migrants." *Journal of Economic History* 75 (2015): 947–92.

Cooley, T. F., and V. Quadrini. "The Cost of Losing Monetary Independence: The Case of Mexico." *Journal of Money, Credit and Banking* 33 (2001): 370–97.

Cooper, Frederick. *Africa since 1940: The Past of the Present.* Cambridge: Cambridge University Press, 2019.

Cordell, Dennis D., Karl Ittman, and Gregory H. Maddox. "Counting Subjects: Demography and Empire." In *The Demography of Empire: The Colonial Order and the Creation of Knowledge,* edited by Karl Ittmann, Dennis D. Cordell and Gregory H. Maddox, 1–21. Athens: Ohio University Press, 2010.

Cornelius, Janet Duitsman. *"When I Can Read My Title Clear": Literacy, Slavery and Religion in the Antebellum South*. Columbia: University of South Carolina Press, 1991.

Crafts, N. F. R. "English Economic Growth in the Eighteenth Century: A Re-Examination of Deane and Cole's Estimates." *Economic History Review* 29 (1976): 226–35.

"The Golden Age of Economic Growth in Western Europe, 1950–1973." *Economic History Review* 48, no. 3 (1995): 429–47.

Cummins, Neil. "The Hidden Wealth of English Dynasties, 1892–2016." *Economic History Review* 75, no. 3 (2022): 667–702.

Curtin, Philip D. *Death by Migration: Europe's Encounter with the Tropical World in the Nineteenth Century*. Cambridge: Cambridge University Press, 1989.

d'Azevedo, Warren L. "Common Principles of Variant Kinship Structures among the Gola of Western Liberia." *American Anthropologist* 64, no. 3 (1962): 504–20.

"Tribe and Chiefdom on the Windward Coast." *Liberian Studies Journal* XIV, no. 2 (1989): 90–116.

Dal Bo, E. "Regulatory Capture: A Review." *Oxford Review of Economic Policy* 22, no. 2 (2006): 203–25.

Dalton, George. "History, Politics and Economic Development in Liberia." *Journal of Economic History* 25, no. 4 (1965): 569–91.

Davies, Norman. *Vanished Kingdoms: The History of Half-Forgotten Europe*. New York: Penguin, 2011.

Davis, Lance E., and R. Huttenback. *Mammon and the Pursuit of Empire: The Political Economy of British Imperialism 1860–1912*. Cambridge: Cambridge University Press, 1986.

Davis, Ronald W. "Two Historical Manuscripts from the Kru Coast." *Liberian Studies Journal* 1, no. 1 (1968): 42–55.

"The Liberian Struggle for Authority on the Kru Coast." *International Journal of African Historical Studies* 8, no. 2 (1975): 222–65.

Ethnohistorical Studies on the Kru Coast. Liberian Studies Monograph Series. Newark: Pencader, 1976.

de Haas, Michiel, and Ewout Frankema, eds. *Migration in Africa: Shifting Patterns of Mobility from the 19th to the 21st Century*. London: Routledge, forthcoming.

de Roo, Bas. "The Trouble with Tariffs: Customs Policies and the Shaky Balance between Colonial and Private Interests in the Congo." *Low Countries Journal of Social and Economic History* 12, no. 3 (2014): 1–21.

de Wet, J. M. J. "Domestication of African Cereals." *African Economic History* 3 (1977): 15–32.

Deane, Phyllis. *Colonial Social Accounting*. Cambridge: Cambridge University Press, 1953.

Deane, Phyllis, and W. A. Cole. *British Economic Growth, 1688–1959: Trends and Structure*. Cambridge: Cambridge University Press, 1962.

Dharmapala, Dhammika, and James R. Hines Jr. "Which Countries Become Tax Havens?" *Journal of Public Economics* 93 (2009): 1058–68.

Dincecco, Mark. *Political Transformations and Public Finances Europe, 1650–1913*. Cambridge: Cambridge University Press, 2011.

Dorward, D. C. "British West Africa and Liberia." In *The Cambridge History of Africa, Volume 7: From 1905 to 1940*, edited by A. D. Roberts, 399–459. Cambridge: Cambridge University Press, 1986.

Downes, Alexander B., and Jonathan Monten. "Forced to Be Free? Why Foreign-Imposed Regime Change Rarely Leads to Democratization." *International Security* 37, no. 4 (2013): 91–131.

Du Bois, W. E. B. "Liberia, the League, and the United States." *Foreign Affairs* 11, no. 4 (1933): 682–95.

Dumett, Raymond E. "John Sarbah, the Elder, and African Mercantile Entrepreneurship in the Gold Coast in the Late Nineteenth Century." *Journal of African History* 14, no. 4 (1973): 653–79.

Dunn, D. Elwood. *Liberia and the United States During the Cold War*. Basingstoke: Palgrave Macmillan, 2009.

ed. *The Annual Messages of the Presidents of Liberia 1848-2010*. Berlin: Walter de Gruyter, 2011.

Dunning, John H. "The Eclectic (OLI) Paradigm of International Production: Past, Present and Future." *International Journal of the Economics of Business* 8, no. 2 (2001): 173–90.

Dyson, Tim. *Population and Development: The Demographic Transition*. New York: Zed Books, 2010.

Dyson, Tim, and Mike Murphy. "The Onset of Fertility Transition." *Population and Development Review* 11, no. 3 (1985): 399–440.

Eggertsson, Thrainn. *Economic Behavior and Institutions*. Cambridge: Cambridge University Press, 1990.

Eichengreen, Barry. "When to Dollarize." *Journal of Money, Credit and Banking* 34 (2001): 1–24.

Globalizing Capital: A History of the International Monetary System. Princeton: Princeton University Press, 2008.

Eichengreen, Barry, Marc Uzan, Nicholas Crafts, and Martin Hellwig. "The Marshall Plan: Economic Effects and Implications for Eastern Europe and the Former USSR." *Economic Policy* 7, no. 14 (1992): 130–75.

Ekbladh, David. *The Great American Mission: Modernization and the Construction of an American World Order*. Princeton: Princeton University Press, 2011.

Ellis, Stephen. *The Mask of Anarchy: The Destruction of Liberia and the Religious Dimension of an African Civil War*. 2nd ed. New York: New York University Press, 2007.

Ellwood, David W. "Was the Marshall Plan Necessary?" In *Alan S Milward and a Century of European Change*, edited by Fernando Guirao, 240–54. London: Routledge, 2012.

Eloranta, Jari, Peter Hedberg, Maria Cristina Moreira, and Eric Golson. "Introduction." In *Small and Medium Powers in Global History: Trade, Conflicts and Neutrality from the 19th to the 20th Centuries*, edited by Jari Eloranta, Eric Golson, Peter Hedberg and Maria Cristina Moreira, 1–26. London: Routledge, 2018.

Eltis, David. "Free and Coerced Transatlantic Migrations: Some Comparisons." *American Historical Review* 88, (1983): 251–80.

Englebert, Pierre. *Africa: Unity, Sovereignty and Sorrow*. London: Lynne Rienner, 2009.

Erasmus, L., J. Leichter, and J. Menkulasi. "Dedollarization in Liberia: Lessons from Cross-Country Experience." *International Monetary Fund Working Paper* WP/09/37 (2009).

Esposito, Chiarella. *America's Feeble Weapon: Funding the Marshall Plan in France and Italy*. Westport: Greenwood Press, 1994.

Esteves, Rui. "The Bondholder, the Sovereign, and the Banker: Sovereign Debt and Bondholders' Protections before 1914." *European Review of Economic History* 17, no. 4 (2013): 389–407.

Evans, Peter. *Embedded Autonomy: States and Industrial Transformation*. Princeton: Princeton University Press, 1995.

Everill, Bronwen. "'Destiny Seems to Point Me to That Country': Early Nineteenth-Century African American Migration, Emigration and Expansion." *Journal of Global History* 7, no. 1 (2012): 53–77.

Abolition and Empire in Sierra Leone and Liberia. Basingstoke: Palgrave Macmillan, 2013.

Federico, Giovanni and Antonio Tena-Junguito. "World Trade, 1800–1930: A New Synthesis." *Revista Historia Economica* 37 (2019): 9–41.

Feingold, Ellen, Johan Fourie, and Leigh Gardner. "A Tale of Gold and Paper: A New Material History of Money in South Africa." *Economic History of Developing Regions* 32 (2021): 264–81.

Feinstein, C. H. *National Income, Expenditure and Output of the United Kingdom, 1855–1965*. Cambridge: Cambridge University Press, 1972.

Fenske, James. "Ecology, Trade and States in Pre-Colonial Africa." *Journal of the European Economic Association* 12, no. 3 (2014): 612–40.

Ferrie, Joseph P., and Jason Long. "Intergenerational Occupational Mobility in Britain and the United States since 1850." *American Economic Review* 104 (2013): 1109–37.

Ferrie, Joseph P., and Werner Troesken. "Water and Chicago's Mortality Transition, 1850–1925." *Explorations in Economic History* 45, no. 1 (2008): 1–16.

Fett, Sharla M. *Recaptured Africans: Surviving Slave Ships, Detention, and Dislocation in the Final Years of the Slave Trade*. Chapel Hill: University of North Carolina Press, 2017.

Field, Kendra T. "'No Such Thing as Stand Still': Migration and Geopolitics in African American History." *Journal of American History* 102 (2015): 693–718.

Findlay, Ronald, and Kevin O'Rourke. *Power and Plenty: Trade, War and the World Economy in the Second Millennium*. Princeton: Princeton University Press, 2009.

Fischer, S. "Seigniorage and the Case for a National Money." *Journal of Political Economy* 90 (1982): 295–313.

Flandreau, Marc, ed. *Money Doctors: The Experience of International Financial Advising, 1850–2000*. London: Routledge, 2003.

Flandreau, M., and J. H. Flores. "Bonds and Brands: Foundations of Sovereign Debt Markets, 1820–1830." *Journal of Economic History* 69, no. 3 (2009): 646–84.

Fletcher, Marvin E. *America's First Black General: Benjamin O. Davis, Sr., 1880–1970.* Lawrence: University of Kansas Press, 1989.

Floud, Roderick, Robert W. Fogel, Bernard Harris, and Sok Chul Hong. *The Changing Body: Health, Nutrition, and Human Development in the Western World since 1700.* Cambridge: Cambridge University Press, 2011.

Flynn, Dennis O., and Arturo Giraldez. "Cycles of Silver: Global Economic Unity through the Mid-Eighteenth Century." *Journal of World History* 13 (2002): 391–427.

Foley, David M. "Liberia's Archival Collection." *African Studies Bulletin* 11, no. 2 (1968): 217–20.

Foner, Eric. *The Story of American Freedom.* New York: W. W. Norton, 1998.

Forbes Munro, J. "African Shipping: Reflections on the Maritime History of Africa South of the Sahara, 1800–1914." *International Journal of Maritime History* II, no. 2 (1990): 163–82.

Ford, Martin "Kola Production and Settlement Mobility among the Dan of Nimba, Liberia." *African Economic History* 20 (1992): 51–63.

Foreman-Peck, James. *A History of the World Economy: International Economic Relations since 1850.* Brighton: Wheatsheaf Books, 1986.

Fourie, Johan. "The Data Revolution in African Economic History." *Journal of Interdisciplinary History* 47, no. 2 (2016): 193–212.

Frankema, Ewout. "The Origins of Formal Education in Sub-Saharan Africa: Was British Rule More Benign?" *European Review of Economic History* 16 (2012): 335–55.

"The Biogeographic Roots of World Inequality: Animals, Disease and Human Settlement Patterns in Africa and the Americas before 1492." *World Development* 70 (2015): 274–85.

Frankema, Ewout, and Anne Booth, eds. *Fiscal Capacity and the Colonial State in Asia and Africa, C. 1850-1960.* Cambridge: Cambridge University Press, 2019.

Frankema, Ewout, and Morten Jerven. "Writing History Backwards or Sideways: Towards a Consensus on African Population, 1850–2010." *Economic History Review* 67, no. 4 (2014): 907–31.

Frankema, Ewout, and Aline Mase. "An Island Drifting Apart: Why Haiti Is Mired in Poverty While the Dominican Republic Forges Ahead." *Journal of International Development* 26, no. 1 (2014): 128–48.

Frankema, Ewout, and Marlous van Waijenburg. "Structural Impediments to African Growth? New Evidence from Real Wages in British Africa, 1880–1965." *Journal of Economic History* 72, no. 4 (2012): 895–26.

"Metropolitan Blueprints of Colonial Taxation? Lessons from Fiscal Capacity Building in British and French Africa, c. 1880–1940." *Journal of African History* 55 (2014): 371–400.

Frankema, Ewout, Jeffrey Williamson, and Pieter Woltjer. "An Economic Rationale for the West African Scramble? The Commercial Transition and the Commodity Price Boom of 1835–1885." *Journal of Economic History* 78, no. 1 (2018): 231–367.

French, Michael J. "The Emergence of US Multinational Enterprise: The Goodyear Tire and Rubber Company, 1910-1939." *Economic History Review* XL (1987): 64–79.

Fry, Richard. *Bankers in West Africa: The Story of the Bank of British West Africa Limited.* London: Hutchinson, 1976.

Fuller, Thomas. *Journal of a Voyage to Liberia.* Baltimore: John D. Toy, 1851.

Fulton, Richard M. "The Kpelle Traditional Political System." *Liberian Studies Journal* 1, no. 1 (1968): 1–18.

"The Political Structures and Functions of Poro in Kpelle Society." *American Anthropologist* 74, no. 5 (1972): 1218–33.

Gallagher, John, and Ronald Robinson. "The Imperialism of Free Trade." *Economic History Review* 6, no. 1 (1953): 1–15.

Gardner, Leigh. *Taxing Colonial Africa: The Political Economy of British Imperialism.* Oxford: Oxford University Press, 2012.

"The Rise and Fall of Sterling in Liberia, 1847–1943." *Economic History Review* 67, no. 4 (2014): 1089–112.

"The Curious Incident of the Franc in the Gambia: Exchange Rate Instability and Imperial Monetary Systems in the 1920s." *Financial History Review* 22, no. 3 (2015): 291–314.

"Colonialism or Supersanctions: Sovereignty and Debt in West Africa, 1871–1914." *European Review of Economic History* 21 (2017): 236–57.

"New Colonies, Old Tools: Building Fiscal Systems in East and Central Africa." In *Fiscal Capacity and the Colonial State in Asia and Africa, C. 1850–1960,* edited by Ewout Frankema and Anne Booth, 193–229. Cambridge: Cambridge University Press, 2020.

Gardner, Leigh, and Tirthankar Roy. *Economic History of Colonialism.* Bristol: Bristol University Press, 2020.

Gennaioli, Nicola, and Ilia Rainer. "The Modern Impact of Pre-Colonial Centralization." *Journal of Economic Growth* 12 (2007): 185–234.

Gersmehl, Philip J. "Soils Map." In *The History of Cartography, Volume 6: Cartography in the Twentieth Century,* edited by Mark Monmonier, 1443–50. Chicago: University of Chicago Press, 2015.

Getachew, Adom. *Worldmaking after Empire: The Rise and Fall of Self-Determination.* Princeton: Princeton University Press, 2019.

Glaeser, Edward L., and Andrei Schliefer. "The Rise of the Regulatory State." *Journal of Economic Literature* XLI (2003): 401–25.

Goldin, Claudia. "America's Graduation from High School: The Evolution and Spread of Secondary School in the Twentieth Century." *Journal of Economic History* 58 (1998): 345–74.

Goldstein, Markus, and Christopher Udry. "The Profits of Power: Land Rights and Agricultural Investment in Ghana." *Journal of Political Economy* 116, no. 6 (2008): 981–1022.

Goodhart, Charles A. E. "The Political Economy of Monetary Union." In *Understanding Interdependence: The Macroeconomics of the Open Economy,* edited by P. B. Kenen, 448–506. Princeton: Princeton University Press, 1995.

Gootenberg, Paul. *Imagining Development: Economic Ideas in Peru's "Fictitious Prosperity" of Guano, 1840–1880*. Berkeley: University of California Press, 1993.

Gottlieb, Peter. *Making Their Own Way: Southern Blacks' Migration to Pittsburgh, 1916–30*. Urbana and Chicago: University of Illinois Press, 1987.

Guannu, Joseph Saye, ed. *The Inaugural Addresses of the Presidents of Liberia: From Joseph Jenkins Roberts to William Richard Tolbert, Jr., 1848 to 1976*. Hicksville: Exposition Press, 1980.

Gurley, Ralph Randolph. *Life of Jehudi Ashmun, Late Colonial Agent in Liberia with an Appendix Containing Extracts from His Journal and Other Writings, with a Brief Sketch of the Life of the Rev. Lott Cary*. Freeport: Books for Libraries Press, 1971.

Guyer, Jane. "Introduction: The Currency Interface and Its Dynamics." In *Money Matters: Instability, Values and Social Payments in the Modern History of West African Communities*, edited by Jane Guyer, 1–34. London: James Currey, 1995.

Haber, Stephen H., Noel Maurer, and Armando Razo. *The Politics of Property Rights: Political Instability, Credible Commitments, and Economic Growth in Mexico, 1876–1929*. Cambridge: Cambridge University Press, 2003.

Hager, L. Michael. "Taxation of Foreign Investment in Liberia." *Liberian Law Journal* 1, no. 2 (1965): 151–78.

Hahn, Steven. *A Nation Under Our Feet: Black Political Struggles in the Rural South from Slavery to the Great Migration*. London: Belknap Press, 2003.

Haines, Michael R., Lee A. Craig, and Thomas Weiss. "The Short and the Dead: Nutrition, Mortality and the Antebellum Puzzle in the United States." *Journal of Economic History* 63 (2003): 382–413.

Handwerker, W. Penn. "Market Places, Travelling Traders, and Shops: Commercial Structural Variation in the Liberian Interior Prior to 1940." *African Economic History* 9 (1980): 3–26.

Hannah, Leslie. "Marshall's 'Trees' and the Global 'Forest': Were 'Giant Redwoods' Different?" In *Learning by Doing in Markets: Firms and Countries*, edited by Naomi R. Lamoreaux, Daniel M. G. Raff and Peter Temin, 253–94. Chicago: University of Chicago Press, 1999.

Hanson, Earl Parker. "An Economic Survey of the Western Province of Liberia." *Geographical Review* 37, no. 1 (1947): 53–69.

Hargreaves, John. "The Establishment of the Sierra Leone Protectorate and the Insurrection of 1898." *Cambridge Historical Journal* 12 (1956): 56–80.

Harlaftis, Gelina. "Greek Shipowners and State Intervention in the 1940s: A Formal Justification for the Resort to Flags-of-Convenience?" *International Journal of Maritime History* 1, no. 2 (1989): 37–63.

Hazelwood, A. "The Economics of Colonial Monetary Arrangements." *Social and Economic Studies* 3 (1954): 291–315.

Helleiner, E. "The Monetary Dimensions of Colonialism: Why Did Imperial Powers Create Currency Blocs." *Geopolitics* 7 (2002): 5–30.

The Making of National Money: Territorial Currencies in Historical Perspective. Ithaca: Cornell University Press, 2003.

Henderson, Morgan, and Warren Whatley. "Pacification and Gender in Colonial Africa: Evidence from the Ethnographic Atlas." *MPRA Working Paper* 61203 (2014).

Herbert, Christian Gbogboda. *The Liberian Shipping Registry: Strategies to Improve Flag State Implementation and Increase Market Competitiveness.* Malmö: World Maritime University, 1999.

Herbert, Eugenia W. *Red Gold of Africa: Copper in Precolonial History and Culture.* Madison: University of Wisconsin Press, 1984.

Herbst, Jeffrey. "The Structural Adjustment of Politics in Africa." *World Development* 18, no. 7 (1990): 949–58.

States and Power in Africa: Comparative Lessons in Authority and Control. Princeton: Princeton University Press, 2000.

Herranz-Loncan, Alfonso, and Johan Fourie. "'For the Public Benefit?' Railways in the British Cape Colony." *European Review of Economic History* 22, no. 1 (2018): 73–100.

Hill, John S. "American Efforts to Aid French Reconstruction between Lend-Lease and the Marshall Plan." *Journal of Modern History* 64, no. 3 (1992): 500–24.

Hoffman, Philip T. "What Do States Do? Politics and Economic History." *Journal of Economic History* 75 (2015): 303–32.

Hogan, Michael J. *The Marshall Plan: America, Britain and the Reconstruction of Western Europe, 1947–52.* Cambridge: Cambridge University Press, 1987.

Hogendorn, J. S., and H. A. Gemery. "Continuity in West African Monetary History? An Outline of Monetary Development." *African Economic History* 17 (1988): 127–46.

Hogendorn, J. S., and Marion Johnson. *The Shell Money of the Slave Trade.* Cambridge: Cambridge University Press, 2003.

Holsoe, Svend E. "Economic Activities in the Liberian Area: The Pre-European Period to 1900." In *Essays on the Economic Anthropology of Liberia and Sierra Leone,* edited by Vernon R. Dorjahn and Barry L. Isaac, 63–78. Philadelphia: Institute for Liberian Studies, 1979.

Hopkins, A. G. "The Currency Revolution in South-West Nigeria in the Late Nineteenth Century." *Journal of the Historical Society of Nigeria* 3, no. 3 (1966): 471–83.

An Economic History of West Africa. London: Longman, 1973.

"Innovation in a Colonial Context: African Origins of the Nigerian Cocoa Farming Industry, 1880-1920." In *The Imperial Impact: Studies in the Economic History of Africa and India,* edited by Clive Dewey and A. G. Hopkins, 83–96. London: Athlone Press, 1978.

"The New Economic History of Africa." *Journal of African History* 50, no. 2 (2009): 155–77.

Huberich, Charles Henry. *The Political and Legislative History of Liberia.* New York: Central Book, 1947.

Huberman, Michael, and Wayne Lewchuk. "European Economic Integration and the Labour Compact, 1850–1913." *European Review of Economic History* 7 (2003): 3–41.

Huillery, Elise. "History Matters: The Long-Term Impact of Colonial Public Investments in French West Africa." *American Economic Journal: Applied Economics* 1, no. 2 (2009): 176–215.

Hull, Richard W. *African Cities and Towns before the European Conquest*. New York: W. W. Norton, 1976.

Iammarino, Simona, and Philip McCann. *Multinationals and Economic Geography: Location, Technology and Innovation*. Cheltenham: Edward Elgar, 2013.

Inikori, Joseph E. "Africa and the Globalization Process: Western Africa, 1450–1850." *Journal of Global History* 2 (2007): 63–86.

International Monetary Fund. *The Economy of Liberia*. Washington, DC: IMF, 1963.

Surveys of African Economies, Volume 6: The Gambia, Ghana, Liberia, Nigeria and Sierra Leone. Washington, DC: IMF, 1975.

Liberia: Selected Issues and Statistical Appendix. Washington, DC: IMF, 2000.

Irwin, Douglas A. *Against the Tide: An Intellectual History of Free Trade*. Princeton: Princeton University Press, 1996.

"Higher Tariffs, Lower Revenues? Analyzing the Fiscal Aspects of 'The Great Tariff Debate of 1888'." *Journal of Economic History* 58, no. 1 (1998): 59–72.

Jedwab, Remi, Edward Kerby, and Alexander Moradi. "History, Path Dependence and Development: Evidence from Colonial Railroads, Settlers and Cities in Kenya." *Economic Journal* 127, no. 603 (2017): 1467–94.

Jedwab, Remi, Felix Meier zu Selhausen, and Alexander Moradi. "The Economics of Missionary Expansion: Evidence from Africa and Implications for Development." *Journal of Economic Growth* 27, no. 2 (2022): 149–92.

Jedwab, Remi, and Alexander Moradi. "The Permanent Effects of Transportation Revolution in Poor Countries: Evidence from Africa." *Review of Economics and Statistics* 98, no. 2 (2016): 268–84.

Jefferson, Thomas. *Notes on the State of Virginia*. Philadelphia: Prichard and Hall, 1788.

Jerven, Morten. "African Growth Recurring: An Economic History Perspective on African Growth Episodes, 1690–2010." *Economic History of Developing Regions* 25, no. 2 (2010): 127–54.

Poor Numbers: How We Are Misled by African Development Statistics and What to Do About It. Ithaca: Cornell University Press, 2013.

The Wealth and Poverty of African States: Economic Growth, Living Standards and Taxation since the Late Nineteenth Century. Cambridge: Cambridge University Press, 2022.

Johnson, Charles S. *Bitter Canaan: The Story of the Negro Republic*. London: Transaction, 1992.

Johnson, Marion. "Cloth as Money: The Cloth Strip Currencies of Africa." *Textile History* 11, no. 1 (1980): 193–202.

Johnson, Noel D., and Mark Koyama. "States and Economic Growth: Capacity and Constraints." *Explorations in Economic History* 64 (2017): 1–20.

Johnston, H. H. *Liberia*. London: Hutchinson, 1906.

Jones, Geoffrey. *British Multinational Banking*. Oxford: Oxford University Press, 1995.

Judt, Tony. *Postwar: A History of Europe since 1945*. London: Vintage, 2010.

Juif, Dacil. "Skill Selectivity in Transatlantic Migration: The Case of Canary Islanders in Cuba." *Revista de Historia Economica* 33 (2015): 189–222.

Karaman, K. Kivanc, and Sevket Pamuk. "Different Paths to the Modern State in Europe: The Interaction between Warfare, Economic Structure, and Political Regime." *American Political Science Review* 107, no. 3 (2013): 603–26.

Kesner, Richard M. *Economic Control and Colonial Development: Crown Colony Financial Management in the Age of Joseph Chamberlain*. Oxford: Clio Press, 1981.

King, Gary, Robert O. Keohane, and Sidney Verba. *Designing Social Inquiry: Scientific Inference in Qualitative Research*. Princeton: Princeton University Press, 1994.

Kiruthu, Felix M. *Voices of Freedom: Great African Independence Speeches*. Nairobi: Cana Publishers, 2001.

Klein, Martin A., and Richard Roberts. "The Resurgence of Pawning in French West Africa During the Depression of the 1930s." *African Economic History* 16 (1987): 23–37.

Knight, Alan. *The Mexican Revolution: A Very Short Introduction*. Oxford: Oxford University Press, 2016.

Konneh, Augustine. "The Hut Tax in Liberia: The High Costs of Integration." *Journal of the GAH* XVI (1996): 41–60.

Religion, Commerce and the Integration of the Mandingo in Liberia. New York: University Press of America, 1996.

Korshak, Yvonne. "The Liberty Cap as a Revolutionary Symbol in America and France." *American Art* 1, no. 2 (1987): 52–69.

Kory, William. "Liberia's Population Figures." *Liberian Studies Journal* 3, no. 1 (1970): 53–62.

Krasner, Stephen D. "Building Democracy after Conflict: The Case for Shared Sovereignty." *Journal of Democracy* 16, no. 1 (2005): 69–83.

Krasner, Stephen D., and Jeremy M. Weinstein. "Improving Governance from the Outside In." *Annual Review of Political Science* 17 (2014): 123–45.

Kuroda, Akinobu. "The Maria Theresa Dollar in the Early Twentieth-Century Red Sea Regions: A Complementary Interface between Multiple Markets." *Financial History Review* 14 (2007): 89–110.

La Croix, Sumner. *Hawaii: Eight Hundred Years of Political and Economic Change*. Chicago: Chicago University Press, 2019.

Langley, Lester D. *The Banana Wars: United States Intervention in the Caribbean, 1898-1934*. Lanham: SR Books, 2002.

Latham, Michael. *The Right Kind of Revolution: Modernization, Development and Us Foreign Policy from the Cold War to the Present*. Ithaca: Cornell University Press, 2011.

Law, Robin. "Posthumous Questions for Karl Polanyi: Price Inflation in Pre-Colonial Dahomey." *Journal of African History* 33, no. 3 (1992): 387–420.

ed. *From Slave Trade to 'Legitimate' Commerce: The Commercial Transition in Nineteenth-Century West Africa.* Cambridge: Cambridge University Press, 1995.

Leenars, Johan G. B., Lieven Claessens, Gerard B. M. Heuvelink et al. "Mapping Rootable Depth and Root Zone Plant-Available Water Holding Capacity of the Soil of Sub-Saharan Africa." *Geoderma* 324 (2018): 18–36.

Liebenow, J. Gus. *Liberia: the Evolution of Privilege.* Ithaca: Cornell University Press, 1969.

Lindsay, Lisa. *Atlantic Bonds: A Nineteenth-Century Odyssey from America to Africa.* Chapel Hill: University of North Carolina Press, 2017.

Livi-Bacci, Massimo. *A Concise History of World Population.* Chichester: John Wiley, 2017.

Livingstone, Frank B. "Anthropological Implications of Sickle Cell Gene Distribution in West Africa." *American Anthropologist* 60 (1958): 533–62.

Logan, Trevon. "Health, Human Capital and African-American Migration before 1910." *Explorations in Economic History* 46 (2009): 169–85.

Long, Jason, and Henry Siu. "Refugees from Dust and Shrinking Land: Tracking the Dust Bowl Migrants." *Journal of Economic History* 78 (2018): 1018–24.

Lopez-Alonso, Moramay. "Growth with Inequality: Living Standards in Mexico 1850–1950." *Journal of Latin American Studies* 39 (2007): 81–105.

Lovejoy, Paul. "Plantations in the Economy of the Sokoto Caliphate." *Journal of African History* 19, no. 3 (1978): 341–68.

Transformations in Slavery: A History of Slavery in Africa. Cambridge: Cambridge University Press, 2012.

"Pawnship, Dept, and 'Freedom' in Atlantic Africa During the Era of the Slave Trade: A Reassessment." *Journal of African History* 55 (2014): 55–78.

Lyon, J. M. "The Education of Sir Harry Johnston in Liberia, 1900–1910." *The Historian* 51 (1989): 627–43.

Maddison, A. "Statistics on World Population, GDP and Per Capita GDP, 1-2008 AD." Groningen Growth and Development Center Working Paper (2010).

Malanima, P. "The Long Decline of a Leading Economy: Gdp in Central and Northern Italy, 1300–1913." *European Review of Economic History* 15 (2011): 169–219.

Maloney, Thomas N. "African American Migration to the North: New Evidence for the 1910s." *Economic Inquiry* 40, no. 1 (2002): 1–11.

Malvin, John. *North into Freedom: The Autobiography of John Malvin, Free Negro, 1795–1880.* Cleveland, OH: Western Reserve Historical Society, 1996.

Mamdani, Mahmood. *Citizen and Subject: Contemporary Africa and Legacy of Late Colonialism.* Princeton: Princeton University Press, 1996.

Manning, Patrick. "African Population: Projections, 1850–1960." In *The Demographics of Empire: The Colonial Order and the Creation of Knowledge,* edited by K Ittman, D. D. Cordell and G. H. Maddox, 245–75. Athens: Ohio University Press, 2010.

Mansell, John N. K. *Flag State Responsibility: Historical Development and Contemporary Issues*. Berlin: Springer, 2009.

Marcus, Harold G. *A History of Ethiopia*. Berkeley: University of California Press, 2002.

Margo, Robert A. *Race and Schooling in the South, 1880-1950: An Economic History*. Chicago: University of Chicago Press, 1990.

Marinelli, Lawrence A. "Liberia's Open-Door Policy." *Journal of Modern African Studies* 2, no. 1 (1964): 91–98.

Mark-Thiessen, Cassandra. "Of Vagrants and Volunteers During Liberia's Operation Production, 1963–1969." *African Economic History* 46, no. 2 (2018): 147–72.

Martel, Leon. *Lend-Lease, Loans and the Coming of the Cold War*. New York: Routledge 1979.

Matanock, Alia M. "Governance Delegation Agreements: Shared Sovereignty as a Substitute for Limited Statehood." *Governance* 27, no. 4 (2014): 589–612.

Maurer, Noel. *The Empire Trap: The Rise and Fall of U.S. Intervention to Protect American Property Overseas, 1893–2013*. Princeton: Princeton University Press, 2013.

Maurer, Noel, and Leticia Arroyo Abad. "Can Europe Run Greece? Lessons from Us Fiscal Receiverships in Latin America, 1904–31." SSRN Working Paper (2017).

Mauro, Paolo, Nathan Sussman, and Yishay Yafeh. *Emerging Markets and Financial Globalization: Sovereign Bond Spreads in 1870-1913 and Today*. Oxford: Oxford University Press, 2006. DOI: 10.1093/0199272697.001.0001.

Maynard, Geoffrey. "The Economic Irrelevance of Monetary Independence: The Case of Liberia." *The Journal of Development Studies* 6, no. 2 (2007): 111–32.

McDaniel, Antonio. *Swing Low, Sweet Chariot: The Mortality Cost of Colonizing Liberia in the Nineteenth Century*. Chicago: University of Chicago Press, 1995.

McKinnon, R. I. "Optimum Currency Areas." *American Economic Review* 53 (1963): 717–25.

Meyer, Michael C., and William L, Sherman. *The Course of Mexican History*. Oxford: Oxford University Press, 1991.

Michalopoulos, Stelios, and Elias Papaioannou. "Pre-Colonial Ethnic Institutions and Contemporary African Development." *Econometrica* 81 (2013): 113–52.

"Historical Legacies and African Development." *Journal of Economic Literature* 58, no. 1 (2020).

Miers, Suzanne. "Slavery and the Slave Trade as International Issues, 1890–1939." *Slavery and Abolition* 19, no. 2 (1998): 16–37.

Miller, Floyd J. *The Search for a Black Nationality: Black Emigration and Colonization 1787–1863*. Urbana: University of Illinois Press, 1975.

Miller, Robert E., and Peter R. Carter. "The Modern Dual Economy – a Cost-Benefit Analysis of Liberia." *Journal of Modern African Studies* 10, no. 1 (1972): 113–21.

Mills, Brandon. *The World Colonization Made: The Racial Geography of Early American Empire*. Philadelphia: University of Pennsylvania Press, 2020.

Milward, Alan S. *The Reconstruction of Western Europe, 1945–51*. London: Routledge, 1992.

Mitchener, Kris James, and Marc D. Weidenmier. "Supersanctions and Sovereign Debt Repayment." *Journal of International Money and Finance* 29, no. 1 (2010): 19–36.

Mitman, Gregg. *Empire of Rubber: Firestone's Scramble for Land and Power in Liberia*. New York: The New Press, 2021.

Mitman, Gregg, and Emmanuel King Urey. "'Sitting on Old Mats to Plait New' the Gendered Struggle over Land and Livelihood in Liberia." In *The Social Life of Land*, edited by Michael Goldman, Nancy Peluso and Wendy Wolford. Ithaca: Cornell University Press, Forthcoming.

Mokyr, Joel. *Why Ireland Starved: A Quantitative and Analytical History of the Irish Economy 1880–1850*. London and Boston: Allen and Unwin, 1983.

Moore, Mick, Wilson Richard, and Odd-Helge Fjeldstad. *Taxing Africa: Coercion, Reform and Development*. London: Zed Books, 2018.

Moore, Wayetu. *The Dragons, the Giant, the Women: A Memoir*. Minneapolis: Grey Wolf Press, 2020.

Moradi, Alexander, Gareth Austin, and Joerg Baten. "Heights and Development in a Cash-Crop Colony: Living Standards in Ghana, 1870–1980." Working Paper (2013), https://alexandermoradi.org/research/Heights_Ghana_1870_1980.pdf.

Morgan, Mary S. "Exemplification and the Use-Values of Cases and Case Studies." *Studies in History and Philosophy of Science* 78 (2019): 5–13.

Moses, Wilson Jeremiah, ed. *Liberian Dreams: Back to Africa Narratives from the 1850s*. University Park, PA: Pennsylvania State University Press, 1998.

Muller, Hans-Peter, Claudia Kock Marti, Eva Seiler Schiedt, and Brigitte Arpagus. *Atlas Vorkolonialar Gesellschaften*. Berlin: Deitrich Reimer Verlag, 2010.

Murdza, Peter J. "Immigrants to Liberia 1865 to 1904: An Alphabetical Listing". *Liberian Studies Research Working Paper* 4 (1975).

Murphy, Dale D. *The Structure of Regulatory Competition*. Oxford: Oxford University Press, 2004.

Murray, Robert. *Atlantic Passages: Race, Mobility and Liberian Colonization*. Gainesville: University Press of Florida, 2021.

Musaccio, Aldo, and Ian Read. "Bankers, Industrialists and Their Cliques: Elite Networks in Mexico and Brazil During Early Industrialization." *Enterprise and Society* 8, no. 4 (2007): 842–80.

Nicholas, Stephen, and Peter R. Shergold. "Human Capital and Pre-Famine Irish Emigration to England." *Explorations in Economic History* 24 (1987): 158–77.

North, Douglass C., John Joseph Wallis, Steven B. Webb, and Barry R. Weingast, eds. *In the Shadow of Violence: Politics, Economics and the Problems of Development*. Cambridge: Cambridge University Press, 2013.

North, Douglass C., John Wallis, and Barry R. Weingast. *Violence and Social Orders: A Conceptual Framework for Interpreting Recorded Human History*. Cambridge: Cambridge University Press, 2009.

North, Douglass C., and Barry R. Weingast. "Constitutions and Commitment: The Evolution of Institutions Governing Public Choice in Seventeenth-Century England." *Journal of Economic History* 49, no. 4 (1989): 803–32.

Nugent, Paul. *Africa since Independence: A Comparative History*. Basingstoke: Palgrave Macmillan, 2004.

Nunn, Nathan, and Leonard Wantchekon. "The Slave Trade and the Origins of Mistrust in Africa." *American Economic Review* 101, no. 7 (2011): 3221–52.

O'Grada, Cormac, and Kevin H. O'Rourke. "Migration as Disaster Relief: Lessons from the Great Irish Famine." *European Review of Economic History* 1 (1997): 3–25.

O'Rourke, Kevin H., and Jeffrey G. Williamson. *Globalization and History: The Evolution of a Nineteenth-Century Atlantic Economy*. Cambridge, MA and London: MIT Press, 2000.

"When Did Globalization Begin?" *European Review of Economic History* 6 (2002): 23–50.

Ofonagoro, Walter. "From Traditional to British Currency in Southern Nigeria: Analysis of a Currency Revolution, 1880–1946." *Journal of Economic History* 39, no. 3 (1979): 623–54.

Ogle, Vanessa. "'Funk Money': The End of Empires, the Expansion of Tax Havens, and Decolonization and Economic and Financial Event." *Past and Present Online* (2020): 1–38.

Olmstead, Alan L., and Paul W, Rhode. "Cotton, Slavery and the New History of Capitalism." *Explorations in Economic History* 67 (2018): 1–17.

Olson, Mancur. *The Rise and Decline of Nations: Economic Growth, Stagflation and Social Rigidities*. New Haven and London: Yale University Press, 1982.

Power and Prosperity: Outgrowing Communist and Capitalist Dictatorships. New York: Basic Books, 2000.

Orr, Kenneth G. "An Introduction to the Archaeology of Liberia." *Liberian Studies Journal* 4, no. 1 (1972): 55–80.

Osborne, Myles. "A Note on the Liberian Archives." *History in Africa* 36 (2009): 461–63.

Owen, John M. *The Clash of Ideas in World Politics: Transnational Networks, States, and Regime Change, 1510-2010*. Princeton: Princeton University Press, 2010.

Oyebade, Adebayo. "Feeding America's War Machine: The United States and Economic Expansion in West Africa During World War Ii." *African Economic History* 26 (1998): 119–40.

Paczynska, Agnieszka. "Liberia Rising? Foreign Direct Investment, Persistent Inequalities and Political Tensions." *Peacebuilding* 4, no. 3 (2016): 297–316.

Paik, Christopher, and Vechbanyongratana. "Path to Centralization and Development: Evidence from Siam." *World Politics* 71, no. 2 (2019).

Pailey, Robtel. *Development, (Dual) Citizenship and Its Discontents in Africa: The Political Economy of Belonging to Liberia*. Cambridge: Cambridge University Press, 2021.

Painter, Nell Irvin. *Exodusters: Black Migration to Kansas after Reconstruction*. New York: Knopf, 1977.

Palan, Ronen. "Tax Havens and the Commercialization of State Sovereignty." *International Organization* 56, no. 1 (2002): 151–76.

The Offshore World: Sovereign Markets, Virtual Places, and Nomad Millionaires. Ithaca and London: Cornell University Press, 2003.

Palan, Ronen, Richard Murphy, and Christian Chavagneux. *Tax Havens: How Globalization Really Works*. Ithaca: Cornell University Press, 2010.

Pamuk, Sevket. *The Ottoman Empire and European Capitalism, 1820-1913*. Cambridge: Cambridge University Press, 1987.

Parsons, Timothy. "The Military Experiences of Ordinary Africans in World War Ii." In *Africa and World War Ii*, edited by Judith A. Byfield, Carolyn A. Brown, Timothy Parsons and Ahmad Alawad Sikainga, 3–23. Cambridge: Cambridge University Press, 2015.

Patterson, K. D. "Health in Urban Ghana: The Case of Accra 1900–1914." *Social Science Medicine* 13B (1979): 251–68.

Payne, J. S. *A Prize Essay on Political Economy as Adapted to the Republic of Liberia*. Monrovia: G. Killian, 1860.

Peceny, Mark. *Democracy at the Point of Bayonets*. University Park, PA: Pennsylvania State University Press, 1999.

Phelps, C. W. *The Foreign Expansion of American Banks: American Branch Banking Abroad*. New York: Ronald Press, 1927.

Piniella, Francisco, Juan Ignacio Alcaide, and Emilio Rodriguez-Diaz. "The Panama Ship Registry: 1917–2017." *Marine Policy* 77, no. 13–22 (2017).

Porter, Philip Wayland. "Population Distribution and Land Use in Liberia." *London School of Economics*, 1956.

Poyker, Michael. "Economic Consequences of the U.S. Convict Labor System." INET Working Paper No. 91 (2019).

Prados de la Escosura, Leandro. "Output Per Head in Pre-Independence Africa: Quantitative Conjectures." *Economic History of Developing Regions* 27 (2012): 1–36.

Puchalski, Piotr. "The Polish Mission to Liberia, 1934–1938: Constructing Poland's Colonial Identity." *Historical Journal* 60, no. 4 (2017): 1071–96.

Ram, K. V. "British Government, Finance Capitalists, and the French Jibuti-Addis Ababa Railway 1898–1913." *Journal of Imperial and Commonwealth History* 9 (1981): 146–68.

Rathbone, Richard. "Casting "the Kingdome into Another Mold", Ghana's Troubled Transition to Independence." *The Round Table* 97, no. 398 (2008): 705–18.

Reid, Richard J. *Frontiers of Violence in North-East Africa: Genealogies of Conflict since c. 1800*. Oxford: Oxford University Press, 2011.

Reynolds, Susan. "There Were States in Medieval Europe: A Response to Rees Davies." *Journal of Historical Sociology* 15, no. 4 (2003): 550–55.

Ricart-Huguet, Joan. "The Origins of Colonial Investments in Former British and French Africa." *British Journal of Political Science* (2021).

Riguzzi, Paulo. "From Globalisation to Revolution? The Porfirian Political Economy: An Essay on Issues and Interpretations." *Journal of Latin American Studies* 41 (2009): 347–68.

Roberts, Richard. "Coerced Labor in Twentieth-Century Africa." In *Cambridge World History of Slavery, Volume 4: AD1804–AD 2016*, edited by David Eltis, Stanley Engerman, Seymore Drescher and David Richardson, 583–609. Cambridge: Cambridge University Press, 2017.

Rodney, Walter. *How Europe Underdeveloped Africa*. Washington, DC: Howard University Press, 1981.

Rodriguez, Junius P., ed. *Encyclopedia of Emancipation and Abolition in the Transatlantic World*. London: Routledge, 2007.

Rodrik, Dani. "Why Do More Open Economies Have Bigger Governments?" *Journal of Political Economy* 106 (1998): 997–1033.

Ronnback, Klas, and Dimitrios Theodoris. "African Agricultural Productivity and the Transatlantic Slave Trade: Evidence from Senegambia in the Nineteenth Century." *Economic History Review* 72, no. 1 (2019): 209–32.

Rosenberg, Emily S. *Financial Missionaries to the World: The Politics and Culture of Dollar Diplomacy 1900-1930*. Durham: Duke University Press, 2007.

Rostow, Walt. *The Stages of Economic Growth: A Non-Communist Manifesto*. Cambridge: Cambridge University Press, 1960.

Sacerdote, Bruce. "Slavery and the Intergenerational Transmission of Human Capital." *Review of Economics and Statistics* 87 (2005): 217–34.

Saha, Santosh C. "Agriculture in Liberia during the Nineteenth Century: Americo-Liberians' Contribution." *Canadian Journal of African Studies* 22 (1988): 224–39.

Salau, M. B. *Plantation Slavery in the Sokoto Caliphate: A Historical and Comparative Study*. Rochester: University of Rochester Press, 2017.

Sanchez Alonso, Blanca. "Those Who Left and Those Who Stayed Behind: Explaining Emigration from the Regions of Spain, 1880–1914." *Journal of Economic History* 60 (2000): 730–55.

Saul, Mahir. "Money in Colonial Transition: Cowries and Francs in West Africa." *American Anthropologist* 106, no. 1 (2004): 71–84.

Sawyer, Amos. *The Emergence of Autocracy in Liberia: Tragedy and Challenge*. San Francisco: ICS Press, 1992.

Schenk, Catherine. "Monetary Institutions in Newly Independent Countries: The Experience of Malaya, Ghana and Nigeria in the 1950s." *Financial History Review* 4 (1997): 181–98.

The Decline of Sterling: Managing the Retreat of an International Currency 1945-1992. Cambridge: Cambridge University Press, 2010.

Schiltz, Michael. "Money on the Road to Empire: Japan's Adoption of Gold Monometallism, 1873–97." *Economic History Review* 65, 3 (2012): 1147–68.

Schneider, Eric B. *Stunting: Past, Present and Future* (2018). http://doi.org/10.21953/lse.9teyst78nhxh

Schneider, Eric B. and Kota Ogasawara. "Disease and Child Growth in Industrialising Japan: Critical Windows and the Growth Pattern, 1917–39." *Explorations in Economic History* 69 (2018): 64–80.

Schulze, Willi. "Early Iron Smelting among the Northern Kpelle." *Liberian Studies Journal* 3, no. 1 (1971): 113–29.

Schumpeter, Joseph A. "The Crisis of the Tax State." *International Economic Papers: Translations Prepared for the International Economic Association* 4 (1954): 5–38.

Schwab, George. *Tribes of the Liberian Hinterland*. Cambridge, MA: Peabody Museum of American Archaeology and Ethnology, 1947.

Schwartz, A. J. "Currency Boards: Their Past, Present and Possibly Future Role." *Carnegie-Rochester Conference Series on Public Policy* 39 (1993): 147–87.

Selgin, G., and L. H. White. "Credible Currency: A Constitutional Perspective." *Constitutional Political Economy* 16 (2005): 71–83.

Sender, John. "Africa's Economic Performance: Limitations of the Current Consensus." *Journal of Economic Perspectives* 13, no. 3 (1999): 89–114.

Sharples, John P. "The Australian Tradesman's Tokens Project, the James Nokes Proof Halfpenny and Problems of the Kangaroo Office." *Journal of the Numismatic Association of Australia* 17 (2006): 45–52.

Shick, Tom W. *Emigrants to Liberia, 1820-1843*. Newark: University of Delaware Press, 1971.

——— "A Quantitative Analysis of Liberian Colonization from 1820 to 1843 with Special Reference to Mortality." *Journal of African History* 12, no. 1 (1971): 45–59.

——— *Behold the Promised Land: A History of Afro-American Settler Society in Nineteenth Century Liberia*. Baltimore: Johns Hopkins University Press, 1980.

Simson, Rebecca. "Ethnic (in)Equality in the Public Services of Kenya and Uganda." *African Affairs* 118, no. 470 (2019): 75–100.

Staley, Eugene. "The Economic Implications of Lend-Lease." *American Economic Review* 33, no. 1 (1943): 362–76.

Stanley, William R. "Trans-South Atlantic Air Link in World War II." *GeoJournal* 33, no. 4 (1994): 459–63.

Stasavage, David. *The Political Economy of a Common Currency: The CFA Franc Zone since 1945*. Aldershot: Ashgate, 2003.

Steckel, Richard H. "The African American Population of the United States 1790–1920." In *A Population History of North America*, edited by Michael R. Haines and Richard H. Steckel, 433–82. Cambridge: Cambridge University Press, 2000.

Steil, Benn. *The Marshall Plan: Dawn of the Cold War*. New York: Simon and Schuster, 2018.

Stevens, Caleb J. "The Legal History of Public Land in Liberia." *Journal of African Law* 58, no. 2 (2014): 250–65.

Stigler, George J. "The Theory of Economic Regulation." *The Bell Journal of Economics and Management Science* 2, no. 1 (1971): 3–21.

Stolz, Y., and J. Baten. "Brain Drain in the Age of Mass Migration: Does Relative Inequality Explain Migrant Selectivity?" *Explorations in Economic History* 49 (2012): 205–20.

Stone, Ruth. "'Meni-Pelee: A Musical-Dramatic Folktale of the Kpelle'." *Liberian Studies Journal* IV, no. 1 (1972): 31–46.

Sunderland, David. *Managing the British Empire: The Crown Agents, 1833–1914.* Woodbridge: Royal Historical Society, 2004.

Sundiata, Ibrahim K. "Prelude to Scandal: Liberia and Fernando Po, 1880–1930." *Journal of African History* 15, no. 1 (1974): 97–112.

Black Scandal: America and the Liberian Labor Crisis, 1929–1936. Philadelphia: Institute for the Study of Human Issues, 1980.

Brothers and Strangers: Black Zion, Black Slavery, 1914–1940. Durham and London: Duke University Press, 2003.

Suter, Christian. *Debt Cycles in the World-Economy: Foreign Loans, Financial Crises, and Debt Settlements, 1820–1990.* Boulder: Westview Press, 1992.

Suzuki, T. *Japanese Government Loan Issues on the London Market, 1870–1913.* London: Athlone Press, 1994.

Svensson, Jakob. "Foreign Aid and Rent-Seeking." *Journal of International Economics* 51 (2000): 437–61.

Syfert, Dwight N. "The Origins of Privilege: Liberian Merchants, 1822–1847." *Liberian Studies Journal* VI, no. 2 (1975): 109–28.

"The Liberian Coasting Trade, 1822–1900." *Journal of African History* 18, no. 2 (1977): 217–35.

Szereszewski, R. *Structural Changes in the Economy of Ghana, 1891–1911.* London: Weidenfeld and Nicolson, 1965.

Taffet, Jeffrey F. "Foreign Economic Aid." In *Oxford Research Encyclopedia of American History*, edited by John Butler. Oxford: Oxford University Press, 2013.

Temple, Jonathan R. W. "Aid and Conditionality." In *Handbook of Development Economics*, edited by Dani Rodrik and Mark Rosenzweig, 4415–523. Oxford: North-Holland, 2010.

Thornton, John. "Demography and History in the Kingdom of Kongo, 1550–1750." *Journal of African History* 18, no. 4 (1977): 507–30.

Africa and Africans in the Making of the Atlantic World, 1400–1800. Cambridge: Cambridge University Press, 1998.

"Revising the Population History of the Kingdom of Kongo." *Journal of African History* 62 (2021): 201–12.

Tolnay, Stewart E. "Educational Selection in the Migration of Southern Blacks, 1880–1990." *Social Forces* 77, no. 2 (1998): 487–514.

Tomek, Beverly C., and Matthew J. Hetrick, eds. *New Directions in the Study of African American Recolonization.* Gainesville: University Press of Florida, 2017.

Tooze, Adam, and Martin Ivanov. "Disciplining the 'Black Sheep of the Balkans': Financial Supervision and Sovereignty in Bulgaria, 1902–38." *Economic History Review* 64, no. 1 (2011): 30–51.

Tripp, Aili Marie. *Women and Power in Postconflict Africa.* Cambridge: Cambridge University Press, 2015.

Tuncer, Ali Coskun. *Sovereign Debt and International Financial Control: The Middle East and the Balkans, 1870-1914.* Basingstoke: Palgrave Macmillan, 2015.

Twomey, Michael J. *A Century of Foreign Investment in the Third World.* Abingdon: Routledge, 2000.

Tyler-McGraw, Marie. *An African Republic: Black and White Virginians in the Making of Liberia*. Chapel Hill: University of North Carolina Press, 2007.

Uche, C. U. "Bank of England vs the Ibrd: Did the Nigerian Colony Deserve a Central Bank?" *Explorations in Economic History* 34 (1997): 220–41.

"Foreign Banks, Africans and Credit in Colonial Nigeria, c. 1890–1912." *Economic History Review* LII (1999): 669–91.

van der Kraaij, F. P. M. *The Open Door Policy of Liberia: An Economic History of Modern Liberia*. Bremen: Bremer Afrika Archiv, 1983.

van Waijenburg, Marlous. "Financing the African Colonial State: The Revenue Imperative and Forced Labor." *Journal of Economic History* 78, no. 1 (2018): 40–80.

Vansina, Jan. "Towards a History of Lost Corners of the World." *Economic History Review* 35, no. 2 (1982): 165–78.

Veeser, Cyrus. "A Forgotten Instrument of Global Capitalism? International Concessions, 1870–1930." *The International History Review* 35, no. 5 (2013): 1146–55.

Vos, Jelmer. "The Slave Trade from the Windward Coast: The Case of the Dutch, 1740–1805." *African Economic History* 38 (2010): 29–51.

Walters, Sarah. "African Population History: Contributions of Moral Demography." *Journal of African History* 62 (2021): 183–200.

Wantchekon, Leonard, Marko Klasnja, and Natalija Novta. "Education and Human Capital Externalities: Evidence from Colonial Benin." *Quarterly Journal of Economics* 130, no. 2 (2015): 703–57.

Webb, James. "Toward the Comparative Study of Money: A Reconsideration of West African Currencies Neoclassical Monetary Concepts." *International Journal of African Historical Studies* 15, no. 3 (1982): 455–66.

Whatley, Warren. "How the International Slave Trades Underdeveloped Africa," *Journal of Economic History* 82 (2022): 403–441.

Widgren, Mats. "Mapping Global Agricultural History: A Map and Gazetteer for Sub-Saharan Africa, C. 1800 Ad." In *Plants and People in the African Past: Progress in African Archaeobotany*, edited by Anna Maria Mercuri, A. Catherine d'Andrea, Rita Fornaciari and Alexa Hohn, 303–27. Cham: Springer Nature, 2018.

Wiley, Bell I. *Slaves No More: Letters from Liberia 1833-1869*. Lexington: University of Kentucky Press, 1980.

Wilks, Ivor. *Asante in the Nineteenth Century*. Cambridge: Cambridge University Press, 1989.

Williams, Heather. *Self-Taught: African American Education in Slavery and Freedom*. Chapel Hill: University of North Carolina Press, 2005.

Williamson, Oliver E. *The Economic Institutions of Capitalism*. New York: The Free Press, 1985.

Wilson, Charles Morrow. *Liberia: Black Africa in Microcosm*. New York: Harper and Row, 1971.

Winchakul, Thongchai. *Siam Mapped: A History of the Geo-Body of a Nation*. Honolulu: University of Hawaii Press, 1994.

Wulah, M. Teah. *Back to Africa: A Liberian Tragedy*. Bloomington: AuthorHouse, 2009.

Young, Crawford. *The African Colonial State in Comparative Perspective*. New Haven: Yale University Press, 1994.

The Postcolonial State in Africa: Fifty Years of Independence, 1960-2010. Madison: University of Wisconsin Press, 2012.

Zimmerman, Andrew. *Alabama in Africa: Booker T. Washington, the German Empire and the Globalization of the New South*. Princeton: Princeton University Press, 2010.

Zucman, Gabriel. *The Hidden Wealth of Nations: The Scourge of Tax Havens*. Chicago: University of Chicago Press, 2015.

Index

Printed in the United States
by Baker & Taylor Publisher Services